E-Commerce Concepts
Illustrated Introductory

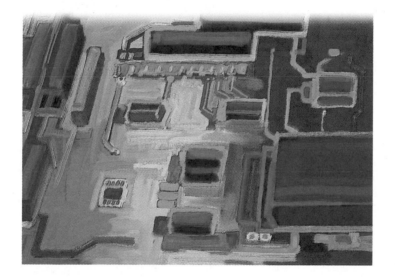

Carol M. Cram

COURSE
TECHNOLOGY

Thomson Learning™

25 THOMSON PLACE, BOSTON, MA 02210

Australia • Canada • Mexico • Singapore • Spain • United Kingdom • United States

E-Commerce Concepts—Illustrated Introductory is published by Course Technology.

Managing Editor:	Nicole Jones Pinard
Production Editor:	Megan Cap-Renzi
QA Manuscript Reviewers:	John Freitas, Ashlee Welz, Andrew Sciarretta
Product Manager:	Emily Heberlein
Developmental Editor:	Barbara Waxer
Text Designer:	Joseph Lee, Black Fish Design
Associate Product Manager:	Emeline Elliott
Composition House:	GEX, Inc.
Cover Designer:	Doug Goodman, Doug Goodman Designs
Manuscript Reviewers:	Dr. Thomas Michael Smith, Rebecca Lawson, Peter L. Partin, Anthony Briggs, Lorraine Bergkuist

For more information contact:

Course Technology
25 Thomson Place
Boston, MA 02210

or you can visit us on the World Wide Web at: www.course.com

For permission to use material from this text or product, contact us by
Tel (800) 730-2214
Fax (800) 730-2215

www.thomsonrights.com

ISBN 0-619-01818-6

Printed in the United States of America

1 2 3 4 5 6 7 8 9 BM 05 04 03 02 01

Exciting New Products

Try out Illustrated's New Product Line: Multimedia Tools

What are Multimedia Tools?

Multimedia tools teach students how to create text, graphics, video, animations, and sound; all of which can be incorporated for use in printed materials, Web pages, CD-ROMs, and multimedia presentations.

New Titles

▶ Adobe Photoshop 5.5—Illustrated Introductory (0-7600-6337-0)
▶ Adobe Illustrator 9.0—Illustrated Introductory (0-619-01750-3)
▶ Macromedia Director 8 Shockwave Studio—Illustrated Introductory (0-619-01772-4)

▶ Macromedia Director 8 Shockwave Studio—Illustrated Complete (0-619-01779-1)
▶ Multimedia Concepts—Illustrated Introductory (0-619-01765-1)

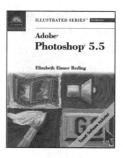

Master Microsoft Office 2000

Master Microsoft Office 2000 applications with the Illustrated Series. With *Microsoft Office 2000—Illustrated Introductory*, students will learn the basics of Microsoft Office 2000 Professional Edition. *Microsoft Office 2000—Illustrated Second Course* focuses on the more advanced skills of Office 2000 applications, and it includes coverage of all of the software in the Premium Edition.

Illustrated also offers individual application books on Access, Excel, Word, and PowerPoint 2000. Each book covers basic to advanced skills for the application and meets Microsoft Office User Specialist (MOUS) certification.

Other titles include:

▶ Microsoft Access 2000—Illustrated Brief, Introductory, Complete, and Second Course

▶ Microsoft Excel 2000—Illustrated Brief, Introductory, Complete, and Second Course
▶ Microsoft FrontPage 2000—Illustrated Essentials, Introductory, Complete, and Second Course
▶ Microsoft Office 2000—Illustrated Introductory and Second Course
▶ Microsoft Office 2000—Illustrated Brief
▶ Microsoft Outlook 2000—Illustrated Essentials
▶ Microsoft PhotoDraw (version 2)—Illustrated Essentials
▶ Microsoft PowerPoint 2000—Illustrated Brief and Introductory
▶ Microsoft Publisher 2000—Illustrated Essentials and Introductory
▶ Microsoft Word 2000—Illustrated, Brief, Introductory, Complete, and Second Course
▶ Microsoft Office 2000—Illustrated Projects

Check Out Computer Concepts

Computer Concepts—Illustrated Brief and Introductory, Third Edition is the quick and visual way to learn cutting-edge computer concepts. The third edition has been updated to include advances to the Internet and multimedia, changes to the industry, and an introduction to e-commerce and security. The Introductory text features a Multimedia CD-ROM.

Create Your Ideal Course Package with CourseKits™

If one book doesn't offer all the coverage you need, create a course package that does. With Course Technology's CourseKits—our mix-and-match approach to selecting texts—you have the freedom to combine products from more than one series. When you choose any two or more Course Technology products for one course, we'll discount the price and package them together so your students can pick up one convenient bundle at the bookstore.

Preface

Welcome to *E-Commerce Concepts— Illustrated Introductory*. This highly visual book offers users a comprehensive hands-on introduction to the business and technology concepts of e-commerce. This book is appropriate for a full semester course, and its modular structure allows great flexibility—you can cover the units in any order you choose.

▶ Organization and Coverage

This text provides a fast-paced and engaging introduction to today's most cutting-edge e-commerce topics. Designed to teach students to explore and evaluate e-commerce technologies, sites, and issues, *E-Commerce Concepts* combines concepts with exploratory exercises. The goal of the text is to encourage students to develop critical thinking skills and to tailor their exploration of e-commerce to suit their individual interests. In addition, a continually updated Student Online Companion allows students to explore relevant sites and articles, ensuring a complete and current learning experience.

▶ About this Approach

What makes the Illustrated approach so effective? It's quite simple. Each concept is presented on two facing pages, with the concepts or step-by-step instructions on the left page, and large screen illustrations on the right page. Students can focus on a single concept without having to turn the page. This unique design makes information extremely accessible and easy to absorb, and provides a great reference for after the course is over. This hands-on approach is ideal for both self-paced or instructor-led classes.

Each two-page spread focuses on a single concept.

Paintbrush icons introduce the real-world case study used throughout the book: MediaLoft, a fictional chain of bookstore cafés.

Easy-to-follow introductions to every lesson focus on a single concept to help students get the point quickly.

Unit A — E-Commerce

Identifying E-Commerce Challenges

From a company's point of view, e-commerce is not necessarily the gold mine that it might become for some of the highest profile dot.com companies. The term **dot.com** is used to describe companies that conduct most—if not all—of their business online. The word *dot* refers to the period that separates the Web site name, or **domain name** (for example, Amazon or Staples) from the word *com* (commercial), which is the **top-level domain** designation. Other top-level domain designations include org, net, and gov. Dot.com usually indicates a Web site that conducts business exclusively on the Internet. Table A-3 shows some of the advantages and disadvantages of conducting business over the Internet. ◆ While MediaLoft management is anxious to develop an e-commerce strategy, they also want to be informed about possible pitfalls. Hiromi asks you to research some of the challenges associated with e-commerce.

Details

▶ Competition

From a Web developer's point of view, one of the most difficult challenges of creating a successful e-commerce Web site is how to keep customers on the Web site until they make a purchase. If a Web site is difficult to navigate, if the products are not described well, if forms are not easy to fill out, or even worse, if links are broken and pictures take too long to load or have disappeared, consumers might simply click to another site. The ease with which consumers can go from site to site on the Internet has shifted the balance of power from the seller to the buyer. A company doing business on the Internet must create a Web site that keeps a potential buyer entertained and informed for as long as it takes that buyer to make a purchasing decision. Web developers call a site that attracts and keeps surfers a **sticky site**.

▶ Costs

In these early years of e-commerce development, much of the up-front costs of building and maintaining a Web site have yet to be recovered. Wild fluctuations in the stock prices of dot.com companies are predicted to continue as stockholders seek a return on their investments. Some analysts predict the demise of purely dot.com companies, and the strengthening of click and mortar companies that have a solid presence and broad recognition in the real world (the brick) along with a comprehensive, user-friendly Web site that generates significant online sales (the click). Some click and mortar companies are expected to vigorously acquire dot.coms as they expand their online presence and take advantage of the latest technological developments.

▶ Disintermediation

In traditional commerce, many businesses operate as **middlemen** to negotiate transactions between a business and the consumer, or between two businesses. Agents, brokers, and sales representatives are all examples of middlemen. These middlemen are fast being made obsolete because consumers can go directly to a company's Web site and purchase products and services without help from an agent or other intermediary. The process of edging out the middleman is called **disintermediation**.

▶ Intermediation

While some intermediaries might be made obsolete by e-commerce, other companies are emerging as a new kind of **intermediary** to exploit markets that could not have existed before the Internet. New intermediaries include auction sites, payment-processing sites, and Web site storefront services. In Figure A-21, a page from Looksmart's Beseen Web site describes the Buy It! button. When a consumer clicks the Buy It! button, credit card information is processed by Beseen, and the original vendor pays Beseen a transaction fee. This new type of intermediation is also referred to as **re-intermediation**. Individuals who develop Internet-based intermediation solutions are referred to as **cyberintermediaries**.

e-byte

"Business-to-Business online revenues will swell to 1.3 trillion over the next three years while Business-to-Consumer e-commerce revenues will only reach 108 billion." *Source: Forrester Research.* [4]

E-bytes are brief facts or ideas that relate to the lesson concept.

Details provide additional key information on the main concept. For lessons that contain activities, clear step-by-step directions explain how to complete the specific task. What students will type is in green.

Every lesson features large-size, full-color illustrations that bring the lesson concepts to life.

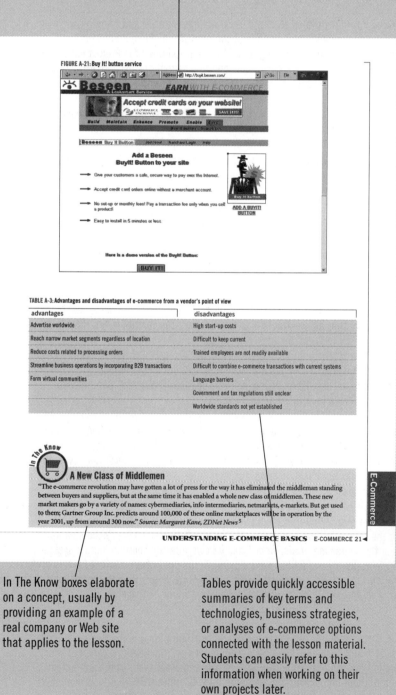

FIGURE A-21: Buy It! button service

TABLE A-3: Advantages and disadvantages of e-commerce from a vendor's point of view

advantages	disadvantages
Advertise worldwide	High start-up costs
Reach narrow market segments regardless of location	Difficult to keep current
Reduce costs related to processing orders	Trained employees are not readily available
Streamline business operations by incorporating B2B transactions	Difficult to combine e-commerce transactions with current systems
Form virtual communities	Language barriers
	Government and tax regulations still unclear
	Worldwide standards not yet established

In The Know
A New Class of Middlemen

"The e-commerce revolution may have gotten a lot of press for the way it has eliminated the middleman standing between buyers and suppliers, but at the same time it has enabled a whole new class of middlemen. These new market makers go by a variety of names: cybermediaries, info intermediaries, netmarkets, e-markets. But get used to them; Gartner Group Inc. predicts around 100,000 of these online marketplaces will be in operation by the year 2001, up from around 300 now." *Source: Margaret Kane, ZDNet News* [5]

E-Commerce

In The Know boxes elaborate on a concept, usually by providing an example of a real company or Web site that applies to the lesson.

Tables provide quickly accessible summaries of key terms and technologies, business strategies, or analyses of e-commerce options connected with the lesson material. Students can easily refer to this information when working on their own projects later.

Other Features

The two-page lesson format featured in this book provides the student with a powerful learning experience. Additionally, this book contains the following features:

▶ **Student Online Companion**
The Student Online Companion, located at www.course.com/illustrated/ ecommerce, contains a wide array of links for students to explore when completing the lessons and end-of-unit material. This innovative online companion enhances and augments the printed page by bringing students onto the Web for a dynamic and continually updated learning experience.

▶ **Real-World Case**
The case study used throughout the textbook, a fictitious chain of bookstore cafés called MediaLoft, is designed to be "real-world" in nature. The MediaLoft case introduces the kinds of questions and issues a company would explore before taking their business online. With a real-world case, the process of investigating e-commerce issues and technology is more meaningful to students.

▶ **End-of-Unit Material**
Each unit concludes with a Focus section. Students explore a controversial issue related to e-commerce or investigate a cutting edge technology and then answer open-ended discussion questions. Review questions, reinforcing the terms and concepts from the unit, follow the Focus section. The Review is followed by Independent Challenges, which pose case problems and involve further exploration of the key concepts and issues covered in the unit. Following the Independent Challenges, the Up to Date Challenge provides an activity where students explore the most recent developments in e-commerce, and compare their research to information in the unit. Each unit concludes with a Visual Workshop, designed to further develop students' critical thinking skills. Students are shown an existing Web page and are asked to evaluate, compare, or research Web sites according to the guidelines provided.

Instructor's Resource Kit

The Instructor's Resource Kit is Course Technology's way of putting the resources and information needed to teach and learn effectively into your hands. With an integrated array of teaching and learning tools that offers you and your students a broad range of technology-based instructional options, we believe this kit represents the highest quality and most cutting edge resources available to instructors today. Many of these resources are available at **www.course.com**. The resources available with this book are:

Student Online Companion The Student Online Companion, located at www.course.com/ illustrated/ecommerce, contains a wide array of links for students to explore when completing the lessons and end-of-unit material. This innovative online companion enhances and augments the printed page by bringing students onto the Web for a dynamic and continually updated learning experience.

Project Files Project Files contain templates students use and questions students answer when completing the lessons and end-of-unit exercises. A Readme file accompanying the Project Files includes instructions for using the files. Adopters of this text are granted the right to install the Project Files on any standalone computer or network. The Project Files are available on the Instructor's Resource Kit CD-ROM, in the Review Pack, and on our Web site at **www.course.com**.

Solution Files Solution Files are Project Files completed with comprehensive sample answers. Use these files to evaluate your students' work.

Figure Files Figure Files contain all the figures from the book in bitmap format. Use the figure files to create transparency masters or to enhance a PowerPoint presentation.

Instructor's Manual Available as an electronic file, the Instructor's Manual is quality-assurance tested and includes unit overviews, detailed lecture topics with teaching tips for each unit, comprehensive sample solutions to lessons and end-of-unit material, and extra Independent Challenges. The Instructor's Manual is available on the Instructor's Resource Kit CD-ROM, or you can download it from **www.course.com**.

Course Test Manager Designed by Course Technology, this Windows-based testing software helps instructors design, administer, and print tests and pre-tests. A full-featured program, Course Test Manager also has an online testing component that allows students to take tests at the computer and have their exams automatically graded.

Course Faculty Online Companion You can browse this textbook's password-protected site to obtain the Instructor's Manual, Solution Files, Project Files, and any updates to the text. Contact your Customer Service Representative for the site address and password.

MyCourse.com MyCourse.com is a quick and easy way to put your course online. MyCourse.com is an easily customizable online syllabus and course enhancement tool. This tool adds value to your class by offering brand new content designed to reinforce what you are already teaching. MyCourse.com even allows you to add your own content, hyperlinks, and assignments. For more information, visit our Web site at www.course.com/at/distancelearning/#mycourse.

WebCT WebCT is a tool used to create Web-based educational environments and also uses Web browsers as the interface for the course-building environment. The site is hosted on your school campus, allowing complete control over the course materials. WebCT has its own internal communication system, offering internal e-mail, a Bulletin Board, and a Chat room. Course Technology offers content for this book to help you create your WebCT class, such as a suggested Syllabus, Lecture Notes, Practice Test questions, Crossword Puzzles, and more. For more information, visit our Web site at www.course.com/at/distancelearning/#webct.

Blackboard Like WebCT, Blackboard is a management tool to help you plan, create, and administer your distance learning class, without knowing HTML. Classes are hosted on Blackboard's server or your school's server. Course Technology offers content for this book to help you create your Blackboard class, such as a suggested Syllabus, Lecture Notes, Practice Test questions, Crossword Puzzles, and more. For more information, visit our Web site at www.course.com/at/distancelearning/#blackboard.

A Note from the Author

If I had to sum up e-commerce in one word, I'd have to say "opportunity." How can you adapt your own interests and abilities to contribute to the e-commerce revolution?

E-Commerce Concepts Illustrated Introductory is all about opportunity. I have tried to present every concept, issue, and technical term in a way that encourages you to think of ways *you* can use it to develop your own e-solutions. Think of *E-Commerce Concepts Illustrated Introductory* as your comprehensive base for future explorations. You can gain an overview of the concepts related to e-commerce and then you can find the areas that intrigue you the most. You might discover that you want to focus on the nuts and bolts of Web page design or the exciting opportunities opening up in marketing or the development of compelling content for that perfect "sticky" Web site.

No one person can be an expert in all areas of e-commerce. However, thousands of opportunities exist for *specialization*. The purpose of *E-Commerce Concepts Illustrated Introductory* is to provide you with the knowledge you need to make informed choices about how you might like to become involved in the e-commerce revolution.

My advice is to spend as much time as possible exploring new areas, reading about the latest e-commerce developments, and thinking about how you could develop new strategies. E-commerce is new for most of us, but that doesn't mean we should shy away from learning as much as we can about it. Use this text to find out for yourself what all the fuss is about!

Writing *E-Commerce Concepts Illustrated Introductory* has challenged me to make new vocabulary and complex issues accessible to anyone interested in learning what e-commerce can mean to them. I can't think of a more exciting and rewarding challenge!

What You Need

To get the most from *E-Commerce Concepts Illustrated Introductory*, you need access to a computer that has an Internet connection and a Web browser such as Internet Explorer or Netscape Navigator. You also need to use a word processing program to complete many of the lesson activities and independent challenges. All of the Project Files supplied for this text are formatted in Microsoft Word 2000. You should be able to open and use these files in most other word processing programs.

Use the Student Online Companion at *www.course.com/illustrated/ecommerce* to supplement your learning and to complete lesson activities and independent challenges. You will find links to a broad range of companies, services, and information Web sites included in the Student Online Companion for each Unit. Use these links as your launching pad into the new and exciting world of e-commerce.

Carol M. Cram

Carol M. Cram

Brief Contents

Contents

E-Commerce

Contents

Contents

Understanding
E-Commerce Basics

Objectives

► Define e-commerce
► Explore Internet history
► Explore e-commerce development
► Understand the self-serve economy
► Define business-to-business e-commerce
► Define business-to-consumer e-commerce
► Identify e-commerce stages
► Analyze e-commerce processes
► Explore online stores
► Identify e-commerce challenges
► Explore e-commerce opportunities

In this unit, you will explore some basic issues and activities related to electronic-commerce (e-commerce). You will define e-commerce, review how e-commerce has developed, and distinguish between Business-to-Business (B2B) and Business-to-Consumer (B2C) e-commerce. You will also explore online stores, identify challenges related to e-commerce activities, and analyze some of the opportunities for e-commerce development. ➤ MediaLoft, a nationwide chain of bookstore cafés that sells magazines, books, videos, software, and CDs, already has a simple Web site. The success of other online bookstores has encouraged MediaLoft to establish an e-commerce presence on the World Wide Web. They have formed the Online Development Group to investigate every aspect of e-commerce. Hiromi Tanaka, leader of the group, has hired you to help assess MediaLoft's e-commerce options. Your first assignment is to familiarize yourself with the basic issues associated with e-commerce.

Defining E-Commerce

On the Internet, you can buy a hot stock, order the latest paperback novel, sell your Beatles bubblegum cards, buy a set of antique Georgian silver, print postage stamps, book a flight, or find and pay for that perfect romantic hideaway in the Tuscan hills. In fact, just about any activity that involves buying and selling has moved from the corner store, the shopping mall, and the office tower to your desktop by way of e-commerce and the Internet. Figure A-1 shows a typical e-commerce transaction from a consumer's point of view. As a member of MediaLoft's new Online Development Group, you decide to review the definition of e-commerce, learn about some of its associated activities, and evaluate its benefits.

Details

► E-Commerce Defined

The term **commerce** refers to all the activities in which a company or individual engages to complete a transaction. When you use the **Internet** to engage in some or all of these activities, commerce becomes **e-commerce**. Therefore, you can define e-commerce as *using the Internet to assist in the trading of goods and services.* Other terms that refer to doing business over the Internet include e-business, e-tailing, and e-trading.

► Activities

E-commerce activities can form some part of just about every stage in the life cycle of a product. Figure A-2 shows the e-commerce activities conducted by a company that sells winter sports equipment. Notice that these activities do not differ significantly from the business activities that companies have always conducted. The difference is that now companies can conduct business by using computers and telecommunications technologies instead of, or in addition to, operating a retail store.

► Characteristics

In theory, the Internet knows no geographical boundaries, political boundaries, or time boundaries. You can order a toaster at three o'clock in the morning, or sell lavender-scented beauty soap to a consumer who lives 10,000 miles away. The universality of the Internet has resulted in the world's largest **level playing field.** As a one-person company operating from a log cabin in the mountains, you can compete with the world's multinational corporations—so long as you have a reliable Internet connection, products or services to sell, and the means of delivering them to customers. In fact, if you sell a product such as software or learning materials that consumers can download directly from a Web site, you don't even need to worry about delivery systems.

► Benefits

Some of the benefits of doing business over the Internet include the ability to engage in the following activities:

- Conduct business 24 hours a day, 7 days a week.
- Sell products to anyone in the world.
- Respond quickly to customers.
- Build a one-on-one relationship with customers.
- Provide customers with up-to-the-minute information.
- Reduce the overhead costs associated with maintaining a brick and mortar retail outlet. The term **brick and mortar** refers to retail locations in the real world, as opposed to the electronic world of cyberspace. Companies that sell products or services both in the real world and online are referred to as **click and mortar** companies.
- Automate business operations to save time and money.

In addition, you can use the Internet to explore new business opportunities, and perhaps build an e-commerce site that meets customer demand for a product or service that no one else has even identified yet!

e-byte

"We are witnessing myriad new forms of business activity, such as electronic marketplaces linking buyers and sellers in seamless global bazaars, and changes in business processes from customer service to product design that harness the new technologies to make businesses more efficient and responsive." *Source: U.S. Secretary of Commerce William M. Daley* [1]

FIGURE A-1: **Summary of an e-commerce transaction**

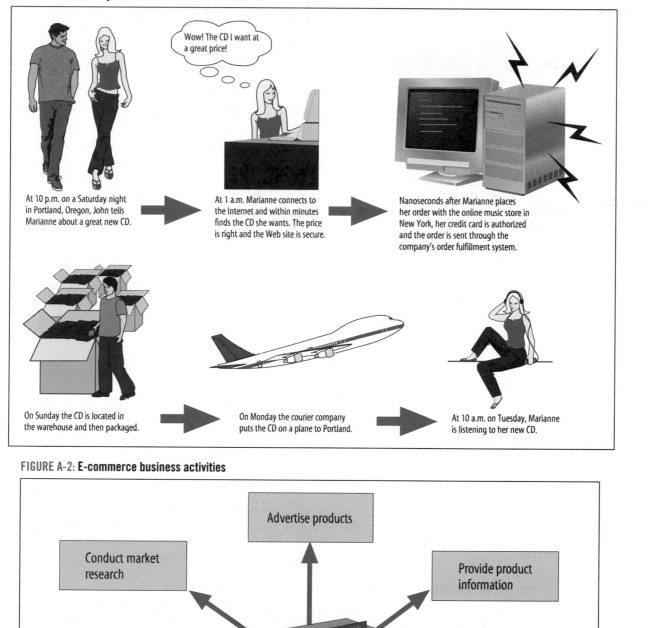

At 10 p.m. on a Saturday night in Portland, Oregon, John tells Marianne about a great new CD.

At 1 a.m. Marianne connects to the Internet and within minutes finds the CD she wants. The price is right and the Web site is secure.

Nanoseconds after Marianne places her order with the online music store in New York, her credit card is authorized and the order is sent through the company's order fulfillment system.

On Sunday the CD is located in the warehouse and then packaged.

On Monday the courier company puts the CD on a plane to Portland.

At 10 a.m. on Tuesday, Marianne is listening to her new CD.

FIGURE A-2: **E-commerce business activities**

Advertise products

Conduct market research

Provide product information

Receive and process payment

Contact customers

Order inventory from suppliers

Track shipping

Order supplies

E-Commerce

Explore Internet History

Millions of computers scattered all across the globe are connected in various ways to form the vast network known as the Internet. In fact, **Internet** means interconnected. More than 200 million users worldwide in more than 100 countries use the Internet to exchange information, communicate with each other, and purchase products and services. ⮕ Hiromi asks you to gather information related to the history of the Internet so that she can have a context for further explorations of e-commerce. You start by learning about the origins of the Internet and the World Wide Web.

Details

► Internet Origin

E-commerce would not exist without the global network of computers called the Internet. In the 1960s, the U.S. Department of Defense developed the Internet to network computers for defense purposes. The agency in charge of developing the Internet was called the Advanced Research Project Agency (ARPA).

► Internet Development

Over the next 30 years, the National Science Foundation (NSF) played a large role in guiding the steady growth of the Internet. In particular, the Internet was used as a communications tool in the scientific and academic communities for electronically transferring and exchanging research materials. Then, in 1989 the NSF opened the Internet to commercial network traffic. In 1992, Tim Berners-Lee created the World Wide Web while working at the European Laboratory for Particle Physics.

► Internet Growth

In just over 10 years, the Internet has grown at an unprecedented rate. Figure A-3 shows a portion of the timeline of Internet growth from 1969 to the beginning of 1995. The timeline appears on the Web site of the National Coordination Office for Computing, Information, and Communications in the United States. Note that the number of Internet hosts first exceeded 100,000 in 1989, and that the White House went online in 1994.

► Graphical User Interface and the World Wide Web

Two factors that enabled the phenomenal growth of the Internet were the development of the **Graphical User Interface (GUI)** and the **World Wide Web (Web)**. The GUI allowed retailers to show pictures, icons and other graphical elements of their products to customers all over the world, and the Web provided consumers with an easy way to navigate from Web site to Web site by way of hyperlinks.

► Use of Hyperlinks

A **hyperlink** is highlighted text on a Web page. You can click a hyperlink to go to another page on the same Web site or to go to a different Web site anywhere on the Web. A hyperlink to another page on the same Web site is called a **local** or **internal** hyperlink; a hyperlink to a different Web site is called a **remote** or **external** hyperlink. Figure A-4 shows some principal components of a typical company Web site. Each component is designed to help people quickly and easily find information and purchase products.

FIGURE A-3: Internet timeline

Timeline	
1969	Defense Department commissions ARPANET to promote networking research.
1974	Bob Kahn and Vint Cerf publish paper which specifies protocol for data networks.
1981	NSF provides seed money for CSNET (Computer Science NETwork) to connect U.S. computer science departments.
1982	Defense Department establishes TCP/IP (Transmission Control Protocol/Internet Protocol) as standard.
1984	Number of hosts (computers) connected to the Internet breaks 1,000.
1986	NSFNET and 5 NSF-funded supercomputer centers created. NSFNET backbone is 56 kilobits/second.
1989	Number of hosts breaks 100,000.
1991	NSF lifts restrictions on commercial use of the Internet.
	High Performance Computing Act, authored by then-Senator Gore, is signed into law.
	World Wide Web software released by CERN, the European Laboratory for Particle Physics.
1993	President Clinton and Vice President Gore get e-mail addresses.
	Mosaic, a graphical "Web browser" developed at the NSF-funded National Center for Supercomputing Applications, is released. Traffic on the World Wide Web explodes.
1994	White House goes on-line with "Welcome to the White House."
1995	U.S. Internet traffic now carried by commercial Internet service providers.

FIGURE A-4: E-commerce Web site components

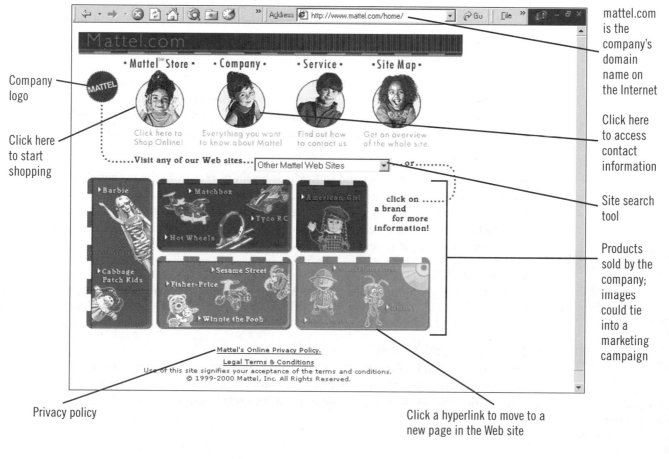

mattel.com is the company's domain name on the Internet

Company logo

Click here to start shopping

Click here to access contact information

Site search tool

Products sold by the company; images could tie into a marketing campaign

Privacy policy

Click a hyperlink to move to a new page in the Web site

Explore E-Commerce Development

Companies have conducted online commercial transactions on a limited scale since the early 1990s. Consumer buying, however, has had a different history. You can count on one hand the years that significant numbers of consumers have been buying products online. Almost daily, Internet developers design new technologies that streamline business operations and automate the purchasing process. The goal of all this rapid development is to attract more customers by making Internet buying and selling procedures as fast, convenient, and easy as possible. Hiromi asks you to help her prepare a presentation for MediaLoft's management. The presentation will include an overview of e-commerce developments.

Details

► Internet Resources

The Internet consists of a vast array of electronic resources that people use to access information, to communicate with each other, and to transmit data. Sometimes people use the words Internet and World Wide Web interchangeably to refer to all of these electronic resources. Internet describes the *entire system* of networked computers; World Wide Web describes the *method* used to access information contained on computers connected to the Internet.

► Global Developments

At present, nations such as the United States, the Scandinavian countries, the United Kingdom, Singapore, and Canada rank among the top ten countries prepared to benefit from e-commerce developments. The rest of the world, however, is fast coming on board. A principal factor that hinders countries in developing an e-commerce presence is the cost of Internet access for its citizens. However, the recent trend to provide free Internet access may result in a stampede of new users to the Internet, particularly in Latin American and Asian countries.

► E-Mail and FTP

Other terms associated with the Internet are e-mail and File Transfer Protocol (FTP). You use **e-mail** to send messages from your computer to another computer. You can use **FTP** to transfer documents and files from one computer to another via the Internet. The World Wide Web, e-mail, and FTP are all tools that you use to access information from the Internet.

► E-Commerce Potential

By the mid-1990s, companies and individuals began to recognize the potential of the Web for reaching both existing and new customers. Businesses in particular identified the potential cost savings they could realize by using the Internet to handle business transactions. For example, a large company could save millions of dollars by sending billing notices via e-mail instead of via the conventional postal system, referred to as **snail mail**.

► Retail Spending

Figure A-5 shows the top Web retailers in May 2000. The figures were compiled by CyberAtlas, a Web site specializing in e-commerce statistics. Of particular interest is the Buy Rate column. On average, about 12 percent of the consumers who enter a Web site will actually purchase a product.

► Government Involvement

Governments could potentially have a profound effect on the future of e-commerce. The policies that governments set can either foster e-commerce, or stop it cold. Check the In The Know to learn more about the U.S. government's current role in e-commerce development.

Address http://cyberatlas.internet.com/markets/retail ▼ | Go | File

Top 20 Web Retailers Among US Home Users
May, 2000

May Rank	April Rank	Web Site	Projected Buyers (000)	Overall Reach (%)	Unique Users (000)	Buy Rate (%)
1	1	amazon.com	1,730	21.1	16,843	10.3
2	2	ticketmaster.com	571	6.6%	5,241	10.9
3	3	barnesandnoble.com	403	7.1%	5,628	7.2
4	13	pets.com	355	2.2	1,754	20.2
5	5	sears.com	329	3.3	2,651	12.4
6	4	cdnow.com	323	7.7	6,122	5.3
7	7	drugstore.com	322	2.7	2,134	15.1
8	9	jcpenney.com	273	2.5	2,009	13.6
9	6	buy.com	272	3.3	2,606	10.4
10	12	1800flowers.com	214	3.0	2,389	9.0
11	17	ftd.com	147	1.7	1,352	10.9

In The Know

Framework for Global Electronic Commerce

The U.S. government developed the five principles listed below as guidelines for conducting e-commerce transactions over the Internet. These principles recognize that the Global Information Infostructure (GII) is beginning to transform how people live and work.

1. The private sector should lead.

2. Government should avoid undue restrictions on electronic commerce.

3. Where government involvement is needed, its aim should be to support it and enforce a predictable, minimalist, consistent, and legal environment for commerce.

4. Government should recognize the unique qualities of the Internet.

5. Electronic commerce over the Internet should be facilitated on a global basis.

These principles are discussed in detail on the government's e-commerce Web site at *www.ecommerce.gov*.[3]

E-Commerce

Unit A
E-Commerce

Understanding the Self-Serve Economy

As consumers, most of us have used some form of **electronic data transmission**, such as phones and faxes, to conduct business for at least the past decade. Now e-mail messages, Personal Digital Assistants (PDAs), and, of course, Web sites on the Internet are almost as readily available as phones and faxes. As a result, we are becoming increasingly more comfortable with using electronic media to conduct all kinds of transactions, from transferring money between bank accounts, to reserving tickets to an upcoming hockey game, to ordering pizza. This willingness to help ourselves and to make new technologies part of our daily lives is the principal characteristic of the **self-serve** economy. Because MediaLoft has built a large part of its business on a self-serve model, Hiromi asks you to investigate this topic further.

Details

▶ **Customer Needs**

The consumer population is becoming more and more demanding. Each day, we are confronted with so many choices of how to spend our money that we can afford to be choosy. Figure A-6 illustrates some of the main consumer needs. One of the most important needs related to online purchasing is "I need to find products on my own." Customers of an online site want to navigate to the exact product they want as quickly and with as little confusion as possible.

▶ **Customer Focus**

A key component of e-commerce is its focus on the customer. A customer interacts with a company's Web site on a one-to-one basis. As a result, each customer expects to be treated with superior service that recognizes his or her individuality. In order to thrive, a business must be designed from the customer's point of view. This requirement is even more crucial when the business is online, because customers can so easily click off a Web site—never to return.

▶ **Self-Serve Components**

- Availability

The Internet brings the whole world to your desktop. In the not-so-distant past, you would need to drive to the library to research a topic or walk to the corner store to pick up a copy of the newspaper. Now, in addition to having online access to news reports from your local newspaper, you can read news reports in newspapers published around the world. This accessibility to information provides you, as a consumer, with unprecedented power. At the click of a mouse, you can access information about companies, compare products, and read reviews that will help you make informed purchasing decisions. Figure A-7 shows the different ways consumers can electronically access information, such as directions to a specific address in the real world.

- Portability

You are no longer bound by your geographical location. The increasing popularity of portable devices such as PDAs, cellular phones, and laptop computers means that you can access information from wherever you are and work with others in ways that were barely imagined just a decade ago. For example, in real-time conferences over the Internet, people scattered across the continent can exchange ideas and provide each other with immediate feedback.

- Speed

You can obtain information at any time and in real time. If your company has an online presence, you can provide your customers with instant updates. For example, when you change a product description, you can post it to your Web site for instant viewing by your customers.

- Convenience

To buy online, you only need to know how to read, use a mouse, and type in a credit card number. To shop for products in a brick and mortar store, you probably need to know how to drive, how to find the store, and how to cope with lines, crowds, and fatigue.

FIGURE A-6: Consumer needs

FIGURE A-7: Access mechanisms

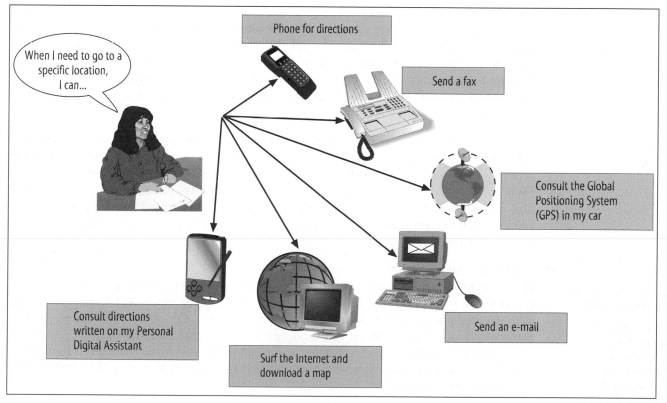

E-Commerce

Defining Business-to-Business E-Commerce

Some Web analysts maintain that 80 percent of e-commerce transactions occur between businesses. **Business-to-Business e-commerce** is defined as sales made by one business to another. You'll also see the abbreviation **B2B** used to refer to Internet transactions conducted between two or more businesses. For example, a printing business that uses the Internet to order paper from a paper company engages in B2B e-commerce. The final consumer of the printing company's products is not yet involved. Hiromi asks you to explore concepts related to B2B e-commerce and determine how MediaLoft can use the Internet to reduce costs and streamline operations.

Details

▶ B2B Activities

One of the key activities associated with B2B e-commerce is the overhaul of inefficient trading processes. Companies can use the Internet to contact suppliers, and then place and track orders as products make their way from the supplier to the company's front door. Companies can also electronically connect with accounting services to record transactions and pay taxes. In fact, just about any transaction that can be conducted with paper or over the phone also can be conducted via the Internet.

▶ B2B Opportunities

Many opportunities exist for Web entrepreneurs to provide businesses with e-commerce solutions. Check the In The Know for information about a B2B venture in the trucking industry.

▶ Intranets

An **Intranet** is a group of connected networks owned by a company or organization and is used for internal business purposes. Only authorized users, such as company employees, can access an Intranet, usually by entering a password. The Web sites on an Intranet can look just like Web sites available to all users on the Internet. The difference between a Web site that can be accessed from the Internet and one that must be accessed from an Intranet is that a firewall surrounds the Intranet to prevent access by unauthorized users. A **firewall** examines each message that enters and exits an Intranet, and then blocks any messages that do not conform to specific criteria.

▶ Extranets

An **Extranet** is an extension of a company's Intranet. The difference is that an Extranet can be made accessible to selected people or groups outside the company. Many B2B transactions occur over Extranets. An individual can enter a company's Web site on the Internet, obtain a password, and then join the company's Extranet to conduct transactions and obtain information not available to the public. Extranets are also used to connect a company's corporate Intranet with the Intranets of the company's suppliers, distributors, and corporate customers, as shown in Figure A-8.

▶ Contract Bidding Process

One of the most interesting—and potentially lucrative—ways that companies can use B2B e-commerce is to facilitate the contract bidding process. For example, two companies that manufacture plastic bubble wrap can electronically bid on a contract to supply packing materials to an online toy store. The bidding process can take place online in real time, and the contracting company can notify the winning bidder instantaneously. Both the bidding and the contracting companies save time and money. Figure A-9 shows a demonstration of the online bidding process.

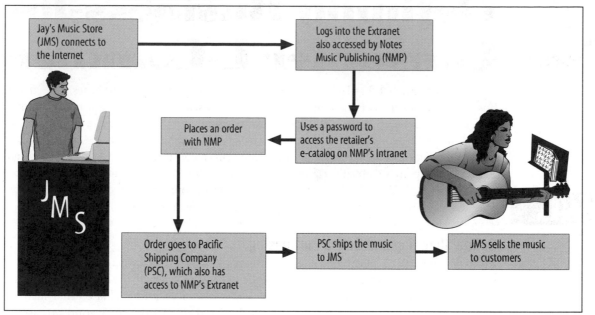

Trade Partnership .
Traders Menu.
Join the o mail list.
View bids to buy.
View bids to sell.
Open a bid to sell.
Open a bid to buy.
Online Trade Office
More Trade Tools
Company Info Index
Market Directory
Trading Services
How to Contact Us

Office of Johance Gruberman
Import & Export Manager
Gutzmann Natural Fruits, Inc.

Purchase Bids Published: 25
Sales Bids Published: 31
Sales Offers from Sellers. 7
Responses From **Buyers**: 5

Summary
of bidding
activity

1. Gutzmann Natural Fruits, Inc. as a **Buyer/Importer**

This section shows the bidding results to the product search posted by Gutzmann Natural Fruits, Inc. earlier. (Gutzmann wants to buy and import **Lemon Juice Makers**.)

Bidding
results

Final Bid	Item	Country	Bidder	Time Mailed
US$0.45 FOB	24	Hong Kong,	San Yuan Food Distributor	12:34 PM, 612/2000
US$0.43 FOB	24	Canada	Smetson Import & Export	1:33 PM, 6/12/2000
US$0.45 FOB	24	Korea	Dae WangLee Food Ltd.	3:21 PM, 6/12/2000
US$0.47 FOB	24	Germany	Hundaart - Hettwettz Enterprise	8:33 AM, 6/13/2000
US$0.42 FOB	24	Malaysia	Malaya Beverages Exporter Inc.	10:11 AM, 6/13/2000
US$0.49 FOB	24	United States	James & Derr. United Wholesalers	1:22 PM. 6/13/2000
US$0.51 FOB	24	Japan	Michimatsu Food Export Inc.	2:49 PM, 6/13/2000
US$0.55 FOB	24	China	Ling Guang Farm Export Asso.	5:37 PM, 6/13/2000

In The Know

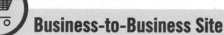

Business-to-Business Site

Truckers Co-Op.com operates a B2B Web site for small- to mid-size trucking companies. The co-op purchases large quantities of the products and services used to run a trucking business and then sells them at discounted rates to its members. As a result of this economy-of-scale purchasing, members can realize significant cost savings on products and services such as fuel, tires, insurance, long-distance phone services, trailer leasing, motels, and office supplies.

E-Commerce

Defining Business-to-Consumer E-Commerce

Some analysts predict that B2B e-commerce transactions will become 10 times more frequent than Business-to-Consumer (B2C) transactions. Nevertheless, in the public's mind, the image most closely associated with e-commerce is **B2C**: a consumer using the Internet to buy a product or service. Of course, not every consumer visits an e-commerce Web site with the expressed purpose of buying something. Figure A-10 shows some of the questions a consumer might want to have answered by visiting a company's Web site. MediaLoft will certainly include B2C e-commerce transactions as part of its Web site. Hiromi asks you to examine topics related to B2C e-commerce transactions and determine the types of products most frequently purchased.

Details

▶ **Online Shopping and Online Purchasing**

From a consumer's point of view, two principal activities characterize e-commerce: online shopping and online purchasing. First, you can use the Internet to shop for products and services. That is, you can research a product, compare prices, and evaluate other factors such as return policies, security and privacy safeguards, and delivery options. Second, you can purchase a product from a Web site. The purchasing activity involves several steps: selecting the product, providing payment information such as a credit card number, providing a real-world address so that the credit card can be authorized and the product can be delivered, and providing an e-mail address so that the company supplying the product can immediately confirm your order.

▶ **Online Selling Goals**

The primary goal of a retail Web site is to attract and keep customers so that they can conduct transactions 24 hours a day from anywhere in the world. To accomplish this goal, businesses need to develop a one-on-one relationship with each consumer, decrease operating costs, and reach narrow market segments that could be scattered all over the world.

▶ **Consumer Products**

Some of the first products sold online were books, music, software, and computers. A consumer could confidently buy any of these products without having to physically examine them. As consumers become more and more accustomed to purchasing products online, other product categories will become popular. Already, the success of e-Bay and other auction sites indicates that consumers are willing to make online purchases of collectible items, art, and other products that traditionally they would have physically examined before buying. For several years, conventional wisdom dictated that big-ticket items such as cars and houses would not sell online, yet consumers are flocking to Web sites such as cars.com and move.com. In tight housing markets, such as San Francisco, many middle- and high-end homes are sold sight-unseen, based solely on their Web listing. E-commerce analysts will be tracking the long-term financial success of Web sites that sell products traditionally associated with direct, person-to-person sales and physical inspection. Perhaps the growing number of consumers who maintain a busy lifestyle will demand Web businesses that cater to their preferences for speed and convenience.

▶ **Consumer Incentives**

Ultimately, a B2C e-commerce site must provide the customer with an easy shopping experience. At the same time, the customer needs to feel that shopping online provides an equal or greater benefit than shopping in a brick and mortar store. Table A-1 compares the online shopping experience with the traditional shopping experience for a consumer who wants to purchase a set of cookware. Note that activities shown in blue are easy to accomplish, while activities shown in red are potential barriers to shopping success. E-commerce Web site developers are continually working to remove or reduce these barriers.

FIGURE A-10: Customer questions

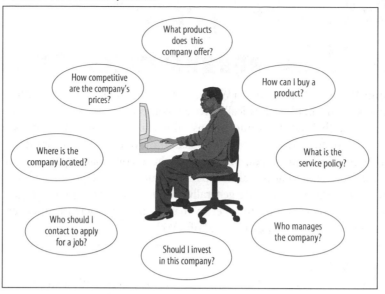

TABLE A-1: Comparison of online and offline shopping experiences

task	online	offline
1. Find cookware	Search for "cookware," "cooking pots," or "pots and pans," then follow links to likely Web sites. • Can search sites all over the world at any time. • Possibly time-consuming. • Need good Web-searching skills.	Check ads for availability, then drive to the shopping mall and check the directory for a store that sells cookware. • Two stores are located. • No shopping malls nearby. • The stores don't carry cookware.
2. Examine cookware	Read product descriptions. • Frequently Asked Questions (FAQs) provide helpful information. • Extensive product descriptions and photos are available. • Cannot physically inspect the cookware.	Inspect cookware and ask questions of the sales clerk. • Sales clerk is knowledgeable and helpful. • No sales clerk is available. • No product information is provided.
3. Comparison shop	Follow links to explore other sites that sell cookware. • Several sites sell the right cookware. • Prices and delivery options vary widely. • Choosing the right options is difficult.	Go to another store. • Find the right cookware. • Can't find cookware; must drive across town. • No other stores in the vicinity.
4. Purchase cookware	Select and purchase cookware that is priced reasonably. • Transaction is processed quickly. • E-mail confirmation is received. • The online site isn't secure. • The ordering system doesn't work. • No method is provided to cancel the order.	Select and purchase cookware. • Transaction is completed quickly and easily. • Long lines detract from the shopping experience. • Cannot get a lower price without going to another location.
5. Receive cookware	Select a reasonably priced delivery option. • Receive the cookware within a few days. • No delivery in your area. • Delivery is too slow. • Delivery charges are too high.	Take the cookware home. • Traffic is light and the distance is short. • Need to pay transportation costs.
6. Use cookware	Start cooking, but find a defect. • E-mail customer service and get a prompt reply and help. • E-mails are not answered. • The online company is out of business. • Delivery charges are too high.	Start cooking, but find a defect. • Return the cookware, wait in line, and get a refund. • The cookware was bought on sale—no refunds are allowed.

Identifying E-Commerce Stages

Some Web watchers say that a Web year is, at best, equal to three months in the real world. While such an assertion can't be statistically proven, you can safely say that developments related to how businesses use the Web to conduct transactions are occurring at warp speed. Companies that wish to conduct business over the Internet need to move quickly. You can divide a company's e-commerce experience into four stages: electronic brochure, corporate expansion, online buying and selling, and integration. Note that not all companies would or could go through all four stages and that transitions from stage to stage are generally gradual and overlapping. ⬗ Hiromi asks you to learn how companies use the Internet to market and sell their products and services so that you can identify the current stage of MediaLoft's Web site.

Details

► Electronic Brochure

Most companies first stake their claim on the Web with a site that is little more than an electronic brochure. These kinds of sites also are called **brochureware** sites. Such sites include limited information about a company, and descriptions of the products or services for sale. Potential customers can contact the company via e-mail, fax, telephone, or snail mail. Some of these sites also include simple order forms that customers can complete and then fax or e-mail. The Web contains many millions of such Web sites. Figure A-11 shows a Web site that sells fibers and yarns for knitting and weaving, and the form that customers can print and then complete to place offline orders.

► Corporate Expansion

In the second stage, companies expand their Web sites to include information about the company: its history, job openings, and relevant press releases. Such Web sites usually focus on providing the consumer with as much information as possible about the company in an effort to build customer loyalty and brand recognition. Figure A-12 shows how Course Technology, the publisher of this book, communicates corporate information on its About page.

► Online Buying and Selling

In the third stage, companies leap into full-scale e-commerce. They provide Web shoppers with the tools to order a product, and to pay for it using a credit card or other form of electronic payment. These e-commerce Web sites include online order forms and links to extensive databases. Designed for convenience and ease of use, third-stage Web sites focus on how best to serve the customer. Figure A-13 shows the home page of Indigo, a large online bookstore. Note the links to value-added features such as news articles, book reviews, holiday gift ideas, special promotions, and account information.

► Integration

In the final and, for most companies, still future stage of development, the lean, mean, customer-focused Web site is tightly integrated with all company operations. Information gathered about customers on the Web site is automatically available to all company departments. A customer need provide contact information only once—by completing a form on the Web site, talking to a sales representative on the phone, or by visiting the brick and mortar store. The difference between a stage 3 and stage 4 online store is not immediately obvious to a consumer, because the appearance of the online store can be the same, regardless of how the business handles customer information and transaction processing. The goal of an integrated Web site is to ensure that the "behind the scenes" activities are conducted in a way that ensures the smooth and efficient operation of all facets of a company's operations.

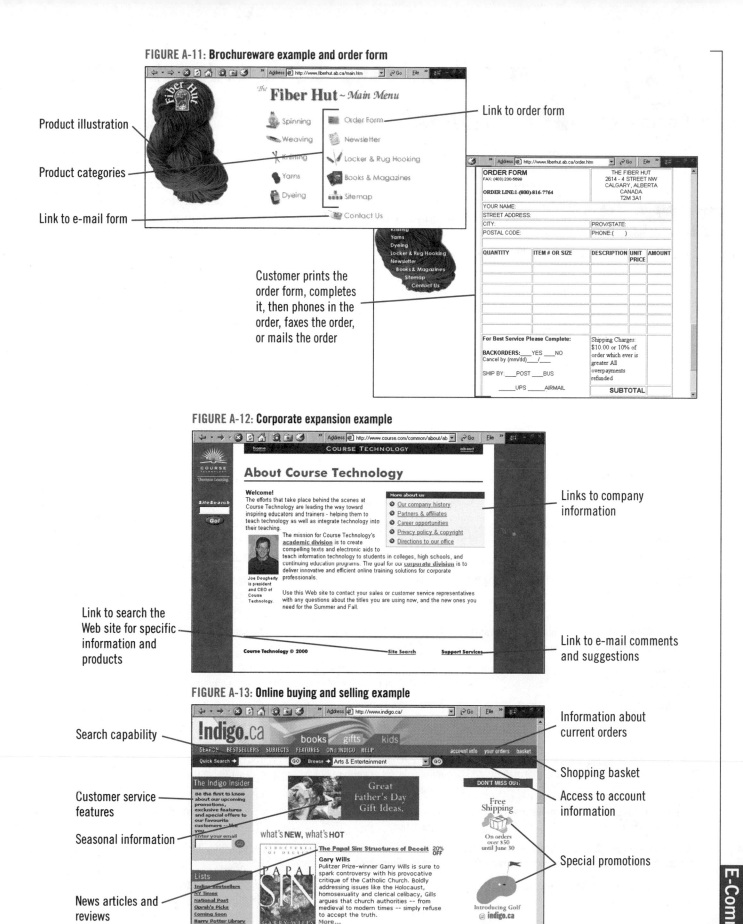

FIGURE A-11: Brochureware example and order form

Product illustration

Product categories

Link to e-mail form

Link to order form

Customer prints the order form, completes it, then phones in the order, faxes the order, or mails the order

FIGURE A-12: Corporate expansion example

Link to search the Web site for specific information and products

Links to company information

Link to e-mail comments and suggestions

FIGURE A-13: Online buying and selling example

Search capability

Customer service features

Seasonal information

News articles and reviews

Information about current orders

Shopping basket

Access to account information

Special promotions

E-Commerce

Analyzing E-Commerce Processes

From a customer's point of view, purchasing a product over the Internet is becoming increasingly easier, thanks to ongoing developments in Web technology. In fact, one of the main goals of e-commerce is to make the purchasing process fast, convenient, and secure. Various technologies are employed to ensure that these goals are met. ✎ You decide to investigate the processes that occur when you click your way through an online shopping site.

Details

► **Online Shopping Example**

Table A-2 presents a typical online shopping experience from both the customer's and the vendor's point of view. A **vendor** is the company that supplies the products sold on the Web site. In this case, Tom the customer wants to purchase art supplies from an art supply store in Denver.

► **Definitions**

As you learn more about e-commerce, you will often encounter some of the terms mentioned in Table A-2, such as cookies and CGI Script. Because many of these terms are integral to the workings of e-commerce, you will explore them in more depth in later units of this book.

TABLE A-2: Online shopping example

Tom the customer	online art store
Tom selects two airbrush paint sets, then clicks a button that will add them to his shopping cart. See Figure A-14.	The art store sends a cookie to the customer's computer where it is stored on the hard drive. The **cookie** contains information about Tom and the products he has selected. The next time Tom visits the art store, that information in the cookie can be accessed by the store.
The list of the items currently in Tom's shopping cart appears. See Figure A-15.	A CGI (Common Gateway Interface) Script or similar application generates the page that displays the items currently in Tom's shopping basket. A **CGI Script** is a standard method used to communicate between computers, regardless of their platform (PC or Mac).
Tom has collected all the art materials he wants for today. He clicks the Checkout button.	Tom's list of items is transferred to a secure server, which allows safe transmission of information, such as credit card numbers.
Tom fills in the form with his contact information, as shown in Figure A-16.	The art store processes the information, and informs Tom when he makes an error. For example, Tom could have left out his zip code or entered an invalid area code.
Tom fixes his error and clicks Continue.	A CGI Script generates a page that displays Tom's contact information along with information about shipping costs. Figure A-17 shows the portion of the page that lists shipping costs.
Tom selects a shipping option, clicks Continue, and then enters his credit card information.	Tom's electronic payment information is **encrypted**, which means that special mathematical algorithms or keys are used to scramble the information into an unreadable form.
Tom clicks Continue to confirm his order.	A payment-processing service verifies the credit card information and completes the transaction.
Tom views a screen that confirms acceptance of the transaction. He can print this page for his records.	An electronic transaction service transfers payment from Tom's credit card account to the art store's business bank.
Tom receives a confirmation e-mail.	The art store sends Tom a confirmation e-mail. The transaction information is stored in a database which is regularly accessed by the order entry system. The order is filled and shipped.
Tom receives his art materials.	The art store has Tom's contact information on file. Based on his purchase history, they now can inform him by e-mail or snail mail about upcoming specials or other promotions that may interest him.

FIGURE A-14: Items selected

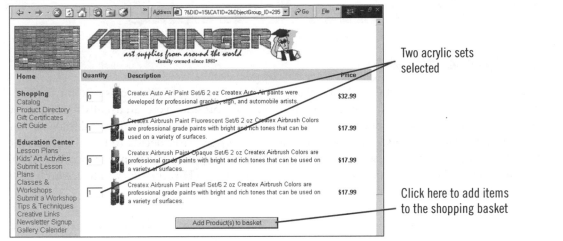

Two acrylic sets selected

Click here to add items to the shopping basket

FIGURE A-15: List of items in the shopping cart

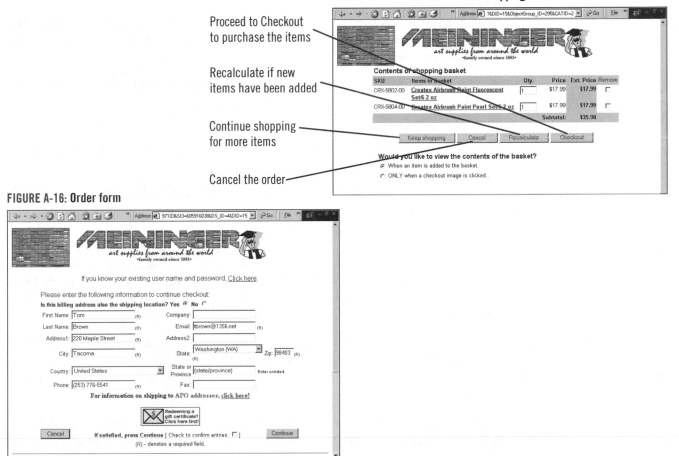

Proceed to Checkout to purchase the items

Recalculate if new items have been added

Continue shopping for more items

Cancel the order

FIGURE A-16: Order form

FIGURE A-17: Sample shipping costs

Click here to cancel order

E-Commerce

E-Commerce

Exploring Online Stores

The best way to understand the various phases of the online shopping process is to buy a product yourself. Even if you don't want to actually purchase a product, you can usually move almost all of the way through the ordering system before you need to provide confidential information such as your name, address, and credit card number. ✎ You decide to learn more about the online purchasing process by analyzing your online shopping experience at two Web sites. The new Online Development Group needs a color printer, so Hiromi asks you to research how you could purchase one online.

Steps

1. Open the Project File **ECA-01.doc** in your word-processing program, then save it as **Online Shopping**

   The document contains a series of questions about your online shopping experience. The purpose of these questions is to provide you with guidelines for evaluating your shopping experience at the two online stores you select.

2. Open your Web browser, go to *http://www.course.com/illustrated/ecommerce*, click the link for **Unit A**, then click the link for **Exploring Online Stores**

3. Select two sites from the list provided

   Any of the choices should provide you with a well-developed Web site from which you can purchase a color printer.

4. Go to one of the sites listed in the Student Online Companion for this lesson, then search the site for the type of color printer that you want to purchase

   You want to purchase the same or a similar product on both sites so that you can meaningfully compare your online shopping experience. You can base your selection on price, features, or brand. For example, you may decide to search for an inkjet color printer that costs approximately $250. Figure A-18 shows the search tool on the Office Depot site that was used to find a color printer. Figure A-19 shows the description of one of the color printers that appeared in the search results.

5. Enter the **brand** and/or **price range** of the printer you've selected in the designated space at the top of the Online Shopping document

   Select the type of color printer that you might actually want to purchase, should you ever be in the market to buy a color printer.

6. Enter the **URL** of the first company you've chosen, then answer the questions provided

   Your goal is to analyze the shopping experience—from searching for the product to purchasing it.

7. Repeat Step 6 to gather information about your shopping experience on the second Web site you selected

   If you find that the exact same brand is not available on the second Web site, select a brand in the same price range. Figure A-20 shows how a similar color printer is described on the Staples site. The printer was found by following a link to "printers" on the Staples home page, then following a series of links to find a description of printers in a price range similar to the printer selected from the Office Depot site.

8. When you have completed all the questions for each company, type **Your Name** at the bottom of the document, save it, print a copy, then close the document

FIGURE A-18: Searching for a color printer

"color printer" entered in the search tool

FIGURE A-19: Selecting a brand

Note the brand name

Note the price

FIGURE A-20: Similar printer on another site

Different brand

Similar price

E-Commerce

E-Commerce

Identifying E-Commerce Challenges

From a company's point of view, e-commerce is not necessarily the gold mine that it might become for some of the highest profile dot.com companies. The term **dot.com** is used to describe companies that conduct most—if not all—of their business online. The word *dot* refers to the period that separates the Web site name, or **domain name** (for example, Amazon or Staples) from the word *com* (commercial), which is the **top-level domain** designation. Other top-level domain designations include org, net, and gov. Dot.com usually indicates a Web site that conducts business exclusively on the Internet. Table A-3 shows some of the advantages and disadvantages of conducting business over the Internet. While MediaLoft management is anxious to develop an e-commerce strategy, they also want to be informed about possible pitfalls. Hiromi asks you to research some of the challenges associated with e-commerce.

Details

► Competition

From a Web developer's point of view, one of the most difficult challenges of creating a successful e-commerce Web site is how to keep customers on the Web site until they make a purchase. If a Web site is difficult to navigate, if the products are not described well, if forms are not easy to fill out, or even worse, if links are broken and pictures take too long to load or have disappeared, consumers might simply click to another site. The ease with which consumers can go from site to site on the Internet has shifted the balance of power from the seller to the buyer. A company doing business on the Internet must create a Web site that keeps a potential buyer entertained and informed for as long as it takes that buyer to make a purchasing decision. Web developers call a site that attracts and keeps surfers a **sticky** site.

► Costs

In these early years of e-commerce development, much of the up-front costs of building and maintaining a Web site have yet to be recovered. Wild fluctuations in the stock prices of dot.com companies are predicted to continue as stockholders seek a return on their investments. Some analysts predict the demise of purely dot.com companies, and the strengthening of click and mortar companies that have a solid presence and broad recognition in the real world (the brick) along with a comprehensive, user-friendly Web site that generates significant online sales (the click). Some click and mortar companies are expected to vigorously acquire dot.coms as they expand their online presence and take advantage of the latest technological developments.

► Disintermediation

In traditional commerce, many businesses operate as **middlemen** to negotiate transactions between a business and the consumer, or between two businesses. Agents, brokers, and sales representatives are all examples of middlemen. These middlemen are fast being made obsolete because consumers can go directly to a company's Web site and purchase products and services without help from an agent or other intermediary. The process of edging out the middleman is called **disintermediation**.

► Intermediation

While some intermediaries might be made obsolete by e-commerce, other companies are emerging as a new kind of **intermediary** to exploit markets that could not have existed before the Internet. New intermediaries include auction sites, payment-processing sites, and Web site storefront services. In Figure A-21, a page from Looksmart's Beseen Web site describes the Buy It! button. When a consumer clicks the Buy It! button, credit card information is processed by Beseen, and the original vendor pays Beseen a transaction fee. This new type of intermediation is also referred to as **re-intermediation**. Individuals who develop Internet-based intermediation solutions are referred to as **cyberintermediaries**.

FIGURE A-21: Buy It! button service

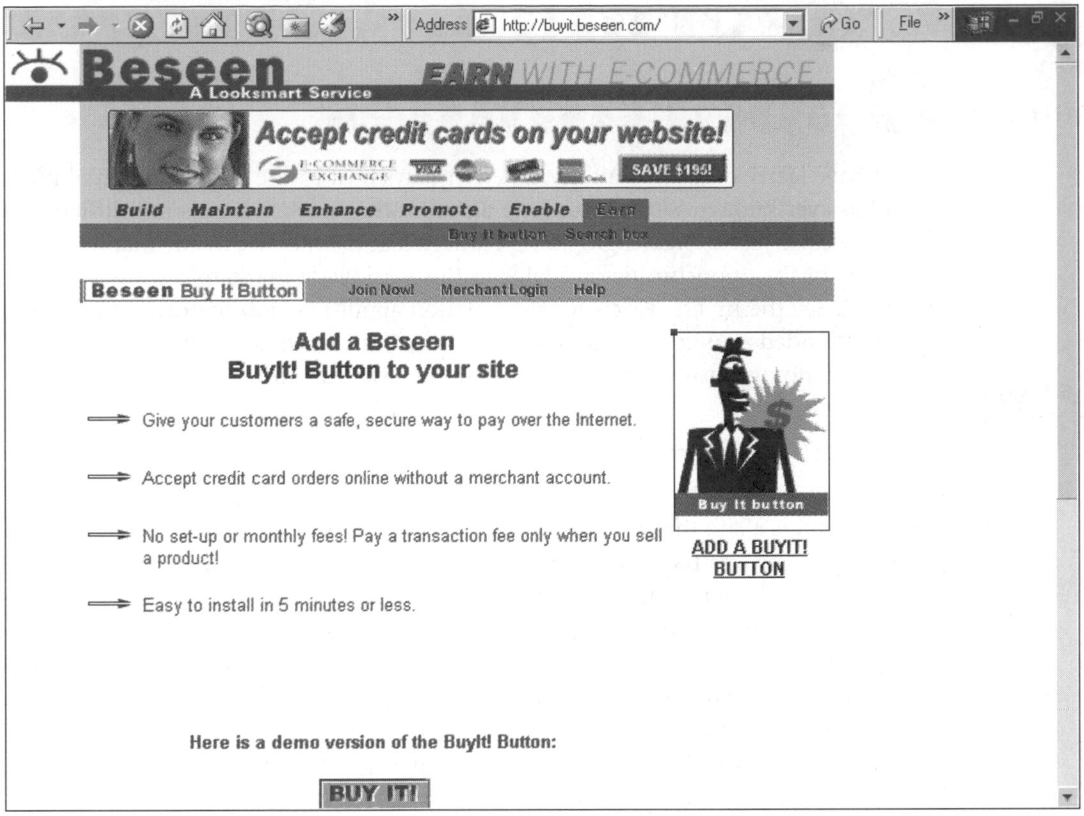

TABLE A-3: Advantages and disadvantages of e-commerce from a vendor's point of view

advantages	disadvantages
Advertise worldwide	High start-up costs
Reach narrow market segments regardless of location	Difficult to keep current
Reduce costs related to processing orders	Trained employees are not readily available
Streamline business operations by incorporating B2B transactions	Difficult to combine e-commerce transactions with current systems
Form virtual communities	Language barriers
	Government and tax regulations still unclear
	Worldwide standards not yet established

In The Know

A New Class of Middlemen

"The e-commerce revolution may have gotten a lot of press for the way it has eliminated the middleman standing between buyers and suppliers, but at the same time it has enabled a whole new class of middlemen. These new market makers go by a variety of names: cybermediaries, info intermediaries, netmarkets, e-markets. But get used to them; Gartner Group Inc. predicts around 100,000 of these online marketplaces will be in operation by the year 2001, up from around 300 now." *Source: Margaret Kane, ZDNet News* [5]

E-Commerce

Exploring E-Commerce Opportunities

As you have learned in this unit, the Internet plays host to the largest potential marketplace the world has ever known. While setting up a stall in this marketplace is not difficult, making your stall a success is just as challenging on the Internet as it would be in any market. The difference is that many of the opportunities available in this worldwide marketplace are just beginning to be identified. See the In The Know for information about new job opportunities. Hiromi recently attended an e-commerce conference where she learned about opportunities available for successfully doing business on the Internet. She asks you to find out more information about these opportunities.

Details

► Web Portals

A Web portal is a site that provides you with your gateway onto the Internet. Usually, the Web portal page is the first page that appears when you launch your Web browser. Figure A-22 shows the Excite portal page. You can customize this portal page by changing its layout and adding content unique to your own needs and interests. For example, some portal pages allow you to include a daily horoscope, stock information, and reminders about upcoming birthdays. Web portals are not new; however, their potential for attracting and keeping consumers is enormous. Portals can be used to foster a sense of community while also providing consumers with search tools, directories, and links to all kinds of content, in addition to sticky features such as free e-mail programs and chat rooms. Portals can even target a specific market, such as sports fans, armchair travelers, or music lovers.

► Virtual Communities

The term **virtual community** is defined as a place where people and businesses gather online. A virtual community does not actually exist in a specific geographical location. Virtual communities aim to attract people with similar interests who can meet online to share experiences, just as the shopping mall has replaced the local town square in many real-world communities. One of the most exciting aspects of the Internet is its capability for bringing people together from all over the world.

► Customization

A key concept that will drive the future of e-commerce is **customization**. The more that a Web site can serve the needs of each individual customer, the greater the site's chance of success. Figure A-23 shows how the Land's End clothing company has customized its services by providing customers with a tool for building a 3-D model based on their own measurements. Customers then can receive personalized fashion tips and even try on clothing. A Web-based company's challenge is to build customer relationships that cannot be formed in the real world. Companies can tailor their Web sites to individual customers, which will help build long-term relationships. Just as most of us like to be recognized when we walk into our corner store, we also like to be greeted and served when we click onto our favorite Web site.

In The Know

Job Opportunities

In addition to the demands for skilled technical workers is the increasing demand for people who can generate content, develop marketing strategies, and develop innovative ways of serving customers via the Internet. Vicki Saunders, CEO of NRG, an Internet advisory, incubator, and venture capital company, maintains that "Traditional business training doesn't necessarily prepare you for something that no one has ever experienced before. We have anthropologists, designers, programmers, historians, and English majors working here."
Source: "From little acorns grow..." The National Post, Linda Frum [6]

FIGURE A-22: **Excite portal page**

Search sites for keywords

Get free voice mail, e-mail, and Internet access

Get stock quotes

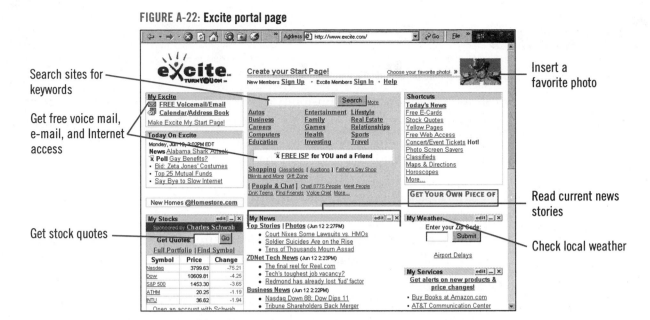

Insert a favorite photo

Read current news stories

Check local weather

FIGURE A-23: **Customization options**

After selecting measurements, various appearance traits are selected

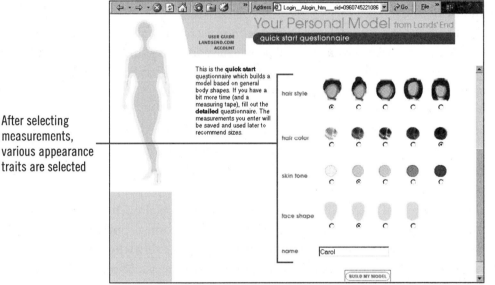

Suit is tried on the personal model

E-Commerce

Focus
Proposed Internet Principles

The Computer Professionals for Social Responsibility (CPSR) is an alliance of computer scientists and other professionals who present information about the impact of computer technology on society. Illustrated below are the CPSR draft principles for their One Planet, One Net initiative. Read the seven principles, then answer the questions that follow.

1. The Net links us all together.

The nature of people and their use of networking technology provides a strong natural drive towards universal interconnection. Because the flow of information on the Net transcends national boundaries, any restrictions within a single country may act to limit the freedom of those in other countries as well.

The true value of the Internet is found in people, not in technology. Since each new user increases the value of the Net for all, the potential of the Net will only be reached when all who desire can openly and freely use the Net.

2. The Net must be open and available to all.

The Net should be available to all who wish to use it, regardless of economic, social, political, linguistic, or cultural differences or abilities. We must work to ensure that all people have the access to the technology, education, and support necessary for constructive, active participation. People in all walks of life should have as much right to send and receive information as do the affluent and powerful.

3. Net users have the right to communicate.

Every use of the Net is inherently an exercise of freedom of speech, to be restricted only at great peril to human liberty. The right to communicate includes the right to participate in communication through interacting, organizing, petitioning, mobilizing, assembling, collaborating, buying and selling, sharing, and publishing.

The Net offers great promise as a means of increasing global commerce and collaboration among businesses, but restrictions on information exchange would eviscerate that promise. Such restrictions include denial-of-service attacks and threats to shut down the connections of users who are not themselves engaged in disruption of the Net. Such restrictions also include the risk of physical, social, and economic retribution.

4. Net users have the right to privacy.

Without assurances of appropriate privacy, users of the Net will not communicate and participate in a meaningful manner.

The right to privacy includes at least three forms:

- Individual Network users should control the collection, use, and dissemination of personal data about themselves, including financial and demographic information.
- Network users should be free to use any available technical measures to help ensure the privacy of all aspects of their communications, including the right to remain anonymous.
- Individuals have the right to control who they communicate with, and how they conduct that communication. The privacy implied by the decision to not communicate must be respected.

5. People are the Net's stewards, not its owners.

Those who want to reap the benefits of the shared global Net are obliged to respect the rights of others who may wish to use the Net in different ways. We must work to preserve the free and open nature of the current Internet as a fragile resource that must be enriched and passed on to our children.

Individual pieces of the Net, such as wires, routers, and servers, have owners whose economic rights and interests must be respected. However, just as the ecosystem in which we live cannot be owned, the Net itself is not owned by anyone.

6. Administration of the Net should be open and inclusive.

The Net should be administered in an open, inclusive, and democratic manner for the betterment of humanity. The needs of all who are affected by the Internet - including current users, future users, and those who are unable to or choose not to be users - must be considered when making technical, social, political, and economic decisions regarding the operations of the Internet.

Although administration of the Net should aim to enhance its efficiency, availability, and security, it should not do so at the cost of discouraging use of the Net. Administration should facilitate and encourage greater use of the Net for communication, rather than inhibit it in any way.

7. The Net should reflect human diversity, not homogenize it.

The Net has the potential to be as varied and multi-cultural as life itself. It can facilitate dialogue between communities and individuals that might previously not have encountered each other in a dozen lifetimes. However, the Net could also become a homogenizing force, working to suppress diversity in favor of a bland globalism.

Individuals and communities should not be forced to forego local cultures and traditions in order to participate in the Net. In order to preserve the vitality that comes with a diversity of viewpoints, we should work toward helping the whole world participate as equals.

Source: Computer Professionals for Social Responsibility [7]

Explore Further...

1. Do you agree with the following statement in Principle 1: "the potential of the Net will only be reached when all who desire can openly and freely use the Net"? Should countries have the right to limit the access their citizens have to the Internet? Research how other countries handle Internet access for their citizens, then write a one-page summary of the policies enforced by at least two countries whose Internet access policies differ from the Internet access policies in your own country.

2. Principle 2 states that the Net must be open and available to all. Find information about how government organizations and companies in your area are working to make the Internet available to all citizens, regardless of their economic, social, or cultural group. Write a two-page paper describing some of the programs available in your area. If you can't find local programs, look for nationwide programs. Your goal is to determine how your community is responding to the need to provide Internet access for all.

3. Do you agree that the Net should be restricted only at "great peril to human liberty"? Write a paper expressing your opinion regarding the rights of society and government to limit Internet access on the grounds of inappropriate content. What constitutes inappropriate content? Check the online news services for stories about the controversies surrounding the restriction of content available on the Internet.

4. Do you agree that the Net cannot be owned by any one organization? Write a one- to two-page paper describing the advantages and disadvantages of preserving the free and open nature of the Internet.

5. Principle 7 states that the Net should reflect human diversity, not homogenize it. Write a one- to two-page paper describing how communities, businesses, and governments can work together to achieve this principle.

Practice

► Review

Fill in the blank with the best answer.

1. You can define e-commerce as using the _____ to assist in the trading of goods and services.
2. E-commerce is also referred to as e-business or _____.
3. You could refer to the Internet as the world's largest _____ playing field.
4. The two factors that enabled the growth of the Internet were the development of the Graphical User Interface and the Web. True/False? _____
5. GII stands for _____ Information Infostructure.
6. Retail locations in the real world are referred to as brickwork stores. True/False? _____
7. Learning how to navigate a Web site requires many hours of training. True/False? _____
8. B2B stands for Business-to-_____ e-commerce.
9. A key activity associated with B2B e-commerce is the overhaul of _____ trading processes.
10. Revenue from B2C e-commerce will far outstrip revenues from B2B e-commerce. True/False? _____
11. Most company Web sites are tightly integrated with all company operations. True/False? _____
12. A Web site that includes limited information about a company and descriptions of its products or services is often called an electronic _____.
13. Traditional middlemen such as agents and brokers are prospering from the opportunities provided by e-commerce. True/False? _____
14. The term _____ is used to describe activities once performed by middlemen.
15. A Web _____ acts like a gateway to the Internet.
16. A Web site that surfers want to visit for a long time is called a _____ site.
17. A _____ community exists only in cyberspace.

► Independent Challenges

1. The Web contains many sites dedicated to providing the most up-to-the minute information about e-commerce. Reports and news articles related to the latest e-commerce developments are appearing every day. As part of your new job as a research assistant for a trade magazine called *Fast Track*, you have been asked to summarize three current articles related to e-commerce.

To complete this independent challenge:

1. Open your Web browser, go to *http://www.course.com/illustrated/ecommerce*, click the link to Unit A, then click the link to Independent Challenge 1.
2. Explore the links provided to find three articles related to the latest developments in e-commerce. You want to find articles that provide a general overview of e-commerce and how it is affecting the global economy. Since hundreds of articles on e-commerce topics are available, be sure to focus your effort on those articles that provide a general overview of e-commerce developments.
3. Open the Project File ECA-02.doc in your word-processing program. This document contains the table that you will use to enter information about the articles you have found.
4. Save the document as *E-Commerce Articles*.

5. Complete the tables with information about each of the three articles you have chosen. If you cannot find information such as the author's name or the date the article was written, indicate Not Available in the appropriate table cell. Note that the Date Accessed is the date that you found and read the article.

6. Summarize each article in approximately 50 words.

7. Type **Your Name** at the bottom of the document, save it, print a copy, then close the document.

2. The Internet is rapidly changing how businesses conduct transactions with each other. While traditional middleman positions are being eliminated, new opportunities are being developed for Web-based companies to facilitate e-commerce between businesses. You are the owner of a medium-sized company that is starting to explore how to use the Internet to streamline operations, save money, and increase profitability. You decide to identify three ways in which your company could replace traditional business processes with e-commerce solutions.

To complete this independent challenge:

a. Fill in the box below with the name of your business and a description of its products and/or services. For example, you could call your company Snowdrift Ski Rentals, and describe it as a ski rental operation that rents ski and snowboard equipment from a small retail location in a ski resort.

Company Name...

Description..

b. Identify three current business activities that are not conducted over the Internet. Make sure at least one of the activities appears to have nothing to do with the Internet. For example, a ski rental operation could order all its equipment from a sales representative, distribute advertising flyers in local parking lots, and use a take-a-number system to guide customers through the rental equipment process. Note that you can choose at least one business practice that involves customers rather than another business. Many e-commerce solutions relate to how a business can streamline its operations to increase efficiency and profitability, regardless of whether the end user is another business or a consumer.

c. Write the business practices you've identified in the table below.

Business Practice 1:...

Business Practice 2:...

Business Practice 3:...

d. List ways you could use the Internet to either replace or assist the business practices you've identified. Note that the Internet probably can't replace *all* business practices. However, you often can find ways of using the Internet in combination with traditional methods to increase efficiency. For example, the ski rental company could have quite a problem with its take-a-number system of guiding customers through the ski rental process. Bottlenecks would inevitably occur, waiting times might be long, and tempers could fray, resulting in a loss of business. To offset these difficulties, the ski rental company could offer customers the opportunity to complete many of the rental procedures online. For example, customers can access the Internet from the comfort of their hotel rooms, and then complete a form that provides the ski rental company with contact information, ski equipment requirements, sizes, and age. When the customer arrives at the ski rental store, the ski equipment would be all ready to go—or at most, the customer might only need to try on a pair of ski boots.

e. Complete the table below with your e-commerce solution(s) for each of the three business practices you identified.

E-commerce solution(s) for business practice 1: ....

E-commerce solution(s) for business practice 2: ....

E-commerce solution(s) for business practice 3: ....

f. Open your word-processing program and create a one- to two-page document that describes your e-commerce solutions in as much detail as possible. Your goal is to identify ways in which your company could save money, more effectively serve its customers or more efficiently accomplish business transactions, and, finally, increase profits.

g. Format the document attractively, type **Your Name** at the bottom, save it as *E-Commerce Solutions*, print a copy, then close the document.

3. While traditional intermediaries such as agents and brokers are being made obsolete by e-commerce, many companies are responding to the challenge by developing intermediary businesses specific to the Internet. An intermediary is a company that helps facilitate transactions. Cyberintermediaries facilitate transactions that are conducted online.
    To complete this independent challenge:

a. Open your Web browser, go to *http://www.course.com/illustrated/ecommerce*, click the link to Unit A, then click the link to Independent Challenge 3.

b. Pick two sites that you think act as intermediaries to facilitate e-commerce transactions.

c. Consider each site with relation to the following questions:
 1. What is the purpose of the site?
 2. Does the site conduct primarily B2B or B2C transactions?
 3. How does the site generate income?
 4. How has the site filled a need that did not exist before the Internet?

d. Open the Project File ECA-03.doc in your word-processing program. This document contains the table that you will use to enter information about the Web sites you have found.

e. Save the document as *E-Commerce Intermediaries.*

f. Complete the table with information about each site.

g. Below the table, write a one-paragraph description of an intermediary that you think could be developed to facilitate e-commerce transactions and related activities. See if you can come up with the next great dot.com idea!

h. Once you have identified your own ideas, see if you can find a company on the Internet that has already implemented a similar idea. Include information about this company in your description.

i. Type **Your Name** at the bottom of the document, save it, print a copy, then close the document.

4. Theoretically, a Web site can sell products and services to anyone anywhere in the world. In practice, however, many Web sites still sell primarily to people in the company's geographical area. For example, a consumer who wishes to purchase a large item such as a sofa or a desk might be reluctant to order it from a Web site half-way across the country because shipping costs could be prohibitive. You decide to investigate Web sites in your area that sell a specific product.
    To complete this independent challenge:

a. Select a product that you might want to purchase from a Web site associated with a company that is either based in your geographical area or has an outlet in your geographical area. Your goal is to find local companies so that you can minimize shipping costs. For example, you could choose a product such as a coffee table, a fruit tree, a tent, or a dishwasher. Try to select a product that you wouldn't normally think of ordering online.

b. Go to the Alta Vista search engine at *http://www.altavista.com* and enter a question such as: "Where are furniture stores in Vancouver?" or "Where are sports equipment stores in Hong Kong?" You can also use Yahoo!, Excite, Infoseek, or another search engine of your choice.

c. Follow links to find two stores in your geographical area that sell the product you want.

d. Open the Project File ECA-04.doc in your word-processing program. This document contains the table that you will use to enter information about the Web sites you have found.

e. Save the document as *Neighborhood E-Commerce Solutions*.

f. Complete the table with information about each site.

g. Type **Your Name** at the bottom of the document, save it, print a copy, then close the document.

► Up To Date

Figure A-24 shows the worldwide statistics for Internet usage as of 1999. As you can see, the estimated worldwide total was 242 million users.

To complete the Up To Date challenge:

1. Open your Web browser, go to *http://www.course.com/illustrated/ecommerce,* click the link for Unit A, then click the link to Up To Date.

2. Follow links to find the latest statistics for worldwide Internet usage. Try to check at least two sites.

3. Fill in the table below with the results of your search. Your goal is to determine how the statistics for worldwide Internet usage have changed since this book was published.

FIGURE A-24: World Wide Web statistics

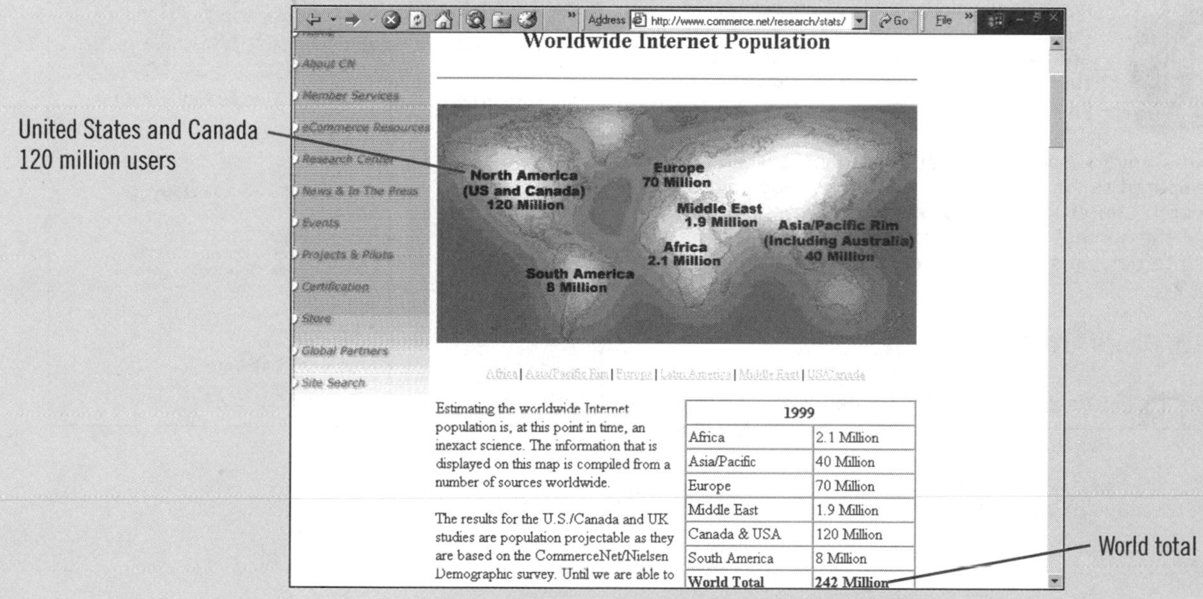

United States and Canada 120 million users

World total

Current date: ....

URL site: ....

Europe ....

Asia/Pacific ....

North America ....

▶ Visual Workshop

Open your Web browser, go to *http://www.course.com/illustrated/ecommerce*, click the link for Unit A, then click the link for Visual Workshop. Follow the link to the current issue of the *E-Commerce Times* will appear on your screen. Compare the issue of *E-Commerce Times* that appears on your screen with the issue of *E-Commerce Times* in Figure A-25. Complete the table with information about the *E-Commerce Times* issue on your screen.

FIGURE A-25

Current date: ....

Titles and summaries of the top three articles: ....

1. ....

2. ....

3. ....

Describe any changes in the appearance of site ....

....

E-Commerce
Options

Objectives

- ► **Identify options**
- ► **Review features**
- ► **Understand Internet access**
- ► **Review Web hosting vocabulary**
- ► **Identify entry-level options**
- ► **Understand storefront services**
- ► **Understand software options**
- ► **Explore storefront software packages**
- ► **Explore e-commerce developers**
- ► **Understand e-business solutions**

The options available for setting up a store in cyberspace are just as numerous as those available for doing business in the real world. You can choose an e-commerce activity that ranges from the online equivalent of a lemonade stand, all the way up to a full-scale e-business that sells thousands of products and employs an army of Web page designers, marketers, order processors, and content developers. You can also choose to adapt an existing Web site to accept online purchasing, or you can use a storefront software program to build a new e-commerce venture from scratch. In this unit, you will look at some of the main options for setting up and maintaining an e-commerce presence on the Internet. ➤ Ian MacDonald has joined the Online Development Group at MediaLoft. His first task is to analyze the various options available for setting up and maintaining an e-commerce Web site.

E-Commerce

Identifying Options

E-commerce entrepreneurs, Internet Service Providers (ISPs), software developers, and Web page designers are all competing to provide small and large businesses with e-commerce opportunities, software, and solutions. In fact, one of the most lucrative e-commerce opportunities could be providing these services to businesses that want to establish an e-commerce Web site. The option a business chooses will depend on the goals it has established for selling its products or services online. Ian asks you to identify the issues related to choosing e-commerce options. In particular, Ian is interested in determining how a brick and mortar company such as MediaLoft can develop an effective online presence.

Details

► Online Goals

Although many options exist to help you create an online presence quickly and inexpensively, establishing a successful online presence is as challenging in cyberspace as it is at your local shopping mall. You first need to determine your business goals, and then you need to select a method of establishing an online presence that meets those goals. Table B-1 lists common goals for e-commerce entrepreneurs, along with possible e-commerce solutions. The option you select depends on your business goals and the resources that you have on hand, or that you can expect to generate.

► Size Considerations

A company's preferred e-commerce solution also depends on the number of visitors they anticipate receiving, and the number of transactions they anticipate processing. If a site becomes busy and cannot handle the volume of visitors it receives, the site might crash, leaving potential customers to click away to another site. To ensure that the e-commerce site you build today can handle the traffic you anticipate tomorrow, the solution you choose must include sufficient bandwidth. The **bandwidth** of a site determines the number of simultaneous visits that the site can handle in a given time period. You can think of bandwidth as the amount of data that is able to traverse a communications circuit in one second.

► Scalability

As a company becomes successful in its e-commerce endeavors, it should be able to move easily from a low-cost, low-maintenance e-commerce solution to a higher-level solution without disrupting service to its customers. One way that a business can enhance **scalability** is to select an appropriate domain name that the business can use for many years. The domain name is the part of the Web site address that identifies the location of the files for that Web site. For example, course.com in the Web site address *www.course.com* is Course Technology's domain name. You need to be aware of the possible limitations of an online business with a Web site address that is a subsection of a larger domain. For example, the address *www.travelbooks.vstorehome.com*, tells surfers that the Travel Books business exists as a subset of a domain called Vstore. An address such as *www.travelbooks.com* tells surfers that the Web site is more likely to belong to a company that specializes in books about travel. The consumer might be inclined to trust the specialist company more because, at the very least, the company is established enough to afford its own domain name.

► Bricks, Clicks, and Dot.Coms

As you learned in the previous unit, a brick and mortar company maintains retail outlets in the real world, while a click and mortar company is one that does business in both the real and cyber worlds. Turning bricks into clicks requires a significant investment in a new electronic infrastructure that can accommodate online orders. In addition, the corporate culture might need to accommodate new or expanded departments, such as online marketing. A dot.com company faces different challenges than its brick and mortar equivalent. On the plus side, dot.com companies use a Web-based business model that allows them to take advantage of the latest Internet technology without the burden of integrating pre-Internet systems. Furthermore, dot.com companies are not generally expected to show a near-term profit. On the minus side, dot.com profitability has yet to prove itself in the long term. Investors might not want to wait for the company to build its infrastructure, develop successful marketing campaigns that drive traffic to the Web site, and finally, show a profit.

TABLE B-1: Goals and Solutions

goals	resources	e-commerce solutions
• Generate extra income without spending much time.	• Very limited money • No products to sell • Limited time	• Link a Web site with other sites that offer affiliate programs. • Sell items in online auctions. • Create a virtual storefront to market other companies' products.
• Sell fewer than 10 products per month.	• Limited money • Limited Web expertise • Limited business experience	• Use a service that hosts your store for free and that processes credit card transactions.
	option 1	
• Sell a limited number of products. • Supplement income from a brick and mortar store.	• Limited money • Limited Web expertise • Some business experience • Customer base	• Open an online store on Yahoo, iCat, or other e-mall-style e-commerce provider.
	option 2	
	• Web site in place • Limited money • Some technical expertise • Some business experience • Customer base	• Use a basic storefront software program to add e-commerce tools such as a shopping cart to an existing Web site.
	option 1	
• Sell a range of products. • Generate income.	• No Web site • Some financial resources • Good technical expertise (or access to expertise) • Business experience • Marketing expertise	• Use a midrange storefront software program to build an e-commerce site.
	option 2	
	• Basic Web site in place • Good financial resources • No technical expertise • Business marketing experience	• Hire an e-commerce developer to upgrade and maintain the site.
• Sell a very wide range of products. • Generate significant profits.	• E-commerce Web site • Top-level financial resources • Experienced technical staff	• Design new software to suit the specific needs of the company. • Run the site from an in-house secure server.
• Increase the size of an existing Web site without disrupting service to customers.	• E-commerce Web site • Experienced technical staff	• Run the site on two parallel servers in order to handle more traffic.

In The Know

Established Companies and E-Commerce

"In theory, many established companies are well positioned to succeed at e-commerce. They possess critical assets—strong brands, established customer relationships, and existing logistics systems—that can give them an edge over start-up competitors. In practice, companies will not be able to exploit these assets unless they can effectively organize for e-commerce. Indeed, for large incumbent companies, the most difficult challenges of e-commerce are not so much strategic as they are organizational." *Source: Boston Consulting Group*[1]

Reviewing Features

A company interested in doing business online needs to develop a Web site that displays products, facilitates transactions, and provides customers with ongoing information about their orders. Just as with a brick and mortar store, an online store must be easy to shop in from the customer's point of view, and efficient to manage from the vendor's point of view. When you compare the shopping process at a brick and mortar store with the shopping process in an online store, only the physical environment and the specific steps required to complete a transaction are different. Instead of pushing a shopping cart up and down crowded aisles, the customer now clicks buttons on a screen. However, the customer still selects products, purchases them, and receives them. ⬤ Before you evaluate the various options for setting up an e-commerce presence on the Internet, you decide to review a cross-section of the features that MediaLoft might want to include in its online store.

Details

► List of Features

Table B-2 describes the principal features of an effective online store. These features are presented in the approximate order in which customers will encounter them. For example, a customer needs to buy something before they receive an e-mail acknowledgement of the purchase. Similarly, a customer will probably browse a catalog and use search tools before adding items to a shopping cart. You will explore each of these features in more detail as you progress through this book. As you read about the features, refer to the illustration of a full-service online store shown in Figure B-1. Some of the features described in Table B-2 are visible on the store's home page.

TABLE B-2: Online Store Features

feature	description
Navigation	Navigation aids make moving from page to page as fast and easy as possible and can inform customers of their exact stage in the purchasing process.
Catalog	Products are organized in a catalog through which customers can browse—either by using a search tool or by following links to product descriptions.
Search tools	Online stores with an extensive catalog of items require a search tool that helps customers quickly locate a product.
Shopping cart	The items that a customer selects are listed on a separate Web page called a shopping cart. A customer can add or remove items before proceeding to the checkout page to enter contact and payment information. Figure B-2 shows five items contained in the shopping cart on the wine.com Web site.
Customer registration	Customers can set up an account so that they enter contact and payment information the first time they purchase products. On subsequent visits to the store, customers need only identify themselves and the site automatically processes their purchases.
Help system	A Help system provides customers with access to information at any stage in the purchasing process. Help can consist of toll-free telephone numbers, e-mail, Frequently Asked Questions (FAQs) pages, and live online help.
Payment processsing	Payments are made online using a credit card or another form of electronic payment. Some payments are made in real time, so the customer receives their order confirmation immediately.
Security	Credit card payments are encrypted and processed on a secure server. **Encryption** refers to the transformation of data into a scrambled form. A **secure server** is the computer that handles the e-commerce transaction so that customer information cannot be accessed or stolen.
Shipping Integration	Shipping costs are automatically calculated, depending on the customer's location and price range. Customers can also choose shipping options at a variety of prices.
Taxation	Taxes for the customer's location are automatically calculated. In the United States, the online merchant must have a location in the same state as the customer to charge sales tax, although this requirement could change as taxation laws related to the Internet are developed and amended.

FIGURE B-1: E-Commerce features

Click navigation aids to access online catalogs

Use the company's domain name to quickly find the Web site

Use search tools to find specific products

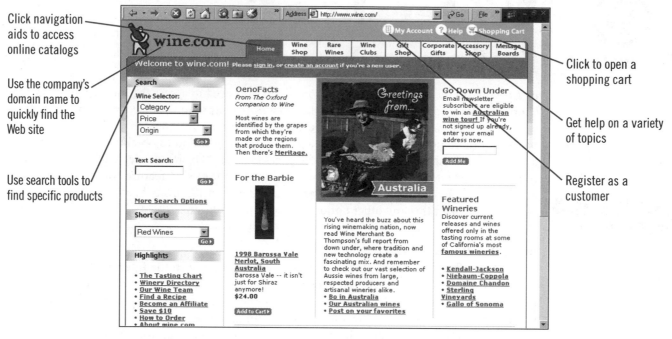

Click to open a shopping cart

Get help on a variety of topics

Register as a customer

FIGURE B-2: Shopping cart that contains selected items

Items to purchase

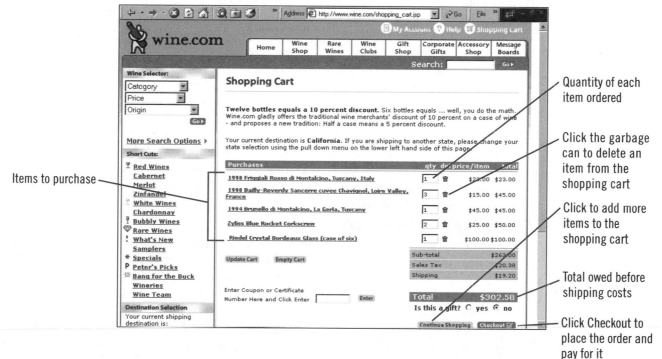

Quantity of each item ordered

Click the garbage can to delete an item from the shopping cart

Click to add more items to the shopping cart

Total owed before shipping costs

Click Checkout to place the order and pay for it

TABLE B-2: Online Store Features (continued)

feature	description
E-mail acknowledgement	Immediately after a customer purchases a product, an e-mail is sent to confirm the order.
Backend integration	Online store transactions are fully integrated with accounting systems and with databases that contain customer information and inventory lists the company uses for other distribution methods.
Tracking	Tracking software on the Web site documents how many visitors have visited the site each hour or day, where they come from, how long they stay, and if they make a purchase.

Understanding Internet Access

Before you can set up an online store in any form, you need to access the Internet and you need to obtain a Web host. You can access the Internet from your school, office, or a community facility, such as a library or recreation center, or you can pay an Internet Service Provider (ISP) to connect your computer via a cable or telephone line. In addition to obtaining an ISP, you need to find a Web hosting provider to store the pages of your Web site for viewing on the Web. The e-commerce solution you choose depends on the functions and features of the Web hosting provider that carries your Web site. At present, an ISP hosts MediaLoft's Web site. Ian asks you to look at this and other options for hosting a Web site.

Details

► **Internet Service Provider**

An **Internet Service Provider** (ISP) connects your computer to the Internet. A basic account with an ISP provides you with an e-mail address and limited or full access to the Internet, depending on the package you purchase. For example, some customers pay for unlimited access, while others pay a lesser sum for only a specified numbers of hours per day, week, or month. Figure B-3 shows a Web site that offers free Internet access to customers who agree to keep advertising materials visible on their screen while they surf.

► **Web Hosting**

The company that hosts a Web site is called a **Web hosting provider.** You can pay your ISP to host your Web site, or you can choose a different company to be the host. Some ISPs provide a limited amount of storage for the files that make up a Web site as part of a basic Internet connectivity package, but these basic sites do not necessarily allow e-commerce activities. You will often need to pay an extra monthly fee to conduct business and you may not be allowed to use custom written Common Gateway Interface (CGI) scripts. A **CGI script** is used to transfer information (such as ordering information) from a computer on the Internet to the host computer. You can also set up a Web site with a free Web hosting service, such as Yahoo Geocities or About.com. However, you will probably not be allowed to conduct business on your free Web site. Ultimately, the Web hosting provider you select will be the one that provides you with the services and the features you want at a price that you are willing to pay. Figure B-4 shows the various packages offered by a typical Web hosting provider.

► **Web Hosting Provider Services**

Once you have selected a Web hosting provider, you can create your own Web pages and upload them to your Web site stored on the Web host's computer, which is, in turn, connected to the Internet. This configuration is known as **client-server**. The Web host's computer is a **server**, and any computer that requests information from the server, such as your home computer, is the **client**. Usually, you use File Transfer Protocol (FTP) to transfer files from the client computer to the server and back again. **File Transfer Protocol** is the protocol commonly used to transfer files over the Internet. FTP includes functions to log onto the Internet, list directories in connected computers, and copy files from one computer to another. Many Web hosting services also provide multiple e-mail accounts, shopping cart software, and access to a secure server to handle credit card processing.

► **Secure Servers**

To conduct e-commerce activities from a Web site on the Internet, you need a Web host that has access to two servers. The first server stores the pages in your Web site. The second server is a **secure server** that processes credit card and other payment transactions in a secure environment.

► **Self-Hosting**

Companies that host their own Web sites usually do so because they anticipate a high-volume of transactions, have the technical and financial resources to invest in special hardware and customized software, and have sufficient staff to maintain the entire system.

FIGURE B-3: Free ISP option

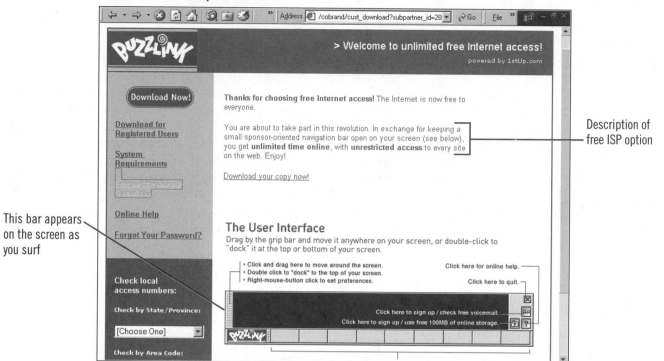

Description of free ISP option

This bar appears on the screen as you surf

FIGURE B-4: Sample Web hosting solutions

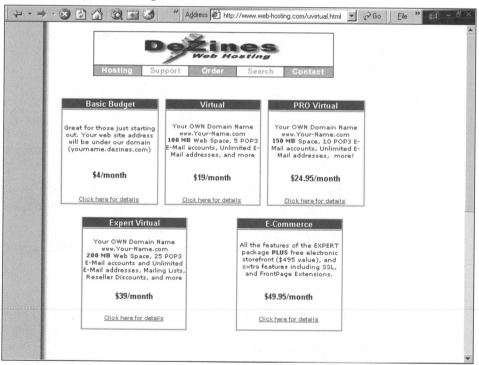

Web Hosting Advantages

One of the greatest advantages of paying for a Web hosting service is that you also have access to technical support. Small-to-medium-sized businesses that cannot afford staff devoted to creating and maintaining their Web sites usually choose a Web hosting service. Many Web hosting services also provide you with Web page templates so that you can quickly create your own site.

Reviewing Web Hosting Vocabulary

Table B-3 defines many of the terms commonly associated with hosting a Web site on the Internet. You will frequently encounter these terms as you explore the various options for hosting an e-commerce site. For example, you will need to know how databases store customer and product information, and the difference between the IP address and host name address of your Web site. You will encounter many of the terms described in Table B-3 in later units. Figure B-5 shows one of the online glossaries that you can use to look up Web vocabulary terms. ◆ Ian asks you to review the terms listed in Table B-3 so that you can help him explain them in a presentation on ISP options he plans to give to the MediaLoft management.

Details

TABLE B-3: Web Hosting Vocabulary

web hosting terms	definition
ADSL	Asymmetrical Digital Subscriber Lines (ADSL) are used to transmit data at high speed over telephone lines. The lines are called asymmetric because the upload and download speeds are different (upload is faster). As a result, ADSL are suitable for Internet access because a Web server sends out much more data than it receives.
Backbone	High-speed lines or connections between large computers that provide a major pathway within a network. Examples include T1 or T3 lines, which are capable of linking thousands of individual users to the Internet.
Bit	Smallest unit of data that a computer can handle. Each bit has a value of zero or one. The abbreviation **bps** stands for bits per second, which measures how quickly data moves across the Internet. For example, in theory, a 56K modem transmits data at a rate of 56,000 bps, although in practice, the transmission speed is closer to 53,000 bits per second, depending on line conditions and the speed of the receiving modem. On the other hand, an ISDN line (see definition below) uses digital technology to transmit data at rates up to 128 kilobits per second (kpbs).
Client	An application or program that contacts a server to obtain data or make requests. For example, an e-mail program is called a client because it sends and receives messages via the server at an ISP.
Database	Structure used to organize and maintain information so that it can be easily retrieved. Databases connected to e-commerce sites typically contain product and customer information.
Download	Process of transferring programs and other files from a computer on the Web to your computer. For example, you can download games, music, software, and videos.
FTP	Method used to transfer files from one computer to another over the Internet, an intranet, a Local Area Network (LAN), a Wide Area Network (WAN), or any other network that uses the TCP/IP protocol and has FTP services running on its computers.
Host name	The unique identification of a computer that is directly connected to the Internet. For example, in an e-mail address such as ccram@course.com, the host name is course.com.
HTTP	HyperText Transfer Protocol (HTTP) is the protocol that defines how messages are formatted and transmitted on the World Wide Web. When you enter a Web site address (a URL) into a Web browser, you are actually sending an HTTP command to the Web server that asks the server to find and display the Web site that matches the address you've entered.
IP	The unique numerical identification of a computer that is directly connected to the Internet. A sample Internet Protocol (IP) address is 125.444.789.2. Usually, you connect with a computer via its host name because most host names are easier to remember than the computer's IP address.

FIGURE B-5: Webopedia online glossary

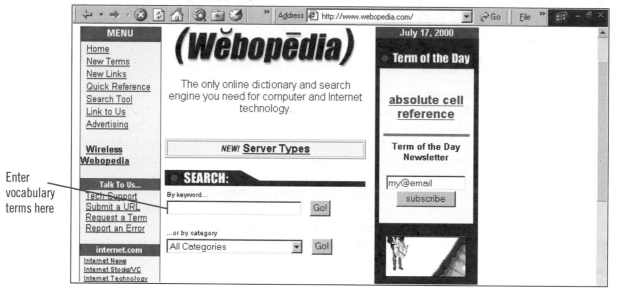

Enter vocabulary terms here

TABLE B-3: Web Hosting Vocabulary (continued)

web hosting terms	definition
ISDN	Integrated Services Digital Network (ISDN) is a digital telephone line that uses Digital Subscriber Protocol (DSP) to offer bandwidths up to 128 kbps.
Login or Logon	Process of identifying yourself to a computer on the Internet or on a local network (including Web sites). A login usually consists of your unique login name (for example, ccram) and a password (for example, marvin).
Mirrored site	A site that is maintained on two servers at once. Large companies might use mirrored Web sites because if one server is very busy or crashes, customers can then access the same site via the other server. A mirrored site can also be contained on one server with partitions set. A partition is a device used to place data in two separate storage areas. Each partition actually behaves like a separate disk drive or server.
Packet switching	Data is separated into packets for transmission over the Internet and then reassembled at the destination point. This method helps expedite transmission of large amounts of data and protects against securily breaches.
Router	The hardware used to connect two or more networks and then to sort and interpret the packets of data as they travel over the Internet.
Server	A computer that accepts requests from other computers that are connected to it.
T1 and T3 lines	High-speed (T1) and super high-speed (T3) digital connections to the Internet. Medium-sized companies that need to transmit large amounts of data use T1 lines. Large corporations and the backbones that connect ISPs use T3 lines.
TCP/IP	The Transmission Control Protocol/Internet Protocol (TCP/IP) is the set of rules (protocol) that determines how packets of data are sent across networks. TCP/IP actually includes a suite of over 100 protocols that includes protocols such as FTP and HTTP.
Upload	The process of transferring a file from your computer to a remote computer on the Internet.

Identifying Entry-Level Options

Not every retailer can aspire to have a 95% market share of its product, and not every business on the Internet needs to be an Amazon.com—an online business that receives thousands of visits every day, carries a broad range of products, and generates sales in the millions of dollars. New opportunities for conducting e-commerce are constantly being developed. Many of these opportunities target individuals and small businesses who want to get their feet wet in e-commerce without investing a great deal of time or money. Some of these entry-level options include virtual storefronts, affiliate programs, and online retailers. ✎ MediaLoft wants to explore entry-level options to see if its customers would enjoy linking to these sites. Ian is particularly interested in auctions as a method to generate revenue with little investment. Based on the information Ian provides, he might recommend that MediaLoft also link to one or two online auction sites. Ian asks you to help him research some of the entry-level options.

Details

► Free Stores

If you only wish to sell an ongoing number of limited items, you can quickly set up an online store through one of the free e-commerce providers. Many of these services handle all the transaction processing for you. All you need to do is market your Web site and have products available to ship when the orders arrive. Figure B-6 shows an example of a small business set up with B-City.

► Virtual Stores

You do not even need to have products to sell to participate in e-commerce. Several sites now provide you with the opportunity to become an e-mall sponsor, even if you don't have products of your own to sell. For example, if you are interested in collectible toys, you can set up a store that sells vintage stuffed teddy bears. You operate the store's Web page, but the products are actually purchased from another online store. The role of your store is to attract customers who are interested in the products you are advertising. As the virtual store intermediary, you collect a commission each time a customer buys a product. When you set up such a store, the e-mall company provides you with a limited number of options for customizing the appearance of the store and its content.

► Affiliate Programs

Hundreds of large Web sites offer affiliate programs as a marketing strategy. To participate in an affiliate program, you place a company's ad banner or other type of link on your Web site. A visitor to your site links to the affiliate program's site by clicking the ad. If a visitor eventually purchases something, you receive a commission. An advantage of affiliate programs is that your Web site does not need to include any other e-commerce elements. For example, your Web site could be a source of information and trivia about classic movies that also includes links to online stores selling movie memorabilia. Figure B-7 shows some of the many affiliate programs available to Web sites that sell travel services.

► Auctions

A relatively inexpensive and low-risk e-commerce option is to register with an auction site such as e-Bay or FirstAuction to sell a wide variety of items—new or used. Auction sites provide consumers with the opportunity to participate in the largest garage sale the world has ever known. You can sell your salad spinner or your signed Picasso. Prices might or might not be a bargain, and some consumers do not receive the products they've purchased, although large auction sites such as e-Bay provide customers with various tools to ensure a transaction's security. As you learned in Unit A, these auction sites are an example of the new brand of intermediary that has emerged because of the Internet. Figure B-8 shows an auction site page. Many of the entry-level e-commerce solutions discussed in this lesson exist because of the activities of the new cyberintermediaries.

FIGURE B-6: Free online store with B-City

Impersonal Web site address

Minimal links

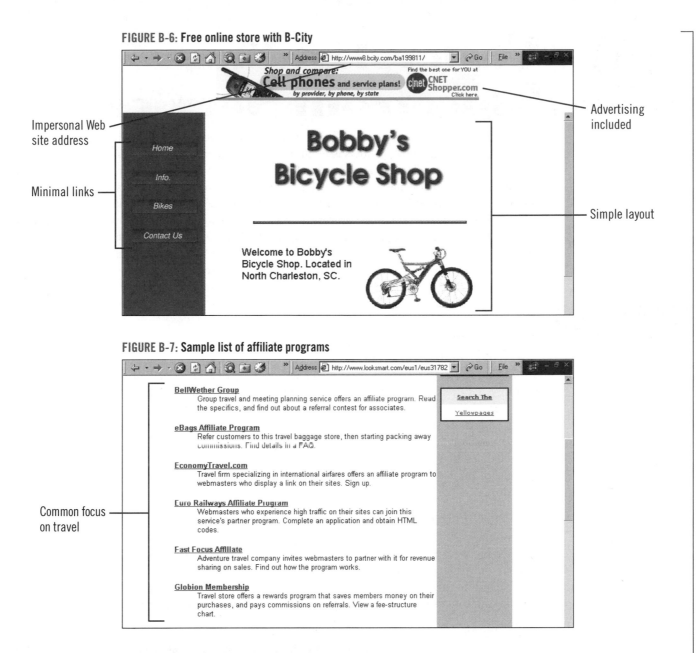

Advertising included

Simple layout

FIGURE B-7: Sample list of affiliate programs

Common focus on travel

FIGURE B-8: Sample page from an auction site

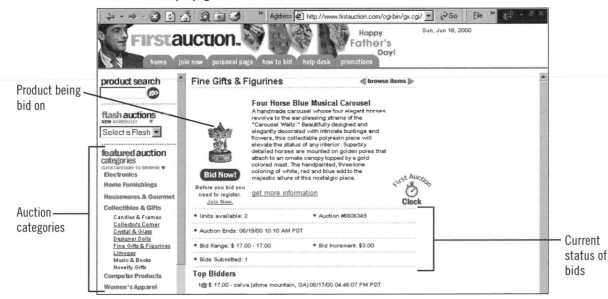

Product being bid on

Auction categories

Current status of bids

Understanding Storefront Services

One of the simplest—but not necessarily the least expensive—ways of building an online store that sells more than a few products is to choose one of the many online storefront services. You can use software downloaded from the storefront service provider to build an online store right in your browser. All you usually need to do is follow the onscreen instructions, often presented in the form of wizards. Most storefront software services charge a monthly fee that includes the Web site building software, transaction processing, and Web hosting. Some solutions are so simple that you don't even need special software or any specific knowledge of how to create a Web site. Although Ian is confident that he has the expertise to modify MediaLoft's existing Web site to accept and process online orders, he wants to explore some of the hosted storefront services available online. In particular, he wants to compare the characteristics of Web sites he can create with storefront service providers with what he has in mind for the Web site he plans to build.

Details

► Storefront Hosting Features

A storefront hosting service is also called a template service, an e-mall, or a storefront solution. Typically, a storefront hosting service supplies online tools that you use to select a design for your Web site, enter information about your products and services, select the products you want to sell, and select payment and shipping options. Most services provide customers with several different templates that offer a variety of designs and features. Storefront services charge varying fees that often include both a setup fee and a monthly fee. Table B-4 compares the pricing options for online stores hosted by Yahoo Store and ShopBuilder. Notice that the price levels for both stores are based on the number of products for sale.

► Web Site Creation

To create a store using a storefront hosting service, you complete a series of forms on your browser. Figure B-9 shows one of the selections you can make while using Merchant Manager to build an online store. Many of the storefront services are so easy to use that you can create a serviceable online store in just a few hours—providing you have products to sell, and can supply all the information about your company that the storefront service requires.

► Web Site Maintenance

Once you have built a store, you can edit it directly in your browser, using the tools provided by the storefront hosting service. For example, you can add new text and insert pictures of your products. The range of activities you can perform depends on the level of service selected.

► Evaluation

You can try out most storefront hosting services before you purchase them. For example, you can try out ShopBuilder's software by following wizards to set up a sample online shop. For many small-to-medium-sized businesses, these storefront services can offer a valuable e-commerce solution. To use them, you do not need to have expertise in Web technology, you do not need to spend a lot of money, and you can be up and running very quickly. In addition, you might not need to obtain a merchant account (an account that a vendor sets up to accept credit card payments), depending on the service you select. LookSmart's store handles all credit card transactions, while Yahoo Store requires that you also obtain a merchant account. The main disadvantage of using some storefront hosting services is the lack of design flexibility. In addition, not all services can be easily customized to meet the specific needs of every business. Figure B-10 shows the features offered by MerchandiZer, which provides a wide range of services for a monthly fee that varies depending on the number of items included in the online store. The MerchandiZer solutions can be customized so that online transactions are fully integrated into the other activities of the company.

FIGURE B-9: Choosing a color template on Merchant Manager

Templates available
in the Home and
Garden theme

FIGURE B-10: MerchandiZer features

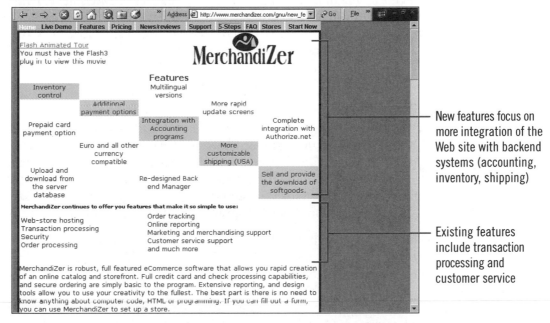

New features focus on
more integration of the
Web site with backend
systems (accounting,
inventory, shipping)

Existing features
include transaction
processing and
customer service

TABLE B-4: Comparison of Yahoo Store and ShopBuilder prices

yahoo store			shopbuilder		
store size	cost	items	store size	cost	items
Small	$100/month	Up to 50	Starter	$20/month	Up to 5
Large	$300/month	Up to 1000	Mini	$40/month	Up to 20
Larger	$100/month for each additional 100 items over 1000		Small	$70/month	Up to 100 items
			Large	$250/month	Up to 1000 items

E-Commerce

Understanding Software Options

You can modify an existing Web site by adding e-commerce capabilities such as a shopping cart and order transaction processing, or you can build an e-commerce Web site from the ground up. Many companies use Web page development software to create a Web site, and then use storefront software to organize and run an online store. In this lesson, you look at the options available for building a Web site and then enhancing it with e-commerce features. MediaLoft has a limited corporate Web site that was designed several years ago using a basic Web page development program. Ian asks you to check out the available options for modifying an existing Web site so that it can accept orders online.

Details

► Web Page Design Software

You can create a Web site yourself by using any number of off-the-shelf software packages such as Microsoft FrontPage, Adobe PageMill, Macromedia Dreamweaver, Cold Fusion, or IBM Top Page. These Web page design programs are also referred to as HyperText Markup Language (HTML) editors. Figure B-11 describes how Web developers use Adobe PageMill features to create a Web site.

► HTML

HTML is the computer language used to create documents that Web browsers read. All documents on the Internet contain HTML tags that tell browsers how to display the document. For example, if you want to display a word in boldface on a Web browser, you need to enclose the word with the <B> tag. Here's how the company name "Artcom Services" is coded so that it appears in boldface in the Web browser: <B>Artcom Services</B>. All HTML codes are hidden when a Web page is shown in a Web browser. You can view the HTML code used to create a Web page by selecting the source option from your browser's View menu.

► Using HTML

You can use most HTML editors to create attractive Web sites even if you are not familiar with HTML. However, the more you know about HTML, the more you can fix little quirks that affect the formatting of a Web page in even the best HTML editors. Fortunately, most programs allow you to switch back and forth between a screen showing HTML codes, and a screen showing the page as it appears in the Web browser, which allows you to become more familiar with HTML. You also can buy software that optimizes your HTML code so that your Web page loads quickly.

► Modifying an Existing Web Site

Many companies build a Web site that initially provides visitors with information about products and services. Then after building an adequate customer base, those companies provide a secure environment in which customers can purchase products online. You can buy storefront packages that modify a Web site you created using Web page design software. Table B-5 lists the steps that a business could take to create, and then modify, a Web site to handle e-commerce transactions. The table also summarizes the skills required to accomplish each step, and specifies what costs might be involved. Figure B-12 describes how a small business could e-commerce-enable its existing Web site by adding links to an e-commerce service provider.

FIGURE B-11: Building a Web page with Adobe PageMill

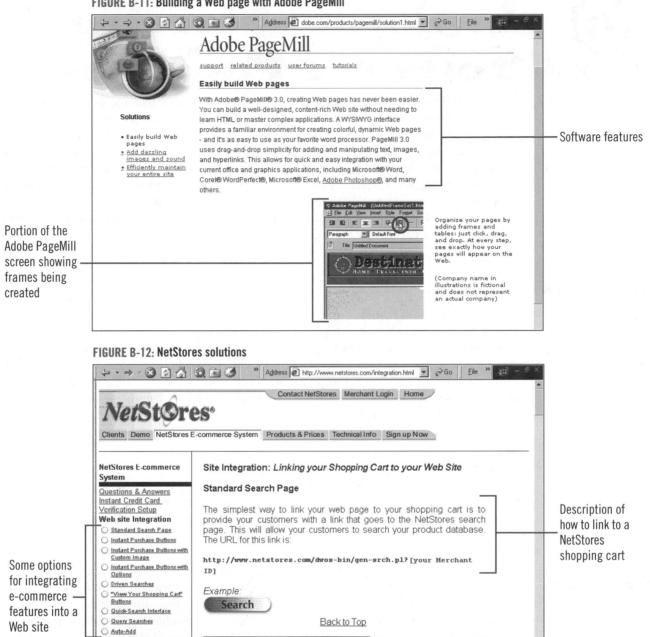

Software features

Portion of the Adobe PageMill screen showing frames being created

FIGURE B-12: NetStores solutions

Description of how to link to a NetStores shopping cart

Some options for integrating e-commerce features into a Web site

TABLE B-5: Web site design and modification steps

activity	skills or costs
Use Microsoft FrontPage, Cold Fusion, or Adobe PageMill to design a Web site.	Basic design and layout skills; elementary knowledge of HTML.
Find a host for the Web site (the ISP or a separate Web host).	Variable monthly rate depending on the size of the Web site. Some ISPs offer free hosting, although generally not for e-commerce.
Insert advertising banners or participate in affiliate programs.	Intermediate knowledge of HTML.
Purchase shopping cart software from the Web hosting provider or from providers, such as RealSoft or EasyCart.	Intermediate knowledge of HTML; good technical support from the Web hosting provider or the company selling the software.
Establish an Internet merchant account with a bank or online merchant account provider or use an Internet payment service such as ibill.	Varying setup costs and per-transaction fees.
Obtain software from an online credit card payment-processing service, such as CyberCash, to access a secure server and enable credit card transactions.	Costs could include software purchase, setup fees, monthly fees, and per-transaction fees.

Exploring Storefront Software Packages

A storefront software package, also called an e-commerce software package, provides you with the tools you need to create a Web site that can handle online transactions. You can choose a storefront package that works with the software used to create your existing Web page, or you can choose a package to create a brand new Web site. Once you have created an online store, you usually need to obtain a merchant account and have access to a transaction-processing service, such as Authorize.net. ▬▬▬ Ian recently saw several storefront software packages demonstrated at a local computer fair. He was impressed by the many features offered, and is considering using a package to build a completely new site for MediaLoft. He asks you to find more information about storefront software packages, particularly about the features they include.

Details

▶ Selection Considerations

Your main concern when selecting a storefront software package is to ensure that the package you select can grow along with your e-commerce Web site. For example, you want to select a package that allows you to include a search tool, even if your business at present does not have a large inventory. In a few years, your inventory could grow to a level where a search tool is needed to locate specific products. Remember the cardinal rule of an e-commerce site—never stand in the way of a customer who wants to purchase a product! That is, you need to make it easy for your customers to find and buy the products they want.

▶ Features

Table B-6 lists the features that should be included in a storefront software package for a small-to-medium-sized business. In addition to these features, the storefront software package might need to support different languages if you plan to sell products around the world.

▶ Software Packages

Storefront software packages, also referred to as merchant software packages, range in price from $100 to $50,000 or higher, depending on the features provided. Figure B-13 describes the features of the Impulse 4.2 storefront software—a relatively low-cost solution. Other packages include StoreFront 2000, Able Commerce Builder, and ecBuilder for small-to-medium sized businesses. IBM Net.Commerce, InterShop, and Maestro Commerce Suite are software packages for high-end e-commerce solutions.

FIGURE B-13: Sample storefront software package

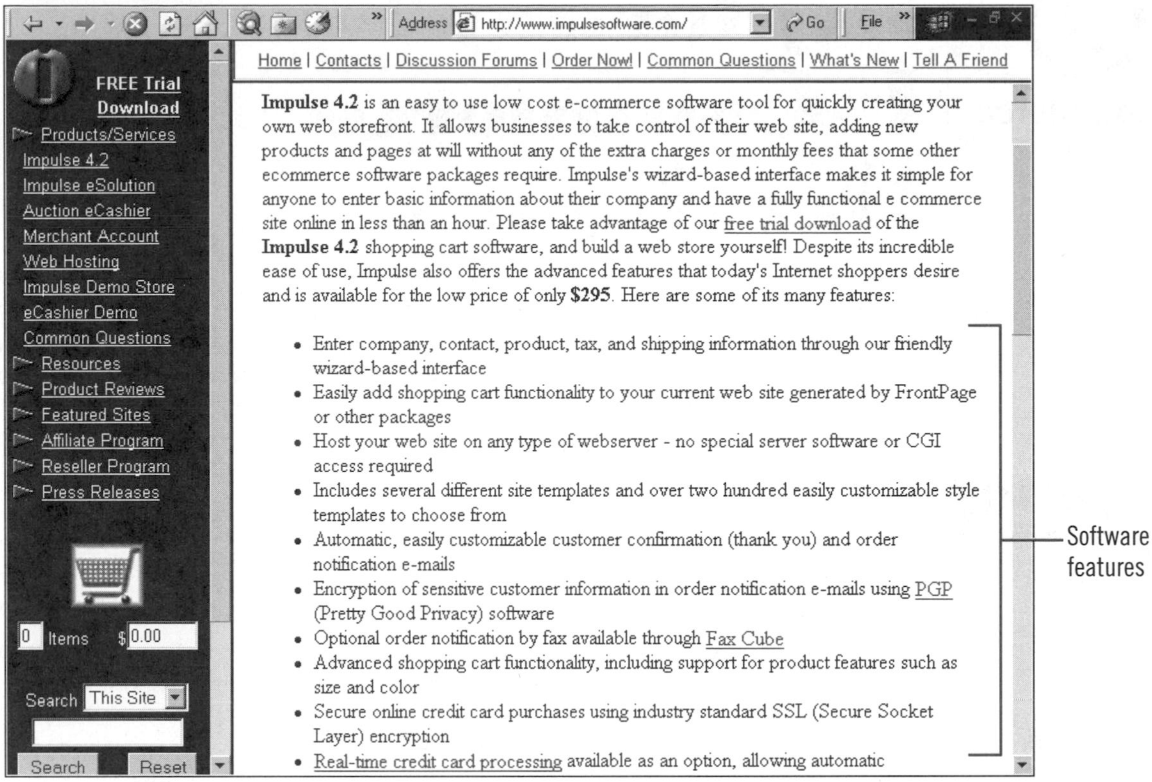

Software features

TABLE B-6: Storefront software features

feature	activity
Accounting integration	Transfers order and transaction information to the company's accounting system.
Secure payment mechanisms	Encrypts payment information, such as credit card numbers, by using Secure Socket Layer (SSL) or SET (Secure Electronic Transaction) technologies.
Shipping integration	Calculates shipping costs based on the customer's location and shipping preferences (for example, overnight delivery, snail mail delivery, and so on).
Tax calculation	Calculates taxes, depending upon the customer's zip code, postal code, or country code.
E-mail notification	Automatically sends an e-mail to customers to confirm an order.
Database access	Links to the company database that stores product information.
Web traffic statistics	Provides information about the number of visitors, their purchasing habits, and other statistics that can be used to drive marketing efforts.
Credit card authorization	Supports electronic payment systems via a secure server.
Search capability	Provides users with an in-site search tool for finding product information quickly.
Technical support	Provides purchasers with the help they need to use the software efficiently. Technical support should be accessible, reasonably priced (or free), and efficient.
Inventory management	Monitors inventory to ensure that stock is replenished following sales.

Unit B

E-Commerce

Exploring E-Commerce Developers

As you have learned, you can use a hosted storefront or template service to quickly set up a small online store. You can also use a variety of software packages to set up your own Web site, and then enhance it with e-commerce tools such as shopping carts and credit card-processing capabilities. You also can hire an e-commerce developer to do everything for you—from designing the Web site, to hosting the Web site, to handing online credit card payments, to updating and maintaining the Web site. Although Ian is confident that the Online Development Group can implement an e-commerce solution for MediaLoft, he wants to explore the services provided by e-commerce developers.

Details

▶ **Cost Considerations**

In some cases, hiring an e-commerce developer could be more cost-effective than building and managing a Web site within a company. This option is an example of **outsourcing**, the term used when one company hires personnel from another company to handle certain operations.

▶ **Web Development and Design Services**

One significant advantage of hiring a company that provides e-commerce development services is that the company usually employs Web marketers and Web designers who will help you develop not just a Web site, but also a Web presence that attracts and holds customers. Every aspect of a Web site, from the choice of color scheme to the layout of the content, to the use of navigation aids, must be integrated into a total Web experience that encourages surfers to return again and again. An e-commerce developer also can help a business with the branding of its Web site. Factors such as the choice of domain name and the way information is communicated should combine to give surfers a positive impression that they associate with a company's Web site. For example, an e-commerce developer might assist a company that sells modeling clay to develop a Web site called artistclays.com that speaks directly to artists in a professional, all-business way. Alternatively, the e-commerce developer might advise the company to target parents and children by calling itself funwithclay.com and including lots of bright colors and cute onscreen games.

▶ **Packages**

Most e-commerce developers provide customers with a selection of services ranging from basic packages that provide little more than access to a Web server, to full-scale e-business solutions that cost many thousands of dollars.

▶ **Basic Packages**

Figure B-14 lists the e-commerce services available in a basic package offered by one e-commerce developer. For $44.95 a month, plus a set-up fee, a small business can build a Web site with its own domain name (for example, *www.companyname.com*) that includes a shopping cart, a catalog for up to 25 products, and SSL (Secure Socket Layer) encryption for sending payment information. Dial-up Internet access is available for an additional $19.95 a month.

▶ **Full-Service Packages**

Figure B-15 lists all the services provided by an Oregon-based e-commerce developer. Studying the services offered provides you with a good overview of the activities involved in creating and marketing an online store.

FIGURE B-14: Basic e-commerce package

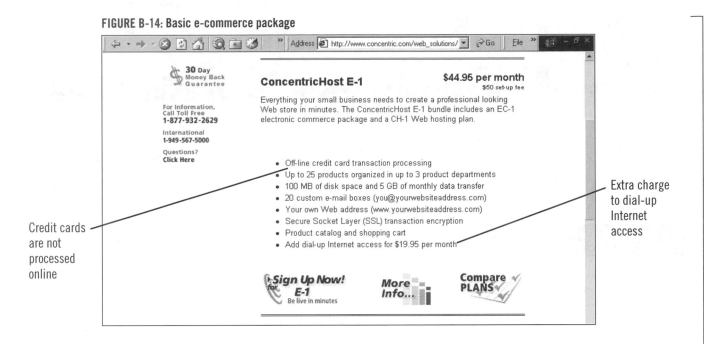

Credit cards are not processed online

Extra charge to dial-up Internet access

FIGURE B-15: E-Commerce developer services

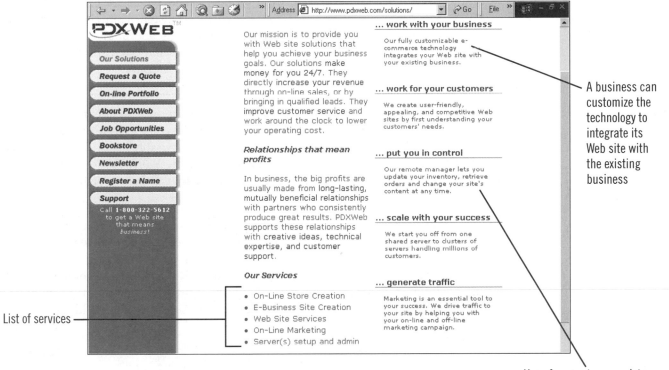

List of services

A business can customize the technology to integrate its Web site with the existing business

Use of a remote server lets customers update inventory and change content

Unit B
E-Commerce

Understanding E-Business Solutions

At the top end of the e-commerce scale are mega sites such as Amazon.com and CDNow, with daily transactions that number in the thousands. Such sites require full in-house e-business or enterprise-scale solutions that involve a significant investment in hardware, software, and personnel. ➤➤➤ While some mid-range storefront software packages look good, Ian is concerned that MediaLoft management expects an even more integrated approach. Their choice depends on the level of financial investment they plan to make in MediaLoft's e-commerce initiative, and the level of online service they want to provide their customers. To help Ian prepare his final report on e-commerce options, you explore the components of a full e-business solution.

Details

► **Hardware**

Large businesses most likely host their own Web site. They require at least one dedicated computer to run the storefront software and at least two servers—an HTTP Web server to receive Web page hits, and an e-commerce secure server (also called a payment server) to process transactions. In addition, a merchant server processes orders and integrates with backend systems such as databases, accounting, and distribution.

► **Architecture**

Figure B-16 shows a sample business system **architecture**, where each layer fulfills a distinct purpose. The customer enters the Web site via a browser and views pages contained on the Web server. Some of these pages are generated from product catalogs that are integrated with a Relational Database Management System (RDMS). When the customer purchases a product, payment information is sent to a Payment server for verification, and information about the product is sent to a Merchant server that calculates shipping costs and taxes, and communicates with the order-processing system, which selects the product and ships it to the customer.

► **Testing**

A full e-commerce solution includes an extensive testing phase prior to launching the company's Web site. Some companies even use their own employee base in a test launch that awards prizes to employees who catch bugs and come up with usable ideas. Even small Web sites should be tested carefully before being launched onto the World Wide Web to ensure that all the various components from payment systems to e-mail links work correctly.

► **Integration**

E-business solutions are fully integrated with all operations of a company, from marketing to order processing to database management to accounting. A company's Web site also is integrated with its Intranet and Extranet sites to facilitate B2B commerce with trading partners, distributors, and resellers. Check the In The Know and Figure B-17 for an example of how Entice!, an e-business solution produced by Multiactive Software, is used to customize the purchasing and delivery process for a company that manufactures and sells specialty building products directly to resellers.

FIGURE B-16: System architecture for a large e-business

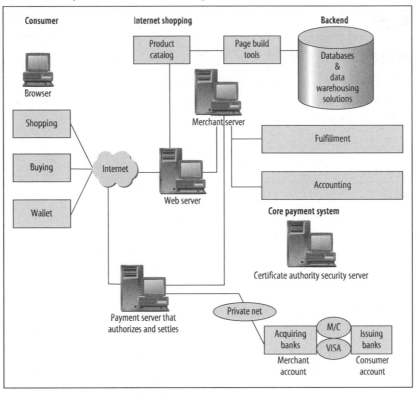

FIGURE B-17: E-Business solution in action

Workers retrieve orders placed by resellers from computers located on the shop floor

Workers on the shop floor assemble the custom-designed products

Sample E-Business Solution

In The Know

Alco Ventures, Inc., a mid-size manufacturer of specialty building products, uses its Extranet to enable resellers to serve themselves. At any time of the day or night, a reseller can log into Alco's Extranet, enter design specifications, and place an order, which is then immediately routed to computers on Alco's shop floor. Figure B-17 shows small parts fabricator Steve Thornton on the shop floor, along with Alco president Ben Hume. Alco's e-business software ensures integration of the entire process—from Web page design to order placement to manufacturing to invoicing to delivery. *Source: Multiactive Software*[3]

E-Commerce

Focus

Online Business Activities

The features of an online store link directly to the series of business activities that must occur regardless of the method customers use to access and purchase products. You can divide these activities into the six stages shown in Table B-7 below.

TABLE B-7: Business stages

stage	activity
One	Meet the customer
Two	Display products
Three	Facilitate shopping
Four	Process payment
Five	Deliver products
Six	Provide customer service

When you take a business online, you need to determine how you will accomplish each of the six stages. You can then select the features that your online store needs to support these stages. Study Figure B-18 to learn about the specific activities related to each of the six stages. For example, Stage One: Meet the Customer occurs when a customer clicks onto a Web site, rather than when the customer walks through the front door of a retail outlet. Because an online store can't have people waiting to greet new customers, how can it meet and serve the people that land on its Web site? One way is to build in capability to recognize repeat customers. Your goal is to think about the activities needed and not worry about the technology required to accomplish them. Some creative Web developers maintain that the most important factor in developing a new e-commerce venture is to think outside the box; that is, think of *what* you want the store to accomplish, before worrying about *how* the activities occur. Technological changes that affect the development of e-commerce activities take place very rapidly. You might identify a need for features that were not covered in this unit simply because they were invented after this book was published. Every day, Web developers construct new and better ways of supporting online business activities.

After you study Figure B-18, answer the following questions. You might also want to look again at the description of online store features presented in the Reviewing Features lesson. However, do not be bound by methods currently in use. Use your imagination to think up new and exciting ways in which online stores could best serve their customers.

FIGURE B-18: Business activities

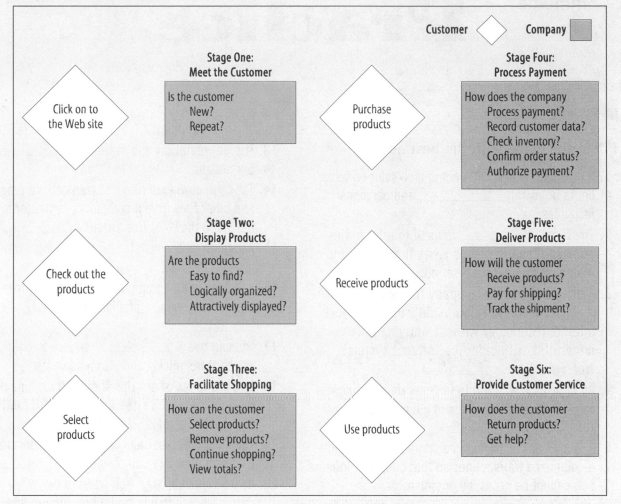

Explore Further...

1. In Stage Two, how could you organize products so that customers can find them quickly and easily?

2. In Stage Two, describe at least two ways in which you could display each product in your inventory.

3. How can customers select multiple products?

4. What information do you think customers would want to know about the products they've selected before they would purchase them?

5. What process do you think occurs when a customer clicks the Buy button and enters credit card information? Don't try to figure out what *really* happens. At this time, you want to think in terms of what steps are required.

6. How could a customer find out where their product is in the shipping process?

Practice

▶ Review

Fill in the blank with the best answer.

1. A company selects an e-commerce solution based on its financial, _____, and personnel resources.

2. The term _____ is used to refer to the number of simultaneous visits that a Web site can handle in a given time period.

3. A brick and mortar company that wants to take its operation online can usually use the latest Internet technology without worrying about integrating with older pre-Internet systems. True/False? _____

4. An individual who wants to generate extra income can consider selling items in online auctions. True/False? _____

5. A _____ server is a computer that handles e-commerce transactions so that customer information cannot be accessed or stolen.

6. Web surfers click _____ aids to move from page to page on a Web site.

7. Customers can get help by checking the Frequently _____ Questions page on a company's Web site.

8. Most individuals need to pay an Internet _____ Provider to connect their computers to the Internet via a cable or telephone.

9. A Web _____ stores the pages of a Web site for viewing on the Web.

10. You cannot use your ISP as a Web host. True/False? _____

11. The connection between a company's computer and the Web host computer is referred to as a _____-server configuration.

12. Asymmetrical Digital _____ Lines are used to transmit data at high speed over telephone lines.

13. The abbreviation bps stands for _____ per second.

14. The term download refers to transferring programs and other files from a company's computer to computers on the Web. True/False? _____

15. A login usually consists of a unique login name and a _____.

16. You can set up an online store through a free e-commerce service provider. True/False? _____

17. You can use a _____ service to build an online store quickly and inexpensively.

18. Two examples of off-the-shelf software packages for designing Web sites are Microsoft FrontPage and Adobe PageMill. True/False? _____

19. The computer language used to create documents that Web browsers can read is called _____.

20. Customers of a large Web site can use a _____ tool to find a specific product.

21. You can set up some storefront software programs to automatically send a(n) _____ to customers to confirm an order.

22. A separate Web page that lists the items a customer has selected is called a shopping _____.

23. The term _____ is used when one company hires personnel from another company to handle certain operations.

24. For companies with enterprise-scale solutions, a _____ server usually processes orders and integrates with backend systems such as databases, accounting, and distribution.

25. Companies with enterprise-scale solutions usually integrate their Web sites with both their Intranet and their _____ sites in order to facilitate B2B commerce with trading partners.

Practice

▶ Independent Challenges

1. More and more companies are using interactive questionnaires on their Web sites to help customers identify their needs. You are the owner of a medium-sized company that sells products you may be able to market and sell online. Your company has a brochureware corporate Web site, and now you want to investigate how you should develop a Web site with e-commerce capabilities.

To complete this independent challenge:

a. Open your Web browser, go to the Student Online Companion at *www.course.com/illustrated/ecommerce*, click the link to Unit B, then click the link to Independent Challenge 1.

b. Select one of the links to go to an online questionnaire designed to determine your e-commerce needs.

c. Complete the online questionnaire so that you can get an idea of what types of questions are asked.

d. Open a new document in a word-processing program, write a brief description of the types of answers you provided, then describe the solutions offered by the Web site in response to your answers. If necessary, complete the questionnaire again to refresh your memory.

e. Write a paragraph that discusses how useful you felt the questionnaire would be for a real business.

f. Type **Your Name** at the bottom of the document, save it as *Web Needs Analysis*, print a copy, then close the document.

2. As Office Manager of a small company, you've been asked to select an e-commerce developer. To help you evaluate some of the services provided, you decide to explore the Web sites of two e-commerce developers, and then compare some of the packages they offer.

To complete this independent challenge:

a. Open your Web browser, go to the Student Online Companion at *www.course.com/illustrated/ecommerce*, click the link to Unit B, then click the link to Independent Challenge 2.

b. Explore the links provided to find two e-commerce developers whose packages offer at least two levels of service.

c. Open the Project File ECB-01.doc in a word-processing program. This document contains the table you will use to compare two e-commerce developers.

d. Complete the table with information about the basic and advanced packages for each of the two e-commerce developers you have chosen.

e. Below the table, in the space provided, write a paragraph describing which e-commerce developer you would choose to host a basic package. Include reasons for your choice.

f. Write another paragraph in the space provided describing which e-commerce developer you would choose for the advanced package. Include reasons for your choice.

g. Type **Your Name**, save the document as *E-Commerce Developer Comparison*, print a copy, then close the document.

3. You can try out storefront or template services by building your own online store. Some services even allow you to post the store on the Web for a short period. As the owner of a small retail operation, you are considering developing an online store. You do not, however, have the time or the expertise to build a store from scratch. You decide to investigate the services, costs, and features offered by three storefront, template, or Web hosting services.

To complete this independent challenge:

a. Fill in the box below with the name of your business and a description of its products. Select a business that sells products related to one of your own interests. For example, if you are interested in water sports, you can choose to sell products such as surfboards, wet suits, or water skis.

E-Commerce

| Store Category: .... |
| Products: .... |

b. Open your Web browser, go to the Student Online Companion at *www.course.com/illustrated/ecommerce*, click the link to Unit B, then click the link to Independent Challenge 3.

c. Explore the links provided to find two template services that offer you the opportunity to try out the software.

d. Open the Project File ECB-02.doc in a word-processing program. This document contains a table that you will use to compare two template services.

e. Follow the procedure required to build an online store for the company and products you have selected. Follow procedures only until the point where you need to enter payment information. Your goal is to compare two template services in accordance with the criteria identified in the table.

f. Complete the table with the required information relating to your experience.

g. Below the table, write a short paragraph describing which template service you would select. Provide reasons for your choice. Remember that cost is not always the only determining factor. Take into account other factors such as ease of use, technical support, appearance of the finished Web site, scalability, and customization.

h. Type **Your Name** at the bottom of the document, save it as *Template Services Comparison*, print a copy, then close the document.

4. Learning any new subject often requires learning what almost amounts to a new language. The more you learn about e-commerce, the more you will come across vocabulary and technical terms with which you might not be familiar. A good way to learn some of these terms is to scan some of the glossary sites available on the Internet to identify terms that you do not yet know. You then can read the definitions and follow any links provided, to at least familiarize yourself with some of the Web vocabulary. Before long, you will easily understand and remember terms such as firewall, SSL, or SQL.

To complete this independent challenge:

a. Open your Web browser, go to the Student Online Companion at *www.course.com/illustrated/ecommerce*, click the link to Unit B, then click the link to Independent Challenge 4.

b. Follow links to one of the glossary sites provided.

c. Find 10 terms that you have encountered, but are not sure of their meaning. Do not just select the first 10 terms in the glossary. Instead, scan the glossary listings available and select terms that you want to understand better. For example, if you have frequently heard the term ActiveX used, but are not sure of its exact meaning, make it one of your selections. For now, your goal is to get an idea of the volume of new terms related to e-commerce and the Internet and what types of activities are connected with these terms. For example, you might find that some terms relate to databases, while other terms relate to connection methods.

d. Open a document in a word-processing program, then type **Glossary Terms** as the title.

e. Copy the Web site address (URL) of the glossary site or sites you have selected to your word-processing document. (*Hint*: To copy a URL, click in the Address or Location box on your browser, press [Ctrl][C], view the document in your word-processing program, then press [Ctrl][V].)

f. In your word-processing program, list the 10 terms that you selected.

g. Read the definition provided for each term.

h. Write your own version of the definition. Avoid just copying technical information that you don't understand. If a definition is just too technical, find a different term. If possible, find other definitions of the term and provide examples. Your goal is to gain some preliminary understanding of the term so that you already have some familiarity with it should you encounter it later in this book, or when you read about e-commerce and other issues related to the Internet.

i. Type **Your Name** at the bottom of the document, save it as *My Glossary*, print a copy, then close the document.

► Up to Date

Figure B-19 shows jobs listed on a large e-commerce developer's Web site. Many of these job titles did not even exist just a few years ago. Part of learning about e-commerce involves learning how you can find a place for yourself within the e-commerce revolution that will use your talents and interests. Decisions that you make about the training you need depend on what kinds of jobs are available.

FIGURE B-19: Job listings

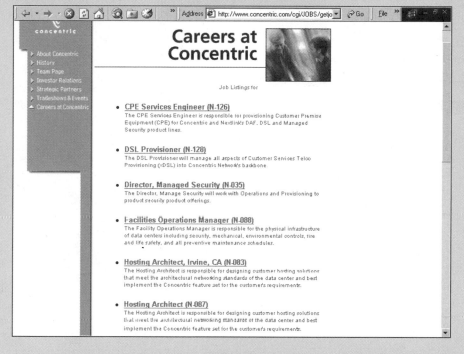

To complete the Up to Date Challenge:

1. Open your Web browser, go to the Student Online Companion at *www.course.com/illustrated/ecommerce*, click the link to Unit B, then click the link to Up To Date.
2. Follow links to find the job listings for two e-commerce developers.
3. Select two similar jobs from each site. Pick one job from each site that you might be interested in, and one job from each site in a field that you've never heard of before.
4. Complete the table below with the required information.

Current Date	Company Name	Position	Qualifications	Salary (if available)

► Visual Workshop

Figure B-20 shows the home page for Office Depot. Study the illustration, then in the space provided, answer questions related to the various features visible. Note that most of the questions will have yes or no answers, or will require you to describe a specific location on the Web page, such as top-right corner.

FIGURE B-20

Question	Answer
Where on the Web page can customers click to create an account?	
How can customers get help?	
Where on the Web page can customers search for a product?	
List three product categories visible on the Web page.	
Can you order a paper catalog from this Web page?	
List three of the resources provided for the business owner.	
How would you find an Office Depot store in your area?	

Unit C

Exploring
Marketing Issues

Objectives

► **Identify marketing issues**
► **Understand market research**
► **Collect customer data**
► **Understand domain names**
► **Explore advertising options**
► **Understand e-mail marketing**
► **Explore search engines and directories**
► **Monitor customer visits**
► **Explore incentives**

Although the e-commerce revolution has brought the world to the doorstep of every online business, the world will not necessarily cross the threshold. Technology only makes an online business accessible; marketing makes Web surfers into customers. In this unit, you will look at marketing issues as they relate to conducting business online. You will learn about market research, the methods used to collect data about customers, online and offline advertising options, and the use of incentives to attract and keep customers on a Web site. You will also learn about Web-specific marketing tools such as domain names, search options, and Web analysis tools. ◄ Parminder Singh, the Marketing Manager assigned to work with the Online Development Group, has asked you to help her learn about online marketing issues. As MediaLoft develops its e-commerce Web site, it needs to determine how to identify, attract, and best serve its online customers.

Identifying Marketing Issues

Details

Marketing efforts must identify customers, determine their needs and their wants, and then develop methods of providing appropriate products or services. In this lesson, you will look at some of the issues related to marketing an online business. Many of these issues are the same in the cyberworld as they are in the real world. Taking a business online does not guarantee success any more than does opening a store and waiting for customers to walk through the door. ➤ Parminder asks you to summarize current marketing issues and e-marketing trends for a presentation that she will give to MediaLoft management.

► **Marketing Questions**

A key component of any company's business plan is the development of viable marketing strategies. One way of establishing a framework for these strategies is to use the 5W questions shown in Figure C-1. Each question relates to one of the issues discussed below.

► **Customer Identification**

Without customers, you do not have an online business—or any kind of business. Therefore, your first priority is to identify the customers who will visit your Web site and buy your products. These customers could be existing customers to a brick and mortar store, brand-new customers, or a combination. You need to determine if your customers are willing to buy online. For example, people who are accustomed to personal attention might not be ready to make the transition to a cyberworld shopping experience. You might need to direct some of your marketing efforts toward educating your customers about the benefits of transacting business online.

► **Location**

Because your customers can be located in any geographical area, you can concentrate on developing a niche market consisting of customers located around the world. The decision whether to target customers spread across a wide geographical area or to target customers in a relatively small area depends on factors such as shipping costs, language, currency, import and export restrictions, and available technology. Even if you want to market your products to customers in Asia, for example, you might not be able to handle high shipping costs and fluctuating foreign currency values. Similarly, you need to ensure that the customers you want to serve have access to the Internet, are interested in or need the products you sell, and can legally purchase your products.

► **Product Identification**

Once you have identified your customers, you need to determine what products they want. For example, if your customers are businesses that purchase printing supplies, you need to determine which brands they prefer and what prices they are willing to pay.

► **Timing**

Marketing strategies must be timed to when customers are willing to buy, such as at holidays or during certain seasons. Usually you don't sell ski equipment in the late spring, or mountain bikes in the middle of winter. The issue of timing also relates to when in the shopping process customers decide to buy. Do your customers require a great deal of information before they buy, or will they buy on impulse?

► **Motivation**

What motivates a customer to purchase a product online rather than from a traditional brick and mortar store? Is the product less expensive online? Can you customize the shopping experience? Can you offer a new experience or better-than-average service? Do customers like to buy in a low-pressure environment? Answers to all these questions will help you determine why your customers will choose to buy from your online business, rather than click away to a competitor.

► **E-Marketing Trends**

Figure C-2 lists some of the trends in **e-marketing**. The one thing that all of these trends have in common is that they aim to build customer loyalty—which means that customers will return to a Web site numerous times, buy more than once, and recommend the Web site to their friends.

FIGURE C-1: Marketing questions

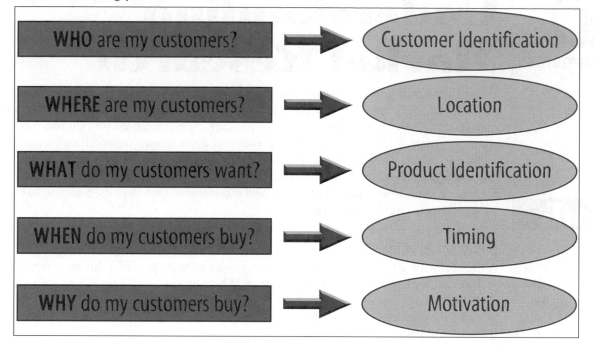

WHO are my customers?	Customer Identification
WHERE are my customers?	Location
WHAT do my customers want?	Product Identification
WHEN do my customers buy?	Timing
WHY do my customers buy?	Motivation

FIGURE C-2: E-marketing trends

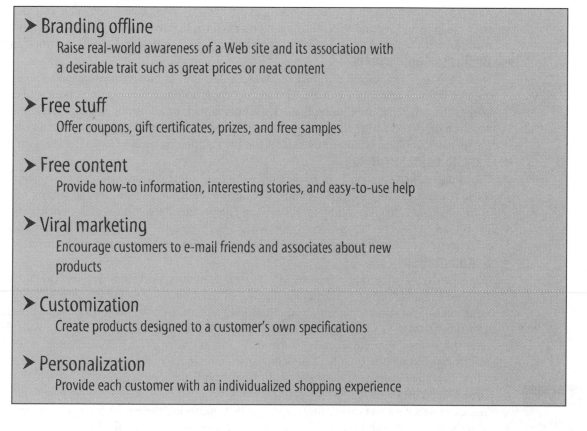

➤ **Branding offline**
Raise real-world awareness of a Web site and its association with a desirable trait such as great prices or neat content

➤ **Free stuff**
Offer coupons, gift certificates, prizes, and free samples

➤ **Free content**
Provide how-to information, interesting stories, and easy-to-use help

➤ **Viral marketing**
Encourage customers to e-mail friends and associates about new products

➤ **Customization**
Create products designed to a customer's own specifications

➤ **Personalization**
Provide each customer with an individualized shopping experience

Understanding Market Research

Market research is the collection and analysis of data about your customers and your competition. You use this data to determine which products you should sell, how much you should charge for them, how you should package them, and how you should interact with your customers. Table C-1 describes how different departments in an online business can use the results of market research to improve a Web site, focus on customer needs, and increase sales. ◄ Parminder wants to use the Internet to conduct market research that will help MediaLoft determine how to best use its new e-commerce Web site. She asks you to investigate issues related to market research.

Details

▶ **Customer Profiles**

A first priority of market research is to develop a customer profile. Who buys your products? Where do they live? How much do they earn? Where do they work? How long have they surfed the Web? What makes them happy? Do they use the Internet at work? Answers to these questions help companies develop effective customer profiles.

▶ **Demographics**

Most customer profiles contain demographic information such as age, gender, income level, occupation, and education. Figure C-3 shows a breakdown of Internet use by language.

▶ **Internet Experience**

Information related to a customer's Internet experience, is referred to as **Webographics**. By analyzing the surfing habits and computer literacy levels of customers, you can determine if they are able and willing to buy online, if you need to educate them about the benefits of buying online, or if you need to find ways to attract them with a Web site that offers something new.

▶ **Business Applications**

If you are involved in B2B e-commerce, you need to find as much information as possible about your customers' corporate climate. The term **corpographics** refers to the gathering of data about corporate structure, purchasing history, and personnel. In addition, you can focus your market research on determining the profitability of a company's clients, and on whether a potential B2B partner has in place, or can easily budget for, the technology needed to do business on the Web.

▶ **Psychological Profiling**

Psychographics, the study of how people think and feel with relation to what they buy, is in itself becoming a big business. Figure C-4 shows a sample psychographic survey offered by a company that collects psychological profiles. The profiles determine which personality types are most likely to buy certain products, and when. Psychographic studies can also be used to test the effectiveness of advertising campaigns, Web site designs, and customer service strategies.

▶ **Segmentation**

You can divide your target market into several segments, and then develop marketing efforts tailored to each segment's particular needs. For example, if your company sells body-building equipment, you can use one method to market your products to professional body builders and another method to market to amateur enthusiasts. Although both groups buy your products, they might not respond equally to the same marketing approach. Professional body builders might want to see the quality of the equipment stressed, while amateurs might want to be reassured that the equipment helps them improve their fitness level.

▶ **Test Marketing**

You can test a new Web marketing campaign by monitoring the responses of various small groups of individuals. For example, you can see how a group—sometimes called a focus group—responds to an online contest. You can also determine what factors contribute to the group's participation. Do more customers respond to the contest information if it is placed in the upper-right corner of the Web page, or if it dominates the page with brightly colored animated text and graphics?

FIGURE C-3: Internet use by language

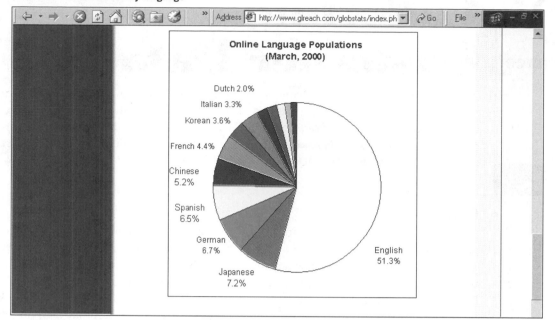

FIGURE C-4: Sample psychographic study

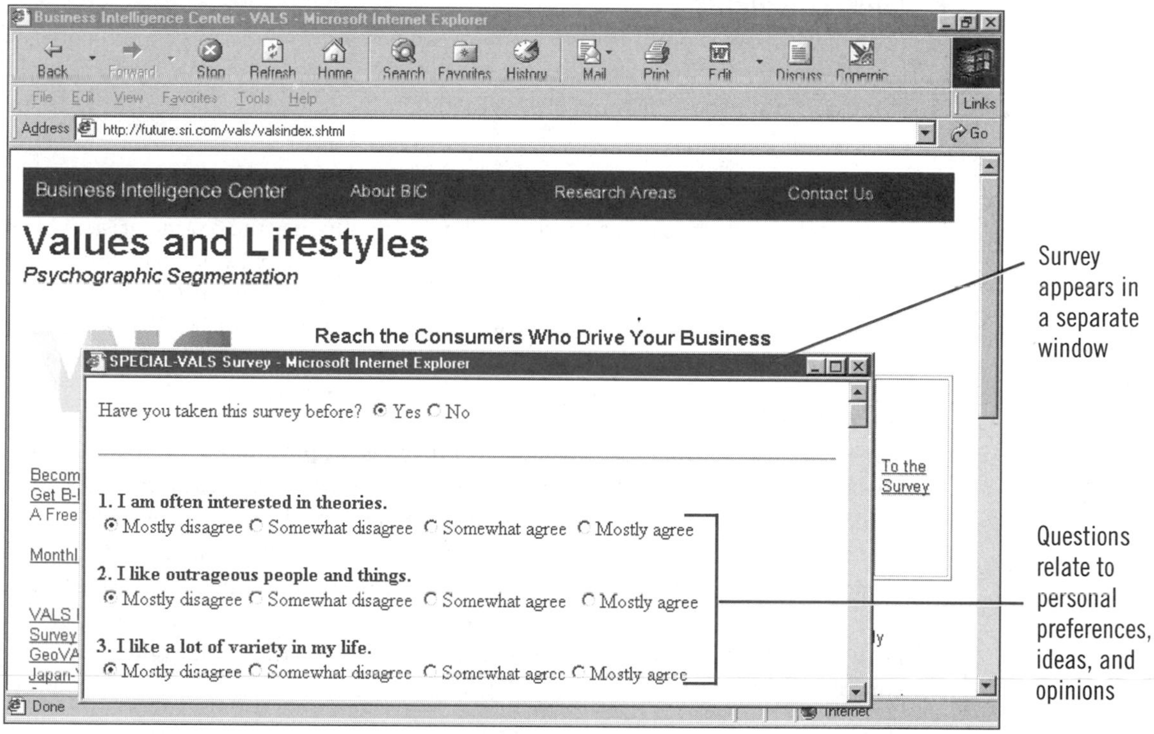

Survey appears in a separate window

Questions relate to personal preferences, ideas, and opinions

TABLE C-1: Uses for market research

department	customer data	application
Marketing	Age and gender	Select advertising outlets
Web development	Internet connection speed	Design the Web site to load quickly for fast and slow connections
Content development	Education level	Use an appropriate writing style
Sales	Income level	Determine pricing levels
Personnel	Occupation	Develop appropriate job listings

E-Commerce

E-Commerce

Collecting Customer Data

Internet technology provides many opportunities for obtaining information about customers and competitors. Some of these methods, such as cookies, are particular to the Internet, while others, such as surveys and usability studies, have been used by marketers for years, and now are adapted to the Internet. ➤ You decide to learn more about how MediaLoft can use the Internet to collect customer data.

Details

► Cookies

A cookie is a small text file containing information for a specific Web site, and is gathered while you surf the Web. When you land on a Web site, your computer picks up a cookie file that stores information about how you navigate the site, which advertisements you click, and which products you purchase. From the customer's point of view, cookies can be useful because they save the customer from indicating preferences at each visit. For example, a customer who frequently buys adventure novels might be informed of the latest releases when they land on the Web site where they purchased other adventure novels.

► Cookies Benefits

From a company's point of view, cookies can be used to build customer profiles and to measure the effectiveness of online advertising. While many companies may appreciate this opportunity, some consumers are becoming concerned that the unregulated use of cookies might lead to an invasion of privacy.

► Online Surveys

You can develop online surveys that will help you identify the characteristics of your target market. This method of conducting market research can yield quality results because the people who complete questionnaires are already visiting your site and are, therefore, more likely to have some interest in the products you offer. Figure C-5 shows a sample online survey designed to determine the Internet usage habits of Web surfers.

► Data Mining

The term **data mining** refers to a class of database applications that searches for patterns within selected groups of data. For example, a company could use data mining software to discover that a target group in Idaho buys more video cameras than the same target group in Louisiana. The company might then create one banner advertisement that appears when customers in Idaho access their Web site, but have a different banner appear when customers in Louisiana access their Web site. Data mining software is designed to discover relationships that had not been previously identified. Figure C-6 presents information about data mining sponsored by a consulting firm.

► Usability Studies

An online business won't be successful if users can't easily figure out how to purchase products. A key component of any marketing initiative is testing the usability of the Web site. To test usability, people with varying levels of Internet experience try to use the Web site to purchase a product, preferably while the person who designed the site looks on. A navigational aid such as a button or graphic element might seem obvious to an experienced user, but might totally confuse a novice user. Once a Web site is launched, you can gather additional information about its usability through surveys and e-mail. The purpose of usability studies is to ensure that nothing gets in the way of the customer who wants to buy. The animated shopping cart might look cute, but it won't help sales if users don't know they need to click it to shop.

FIGURE C-5: Sample online survey

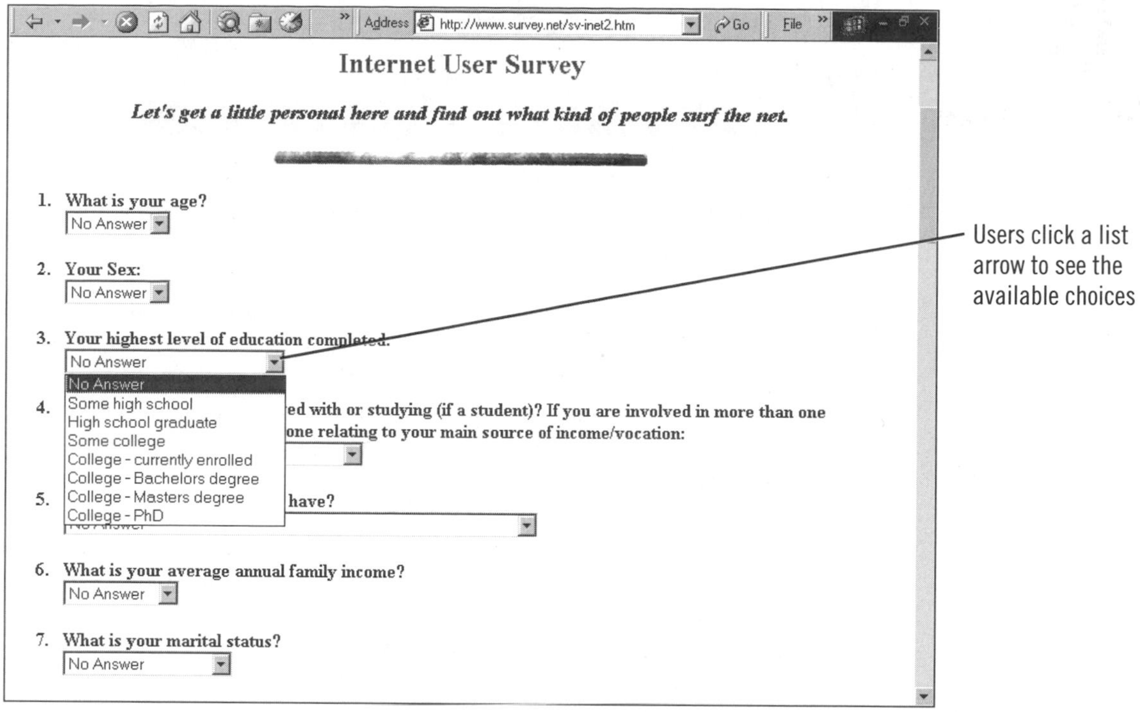

Address http://www.survey.net/sv-inet2.htm
Go
File
Internet User Survey
Let's get a little personal here and find out what kind of people surf the net.
1. What is your age?
No Answer
2. Your Sex:
No Answer
3. Your highest level of education completed:
No Answer
No Answer
Some high school
High school graduate
Some college
College - currently enrolled
College - Bachelors degree
College - Masters degree
College - PhD
4.
ed with or studying (if a student)? If you are involved in more than one
one relating to your main source of income/vocation:
5.
have?
6. What is your average annual family income?
No Answer
7. What is your marital status?
No Answer
Users click a list arrow to see the available choices

FIGURE C-6: Data mining information

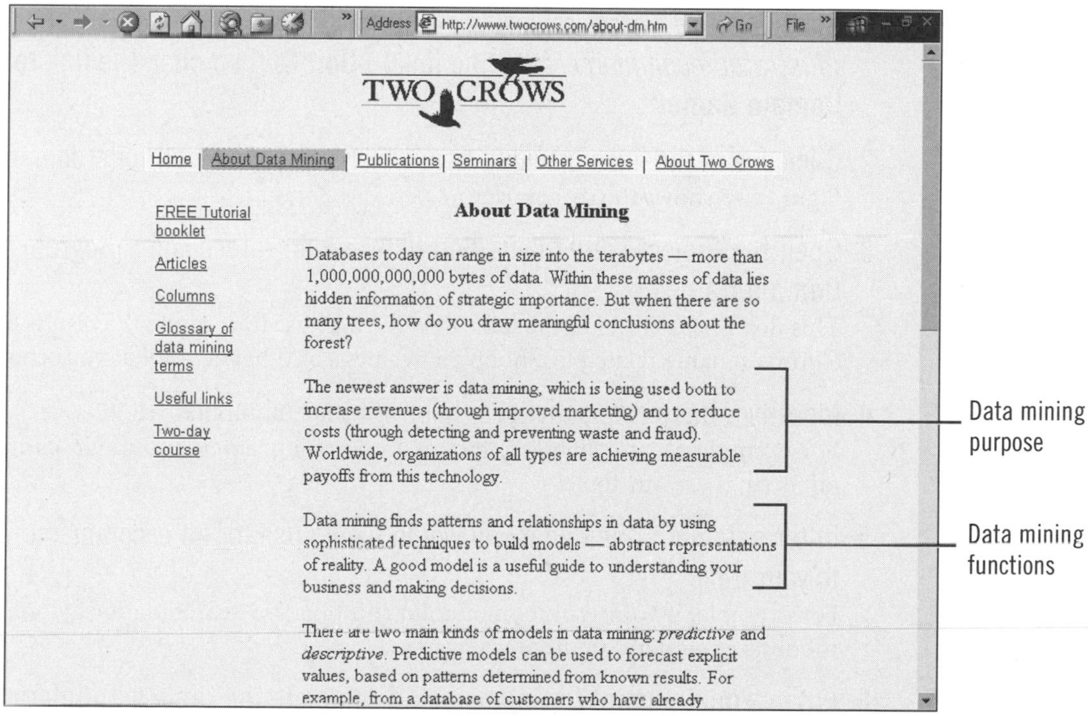

Address http://www.twocrows.com/about-dm.htm
Go
File
TWO CROWS
Home | About Data Mining | Publications | Seminars | Other Services | About Two Crows
FREE Tutorial booklet
Articles
Columns
Glossary of data mining terms
Useful links
Two-day course
About Data Mining
Databases today can range in size into the terabytes — more than 1,000,000,000,000 bytes of data. Within these masses of data lies hidden information of strategic importance. But when there are so many trees, how do you draw meaningful conclusions about the forest?
The newest answer is data mining, which is being used both to increase revenues (through improved marketing) and to reduce costs (through detecting and preventing waste and fraud). Worldwide, organizations of all types are achieving measurable payoffs from this technology.
Data mining finds patterns and relationships in data by using sophisticated techniques to build models — abstract representations of reality. A good model is a useful guide to understanding your business and making decisions.
There are two main kinds of models in data mining: predictive and descriptive. Predictive models can be used to forecast explicit values, based on patterns determined from known results. For example, from a database of customers who have already
Data mining purpose
Data mining functions

In The Know

Tracking Marketing Efforts

As a leading provider of online training solutions, DigitalThink.com must gather customer data to help them make smart decisions. Susan McKenna, DigitalThink's Marketing Manager explains: "We use our Web site to track our programs through three important phases of our marketing efforts: Reach (the number of people who see our brand), Response (the number of people who respond to any given advertisement), and Conversion (the number of people who convert into customers)." *Source: DigitalThink*[2]

E-Commerce

Understanding Domain Names

One of the easiest ways to attract people to your Web site is to provide them with a short, easy-to-remember Web site address. This address should only consist of a **domain** name, such as the name of the company or a descriptive word, and the top-level domain. The most common top-level domain is *.com*, which stands for commercial. Other top-level domains include *.org*, *.net*, *.gov* (for government sites), and two-letter abbreviations for countries, such as *.ca* for Canada and *.fr* for France. Because many of the .com domain names are taken, some companies are now purchasing a .cc domain name, as described in Figure C-7. Getting an effective domain name is one of the first—and most important—marketing decisions a company makes because the domain name chosen must blend with other marketing materials that the company already has in place. A company can also engage in domain prospecting, which involves coming up with a list of hot domain names and then checking their availability. In domain prospecting, investors buy up good domain names and resell them—often at tremendous profits. Companies engaged in domain prospecting, however, need to make sure they avoid **cybersquatting**—which means registering a company name and then trying to resell it to its lawful owner at a profit. Legislation is pending to prevent cybersquatting. MediaLoft already has its domain name. However, in the future it may want to register additional domain names related to the products it sells. Parminder asks you to investigate how to obtain a domain name.

Steps

1. Start your Web browser, go to the Student Online Companion at *www.course.com/illustrated/ecommerce*, click the link to **Unit C**, then click the link to **Understanding Domain Names**

2. Click one of the links provided from which you can search for a domain name
   Figure C-7 shows the search page at Network Solutions.

3. Open the Project File **ECC-01.doc** in your word-processing program, then save it as **Domain Names**
   This document contains the table that you will use to compile the results of your search for a domain name related to a hobby, a business, or other activity of your choice.

4. Identify a business, activity, or hobby in the cell labeled **Topic**
   For example, if your hobby is mountain climbing, enter "mountain climbing" or "mountaineering" as your topic.

5. Enter a domain name that you would like to use for an e-commerce Web site related to your topic
   For example, if your topic is mountain climbing, try searching for a domain name such as mountains.com or xtremeclimbing.com.

6. Enter a minimum of five names, and complete the table with information about the results of your domain name searches
   Your goal is to see what domain names are still available. You will probably find that most common domain names are already taken. However, sometimes you can still find domain names just by altering a few letters, or by using creative combinations. For example, climbing.com might be taken, but cliffhanging.com might not. Figure C-8 shows an example of mountain climbing-related domain name searches.

7. Type **Your Name** at the bottom of the document, save it, print a copy, then close the document

FIGURE C-7: Purchasing a .cc domain name

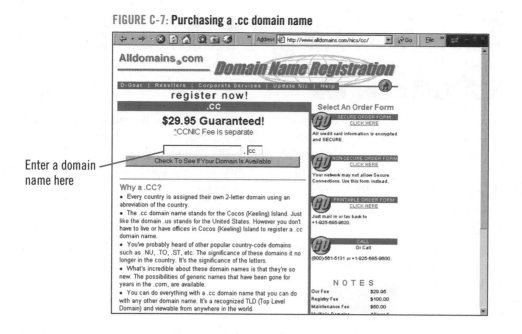

Enter a domain name here

FIGURE C-8: **Domain name search results**

Domain Name Search

Topic: Mountain Climbing

Domain Name	Response	Alternative(s)
mountainclimbing.com	Taken	No alternatives
cliffhanging.com	Available	cliffhanging.net cliffhanging.org
rockclimbing.com	Taken	No alternatives
pitons.com	Taken	No alternatives
rappelling.com	Available	rappelling.net rappelling.org

In The Know

Registering a Domain Name

After you have searched for and found the domain name you want to use, you can register it yourself if you know the IP address of the Web site hosting the domain name, you can contact Network Solutions directly, or you can register a domain name with a registrar. The following steps describe how to register a domain name with a registrar:

1. The customer contacts a registrar and provides contact information (name, company, address) and technical information (computer system, connection).

2. The registrar submits the technical information to the registry—which is a central directory of domain names.

3. The registry provides other computers on the Internet with the customer's e-mail address and Web site address.

4. The customer agrees to a registration contract with the registrar. The contract specifies the terms under which the registered domain name is accepted and maintained.

E-Commerce

E-Commerce

Exploring Advertising Options

An online business can choose from a variety of online and offline advertising options, such as links exchanges, affiliate programs, and news groups postings. In this lesson, you will look at some of the more popular ways of advertising a Web site online. Parminder is particularly intrigued by free or low-cost online advertising methods. She asks you to examine online methods and compare them to conventional advertising methods.

Details

▶ **Links**

One of the least expensive advertising options is to exchange links with related Web sites. This option can also lead to building of a sense of community and loyalty among Web users—a major goal of doing business online.

▶ **Banner Ads**

You can purchase banner ads—sometimes for very high prices—or you can exchange banners with other online companies. A banner ad is always a link to the sponsoring company. Figure C-9 shows an example of a Web site containing several banner ads. The effectiveness of banner ads depends on factors such as their placement on the Web site and their ability to attract clicks. Banner ads might be most effective when placed on sites that attract people in a target market. For example, a banner ad for video games would not be well-placed on a Web site that has a target audience of retirees.

▶ **Affiliate Programs**

When you join an affiliate program, you place a link, banner, or button on your Web site. When a customer clicks the link, they go to the affiliated Web site. If the customer buys a product from the affiliated Web site, you receive a commission. One reason for the increasing popularity of affiliate programs is that they take advantage of the marketing efforts of hundreds of companies at once. No single company can reach every consumer. By linking with Web sites that sell similar products, your range of contacts can be extended almost infinitely.

▶ **Pop-Up Windows**

Pop-up windows usually contain links to other Web sites, to free offers, and to surveys. Another type of pop-up window appears when a surfer clicks a link. The surfer can either read and respond to the message in the window, or close the window. As surfers become more familiar with the Internet, the popularity of pop-up windows—particularly those that appear unbidden—is decreasing. Many surfers find them intrusive and counter-productive. Figure C-10 shows a pop-up window being used effectively to provide a surfer with additional information—but only after a link is clicked.

▶ **Viral Marketing**

The term **viral marketing** describes a message or giveaway that people receive, and then send along to friends and colleagues. The purpose of viral marketing is to encourage customers to tell each other about products or services. Viral marketing is really just the online form of word-of-mouth marketing and can be very successful, because it depends on the relationships between people who already know each other.

▶ **Newsgroup Postings**

Newsgroups exist for virtually every activity on earth—and probably some extra-terrestrial ones, too! You can join newsgroups related to the products or services you sell and participate in discussions. By discreetly placing your company name and URL in your signature, you might even attract business queries, although you need to be careful not to antagonize newsgroup members by cluttering up their postings with blatant advertisements.

▶ **Offline Advertising**

A company should, at the least, include its URL on every print advertisement, business card, and letterhead, along with a statement such as Check Us Out Online or Visit Us Online. Companies can also advertise their online businesses in conventional media such as radio, television, magazines, and newspapers.

FIGURE C-9: Sample banner ads

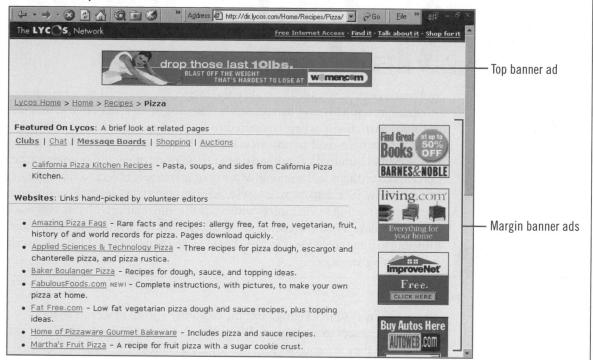

Top banner ad

Margin banner ads

FIGURE C-10: Sample pop-up window

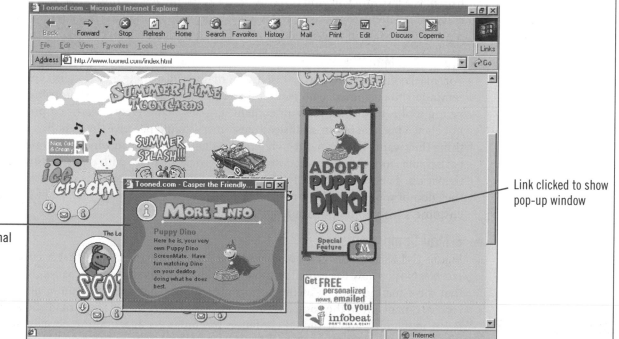

Link clicked to show pop-up window

Pop-up window contains additional information

In The Know

Branding

A key concept related to advertising is **branding**—the association of a company with a particular logo, image, or characteristic, such as high quality or reliability. A challenge faced by the dot.coms—those companies that do all their business on the Internet—is the development of a recognizable brand. In cyberspace, branding has more to do with providing a unique service, product, or value than with physical elements such as logos or designs.

Understanding E-Mail Marketing

Web marketers were quick to realize the incredible potential of e-mail for reaching thousands of customers quickly and inexpensively. The cost of an e-mail marketing campaign is virtually nothing, particularly when compared to the cost of a four-color print advertising campaign. However, using e-mail to spam customers is not effective. **Spamming** means to indiscriminately e-mail hundreds, thousands, or even millions of people at once, in the hopes that a small percentage of them will respond. Most people strongly object to this type of e-mail marketing. In fact, many ISPs discontinue service to customers who spam. E-mail can be most effectively used for marketing to customers who want the information offered. MediaLoft is anxious to explore e-mail methods of marketing their products to both existing and new customers. Parminder asks you to investigate some of the ways MediaLoft can use e-mail as part of its marketing strategy.

Details

▶ **Goals**

The goal of e-mail marketing from the customer's point of view is to provide the means of indicating preferences to a company. When the customer decides to purchase, the company already knows who they are and can provide quick and efficient service.

▶ **Characteristics**

E-mail is a fast, efficient, and cost-effective way to contact customers. However, these characteristics can be dangerous. An e-mail is a legal communication, just like a letter. As a result, nothing should be said in an e-mail that would not be typed on paper.

▶ **Types of E-Mail**

For marketing purposes, you can use e-mail to distribute newsletters, announcements, or reminders to customers who request them. The fundamental rule when using e-mail as a marketing tool is to include relevant content. E-mails that merely advertise a product usually will not elicit a positive response. Instead, customers should perceive the e-mail as containing something they want. The term **opt-in** refers to e-mail campaigns in which customers have agreed to participate. You attract opt-in customers by providing them with opportunities to request participation. The term **opt-out** refers to e-mail options that a customer must actually deselect if they do not want to receive e-mail. Figure C-11 shows a Web page on Disney.com that provides customers with both opt-in and opt-out selections.

▶ **E-Mail Components**

Figure C-12 shows the components of a typical marketing e-mail that a customer agreed to receive. Notice how the e-mail reminds the customer that they asked to receive the e-mail, and that the e-mail includes a method of unsubscribing. That is, if a customer no longer wishes to receive e-mails from the company, they can easily cancel them. The e-mail should be addressed to an individual, and it should contain a meaningful subject. Some e-mails, such as the one shown in Figure C-12, are presented in the form of newsletters and have a list of topics. In addition, the e-mail should include a link to the company's home page.

▶ **Personalization**

Using e-mail as a marketing strategy allows a company to build personal relationships with their customers. People can reply to e-mails and feel as if their preferences and needs are being taken into consideration. To be effective, companies must answer e-mails promptly and include personal messages. Form letter e-mails are not as effective as personal e-mails, although sometimes using form letter e-mails can be an efficient way of marketing to existing customers. Many e-mail programs include mail-merge capabilities similar to those found in most word-processing programs.

e-byte

Forrester Research estimates that by 2004, marketers will send more than 200 billion e-mails in the United States alone and that the volume of e-mail will surpass the amount of marketing material sent by traditional mail in 2002. *Source: E-Commerce Times*[3]

FIGURE C-11: Sample opt-in and opt-out selections

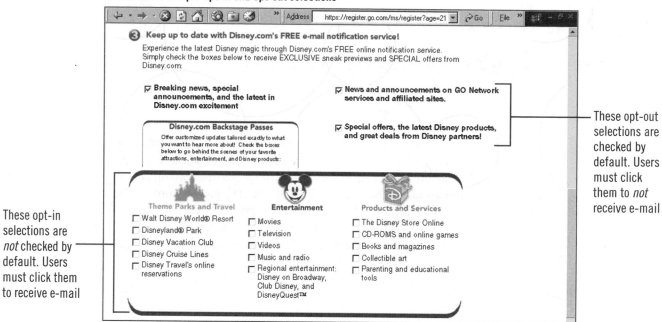

These opt-in selections are *not* checked by default. Users must click them to receive e-mail

These opt-out selections are checked by default. Users must click them to *not* receive e-mail

FIGURE C-12: Sample marketing e-mail

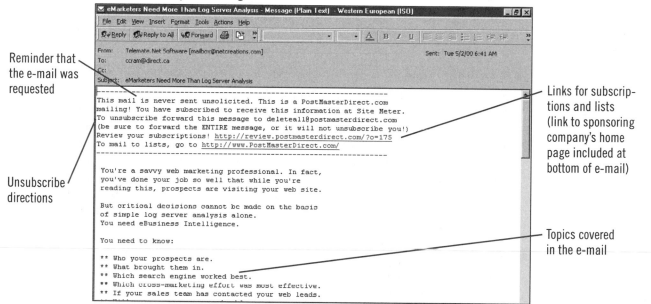

Reminder that the e-mail was requested

Unsubscribe directions

Links for subscriptions and lists (link to sponsoring company's home page included at bottom of e-mail)

Topics covered in the e-mail

Exploring Search Engines and Directories

You can find products and services on the Internet by entering keywords into search engines, or by navigating through directories and cybermalls. Most search engines use a software program called a **Web robot** (also known as a **spider** or **bot**) to find pages that contain keywords related to specific topics. Once the search engine finds the Web sites containing keywords, it lists these Web sites in a specific ranking order or index. From a marketer's point of view, having a Web site ranked in the top 10 search results is of paramount importance, because most Web surfers explore links to only the first few Web sites listed on the first page of the search results. ➤ Parminder asks you to explore issues related to search engines and directories. She plans to use the information you provide in a report for MediaLoft that recommends ways to help customers find the MediaLoft site.

Details

► Search Engines

Figure C-13 shows the top single-use search engines listed by the percentage of Web surfers who are estimated to have visited each search engine. A company should submit their Web site to as many of these top search engines as possible, along with meta search engines such as Dogpile and Web Crawler. A meta-search engine transmits a search expression to several search engines at once.

► Keywords

Search engines index pages by keywords provided by the Web site's company. As a result, a company needs to identify keywords that relate to the content on its Web site before submitting the site to a search engine.

► Site Preparation

You should include keywords in three locations on your Web site so that search engines can find them. First, include at least one or two keywords in the Web page's title. For example, in a search for "gardens," a site named Gardens Unlimited might show up ahead of a site named Mark's World of Green, even if Mark's World of Green really is a gardening center. Second, include keywords between the meta tags at the top of a Web page. A **meta tag** is the HTML code used to enclose a description of a site's contents. This description can consist of a list of keywords. Figure C-14 displays meta tags that contain keywords related to art, because the Web site displays and sells an artist's paintings and drawings. Third, include some of the keywords on the Web page, preferably toward the top of the page.

► Site Submission

Submitting a Web site to several search engines can take a great deal of time. In addition, not every search engine accepts every site submitted to it. You can pay a service to submit your site to several search engines at once, or you can go to each search engine in turn to read and then follow their submission guidelines. A company can also pay to appear in the top search results for specific keywords. Figure C-15 shows the search results on the Go To Search engine that appeared after searching for "Hotels in Italy."

► Directories

Directories categorize Web sites by topic, such as flowers or pets. Yahoo is both a directory and a search engine, while other directories function more as cybermalls that only contain products. On the Web, **cybermalls** are becoming increasingly popular because they provide surfers with a fast and convenient way of accessing numerous stores—not unlike a real-world shopping mall, but without the tired feet.

FIGURE C-13: Top search engines

Address http://www.searchenginewatch.com/report
Current Comparison
Below is a look at the latest Media Metrix's ratings. They show audience reach, which is the percentage of web surfers estimated to have visited each search engine during the month. Because a web surfer may visit more than one service, the combined totals exceed percent.
YH 63.5%
MSN 51.4%
LY 38.5%
NS 31.9%
GO 27.7%
EX 22.1%
AV 17.0%
SP 15.5%
LS 12.5%
AJ 10.8%
GT 10.2%
iWon 9.2%
G2N 7.5%
DH 6.3%
0% 10% 20% 30% 40% 50% 60% 70%
KEY: YH=Yahoo, MSN=MSN, LY=Lycos, NS=Netscape, GO=Go (Infoseek), EX=Excite, AV=AltaVista, SP=Snap, LS=LookSmart, AJ=AskJeeves, GT=GoTo, iWon=iWon, G2N=Go2Net, DH=Direct Hit. Also use this key for charts below. See the Major Search

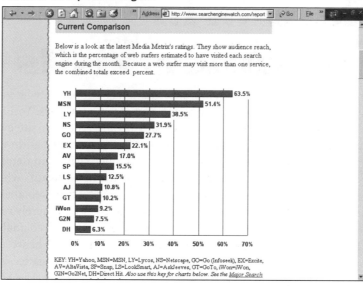

FIGURE C-14: Keywords inserted between meta tags

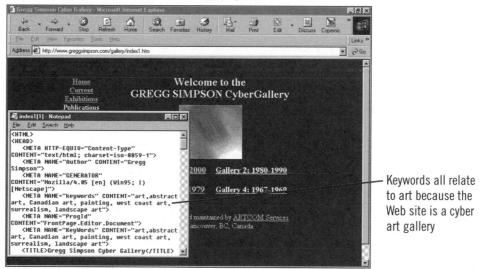

Gregg Simpson Cyber Gallery - Microsoft Internet Explorer
Address http://www.greggsimpson.com/gallery/index1.htm
Home
Current
Exhibitions
Publications
Welcome to the
GREGG SIMPSON CyberGallery
index1[1] - Notepad
<HTML>
<HEAD>
<META HTTP-EQUIV="Content-Type" CONTENT="text/html; charset=iso-8859-1">
<META NAME="Author" CONTENT="Gregg Simpson">
<META NAME="GENERATOR" CONTENT="Mozilla/4.05 [en] (Win95; I) [Netscape]">
<META NAME="keywords" CONTENT="art,abstract art, Canadian art, painting, west coast art, surrealism, landscape art">
<META NAME="ProgId" CONTENT="FrontPage.Editor.Document">
<META NAME="KeyWords" CONTENT="art,abstract art, Canadian art, painting, west coast art, surrealism, landscape art">
<TITLE>Gregg Simpson Cyber Gallery</TITLE>
Gallery 2: 1980-1990
Gallery 4: 1967-1969
maintained by ARTCOM Services
ancouver, BC, Canada
Keywords all relate to art because the Web site is a cyber art gallery

FIGURE C-15: Paid search results

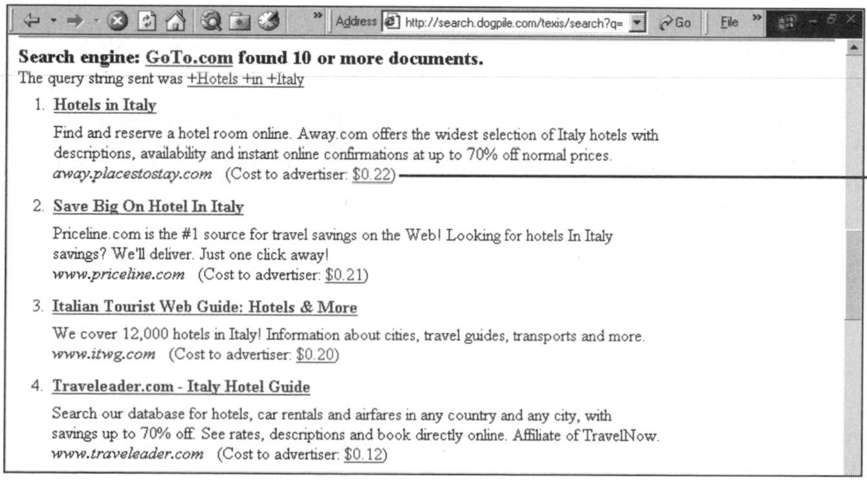

Address http://search.dogpile.com/texis/search?q=
Search engine: GoTo.com found 10 or more documents.
The query string sent was +Hotels +in +Italy
1. Hotels in Italy
Find and reserve a hotel room online. Away.com offers the widest selection of Italy hotels with descriptions, availability and instant online confirmations at up to 70% off normal prices.
away.placestostay.com (Cost to advertiser: $0.22)
2. Save Big On Hotel In Italy
Priceline.com is the #1 source for travel savings on the Web! Looking for hotels In Italy savings? We'll deliver. Just one click away!
www.priceline.com (Cost to advertiser: $0.21)
3. Italian Tourist Web Guide: Hotels & More
We cover 12,000 hotels in Italy! Information about cities, travel guides, transports and more.
www.itwg.com (Cost to advertiser: $0.20)
4. Traveleader.com - Italy Hotel Guide
Search our database for hotels, car rentals and airfares in any country and any city, with savings up to 70% off. See rates, descriptions and book directly online. Affiliate of TravelNow.
www.traveleader.com (Cost to advertiser: $0.12)
Cost to advertiser when a consumer clicks through to the Web site

E-Commerce

Monitoring Customer Visits

You use Web analysis tools to gather information about people who visit online businesses. Most Web hosts or ISPs can provide you with daily traffic statistics. You also can link to one of the many Web tracking sites to count how many people visit your site every hour, day, and month, to view information about where the visitors found your site, and to see how long they stay on your site. A key task related to monitoring customer visits is to determine how much qualified traffic visits a Web site. You can define **qualified traffic** as visitors who already match the profile of previous buyers. Figure C-16 shows data gathered by two Web analysis tools. At present, MediaLoft's Web site includes a simple hit counter that merely records the number of times a page has been viewed. Parminder heard that she can use a Web analysis tool to actually log the IP address of each computer that accesses the site. She's also heard that many free or low-cost Web analysis tools are available online. She asks you to investigate.

Steps

1. Start your Web browser, go to the Student Online Companion at *www.course.com/ illustrated/ecommerce*, click the link to **Unit C**, then click the link to **Monitoring Customer Visits**

   You will see a list of links to Web sites that provide various types of Web analysis tools such as site meters and Web counters. Some of these tools can be downloaded and placed on a Web site for free.

2. Open the Project File **ECC-02.doc** in your word-processing program, then save it as **Site Trackers**

   This document contains the table that you will use to complete your comparison of the information provided by three tracking services.

3. Explore three Web sites that offer tracking services, and complete the table with the required information

   On the Web sites, look for links to pages that display sample tracking information or demonstrations. Your goal is to find the kind of information that each tracking tool gathers, and to analyze the efficiency and effectiveness of the sponsoring Web site.

4. Scroll to the second page of the document, then complete the two tables with the required information

   The tables will expand as you type your responses. Your goal is to determine which Web analysis tool provides you with the most useful information, and then to determine how to use selected information to aid marketing efforts. For example, if a Web analysis tool shows that the majority of your customers are from Europe, you might want to explore options for placing advertisements in relevant European publications, or you might decide to buy software that translates your Web site's content into different languages.

5. Type **Your Name** at the bottom of the document, save it, print a copy, then close the document

FIGURE C-16: Web analysis data from two tracking programs

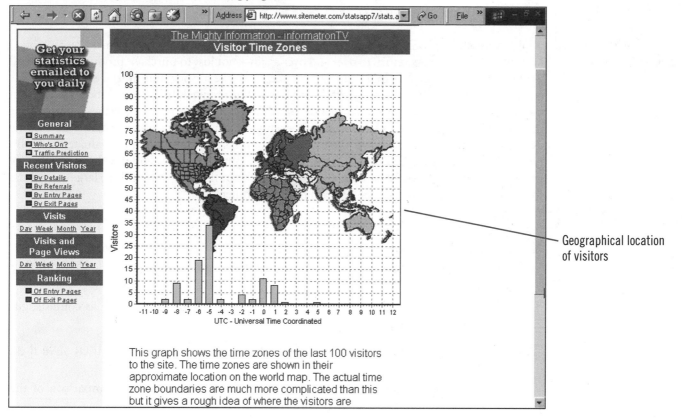

Geographical location of visitors

This graph shows the time zones of the last 100 visitors to the site. The time zones are shown in their approximate location on the world map. The actual time zone boundaries are much more complicated than this but it gives a rough idea of where the visitors are

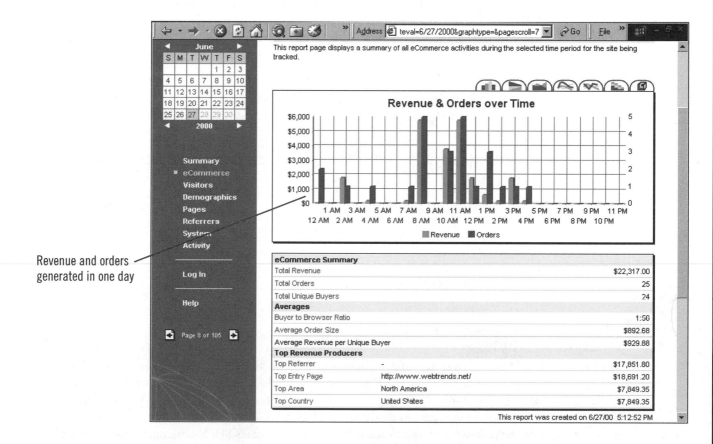

Revenue and orders generated in one day

Exploring Incentives

To be successful, an online business must build a relationship with its customers by creating a Web site that customers return to over and over again—not just to purchase products, but to read content, play contests, or explore the latest offers. Just like a brick and mortar store, an online store must offer its customers incentives in several areas: buy while at the site, become a repeat buyer, and recommend the site to friends and colleagues. Figure C-17 describes some sample incentives, and Figure C-18 shows a specific example. Web marketers are constantly developing new ideas for attracting customers to Web sites. However, incentives need to be evaluated carefully. Some surfers will visit a Web site just to participate in a contest or special offer with no intention of buying anything. Parminder asks you to check out the Web sites of three large companies to find out what incentives they are offering their customers.

Steps 1234

1. Start your Web browser, go to the Student Online Companion at *www.course.com/illustrated/ecommerce*, click the link to **Unit C**, then click the link to **Exploring Incentives**

   You will see a list of links to Web sites that might provide incentives such as contests, gift certificates, or free gifts.

2. Open the Project File **ECC-03.doc** in your word-processing program, then save it as **Incentives**

   This document contains the table that you will use to complete your comparison of the incentives offered by three online businesses.

3. Select three companies from the list, then follow the links to explore the incentives offered

   Some of the companies might no longer offer incentives. If so, try another company or conduct a search to find a company that is not included in the list on the Student Online Companion.

4. Complete the table by entering the required responses

   Your goal is to evaluate the existing incentives to determine how these incentives could be improved or new ones developed.

5. Type **Your Name** at the bottom of the document, save it, print a copy, then close the document

Qualified Traffic

Magictricks.com has found an effective way of driving qualified traffic to its Web site. People interested in magic can send a free, magic-related postcard, such as the one shown in Figure C-18, to a friend who must then visit the site to claim the postcard. While on the site, the new visitor can also choose to purchase a poster of the same image. Jackie Monticup, the co-owner of Magictricks.com, reports a significant increase in poster sales as a result of the free postcard offer. The key to success, states Ms. Monticup, is that the postcard offer attracts people who are already interested in magic, and, therefore, predisposed to stay awhile on the site and check out the extensive range of magic-related contents and products. *Source: Magictricks.com*[4]

FIGURE C-17: Incentives for online businesses

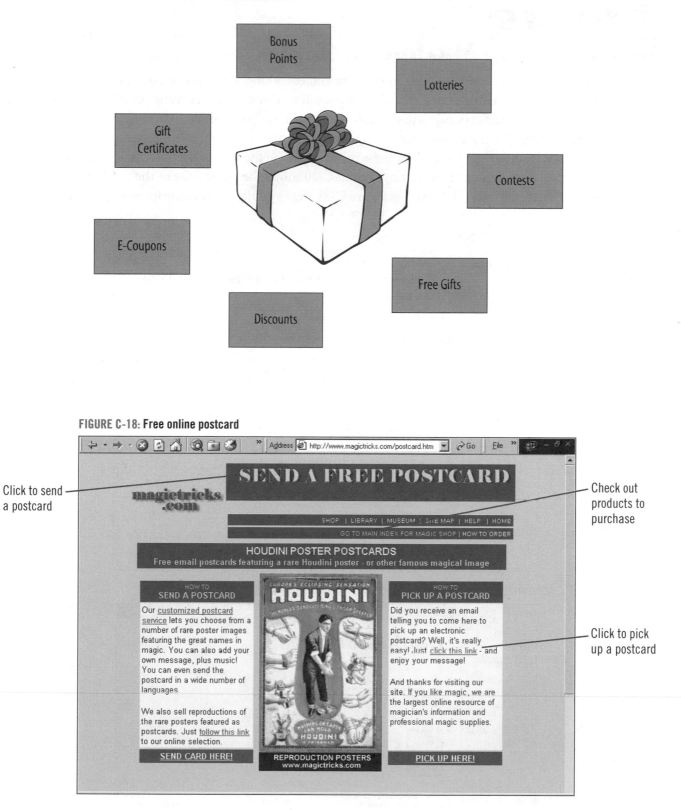

Bonus Points

Lotteries

Gift Certificates

Contests

E-Coupons

Free Gifts

Discounts

FIGURE C-18: Free online postcard

Click to send a postcard

Check out products to purchase

Click to pick up a postcard

Focus

Controversial Marketing Topics

Many of the topics covered in this unit are the subject of ongoing controversy. Chief among these topics are cybersquatting, cookies, and junk e-mailing. Cookies bother some people because of privacy concerns, while cybersquatting relates to the ownership of domain names and the practice of cyberpiracy. Junk e-mail, also known as spamming, is becoming quite a nuisance for many consumers. Web sites related to each of these issues appear in the figures shown below. Figure C-19 shows an article about cybersquatting, Figure C-20 shows the home page of the Cookie Central Web site, and the JunkBusters Web site in Figure C-21 shows guidelines relating to spam prevention.

FIGURE C-19: Cybersquatting article

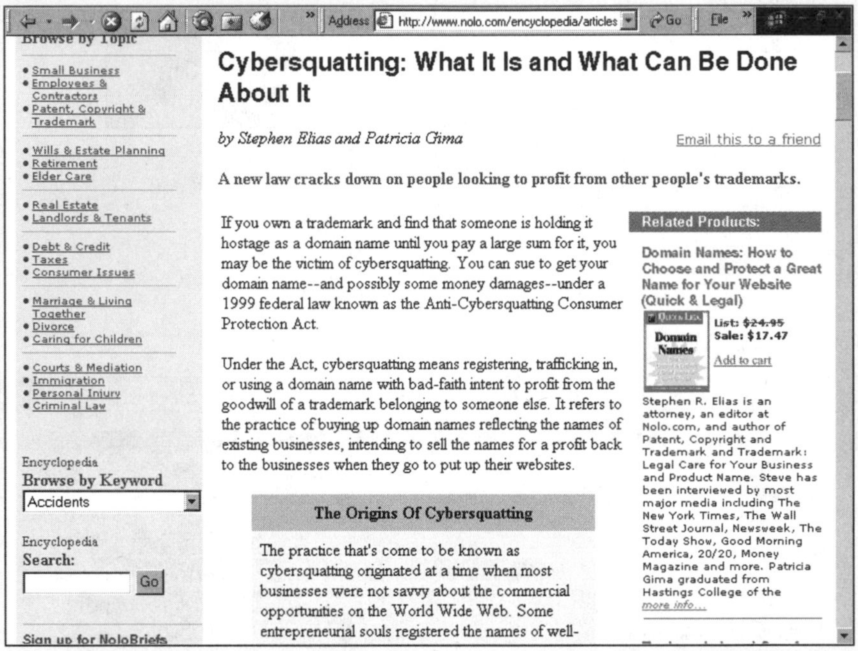

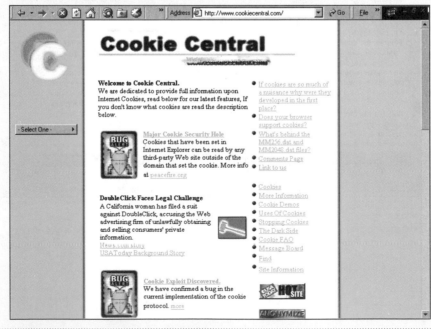

FIGURE C-20: Cookie Central Web site

FIGURE C-21: JunkBusters spamming information

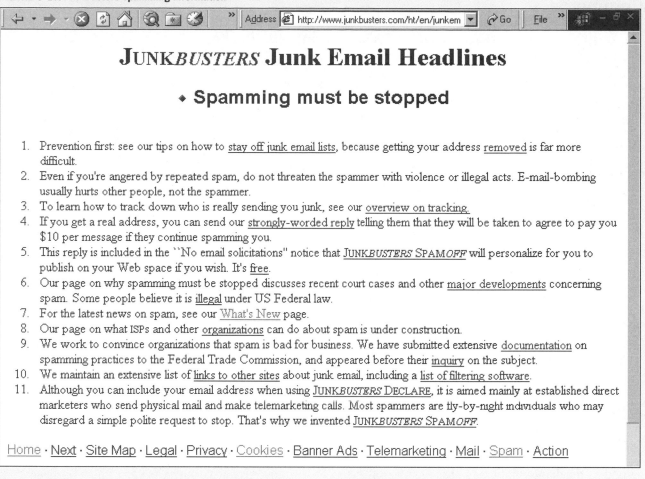

JUNK*BUSTERS* Junk Email Headlines

◆ Spamming must be stopped

1. Prevention first: see our tips on how to <u>stay off junk email lists</u>, because getting your address <u>removed</u> is far more difficult.
2. Even if you're angered by repeated spam, do not threaten the spammer with violence or illegal acts. E-mail-bombing usually hurts other people, not the spammer.
3. To learn how to track down who is really sending you junk, see our <u>overview on tracking.</u>
4. If you get a real address, you can send our <u>strongly-worded reply</u> telling them that they will be taken to agree to pay you $10 per message if they continue spamming you.
5. This reply is included in the ``No email solicitations'' notice that JUNK*BUSTERS* SPAM*OFF* will personalize for you to publish on your Web space if you wish. It's <u>free</u>.
6. Our page on why spamming must be stopped discusses recent court cases and other <u>major developments</u> concerning spam. Some people believe it is <u>illegal</u> under US Federal law.
7. For the latest news on spam, see our <u>What's New</u> page.
8. Our page on what ISPs and other <u>organizations</u> can do about spam is under construction.
9. We work to convince organizations that spam is bad for business. We have submitted extensive <u>documentation</u> on spamming practices to the Federal Trade Commission, and appeared before their <u>inquiry</u> on the subject.
10. We maintain an extensive list of <u>links to other sites</u> about junk email, including a <u>list of filtering software.</u>
11. Although you can include your email address when using JUNK*BUSTERS* DECLARE, it is aimed mainly at established direct marketers who send physical mail and make telemarketing calls. Most spammers are fly-by-night individuals who may disregard a simple polite request to stop. That's why we invented JUNK*BUSTERS* SPAM*OFF*.

<u>Home</u> · <u>Next</u> · <u>Site Map</u> · <u>Legal</u> · <u>Privacy</u> · Cookies · <u>Banner Ads</u> · <u>Telemarketing</u> · <u>Mail</u> · Spam · <u>Action</u>

Explore Further...

To complete the following questions, you need to conduct some research about the issues discussed in Figures C-19, C-20, and C-21. First, start your Web browser, go to the Student Online Companion at *www.course.com/illustrated/ecommerce*, then click the link to Focus. You will find a series of articles related to cookies, cybersquatting, and e-mail marketing. Spend some time following the links and scanning some of the articles. Your goal is to learn about the topics while also familiarizing yourself with some of the current controversies. Complete the following questions.

1. What is the Anticybersquatting Consumer Protection Act? How does this act protect people from cybersquatting? Write a one-page paper that summarizes your opinion—either for or against—on this new act.

2. Write a one-page paper that describes the activities of domain name speculators (called prospectors), and explores some of the opportunities that might still exist for them. Make sure you include and support your own opinion about whether domain name speculation should be considered a legitimate business activity.

3. Write a one- to two-page paper that describes some of the main issues related to the cookie controversy. Make sure you include and support your own opinion in relation to cookies. For example, do you think cookies are something that should concern consumers?

4. Describe two or three ways that you can avoid receiving junk e-mail. Also include information about how you can track down a spammer and what you can do to avoid future spam attacks.

Practice

► Review

Fill in the blank with the best answer.

1. While technology makes an online business accessible, marketing makes Web surfers into _____.

2. Some customers might need to be educated about the benefits of transacting business online. True/False? _____

3. Every online business should strive to serve consumers all over the world. True/False? _____

4. Market _____ is the collection and analysis of data about customers and competition.

5. A customer _____ usually contains information about the location, age, occupation, and Internet usage habits of customers.

6. Information related to a customer's Internet experience is referred to as _____.

7. A company engaged in B2B e-commerce needs to find as much information as possible about the _____ climate of their customers.

8. The term _____ describes the study of how people think and feel, particularly as related to their buying behaviors.

9. You can divide your target market into several _____ in order to develop tailored marketing efforts.

10. A small text file that contains information gathered while you surf the Web is called a _____.

11. The term data mining refers to a class of _____ applications that searches for patterns within selected groups of data.

12. A key concept related to data mining is that it discovers relationships that had not been previously identified. True/False? _____

13. The most common top-level domain is _____.

14. Most government sites use the _____ top-level domain.

15. You test the _____ of a Web site to determine how people navigate it to purchase products.

16. The association of a company with a particular logo, image, or characteristic is called _____.

17. One of the least-expensive advertising options is to exchange _____ with related Web sites.

18. Every time a customer clicks a link from your Web site to an affiliated Web site, you receive a commission. True/False? _____

19. The term _____ marketing describes a message that people receive and then send along to friends.

20. A company can promote its Web site by always including its _____ on every print advertisement, business card, and letterhead.

21. Sending out e-mails to thousands of people indiscriminately is an effective online marketing method. True/False? _____

22. The term _____ refers to e-mail campaigns in which customers have agreed to participate.

23. A search engine uses a software program called a Web _____ to find pages that contain keywords related to specific topics.

24. All search engines index pages by the keywords provided by the submitting company. True/False? _____

25. Some Web analysis tools can be downloaded and placed on a Web site for free. True/False? _____

26. Some Web analysis tools categorize visitors to a Web site by language and geographical location. True/False? _____

► Independent Challenges

1. A key component of any marketing strategy is analyzing the competition. On the Web, the competition can appear to be virtually unlimited because an online business competes with businesses all over the world, not just the two or three businesses in its geographical location that sell the same type of products or services. When you set up an online business, you can gain valuable ideas on how to market your products or services by investigating what the competition is doing. For example, if one of the companies selling the same kinds of products or services you sell is offering free samples, you might want to offer a similar program from your Web site. In particular, you want to check out what kind of content your competitor includes on its Web site.

To complete this independent challenge:

a. Fill in the box below with the name of a business that you want to pursue online, and include a description of the products or services your Web site will sell. For example, you could be interested in selling sailboats, online tarot readings, or a new line of children's clothing. Select a business that sells products related to one of your own interests. The business does not need to be real.

Business Category...

Products or Services..

b. Conduct a search for three companies that sell the product or service that you want to sell. Try a variety of search methods. For example, you can enter generic domain names such as *www.sailing.com* or *www.clothesforkids.com*. You can also search for product categories in search engines such as AltaVista and Infoseek, or in directories such as Yahoo.

c. Open the Project File ECC-04.doc in your word-processing program. This document contains the tables that you will use to analyze each of the three sites.

d. Identify the name of the URL of each of the three Web sites in the tables provided.

e. Answer the questions provided for each Web site. Include as much information as you can. Your goal is to determine which features of the competition's Web sites you would like to modify. As you complete your competition analysis, you might identify marketing strategies and features a sample Web site doesn't include, but that you think would help market your products or services. Often, you get ideas about new marketing strategies from checking what the competition is *not* doing.

f. Type **Your Name** at the bottom of the document, save it as *Competitor Analysis*, print a copy, then close the document.

2. E-business is so new that everyone involved can learn from each other's experiences. A great way to learn new marketing ideas and share tips and suggestions is to join a discussion group. Several free discussion groups exist on the Internet. You can join any of these mailing lists and monitor the postings to find valuable advice and information.

To complete this independent challenge:

a. Start your Web browser, go to the Student Online Companion at *www.course.com/illustrated/ecommerce*, click the link to Unit C, then click the link to Independent Challenge 2.

b. Select one of the links to go to a site from which you can subscribe to a free mailing list related to selling products and services online.

c. Follow the steps provided on the site to join the mailing list. Note that you need to have an e-mail address to join the mailing list.

d. Over the next week, read the postings that you receive from the mailing list. Note any suggestions that you feel are particularly useful.

e. Open your word-processing program and write a summary of the most valuable advice and tips you obtained from reading the mailing list postings over the week. If you did not find any useful information, describe the information you did find, and state why you did not think it was useful. Your critique should be approximately two pages long, double-spaced.

f. Type **Your Name** at the bottom of the document, save it as *Mailing List Critique*, print a copy, then close the document.

3. Surveys can provide companies with the information they need to develop effective marketing campaigns. If you own a small business, what kind of questions would you ask the people in your target market? For example, suppose you wanted to sell costume jewelry to teenagers. You could develop a survey for distribution to high school girls that includes questions about design and color preferences, price tolerance, and buying power. You decide to try developing a simple survey that you could use to find out about customers for a business of your choice.

To complete this independent challenge:

a. Fill in the box below with the name of a business you might wish to pursue, and a description of your products or services. You can choose a completely online business or a click and mortar business.

Business Name	
Products/Services	

b. Identify the general characteristics of your target market in the box below. For example, if you want to sell kayaks, your target market could be twenty-something athletes who are attracted to outdoor sports and live near rivers with white water.

Average Age ....

Gender(s) ....

Income level ....

Location ....

Internet usage ....

Most common employment (for example, professional, administrative, retail) ....

Other characteristics ....

....

....

....

c. Open your word-processing program, then write 10 questions that you would ask in a survey designed for people in your target market.

d. At the end of your document, write a paragraph describing how you would develop marketing strategies based on the answers to at least three of the questions. For example, if most of your target market prefers competitive whitewater kayaking to sea kayaking, you might run an online contest that gives away a trip to a local kayaking championship.

e. Type **Your Name** at the bottom of the document, save it as *Sample Survey*, print a copy, then close the document.

4. As the owner of a small business that has just recently established an online presence, you need to determine the best keywords to use when submitting your site to search engines. To help you decide, you use five keywords related to your product or service, and you conduct searches on three search engines.

To complete this independent challenge:

a. Fill in the box below with the name of a business you might want to pursue, and a description of your products or services.

Business Name ....

Products/Service ....

....

....

b. Open the Project File ECC-05.doc in your word-processing program. This document contains the table that you will use to list your five keywords and the results of three search engines of your choice.

c. Identify three search engines in the boxes of the table. For example, you could choose Excite, Infoseek, and MSN.

d. List your keywords in the boxes provided. Choose keywords related to the products or services you already identified. For example, keywords related to a company that sells sewing supplies could be sewing, stitchery, fabric, zippers, and patterns.

e. Use the Keywords to conduct searches on each of the three search engines you've identified.

f. Rank the search results according to the following criteria:

Excellent: The top Web sites were obviously relevant
Good: Most of the top Web sites were somewhat relevant
Fair: Only one or two of the top Web sites were relevant
Poor: None of the top Web sites were relevant

g. Complete the two boxes below the table with your responses. Note that the boxes will expand as you type.

h. Type **Your Name** at the bottom of the document, save the document as *Search Engine Analysis*, print a copy, then close the document.

▶ Up to Date

Neilson Net Ratings provides a top-ten list in categories such as Top Ten Banners, Top Ten Properties, and Top Ten Advertisers. Figure C-22 shows the Top Ten Banners list page for a week in June.

FIGURE C-22: Top ten banners

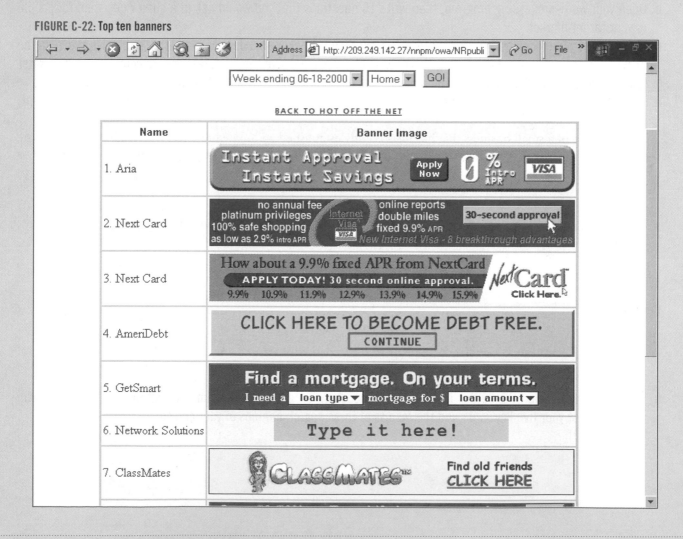

To complete the Up to Date Challenge:

a. Start your Web browser, go to the Student Online Companion at *www.course.com/ illustrated/ecommerce*, click the link to Unit C, then click the link to Up to Date.

b. Click the link to Nielson's Net Ratings Web site, then follow links to find the top 10 banners for the current week.

c. List the top five banners in the table below.

d. Answer the following questions about the banners listed on the week you checked the Neilson Net Ratings site.

Banner 1 ....

Banner 2 ....

Banner 3 ....

Banner 4 ....

Banner 5 ....

What is the most common type of business represented?

The majority of the banners shown in Figure C-22 relate to financial matters such as debt consolidation, credit cards, or mortgages. Discuss why you think these banners attracted customers.

Choose one of the top three banners that appear on the page you accessed. Describe why you think a large number of Web surfers clicked on it. Do you think people were attracted by the message or the graphics?

Visual Workshop

Figure C-23 below shows a home page for *www.mercedes.com*. Study the figure, then go online to the current mercedes.com home page. Answer the questions provided to determine how the site has been updated, and how the current site aids the marketing efforts of the Mercedes-Benz company.

FIGURE C-23

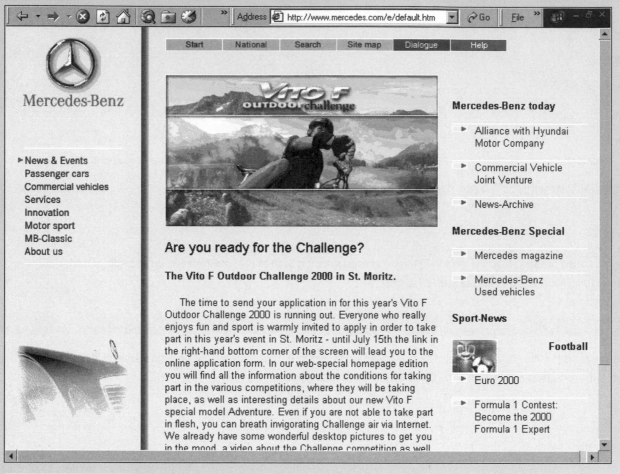

What content is now included on the home page that was not included in Figure C-23?

How do you think this new content encourages customers to enter the site and develop loyalty for Mercedes-Benz?

What products are now featured on the home page?

What customer preferences is Mercedes-Benz attempting to appeal to by highlighting these products?

What new free offers or contests are offered?

What goals do you think the company hopes to achieve by offering these contests? Do you think these goals are achievable? Why, or why not?

Planning
and Development

Objectives

► **Determine goals**

► **Explore international issues**

► **Identify planning stages**

► **Allocate resources**

► **Explore site maps**

► **Develop content**

► **Explore Web site design principles**

► **Define Web site design tools**

► **Define Web page programming tools**

► **Define data-processing tools**

Imagine a customer surfing the Web looking for a site that sells rare stamps. The click of a hyperlink lands them on your lovingly constructed rare stamp site. Five seconds later, they click away. What happened? Presuming your site was selling the right kind of rare stamps, the rapid click away probably had something to do with the site's appearance. Perhaps the rainbow background, dancing stampettes, and multiple frames made the site appear amateurish, or the links were too hard to read, or the graphics took too long to load, or the page did not provide enough information to entice the surfer to investigate further. With the competition only one click away in the fast-paced world of the Web, any company that wants to conduct business online must design its Web site to both attract and keep customers. In this unit, you'll learn about the issues and technologies related to the planning, appearance, and construction of e-commerce Web sites. ✐━━ In a previous unit, you worked with Ian MacDonald to evaluate options for setting up an online business. Now you will work with Ian to identify the steps that MediaLoft needs to take to construct a Web site that will welcome and serve its customers.

Determining Goals

Most successful online businesses are much more than just electronic storefronts. Their Web sites entertain and educate customers, offer incentives, provide customer service, and streamline transaction processing. An online business can also extend online activities beyond its own Web site to monitor the activities of its competitors, explore new markets, and find new trading partners. In order to focus its efforts effectively, an online business—just like any business—requires a comprehensive business plan. The plan should identify specific goals and describe the activities in which the business will engage to fulfill those goals. MediaLoft wants to use its Web site as an extension of its brick and mortar operation. Ian has asked you to help him identify what questions to ask to determine appropriate goals and related activities for a Web site.

Details

► Strategic Questions

The first and most important question to ask is "Why should someone come to my Web site?" The answer "to buy my products" won't get you too far, because plenty of other Web sites and real-world stores probably sell products similar to yours. Even if you sell unique handmade items, such as leather clothing or herb wreaths, thousands of other sites also sell unique items. Your site needs to provide customers with a *reason* to stop by and, more importantly, a reason to stay and, ultimately, a reason to buy and then return to buy again. Figure D-1 lists strategic questions and sample answers related to a company that sells scuba-diving equipment. The answers should help the scuba-diving equipment company determine appropriate goals for its Web site.

► Web Site Activities

Table D-1 lists some of the principal activities for a Web site, and includes suggested methods for accomplishing these activities. These methods could well take advantage of new technological advancements related to the development of Web sites. For example, if one activity is to build a community of customers, you could encourage customers to participate in real-time online discussions. If another activity is to build branding, you want to make sure that every page on your Web site includes a distinctive logo that loads as quickly as possible.

► Web Site Goals

You ask strategic questions and consider possible activities for your Web site in order to develop tangible goals that you can both measure and evaluate. Figure D-2 lists goals commonly established both for online businesses, and for click and mortar businesses. Stores such as TicketMaster, Kodak, and Odwalla Juice are examples of click and mortar operations.

► Practical Considerations

Once you have answered strategic questions, identified appropriate activities for your Web site, and established tangible goals, you need to focus on practicalities. Can you, indeed, accomplish the goals you've set for your Web site? Ask yourself the following list of practical questions:

1. Does my company have the time and expertise to build our Web site, or to oversee a third party that builds our site?
2. Does my company have enough money to build and maintain the Web site effectively?
3. What prices should I charge for my products?
4. What are the shipping costs for my products?
5. Could my company handle sudden increases in orders?
6. How do I know when I need to hire additional personnel?
7. Can I serve international customers?

Answers to these questions might well preclude some of the activities and goals you've planned for the Web site. For example, you might find that high international shipping costs will make your products too expensive for customers in countries outside your own. Alternatively, your answers could indicate that the steps required to accomplish your goals might be less challenging than you first conceived.

e-byte

"Your Web site has to solve my problems—I need a new camera, I need a book, I need someone to design a logo, or I need someone who understands Ampex™ reel-to-reel tape decks. And since this is the Web, I want someone who can solve my problems now!"
Source: Vincent Flanders, Web Sites That Suck[1]

FIGURE D-1: Sample answers to strategic questions

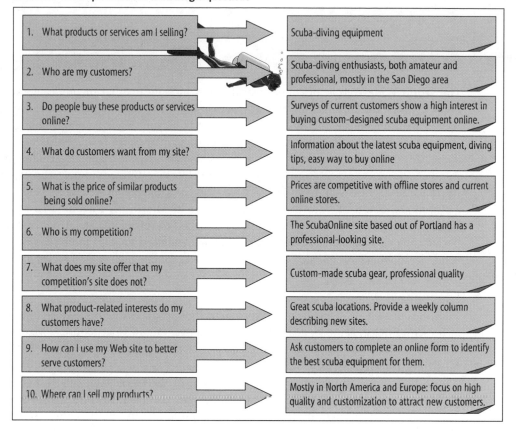

1. What products or services am I selling?	Scuba-diving equipment
2. Who are my customers?	Scuba-diving enthusiasts, both amateur and professional, mostly in the San Diego area
3. Do people buy these products or services online?	Surveys of current customers show a high interest in buying custom-designed scuba equipment online.
4. What do customers want from my site?	Information about the latest scuba equipment, diving tips, easy way to buy online
5. What is the price of similar products being sold online?	Prices are competitive with offline stores and current online stores.
6. Who is my competition?	The ScubaOnline site based out of Portland has a professional-looking site.
7. What does my site offer that my competition's site does not?	Custom-made scuba gear, professional quality
8. What product-related interests do my customers have?	Great scuba locations. Provide a weekly column describing new sites.
9. How can I use my Web site to better serve customers?	Ask customers to complete an online form to identify the best scuba equipment for them.
10. Where can I sell my products?	Mostly in North America and Europe: focus on high quality and customization to attract new customers.

FIGURE D-2: Web site goals

TABLE D-1: Web site activities

web site activity	sample methods
Build customer loyalty	Provide live online help
Sell products	Securely process transactions electronically
Conduct market research	Include online surveys and use cookies to track where customers travel on your Web site
Create customer communities	Create discussion forums or chat rooms
Support customers	Include FAQ (Frequently Asked Questions) pages
Build branding	Customize the buying experience
Manage purchasing processes and interact with suppliers	Register corporate customers and provide one-click order processing

Exploring International Issues

The World Wide Web is, of course, worldwide, which means that theoretically every company in every country can do business with any person anywhere on the planet. In reality, the challenges related to doing business with countries other than your own have not changed. All that has changed is access. With a Web site and e-mail, you can advertise your products or services around the world, and you can accept electronic payments from anyone. However, you might not be able to ship your products quickly and inexpensively to all locations, meet import and export restrictions, communicate effectively in different languages, or collect required taxes. On the other hand, going global could be your best option. See the In The Know for one analyst's point of view. MediaLoft will soon open outlets in selected countries in Latin America, Europe, and Asia. Because the new MediaLoft e-commerce Web site will need to serve these new customers, Ian asks you to learn what issues MediaLoft should address for online international sales.

Details

▶ **Language**

English is not the principal language spoken by the vast majority of the world's population, even if, at present, English is the language spoken by just over half of Internet users. Many analysts predict that one of the greatest growth areas will be in the number of non-English speakers coming online.

▶ **Multilingual Web Sites**

Figure D-3 shows the Spanish-language version of the Hertz Web site. If a company provides multilingual versions of its Web site, then it might also need to conduct business in those languages. For example, a customer who orders products from the Russian version of a company's Web site would probably communicate via e-mail in Russian, and expect Russian versions of documents and instructions to accompany the products purchased.

▶ **Content and Appearance**

A Web site built to appeal to consumers in foreign countries must take into account cultural preferences and traditions. For example, certain color combinations might offend some cultures, while slogans don't always translate as expected. A famous example is General Motors' discovery that the name of one of its most popular Chevrolets, the Nova, translates into Spanish as "it won't go."

▶ **Currency**

Currency issues relate to customer service because customers can pay for products with credit cards that automatically convert charges to the customer's own currency. A Web site should clearly indicate the currency of the product prices, and even provide customers with a convenient method to convert prices into the currency of their choice, as shown in Figure D-4.

▶ **Import/Export Laws**

At present, you cannot ship any product you want anywhere in the world. Restrictions are placed on which products you can export from your own country, and on which products you can import into another country. To find information about exporting and importing products, you need to contact the government agency responsible for commerce in your own country, and in each country to which you want to export products. To conduct business with overseas customers, you might need to use intermediaries such as shipping agents, export management companies, or export trading companies. Because many of these intermediaries have Web sites, finding the information you need to export products is becoming increasingly easier.

▶ **Taxation**

Taxation laws vary from country to country but, at present, no central information source exists. As with import and export laws, a company must contact government agencies in the countries in which they want to do business.

▶ **Shipping**

A Web site should inform customers about shipping costs at the beginning of the purchasing process. Some Web sites ask customers to first identify their location. They are then advised that shipping is not available to their location, or running totals are provided that include shipping costs for each item customers add to their shopping baskets.

FIGURE D-3: Spanish language version of the Hertz Web site

Currently selected language

Other languages

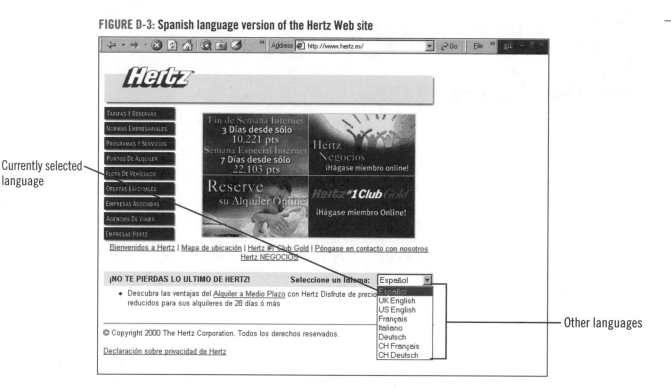

FIGURE D-4: Room rates quoted in multiple currencies

Deutsche Mark is the currently selected currency

Customers can choose a currency

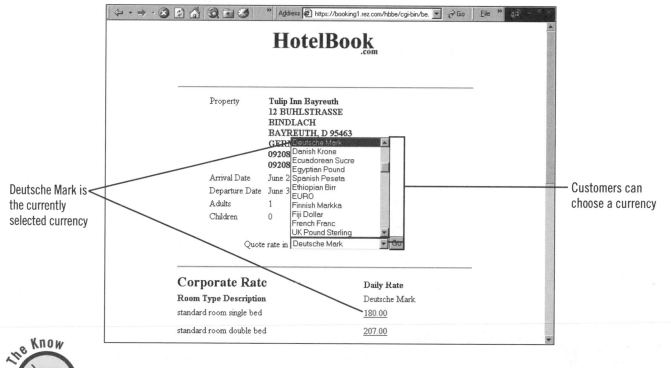

In The Know

🛒 Web Globalization

"WorldPoint is an Internet globalization company that combines multilingual content management systems and Internet translation solutions with a network of professional language translators. The chief architect at WorldPoint, Olin Lagon, writes that pioneers are forging a global Internet marketplace defined by the Web, not geography, borders, or policies. [Businesses] should start mapping out a Web globalization strategy now, or they'll have to compete for scarce resources and face stiff competition. E-Commerce does not happen unless there is trust. And culturally sensitive communication forms a strong foundation of trust."

Source: www.designshops.com²

Identifying Planning Stages

In less than an hour, you can create a simple e-commerce Web site that sells a limited number of products. To run a successful online business—just like any business—you must plan carefully and follow several distinct steps. Even then, success can still be elusive. Many of the largest dot.coms have yet to turn a profit, even though they are run with as much rigor as any real-world business. What sets an online business apart from other kinds of business initiatives are the timelines involved. Web sites can be updated almost instantly to feature new ideas, products, or policies. Adding to the time pressure is the fact that new technologies and competing Web sites can, without warning, make an online business obsolete. To survive, companies must create and implement plans that they can adapt to meet the demands of constant change. Ian asks you to clarify the steps required to take a business online, so he can determine where MediaLoft's e-commerce initiative stands.

Details

► Project Management

You need to handle the creation and maintenance of an e-commerce site as a distinct project that uses formal planning and controlling techniques to achieve specific goals. Companies can use project management software programs such as Microsoft Project to plan costs and schedules, to determine tasks, and to monitor performance against benchmarks. A **benchmark** is a reference or standard used for measurement or comparison purposes.

► Customer Interaction

Once you have determined the goals of your Web site, you need to plan how customers will interact with the site. Suppose that you have launched a Web site to help travelers find accommodations in Mexico. Figure D-5 lists the questions that a customer to your site might have. The answers to these questions will help you determine crucial factors such as the size of your Web site, the level of interactivity required, and how frequently you should update the site.

► Sample Interaction

Referring to Figure D-5, if you decide that customers might ask "Which three-star hotels in Mexico City cost less than $150 per night?" you can place a form on your site that includes drop-down lists with options that customers can choose. After customers indicate their preferences, your database of hotels is searched and the results are listed on a new Web page.

► Purpose of Questions

By anticipating the kind of information your customers might want from your Web site and how they might want to gain it, you avoid spending money on programming that might not be necessary. Instead, you can focus on developing the features that your customers really want.

► Technology Levels

You also need to anticipate the technology your customers are likely to use. For example, if your target market is Web developers, you might safely use more high-tech features on your Web site because most Web developers will have high-speed computers and up-to-date browsers. If, on the other hand, your customers rarely upgrade their computer equipment, you might want to avoid including features that require the latest browsers and fastest computers to enjoy.

► Implementation

Table D-2 provides a sample step-by-step plan for taking a business online. Note that many of these steps occur simultaneously over several months or even years. Often a company launches a simple Web site, and then expands and enhances it in response to customer needs and in relation to the company's changing financial and personnel resources. A company's business plan also must allocate time to update, improve, and maintain its Web site constantly.

e-byte

"Fifty percent of small- and mid-sized business owners predict they will use the Internet to fuel growth during the next 12 months—more than any other strategy mentioned and up from 33 percent in 1998."
Source: Arthur Andersen[3]

FIGURE D-5: Customer questions

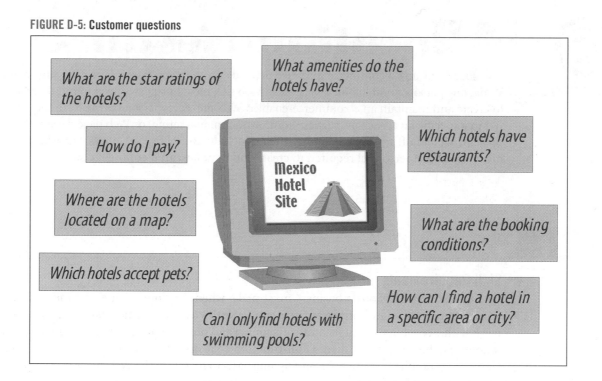

TABLE D-2: **Steps for taking a business online**

step #	description
1	Conduct market research to identify your customers, determine their need for your products, and monitor the activities of competitors
2	Set goals for the Web site and develop a business plan
3	Obtain access to the Internet—through an Internet Service Provider or via an in-house server
4	Obtain a domain name
5	Identify customer needs and interactivity requirements
6	Establish a **layout** for the Web site that roughs out its overall appearance and approximate number of pages
7	Create a catalog of products
8	Identify and set up accounts with suppliers
9	Set up e-commerce payment mechanisms
10	Establish viable delivery methods for local and international customers
11	Identify and implement security systems
12	Establish inventory-tracking systems
13	Design the Web site: set up and program pages, add interactive elements
14	Update content for the Web site (ongoing)
15	Develop systems for handling customer service
16	Maintain the Web site and monitor its security (ongoing)

E-Commerce

Allocating Resources

The success of any e-commerce initiative depends on the people who launch it and maintain it. While one person could handle a very small Web site, most businesses need to put together a team to create and maintain an e-commerce-enabled Web site. Each person on the team requires expertise in a specific area, such as database administration, marketing, or Web page design. At present, MediaLoft's Web Development Team includes only a few members. Ian asks you to learn more about the personnel required to create and maintain an e-commerce site.

Details

► Skill Requirements

One of the first decisions a business must make when developing an e-commerce initiative is whether to create an in-house team, to contract with Web specialists outside the company, or to work with a combination of in-house personnel and outside consultants. Keeping up with technology has become more than a full-time job that doesn't stop once a Web site is created. Companies require personnel on an ongoing basis to maintain the Web site, to add new content, to respond to technological advancements, and to provide customer service. To understand how many different skills are required to build and maintain a large Web site, see Figure D-6 for a list of job categories advertised by Excite.com. As you can see, an extensive range of jobs is available in virtually all business areas.

► Outsourcing

Outsourcing is the term used when a company hires another company to handle some of the tasks related to the creation and maintenance of a Web site. For example, a company might hire a professional Web site designer to create its Web site and then pay your Web hosting provider (who might also be your ISP) to host the site. Most small-to-medium-sized companies outsource at least some of the tasks related to creating and maintaining their Web site.

► Types of Outsourcing

A company that chooses **early outsourcing** hires an outside consultant to design the Web site, while a company that chooses **late outsourcing** designs the Web site in-house, and then hires outside consultants to maintain it. Many companies choose **component outsourcing**, which involves having an outside company handle specific portions of an e-commerce initiative. For example, after their Web site has been e-commerce-enabled, a company could hire one outside firm just to manage electronic payment systems. Other examples of component outsourcing include network consulting and support, content development, customer support, and security. Companies can also choose to use Applications Service Providers to set up and maintain a Web presence. See the In The Know for additional information.

► Team Composition

The first step a company takes when launching an e-commerce initiative is to set up an internal team—even if most of the work related to the creation and maintenance of the Web site will be outsourced. The in-house team needs to include people from the company's technical and business functional areas. The team can then decide what functions to outsource and what functions to complete in-house. Many companies hire an outside consultant to design the Web site, and then teach in-house team members how to maintain it. Table D-3 describes the various functional areas commonly involved in creating and maintaining a Web site.

FIGURE D-6: Sample job categories on Excite.com

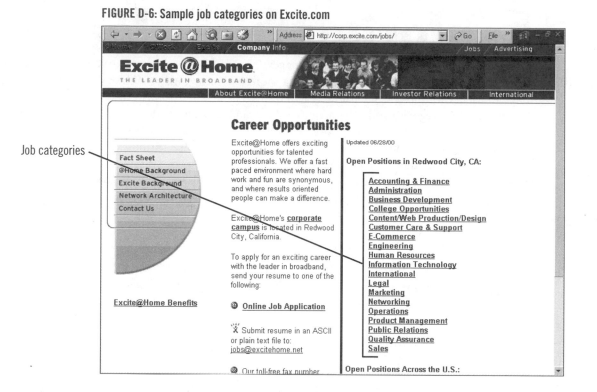

Job categories

TABLE D-3: Web development team composition

functional area	responsibilities
Business management	Develop proposals, ensure that business plan goals are met, oversee project components, administer the budget.
Applications specialists	Design and maintain the Web site, create and edit Web pages. If Web site design is outsourced, in-house staff might receive training in site maintenance.
Systems administrators	Maintain the server and operating systems, and ensure secure and reliable operations. Companies that do not own a server outsource systems administration to an ISP.
Network operations	Manage internal networks, develop firewalls (security systems), solve network problems.
Database administration	Create and maintain product databases, support transaction processing, coordinate shipping options.
Accounting	Process payments and refunds.
Customer service	Handle e-mail requests, provide phone or live online support, handle customer registration, develop FAQ pages, customize orders where applicable, personalize the shopping experience, handle exchanges and returns.
Content specialists	Develop content that supports product information on an ongoing basis; frequently update content.
Marketing consultants	Conduct usability and test-marketing studies, monitor competitors' Web sites, develop marketing materials, submit the site to search engines.

In The Know

Application Service Providers

"Application Service Providers (ASPs) deliver and manage applications and computer services from remote data centers to multiple users via the Internet or a private network. ASPs give customers a viable alternative to procuring and implementing complex systems themselves. In some cases, ASPs even provide customers with a comprehensive alternative to building and managing internal information technology operations. ASP customers also are able to control more precisely the total cost of technology ownership through scheduled payment schemes."

Source: ASP Industry Consortium[4]

E-Commerce

Exploring Site Maps

A Web site is a collection of related Web pages. The number of pages in a Web site can range from one or two to several thousand, or even more. Therefore, many Web developers create site maps so users can find specific pages in a Web site. The **site map** illustrates how the Web site is organized into categories and sub-categories. You can learn a great deal about how e-commerce sites are organized by studying their site maps. Figure D-7 shows the site map included on a Web site that sells Web site hosting services. Web developers can use various site-mapping tools to quickly create a site map of all the pages in a Web site. Figure D-8 shows the various site map styles available for creating a site map using the Xtreeme SiteXpert tool. ◄▬▬ Ian will need to develop a comprehensive site map for MediaLoft's Web site. To help him determine how best to organize the site map, he asks you to explore the site maps of three large e-commerce sites.

Steps 1 2 3 4

1. Open your Web browser, go to the Student Online Companion at *www.course.com/ illustrated/ecommerce*, click the link to **Unit D**, then click the link to **Exploring Site Maps**

2. Select three sites from the list provided

3. Open the Project File **ECD-01.doc** in your word-processing program, then save it as **Web Site Maps**

   The document contains a series of questions about the site maps on each of the three Web sites you have chosen.

4. Go to one of the sites you chose in Step 2 then follow links to find the site map

   Some Web sites provide access to their site maps from an About Us or More Information link. A site map should be featured quite prominently on a Web site, preferably on the home page. In your analysis, you can also include information about any difficulties you experienced finding or navigating the site map.

5. Answer the questions provided for the first Web site

   Your goal is to analyze how the site map is organized, and how it helps (or does not help) the user find information. Include your opinion where appropriate.

6. Repeat Steps 4 and 5 to analyze the site maps in two other Web sites

7. When you have completed all the questions for each site map, type **Your Name** at the bottom of the document, save it, print a copy, then close the document

FIGURE D-7: Sample site map

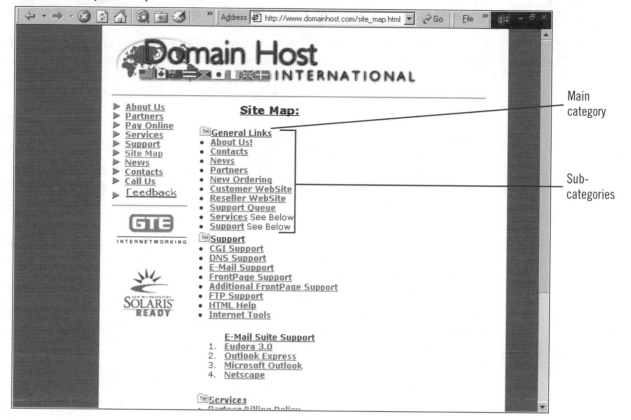

Main category

Sub-categories

FIGURE D-8: Xtreeme SiteXpert site map samples

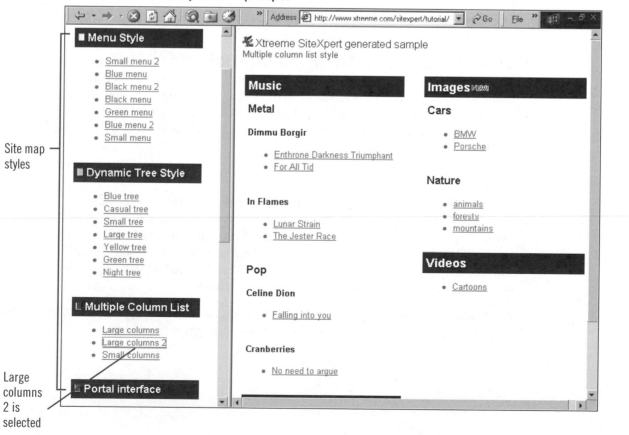

Site map styles

Large columns 2 is selected

Developing Content

Just like stores in the real world, a Web site needs to attract visitors who will, hopefully, become customers. One way a business can attract visitors to its Web site is to provide plenty of intriguing **content** in the form of interesting articles, games, questionnaires, and contests. In fact, many people say that the Internet is all about content and, as such, is similar to television, but with the added attraction of being potentially interactive and not limited by schedules.

People primarily surf the Web to find information, to be entertained, and to find and communicate with people who have similar interests. Purchasing a product is often a secondary activity that results from surfing, but was not the surfer's initial reason for going online. For example, someone interested in cycling could be looking for information about great cycling routes. After landing on a cycle shop's site that provides that information, they spot and buy a new pair of cycling gloves.

Figure D-9 shows how MotherNature.com handles content related to interests that surfers to its site are likely to have. As surfers click articles that interest them, they can also purchase related products. The content helps keep surfers on the site—learning new information, being entertained, and eventually purchasing. MediaLoft already plans to include monthly book reviews and author interviews on its new Web site. To get more ideas for suitable Web site content, you decide to identify the content included on three e-commerce Web sites, and then evaluate how you think the content helps attract and keep new customers.

Steps

1. Open your Web browser, go to the Student Online Companion at *www.course.com/illustrated/ecommerce*, click the link for **Unit D**, then click the link for **Developing Content**

2. Select three sites from the list provided

3. Open the Project File **ECD-02.doc** in your word-processing program, then save it as **Content Evaluations**
   The document contains guidelines to help you explore and evaluate the content provided by the three Web sites you have chosen.

4. Go to one of the sites you chose in Step 2, then follow the links to find content
   Concentrate on finding content that is not directly related to product information. For example, a description of a specific brand of VCR is product information; an article on how to program your VCR is content. Note that some sites might include more than one kind of content. For example, a site could include how-to articles, news links, a contest, and pages that the user can customize.

5. Complete the guidelines for each of the three sites

6. As you work, refer to the sample content evaluation shown in Table D-4
   The sample evaluation explores the content of a Web site that sells art. On this Web site, many different types of content are available, including an extensive Learn About Art section that provides information about museum exhibitions, art history, and artist biographies. The site also offers framing tips, and even has a section titled My Gallery where users can store images that they like, but are not ready to purchase.

7. When you have completed your exploration of the three sites, type **Your Name** at the bottom of the document, save it, print a copy, then close the document

FIGURE D-9: Links to content on MotherNature.com

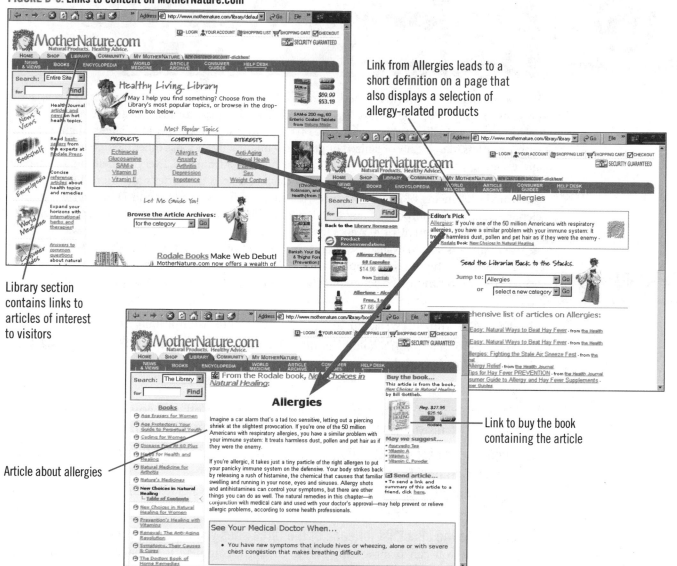

Link from Allergies leads to a short definition on a page that also displays a selection of allergy-related products

Library section contains links to articles of interest to visitors

Article about allergies

Link to buy the book containing the article

TABLE D-4: Sample content evaluation

Company 1 Name:	Art.com
Company 1 URL	http://www.art.com/

What content categories (for example, articles, contests, games) are included on the Web site?

Extensive information about art, including art history, artist biographies, how-to framing tips, museum exhibitions, and art terms; a section entitled "My Gallery" where users can store images that they like, but are not ready to purchase; two contests.

Select one of the content categories and explore it. Do you think the content is useful and/or entertaining? Give reasons for your answer.

The "Learn About Art" section provides several interesting categories, but not every category includes an extensive amount of information. For example, the museum exhibitions section lists exhibitions only in the United States, and the framing tips section is just one page. Over 2,500 artist biographies are included in the Artist Biographies section, but biographies are quite short. Pictures of the artist's work accompanies some biographies, along with links to buy prints or originals.

If you wanted to find and purchase a product, describe how you could quickly find your way to it.

A search capability that allows for three types of searches is always visible in the left pane.

How do you think the content could be improved or expanded to attract more Web surfers?

The framing information could be expanded, and every artist's biography should be accompanied by pictures. The museum section should be expanded to include exhibitions worldwide.

Exploring Web Site Design Principles

Even more than a real-world business, an online business must pay careful attention to the image it presents to the world. The average Web surfer checks out a page for just two-to-five seconds before deciding to investigate further, or to move on to another site. A real-world business might get away with being less than ideally organized or physically unattractive if it has other factors such as location and exclusivity to recommend it. A Web site has no such advantages. Every element on a Web page must coordinate with every other element to catch and keep the surfer's attention. Table D-5 lists seven major elements of an e-commerce Web site, and lists some Dos and Don'ts related to each element. The main purpose of any e-commerce Web site is, of course, to transform surfers into customers. Each element of a Web site's design must facilitate this goal in every way possible.

Ian asks you to evaluate several Web sites with relation to the seven elements identified in Table D-5. When he starts developing a new design for the MediaLoft e-commerce Web site, Ian wants to avoid common Web design pitfalls. He also wants to gather some new design ideas.

Steps

1. Open your Web browser, go to the Student Online Companion at *www.course.com/ illustrated/ecommerce*, click the link to **Unit D**, then click the link to **Exploring Web Site Design Principles**

2. Select three sites from the list provided
   Try to select three sites that differ significantly from each other. If possible, select at least one site from a large company and one site from a small company.

3. Open the Project File **ECD-03.doc** in your word-processing program, then save it as **Design Comparisons**
   The document contains a checklist that you can use to evaluate the three Web sites in terms of seven design elements.

4. Complete the checklist for each of the three sites you chose in Step 2
   Note that you can print a copy of the checklist, complete it by hand, and calculate the required totals. Try to be as objective as possible in your evaluations. Your goal is to determine how various design elements contribute to or detract from a customer's successful use of the Web site.

5. As you work, refer to the sample Web site shown in Figure D-10, and to the design elements described in Table D-5
   The Web site shown in Figure D-10 is neatly designed and easy to navigate. Note how the designer uses interesting graphics and images, yet still maintains the Web surfer's focus on the product descriptions. This site fulfills the goal of an effectively designed Web site, which is to ensure that as many surfers as possible can use the Web site to obtain information and, ultimately, to make purchases.

6. Choose the Web site that received your lowest rating, then, in the space provided, write a paragraph that describes how you think the Web site could be improved
   For example, you might decide that the Web site would be easier to navigate if the black background and green text were replaced by a white background and black text. Or, you might recommend that the large, slowly loading graphics be removed or replaced with small pictures that load quickly.

7. Type **Your Name** at the bottom of the document, save it, print a copy, then close the document

FIGURE D-10: Effective Web page design

Interesting design elements reflect the focus on mountain bike products

Picture is eye-catching without being intrusive

White background sets off product descriptions

Navigation aids are clear and easy to read

Products are clearly presented

TABLE D-5: Web site design elements

element	what's good	what's not so good
Background	• Doesn't intrude • Complements the foreground • Very light colors or white • Very subtle patterns or textures	• Overwhelms the text • Draws attention to itself • Very dark colors or black • Loud, aggressive patterns • Background image takes too long to download
Text	• Clear and easy to read • Standard fonts • Concise and easy-to-understand • Free of grammatical errors and misspellings	• Blends into the background—difficult to read • Fancy fonts detract from the meaning • Poorly written, misspelled words
Loading time	• Text loads almost immediately • Pictures are small and load quickly	• Text is part of graphics that load very slowly • Nothing much appears on the screen for long periods of time
Graphic elements (logos, icons, design elements)	• Easy to understand • Colorful, but not intrusive • Complements the content	• Irrelevant to the content • Take up too much space • Clash with text and pictures • Take too long to download
Images	• Clearly presented and easy to see • Interesting and/or dynamic • Appropriate for the content • Fast loading	• Out-of-focus, over-exposed, or under-exposed • Irrelevant or intrusive • Take too long to download • Too many images distract from the site content • Images are not balanced properly between the left, center, and right of the page, and interrupt the normal flow of reading
Navigation aids	• Immediately obvious • Include text • Inform the user exactly where they are within the site	• Difficult to find • No text included; contains icons that might not be immediately understood
Plug-ins	• Informs the user that a plug-in is necessary and available for both Windows- and Mac-based computers • Provides a hyperlink to the plug-in Web page	• Web browser may freeze or shut down • The plug-in is difficult to download or install

E-Commerce

Defining Web Site Design Tools

As you learned in Unit B, you can choose from a wide variety of methods to design an e-commerce Web site. For example, you can select a template service, use storefront software packages, or hire an e-commerce developer. You can also create a Web site in-house using Web design software such as Microsoft FrontPage, Adobe PageMill, or Macromedia Dreamweaver, and then add e-commerce capabilities. To help you make informed choices, you need to learn about the basic tools used to create Web sites. ✐ Ian asks you to help him summarize the principal characteristics of Web site design tools so that the non-technical members of MediaLoft's management team can gain a basic understanding of how a Web site is constructed.

Details

► HTML

You can define **HyperText Markup Language (HTML)** as the formatting language used to identify the structure and layout of a Web document. Different types of **tags** designate how text and other objects appear on the Web page. Structural tags such as <HEAD> and <BODY> define different sections of a Web page. Formatting tags such as <B> (for bold) define how text appears in the Web browser. With a few exceptions, most tags come in pairs. For example, all text typed between the <I> and </I> tags appears in *italics*. The <I> is the opening tag and the </I> tag is the closing tag. To view all the HTML tags used to create a Web page, select the source command from the View menu in your browser. You can create a Web page by entering HTML codes into a text editor, such as Notepad.

► Web Page Design Software

If you don't want to enter all the HTML codes manually, you can use a Web page design program to create Web pages. With Web page design software, you can work in a WYSIWYG environment. The acronym **WYSIWYG** stands for <u>W</u>hat <u>Y</u>ou <u>S</u>ee <u>I</u>s <u>W</u>hat <u>Y</u>ou <u>G</u>et and means that you can format text just as you would in a word-processing program, but you don't have to enter codes. The program enters the codes for you in a separate screen that you can view at any time. Figure D-11 shows how a Web page appears in three views in Microsoft FrontPage—a popular user-friendly Web page design program. Other popular programs include Allaire HomeSite, Cold Fusion, and H<u>o</u>T M<u>e</u>taL Pro.

► DHTML

DHTML, or **Dynamic HTML**, is used to create Web sites with which a surfer can interact without downloading additional plug-in programs. To view pages constructed with DHTML, a user must have version 4.0 or higher of either Netscape Navigator or Internet Explorer. DHTML can be used to create Web page effects that do not require long download times and also can provide users with new ways to navigate Web sites. For example, you can use DHTML to create an image that changes into another image when a user moves the mouse over it.

► XML

XML (eXtensible Markup Language) is a markup language that can be used in conjunction with HTML to create completely new sets of custom tags. XML is used to define the actual data or content included in a Web page, while HTML defines the way in which a page is formatted (its appearance). Information can be tagged just once with XML tags, and then formatted in many different ways, depending on how much text can be displayed on any given browser or device. For example, the information on a Web site could appear in a compressed version with little or no extra formatting on a Personal Digital Assistant, and appear in its expanded version on a desktop computer. The **World Wide Web Consortium (W3C)** has recommended development of a Web-specific vocabulary called **XHTML** that might become the new language of the Web.

► VRML

Virtual Reality Modeling Language (VRML) is used to create three-dimensional virtual worlds. Referred to as a scene description language, VRML tells a browser how to place objects in order to construct a 3-D environment. To view a page that has been constructed with VRML, you need to download a special plug-in.

FIGURE D-11: Web site in three views in Microsoft FrontPage

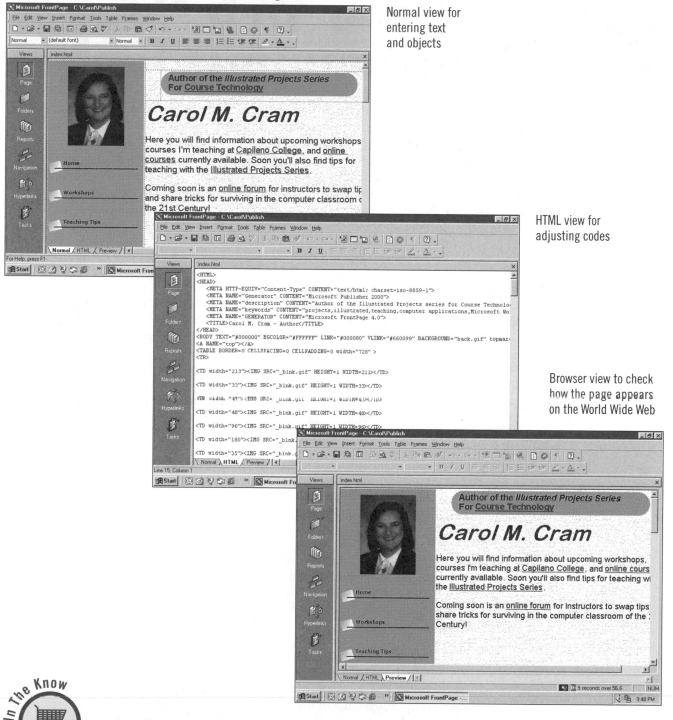

Normal view for entering text and objects

HTML view for adjusting codes

Browser view to check how the page appears on the World Wide Web

Choosing Tools

Each tool described in this lesson is used for a different level of site design, depending on the level of inter-activity and database interaction required. For example, you can use HTML to build a simple Web site that primarily provides information and does not change in response to input from the user. You use high-level tools such as DHTML, VRML, other programming tools to build in interactivity. An **interactive** Web site displays pages based on user input. For example, the Web site might generate a page that lists all the items the user has placed in a shopping cart. The page is often generated from a database containing information about all the products sold by the company.

E-Commerce

Defining Web Page Programming Tools

Once you have created a Web site, you can use a variety of programming tools to make the Web site more powerful and interactive. For example, if you buy a gift online, you can design and send a personalized greeting card that contains animated images you've uploaded from your computer. If you want to offer customers the chance to win a prize or a discount, you can design an electronic version of a scratch and win card. Two of the primary tools used to make a Web site interactive are the Java programming language and JavaScript. Web developers can also create special effects that Web surfers can view by using plug-in programs downloaded from the Internet. ◀━━ MediaLoft wants to add some interactive elements to its Web site. Ian asks you to research the most popular Web page programming tools so that he can determine what kinds of interaction would work best on MediaLoft's Web site.

Details

► Java

Sun Microsystems developed the Java programming language so that Web developers could write **Java Applets**—programs that users can download safely from the Internet and run on any system. When a user requests a Web page containing Java applets, both the page and the applets are downloaded and then run on the user's computer. As a result, Java applets are said to run **client-side applications**—tasks and applications that run on the user's computer rather than on the server. Java is platform-independent—any program written in Java can run on a wide range of computer platforms, including Mac and PC. Table D-6 lists some of the ways Web developers use Java to make a Web site interactive.

► JavaScript

JavaScript is a scripting language used to provide feedback to the Web surfer, to generate new Web pages, and to execute tasks defined by the user. JavaScript actually works in conjunction with HTML source code to enable Web developers to add dynamic content to a Web page. The term **dynamic** describes actions or events that occur as they are needed.

► Using JavaScript

You use JavaScript to create and interact with objects in a Web page. For example, each form in a document is an object that is made up of other objects such as option buttons, and text boxes. You use JavaScript to define an object's properties and methods. The **properties** of an object are characteristics such as height and color. The actions you either perform with an object or perform on an object are **methods**.

► Adding JavaScript to Web Pages

You can access hundreds of JavaScripts from various free archives and libraries on the Web. Before you download a script, however, you need to make sure that you are permitted to use it. Many sites permit only personal use of copied scripts. Figure D-12 shows a page where you can copy a JavaScript that defines any word you click. To copy this JavaScript for personal use, you first need to check any copyright restrictions and then, if permitted, you can copy the codes provided and paste them into the HTML view of your Web page.

► Plug-in Programs

A plug-in program enhances the capabilities of the Web browser. Most often, plug-in programs are used to run movies, play music, and show animations. Popular plug-in programs include Flash, Shockwave, RealPlayer, and QuickTime. Table D-7 describes the functions of these plug-ins.

FIGURE D-12: Sample JavaScript used to open word definition windows

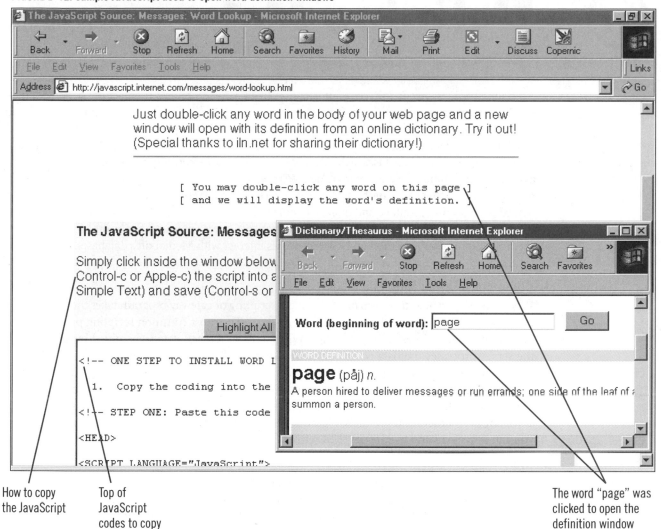

How to copy the JavaScript

Top of JavaScript codes to copy

The word "page" was clicked to open the definition window

TABLE D-6: Tasks accomplished with Java

task	description
Animation	Create static images that are programmed to move within preset parameters, or create interactive animations that the user can change by clicking certain locations
Interactivity and Computation	Create objects such as crossword puzzles, mazes, and simulations with which users can interact
Communications	Create chat rooms that users can visit to engage in real-time conversations

TABLE D-7: Plug-in programs

program	description
Flash	A low-bandwidth animation technology that is created using Macromedia's Flash animation application. Low-bandwidth means that the animations load quickly on most computers. Sites that use Flash can feature exciting animations, sounds, and other special effects
Shockwave	A Macromedia application that plays movies on newer versions of Web browsers
RealPlayer	Widely used plug-in that is used to play audio and video files. Newer versions help users find the Web locations of audio and video files they want, and then customize their preferences
QuickTime	Plug-in used to view video and audio files downloaded from the Web

Defining Data-Processing Tools

An online business needs to receive information from a customer and then act on it. For example, when a customer to a florist's Web site places an order for a bouquet of roses, the information in the order must be processed so that, in as short a time as possible, the customer receives the roses. Web developers use data-processing tools to perform specific tasks with the information that customers enter into a Web site. These tasks include registering a new customer, adding customer information to a database, and fulfilling a customer's order. ⬤⬤⬤ The more you investigate e-commerce sites, the more you realize that many of the activities you perform on a Web site depend on access to databases that contain product, contact, and financial information. You agree with Ian that you need to find out what tools are available to process information that customers enter into forms on MediaLoft's Web site. You also need information on how those tools interact with MediaLoft's databases.

Details

► Common Gateway Interface

When you enter data into a form on a Web site, a scripting or gateway program takes the information from the HTML form and interprets it for the server. The most common scripting program is the Common Gateway Interface (CGI) script. When a server receives data transmitted by a CGI script, the server processes the data according to predetermined requirements found in the script. Some processed information can go to a database to complete the order, and another part can produce a confirmation page that thanks the customer for the order. Sometimes scripting programs are referred to as the glue that connects Web pages to the databases containing information about a company's customers and products. Figure D-13 shows a Web page with links to CGI resources that you can download and use, if copyright restrictions allow.

► PERL

You can use the **PERL** programming language to write the scripts required to run a CGI program. You can also use other programming languages such as C, C++, and Python, as long as the programming language produces an executable file. An **executable file** is one created in a format that a computer can run independently of the programming language environment in which the program was written.

► Active Server Pages

Active Server Pages (ASP) were developed by Microsoft to provide Web developers with a server-side scripting environment. ASP creates Web pages in direct reaction to events caused by the Web visitor. The term **server-side** means that the scripts a Web developer writes actually run on the server, rather than on the Web surfer's own computer. This results in faster and more efficient processing speeds. You can use ASP codes to create a wide variety of functions—many related to how a Web page interacts with a database. For example, you can write an ASP script to direct the server to request information from a company's Microsoft Access database that contains product information. Figure D-14 shows a list of sample ASP scripts, along with a sample page generated by the Shopping Cart script.

► ActiveX

ActiveX refers to a set of technologies developed by Microsoft that includes a set of rules related to how information should be shared between applications. You use ActiveX technologies to create **ActiveX controls**—objects that Web designers place on Web pages to perform specific tasks, such as displaying a drop-down menu in a form, or showing an up-to-date calendar. A significant difference between ActiveX controls and Java or JavaScript codes is that ActiveX controls work only on computers that run Windows and use browsers that support ActiveX controls. When a user visits a Web site containing an embedded ActiveX control, the control is executed on the user's computer. Hundreds of ActiveX controls are available for Web developers from Web sites such as *www.active-x.com*.

FIGURE D-13: CGI resources

Programs and scripts available

Web hosting information

Links to books about CGI

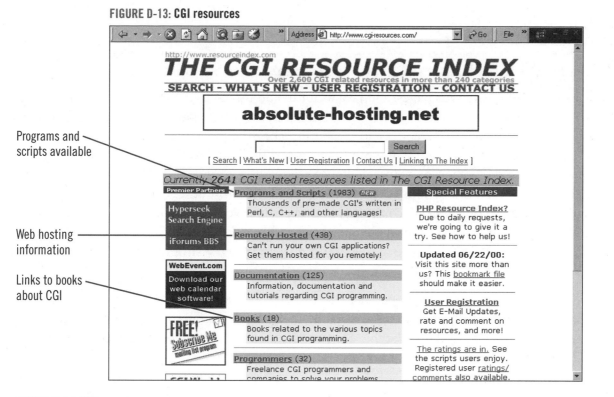

FIGURE D-14: ASP sample

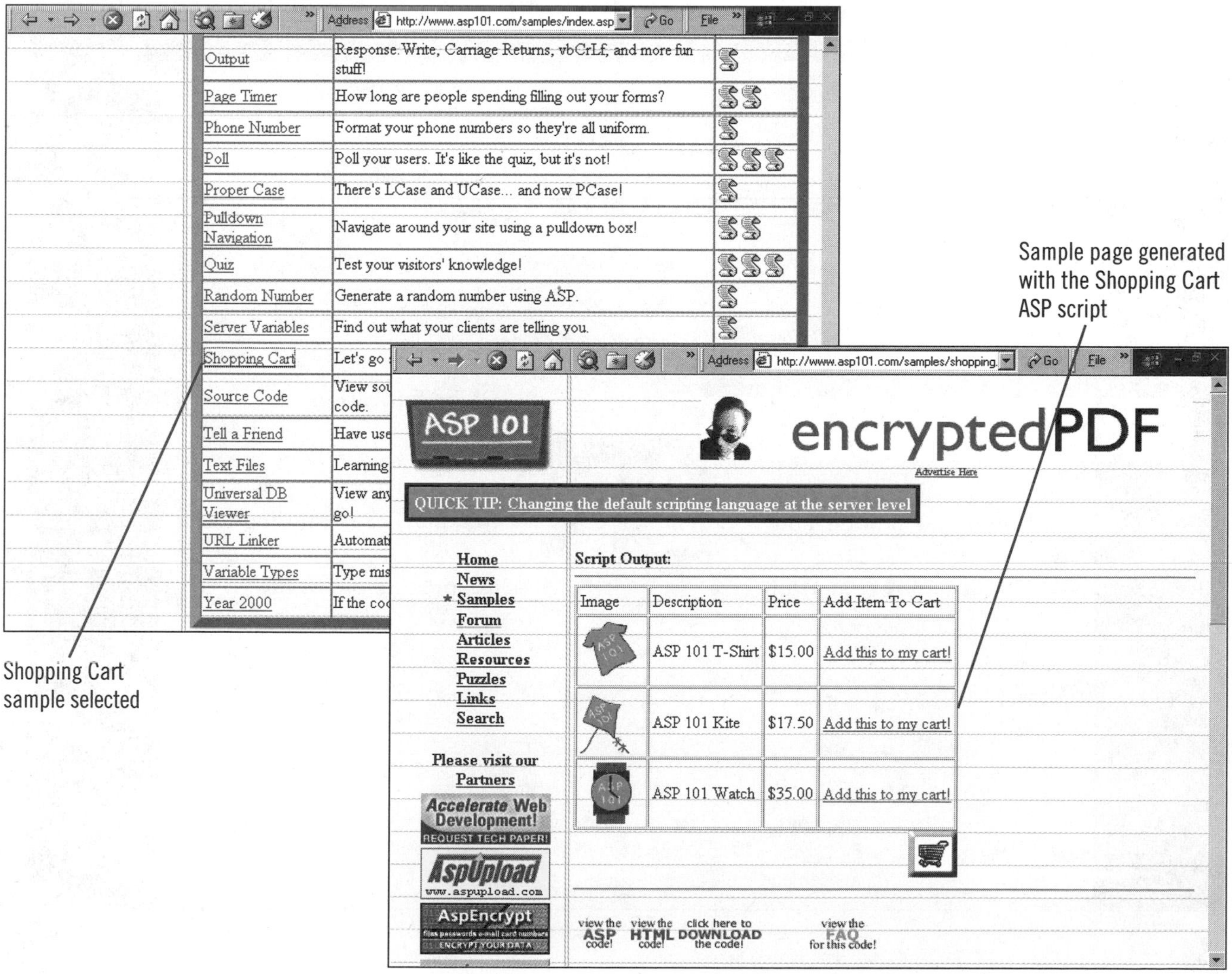

Sample page generated with the Shopping Cart ASP script

Shopping Cart sample selected

Focus

Learning HTML and JavaScript

You use HTML to create Web pages, and JavaScript to add interactivity. Even if you are not a Web page developer, you will occasionally need to check the source pages of Web pages in order to view and manipulate HTML codes and JavaScript. For example, you might decide to insert the HTML tags that will activate a site counter, or insert the JavaScript that runs a game you've downloaded from the Web. A principal challenge related to working with HTML and JavaScript is learning how to read the various codes. At first, the jumble of brackets, letters, and numbers that make up source code appears confusing. However, once you start to identify specific codes and understand their purpose, the whole muddle starts to make sense. Within no time, you see that <body bgcolor="#FFFFFF" text="#000000" link="#333399"> simply lists the colors of the Web page's background, text, and link text.

Figure D-15 shows how a Web page appears in the browser and Figure D-16 shows the HTML source code for the Web page. Study the two pages carefully, then answer the questions provided. Your goal is to start learning how to read some of the HTML codes used to create and format a Web page.

FIGURE D-15: Browser version

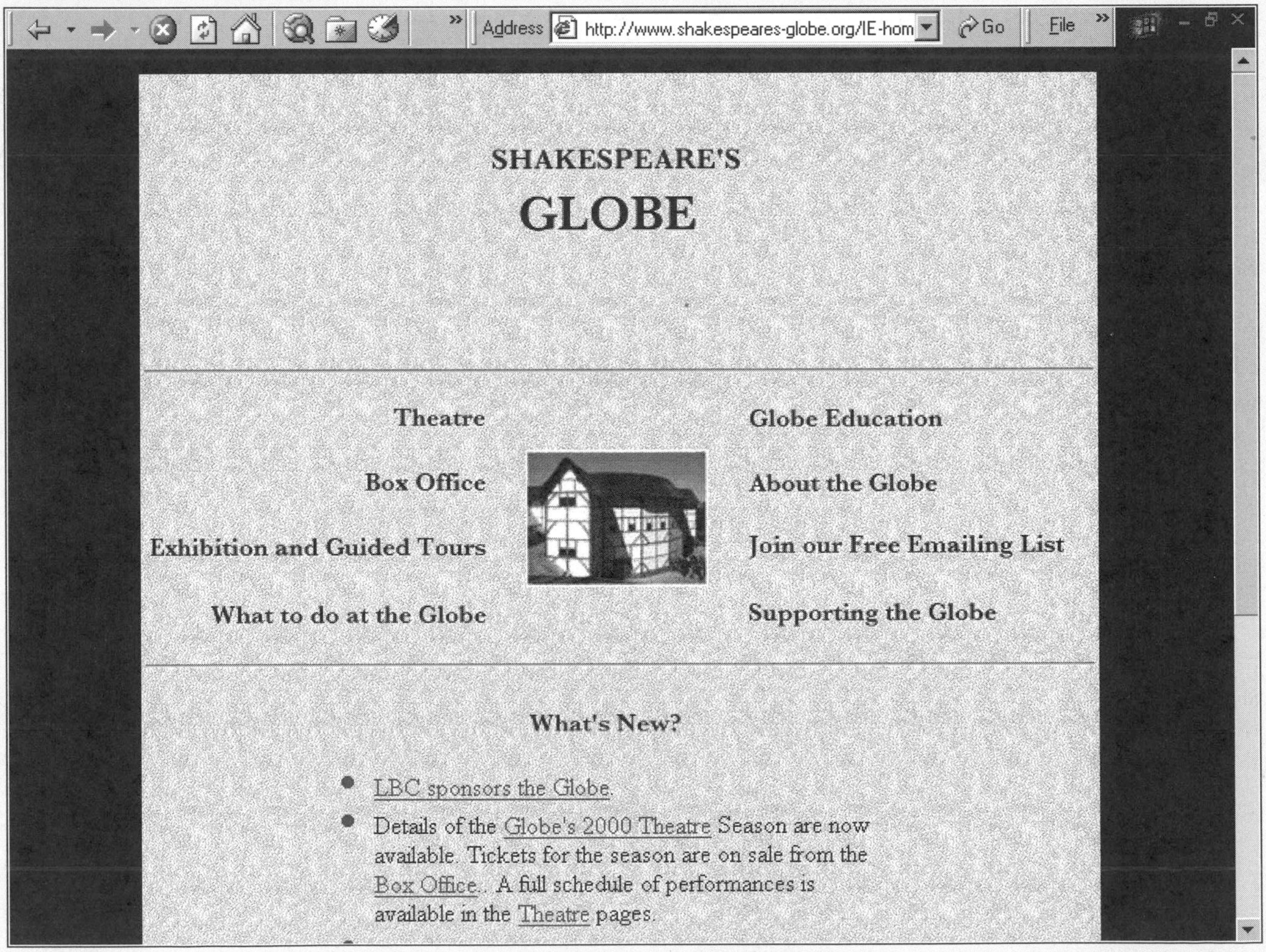

Address: http://www.shakespeares-globe.org/IE-hom

SHAKESPEARE'S
GLOBE

Theatre   Globe Education

Box Office   About the Globe

Exhibition and Guided Tours   Join our Free Emailing List

What to do at the Globe   Supporting the Globe

What's New?

- LBC sponsors the Globe.
- Details of the Globe's 2000 Theatre Season are now available. Tickets for the season are on sale from the Box Office. A full schedule of performances is available in the Theatre pages.

```
IE-home[1] - Notepad                                                    _ 8 X
File  Edit  Search  Help

<html>

<head>
<meta name="description" content="The reconstructed Shakespeare's Globe on London's Bankside,
including Theatre, Education and Exhibition departments.">
<meta name="keywords" content="Shakespeare, Globe, Shakespeare's Globe, theatre, theater,
workshop, workshops, lecture, lectures, seminar, seminars, exhibition, education, plays, London,
Wanamaker, entertainment, performing arts, school, schools, college, colleges, London, England,
UK, United Kingdom">
<title>Shakespeare's Globe Theatre, Bankside, Southwark, London</title>


<meta name="Microsoft Border" content="none">
</head>

<body bgcolor="#000000" text="#000000">
<div align="center"><center>

<table border="0" width="80%" background="images/parchment.gif">
  <tr>
    <td width="150%" colspan="4"><p align="center">   </p>
    <p align="center"> <img src="images/TITLE.gif" WIDTH="240" HEIGHT="80"><br>
    <strong><br>
    <marquee border="1" scrollamount="1" scrolldelay="40"> </marquee></strong></p>
    <hr>
    </td>
  </tr>
  <tr>
    <td width="46%" align="right"><map name="FPMap8">
      <area href="theatre/Default.htm" shape="rect" coords="2, 1, 199, 19"></map><img border="0"
src="images/theatre.gif" usemap="#FPMap8" width="200" height="20"></td>
    <td width="34%" valign="middle" align="center" rowspan="4" colspan="2"> <p><img
src="images/globe.jpg" WIDTH="116" HEIGHT="87"></p>
    <p> </td>
    <td width="70%" align="left"><map name="FPMap1">
```

Explore Further...

1. What description appears next to the content= code?

2. What is the title of the Web page?

3. What is the width of the table border?

4. What is the name of the .gif file used to fill the table background?

5. What code appears at the very top of the source code page?

6. What do you think the <tr> tag stands for?

7. Toward the bottom of the source code screen, what is the name of the file following the href= code?

8. What is the name of the .jpg file that contains the picture of the Globe Theater that appears in the middle of the page?

9. List five keywords included in the meta information. Keywords are not visible in the browser view. Search engines use them to compile search results.

10. What is the width of the globe.jpg file?

Practice

▶ Review

Fill in the blank with the best answer.

1. An online business requires a comprehensive _____ plan that identifies specific goals and describes the activities in which the business will engage to fulfill those goals.

2. You ask strategic questions and consider possible activities for your Web site in order to develop tangible _____ that you can both measure and evaluate.

3. English will continue to be the language spoken by the majority of Web surfers for many years to come. True/False _____

4. To conduct business with overseas customers, you might need to use _____ such as shipping agents, export management companies, or export trading companies.

5. To survive, companies must create and implement plans that they can adapt to meet the demands of constant _____.

6. A _____ is a reference or standard used for measurement or comparison purposes.

7. Most businesses will need to put together a _____ of people to create and maintain an e-commerce-enabled Web site.

8. A company that hires another company to create and maintain its Web site is _____ its web design tasks.

9. Many Web developers create site _____ that users can access to help them find specific pages in a Web site.

10. One way a business can attract visitors to its Web site is to provide plenty of intriguing _____ in the form of interesting articles, games, questionnaires, and contests.

11. Every element on a Web page must coordinate with every other element to catch and keep the surfer's attention. True/False _____

12. You can define _____ as the formatting language used to identify the structure and layout of a Web document.

13. The acronym WYSIWYG stands for What _____ _____ Is What You Get.

14. You can use _____ to create an image that changes into another image when a user moves the mouse over it.

15. The World Wide Web _____ (W3C) is the organization that sets the standards to which browsers and other web technologies should conform.

16. An _____ Web site is one that displays pages based on input from a user.

17. When a user requests a page containing Java _____, both the Web page and the applets are downloaded and then run on the user's computer.

18. JavaScript actually works in conjunction with HTML source code to enable Web developers to add _____ content to a Web page.

19. The _____ of an object are characteristics such as height and color.

20. When you enter data into a form on a Web site, a scripting or gateway program takes the information from the HTML form and _____ it for the server.

21. Sometimes scripting programs are referred to as the _____ that connects Web pages to the databases that contain information about a company's customers and products.

22. An _____ file is one created in a format that a computer can run independently of the programming language environment in which the program was written.

23. Active _____ Pages (ASP) were developed by Microsoft to provide Web developers with a server-side scripting environment for creating Web pages in reaction to events caused by the Web visitor.

▶ Independent Challenges

1. Many Web sites on the Internet do not obviously sell anything, yet they are online businesses. For example, the Ask Jeeves Web site provides surfers with a user-friendly search engine, while the weather.com Web site provides up-to-the-minute information about the weather in almost every city in the world. How do these Web sites make money? What would their goals be? You decide to analyze several Web sites that are not actually selling anything, so that you can figure out how they could be generating profits.

a. Open the Project File ECD-04.doc in your word-processing program. This document contains the table you will use to enter information about the Web sites that appear to be businesses, yet do not appear to sell any products.

b. Save the document as *Web Site Goals*.

c. Open your Web browser, go to the Student Online Companion at *www.course.com/illustrated/ecommerce*, click the link to Unit D, then click the link to Independent Challenge 1.

d. Select three of the companies listed, then explore their Web sites.

e. Identify the company name and the URL of each of the three Web sites in the tables provided.

f. Answer the questions for each of the three Web sites you have chosen. Your goal is to analyze the purpose of the Web site, and to determine how profits are generated or what the sponsoring business hopes to gain by providing the information or service.

g. Type **Your Name** at the bottom of the document, save the document, print a copy, then close the document.

2. Many companies have discovered that the most effective way of doing business internationally is to focus efforts on one or two countries, rather than try to market to every country in the world—an impossible task without unlimited financial resources. Success is most likely achieved if the online company thinks locally in its chosen market. That is, product descriptions are customized to the preferences of the country's population, shipping costs are manageable, and customer support is provided in the appropriate language. As the owner of a small business, you've decided to research the requirements for selling your product to one of three countries. You will need to identify the language and currency of the people in your target market, find sample shipping costs for your product, and determine any relevant import and export laws.

To complete this independent challenge:

a. Fill in the box below with the name of a business you might want to pursue internationally, and a description of your products or services. You can choose a completely online business, or a click and mortar business.

Business name...

Products/services...

b. Choose one of the following countries: Japan, France, or Brazil.

c. Open the Project File ECD-05.doc in your word-processing program. This document contains the table that you will use to enter information related to doing business with the country you have chosen.

d. Save the document as *International Business*.

e. Open your Web browser, go to the Student Online Companion at *www.course.com/illustrated/ecommerce*, click the link to Unit D, then click the link to Independent Challenge 2.

f. Follow links for the country you've chosen to find the information required for the table.

g. Complete the table as fully as possible. Your goal is to provide a general overview of the issues related to selling your products to people living in the country you've chosen. If the regulations for a particular category are too complicated, summarize them as briefly as possible, or provide a link to the relevant Web site.

h. Type **Your Name** at the bottom of the document, save it, print a copy, then close the document.

3. Thousands of new jobs have been created because of the Internet and e-commerce. Web sites need to be created, marketing plans formulated, Web-based projects supervised, content developed, and international contacts established. A quick browse through most large Web sites usually brings you to a page that lists available jobs. Now that you have read quite a bit about doing business on the Internet, you are starting to get some idea about the areas of e-commerce that interest you. Do you want to learn how to make a Web site interactive, how to use search engines as marketing tools, how to manage a Web site, or how to design security systems for an e-commerce-enabled Web site?

To complete this independent challenge:

a. Fill in the box below with two functional areas that interest you related to doing business on the Internet. For ideas, refer to the lesson on Allocating Resources. For example, you might be interested in business management and marketing, or systems administration and database administration.

Functional Area 1 ....

Functional Area 2 ....

b. Open a new document in your word-processing program, then save it as *Job Descriptions*.

c. Open your Web browser, go to the Student Online Companion at *www.course.com/illustrated/ecommerce*, click the link to Unit D, then click the link to Independent Challenge 3.

d. Follow links to find job descriptions at some of the companies listed.

e. Select at least three jobs in an area that interests you.

f. Copy the job descriptions into your word-processing program, then format them attractively.

g. Under each job description, write a paragraph describing why you'd be interested in the job, what further training and experience you'd require before you could apply for the job, and how you could receive the required training and experience.

h. Type **Your Name** at the bottom of the document, save it, print a copy, then close the document.

4. One way to learn about the various programming languages and plug-ins available is to contact Web developers directly. For example, you can find examples of Web sites that include interactive elements or other interesting effects, and then e-mail the Web developer and ask what tools they used to create the effects. Chances are good that at least some developers will be pleased to share information with you. Your goal is not necessarily to learn *how* to use the programming tools at this point, but rather to learn *what* tools are available, what tasks they can help accomplish, or what effects they can produce.

To complete this independent challenge:

a. Select an activity you are interested in, such as bird watching, cake decorating, or baseball.

b. Open your browser, then open a search engine such as Yahoo, Infoseek, or AltaVista.

c. Spend about 30 minutes searching for sites related to the activity you have chosen. Your goal is to find sites that feature some kind of interactive element. For example, the site could include a form, an animated sequence, or a game.

d. Select at least three sites that include interesting interactive elements.

e. Find links on the sites to the Webmaster, Web developer, or Web design company that created the Web site. Usually, these links appear at the very bottom of the home page.

f. Send an e-mail to the developer, asking for information about how the interactive effect you've admired was created. Assure the developer that you are a student who is just starting to learn about the tools used to create interactive Web pages.

g. Print any replies you receive. You might need to send e-mail to several developers in order to receive two or three replies. Some Web developers will be too busy to reply, while others will be pleased to share information with you.

h. Open a new document in your word-processing program, then write a paragraph describing your reaction to the reply or replies you received. Explain whether you understood the information provided, and whether the information was useful.

i. Type **Your Name** at the bottom of the document, save it as *Web Developer Information*, print a copy, then close the document.

► Up to Date

New technologies are constantly being developed to aid in the design and construction of interactive Web sites. Several Web sites provide up-to-date information about new technologies. For example, Figure D-17 shows a list of articles on the ec-trends Web site. As you can see, one of the articles describes new technology that facilitates access to e-commerce for the visually impaired.

FIGURE D-17: Sample ec-trends articles

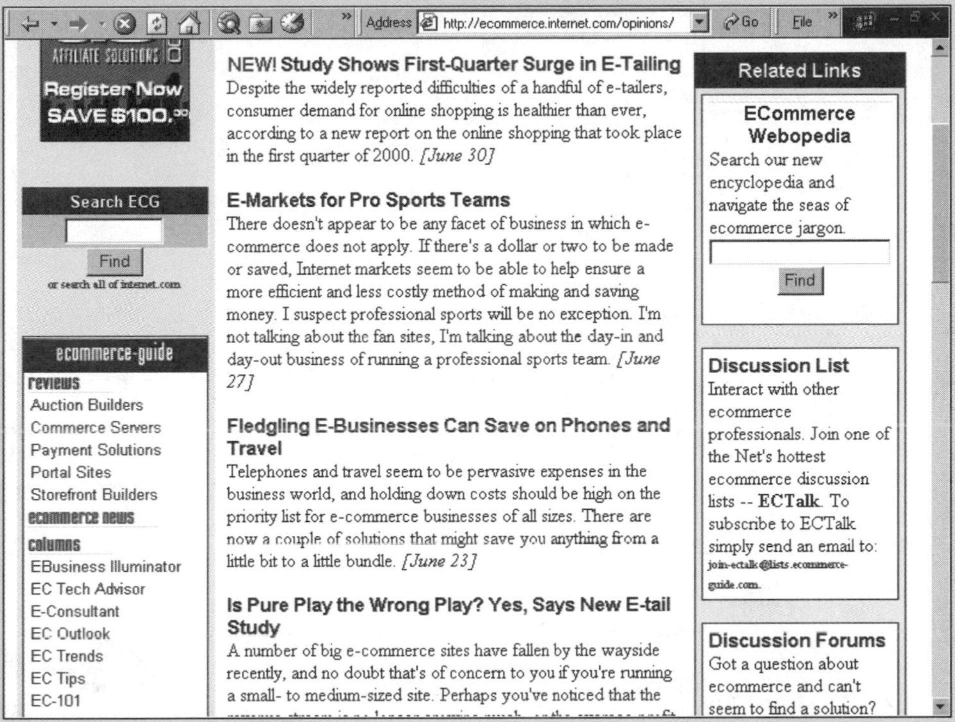

To complete the Up to Date Challenge:

a. Open your Web browser, go to the Student Online Companion at *www.course.com/illustrated/ecommerce*, click the link to Unit D, then click the link to Up To Date.
b. Click the link to ec-trends.
c. Select an article that appeals to you, then complete the box below with the required responses.

Enter the title, author, and date of the article you've selected.

Briefly describe the technology or trend presented in the article.

Do you think the technology or trend will catch on or be useful? Give reasons for your answer.

▶ Visual Workshop

As you learned in this unit, taking an online business to an international audience involves more than just uploading a Web site to the Internet. Language and cultural issues must be addressed, as must practical issues related to shipping, import and export laws, and taxation. Finally, a Web site's appearance might need to change, depending on its target audience. Shown below are two different versions of eBay's Web site. Figure D-18 shows the home page for the Japanese eBay, and the home page for the British eBay. Study the two home pages, then answer the questions below. Your goal is to determine how the appearance of the two eBay sites differs to accommodate the needs and tastes of the target audiences.

FIGURE D-18

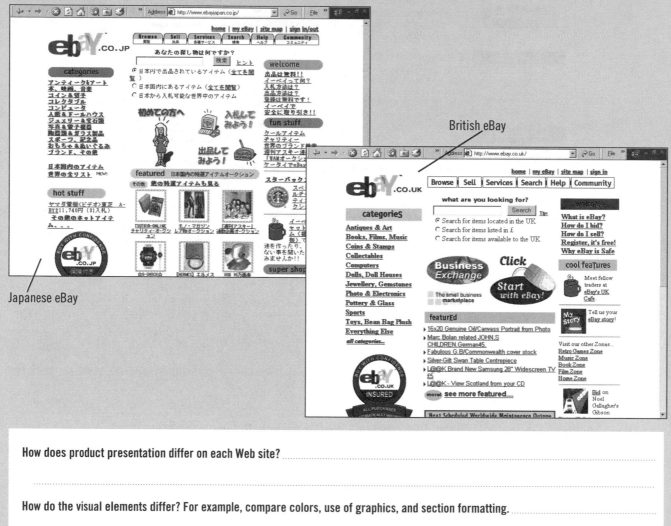

British eBay

Japanese eBay

How does product presentation differ on each Web site?

How do the visual elements differ? For example, compare colors, use of graphics, and section formatting.

How do the main elements differ? For example, compare the presention of the tabs and category sections.

What conclusions about various target markets could you make just by viewing how eBay presents its Web site to Japanese and British consumers?

E-Commerce
Components

- ► **Understand navigation aids**
- ► **Explore navigation aids**
- ► **Identify Web site search tools**
- ► **Understand databases**
- ► **Understand forms**
- ► **Identify ordering methods**
- ► **Understand shopping carts**
- ► **Explore checkout procedures**
- ► **Identify shipping options**
- ► **Monitor speed issues**

Imagine how customers at a retail store would feel if the staff suddenly barred the doors or hid the merchandise. Now imagine how online customers feel when they must click numerous links to find a product or, after shopping for a half-hour, are suddenly informed that shipping costs are twice the price of the items they want to purchase. Just as most retail stores strive to create an environment that facilitates the purchasing process, so must a Web site be designed to help customers find, order, pay for, and receive the products they want. In this unit, you will examine each step in the purchasing process—from finding the product, to receiving it on your doorstep. ◀━━━ Javad Shiraz is in charge of developing the components required to make the MediaLoft Web site as customer-friendly as possible. You will help him identify these components and learn how they can be incorporated into an e-commerce Web site.

Unit E
E-Commerce

Understanding Navigation Aids

One of the most important questions that an online business can ask is "How can Web surfers find and purchase our products?" The most common answer is "by following links." A Web site is a collection of pages connected by **hyperlinks**, or **links**. When a customer clicks a hyperlink labeled Checkout, for example, the Web page that appears contains information about how the customer can pay for the products shown in the electronic shopping basket. MediaLoft's current Web site includes a set of text links along the left side of each page. While these links are generally easy to understand, Javad wants you to check out more dynamic navigation systems.

Details

► Definition of Navigation Aids
Web site developers create navigation aids to help surfers find their way around a Web site. A **navigation aid** can be hyperlink text, buttons, or other graphic elements such as symbols, icons, and pictures that a Web surfer clicks to go to a new page in a Web site.

► Accessibility
Navigation aids must enable customers to go from Point A to Point Z and back again. For example, a customer who has navigated to a page that lists shipping options should have immediate access to the home page, to the shopping cart, or to any other area of the Web site. On most Web sites, navigation aids to the main areas of the Web site, such as the home page and checkout page, are always visible because surfers could first arrive at any page in a Web site—not just the home page. For example, a customer could search for "houses in Albuquerque" and then enter a page on a realtor's Web site that describes passive-solar homes in New Mexico. On this page, the surfer should be able to determine whose site they're in, where they are in that site, and how to move to another page in the site. If the page doesn't include a link to other pages, or even the company name or logo, the surfer might just click away without ever learning about the company or its services.

► Navigation Aid Design
Navigation aids need to be clear and easy-to-understand for both new and experienced Web users. An experienced Web surfer would probably know to click a link labeled Shopping Cart to initiate the shopping process, but a new user might not understand what a shopping cart refers to in the context of an e-commerce-enabled Web site. To make sure that both kinds of surfers know how and where to start shopping, the navigation aid could be labeled Start Shopping or Buy It Now. Navigation aids that consist solely of graphic objects or icons are often difficult to understand. These cryptic symbols can easily confuse and even alienate potential customers. A good rule of thumb is to always include text in a navigation aid, especially because some experienced surfers set their browsers so that only text appears.

► Navigation Bars
Increasingly, Web developers are streamlining Web sites to enhance their navigability. A common trend is to position links to the Web site's main sections so they appear along the top of the screen. Sometimes the links are presented in the form of tabs that mimic file folders, or as simple text entries in color-coordinated rectangles. A series of the tab links is sometimes referred to as a **navigation bar.** Some Web designers maintain that no more than six or seven items should appear on a navigation bar so the Web site is kept clear, uncluttered, and focused. Figure E-1 shows different designs for navigation aids.

► Table of Contents
The table of contents that appears at the bottom of the page in many Web sites often includes links to the main Web site pages, as well as links to less-traveled areas of the site, such as the About Us or Jobs sections. Links to Web pages can also appear along the left or right sides of the screen. Check the In The Know for information about links in frames and tables.

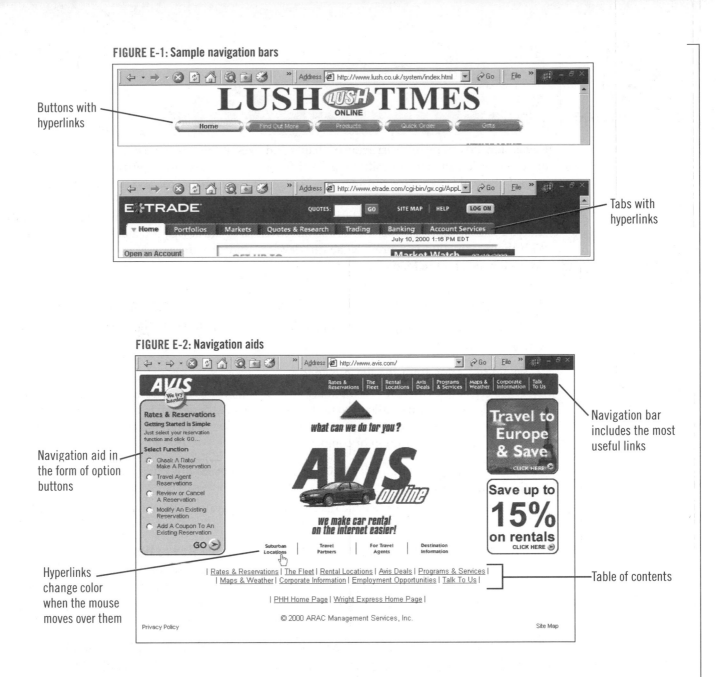

FIGURE E-1: Sample navigation bars

Buttons with hyperlinks

Tabs with hyperlinks

FIGURE E-2: Navigation aids

Navigation bar includes the most useful links

Navigation aid in the form of option buttons

Hyperlinks change color when the mouse moves over them

Table of contents

In The Know

Frames and Tables

Navigation aids can also appear along the left side of the screen—often in a frame. A Web site that uses frames is divided into two or more sections. Each section loads separately and functions as a separate Web page that can have its own scroll bar. One frame always contains links to other pages in the Web site. Not all Web browsers support frames. The trend in recent years has been to remove frames from Web sites and instead construct pages that fill no more than the average-sized screen at a resolution of 800 x 600 pixels. Instead of frames, Web page designers use **tables** to divide a page into several sections. Figure E-2 shows a Web site that includes navigation aids in a navigation bar along the top of the screen, in a graphic object containing option buttons along the left side of the screen, and in the table of contents at the bottom of the screen. Additional hyperlinks to special areas of the Web site are included above the table of contents. All of these aids were created in tables.

Exploring Navigation Aids

Navigation aids come in a vast array of shapes and sizes. While many Web sites use similar top-of-screen or left-of-screen positioning for their navigation aids, the appearance and effectiveness of these aids can vary considerably. You can learn a great deal about how to design an efficient e-commerce Web site by studying the ways in which you can navigate it. Exploring inefficient navigation systems can be just as useful as exploring efficient systems. Javad asks you to analyze the characteristics and effectiveness of the navigation aids on two Web sites. With the information you provide, he can develop guidelines to help him create appropriate navigation aids for the MediaLoft site.

Steps

1. Open your Web browser, go to the Student Online Companion at *www.course.com/illustrated/ecommerce*, click the link for **Unit E**, then click the link for **Exploring Navigation Aids**

2. Select two sites from the list provided
   Try to select one site that you think uses navigation aids well and select another site where the navigation aids are difficult to understand or poorly designed. If you want, you can use sites that you've visited in your own surfing activities, keeping in mind the surfing policies of your educational institution or company.

3. Open the Project File **ECE-01.doc** in your word-processing program, then save it as **Navigation Aids**
   The document contains the table that you will use to evaluate the navigation aids included on the two Web sites you selected in Step 2.

4. Evaluate each Web site, using the criteria noted in the **Navigation Aids** document
   Your goal is to evaluate how the navigation aids help you find selected areas of the Web site. If you are confused by a navigation aid, or are unable to find a link, describe your experience. Not all sites are well organized. See if you can determine why the existing navigation aids are inadequate, and then suggest ways they could be improved.

5. When you have completed all the questions for both Web sites, type **Your Name** at the bottom of the document, save it, print a copy, then close the document

In The Know

Creating Navigation Bars

The navigation bars along the top of many Web sites are relatively simple to create. The hyperlinks to each site are positioned on a graphic image that depicts a series of tabs or other dividers. To find out exactly how a navigation bar is constructed, you can check the HTML source for the page. Both the Netscape Navigator and Internet Explorer Web browsers allow you to view the source code. In Netscape, click View on the menu bar, then click Page Source. In Internet Explorer, click View on the menu bar, then click Source. On the source page, each tab on the browser consists of an image for the tab and the hyperlink for the page to which the image links. Figure E-3 shows a typical navigation bar, along with a portion of the source code used to create it.

FIGURE E-3: Navigation bar with source code

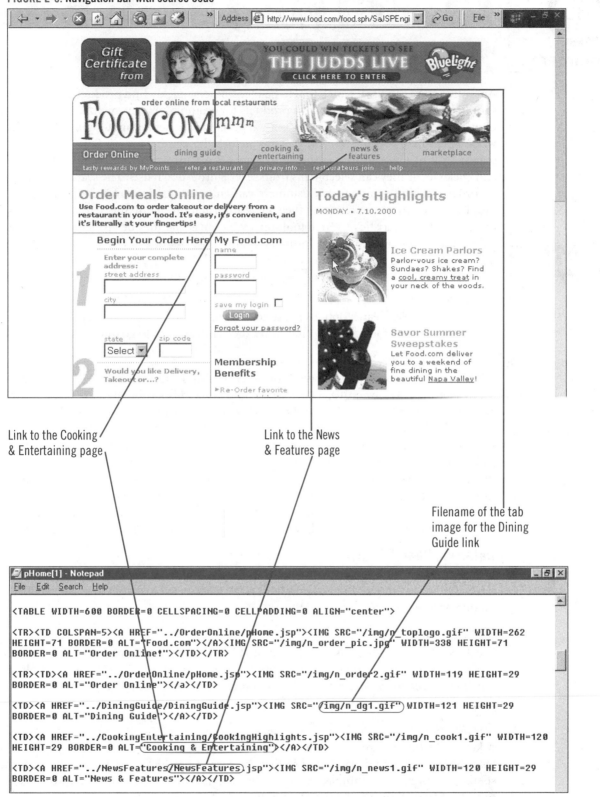

Link to the Cooking & Entertaining page

Link to the News & Features page

Filename of the tab image for the Dining Guide link

E-Commerce

Identifying Web Site Search Tools

An online store can use a search tool to help customers quickly find products. Ideally, a customer should be able to enter the name of a product (for example, pepperoni pizza), click a button, and then be presented with a list of every pizza that includes a pepperoni topping. A really useful list would present the pepperoni-only pizzas before the combo pizzas. Some Web sites include search tools in a special area, as shown in Figure E-4. Customers to this site can enter a keyword and click Go, or they can select items from several drop-down lists. The search area also includes an order-tracking component. Customers can enter unique information, such as their phone number and order number, and then view information about the status of their order. An important characteristic of search tools on a Web site is that they be visible on every page so that a customer can search for a new product at any time. ━━━ Javad asks you to research how MediaLoft can add search tools to its Web site.

Details

► **Drop-Down Lists**
One of the simplest search options is a series of drop-down lists. Customers click the down arrow to display a list of products or specifications, then click an item to go directly to a page of details.

► **Site Search Tools**
A Web site search tool finds keywords or other data in the normal HTML Web pages on one or more Web sites. For example, a customer could enter "Lisbon hotels" into a travel Web site to generate a list of hotels in Lisbon, Portugal. You can download site search tools from various sites on the Web, or you can purchase more robust tools, depending on the complexity of your site. Figure E-5 shows the features of a Web site search tool you can download from SiteMiner. This tool is hosted remotely, which means that the site indexer is not located on the same server that hosts the Web site. The e-commerce company that wants to add a search tool to one or more Web sites just needs to follow the directions to sign up for the service, open an HTML editor, copy the HTML and JavaScript codes, then paste them into an appropriate location on one or more Web pages. Figure E-6 shows the code that was used to generate a search tool.

► **Database Search Tools**
Web site search tools are appropriate for Web sites where all the data is contained on HTML pages. Online businesses that sell hundreds of products need to search databases that are located on one or more servers.

► **Site Search Process**
Most Web site search tools use **indexing robots** that electronically visit a site, follow the links, and index the contents. These robots work most efficiently on sites that already contain a comprehensive site map. A site map presents links to all the pages in a Web site, and is well-organized in an easy-to-read format.

► **Keywords**
A key task when designing search tools is to anticipate as many keywords as possible. You can also choose to design a search tool so that the correct products appear even if a customer misspells a keyword. For example, you want the customer who enters the keyword "pokman" in a toy site to find all the products related to Pokémon characters.

► **Presentation**
The results of a search should be easy to read and contain appropriate links. In addition, the results should be embedded in a Web page that is formatted with the same colors and includes the same navigation aids as the other pages in the Web site. Embedding information that has been generated as a result of a customer's request is called **inline personalization**.

FIGURE E-4: Sample search areas

Search tool ⎯

Series of drop-down lists of product categories

Order-tracking tool ⎯

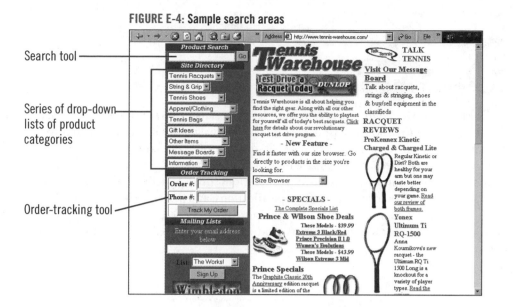

FIGURE E-5: Sample Web site search tool service

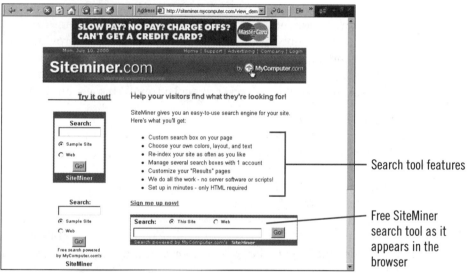

Search tool features

Free SiteMiner search tool as it appears in the browser

FIGURE E-6: Code to generate the search tool

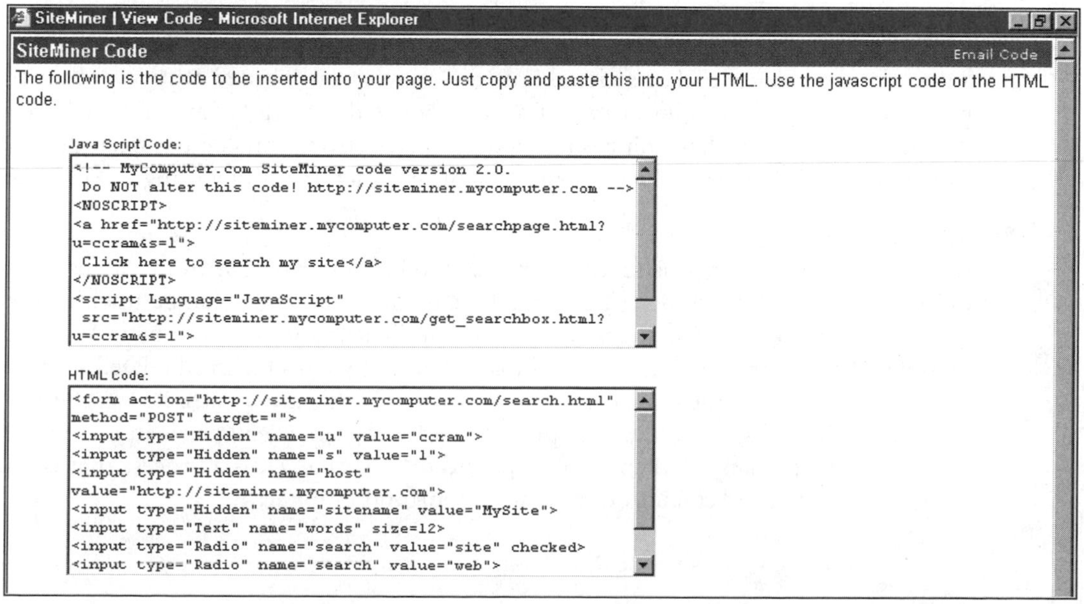

SiteMiner | View Code - Microsoft Internet Explorer

SiteMiner Code   Email Code

The following is the code to be inserted into your page. Just copy and paste this into your HTML. Use the javascript code or the HTML code.

Java Script Code:

```
<!-- MyComputer.com SiteMiner code version 2.0.
 Do NOT alter this code! http://siteminer.mycomputer.com -->
<NOSCRIPT>
<a href="http://siteminer.mycomputer.com/searchpage.html?
u=ccram&s=1">
 Click here to search my site</a>
</NOSCRIPT>
<script Language="JavaScript"
 src="http://siteminer.mycomputer.com/get_searchbox.html?
u=ccram&s=1">
```

HTML Code:

```
<form action="http://siteminer.mycomputer.com/search.html"
method="POST" target="">
<input type="Hidden" name="u" value="ccram">
<input type="Hidden" name="s" value="1">
<input type="Hidden" name="host"
value="http://siteminer.mycomputer.com">
<input type="Hidden" name="sitename" value="MySite">
<input type="Text" name="words" size=12>
<input type="Radio" name="search" value="site" checked>
<input type="Radio" name="search" value="web">
```

E-Commerce

E-Commerce

Understanding Databases

Online businesses need to access, store, and generate data in a wide variety of forms. For example, they might need to produce a list of customers who live in Omaha, create an archive of company press releases, or display information about all the products a customer just ordered. Databases contain all the data needed to facilitate these activities. Figure E-7 notes some of these activities in relation to an e-commerce-enabled Web site. A **database** is defined as a collection of information, such as names, addresses, product specifications, and prices, that is organized so that a computer can quickly retrieve specific information. MediaLoft has developed an extensive database of its products and customers, and now needs to make the database accessible to the company Web site.

Details

► **Open Database Connectivity**

The term Open Database Connectivity (ODBC) defines the standard interface used to access a database from another source, including a Web page. An **interface** is a program or an actual device that connects two entities. The ODBC interface provides access to data that has been created and stored in any database application, no matter which Database Management System (DBMS) is used to handle the data. For example, ODBC can make files in databases such as dBase and Microsoft Access accessible from Web pages on the Internet.

► **SQL**

Structured Query Language (SQL) is the standardized language used to request information from a database. Pronounced *see-kwell* (or just as separate letters), SQL enables many users to access the same databases at the same time. The ODBC technology relates closely to SQL because it acts as an interface between the SQL queries and the individual database. In effect, ODBC translates the SQL query into a language that the database can understand and then act on. The result is the generation of a Web page containing variable data. **Variable** data can be a description of products ordered, a customer's contact information, or other information generated as a result of customer input. The Web site shown in Figure E-8 provides a basic introduction to SQL.

► **Electronic Catalogs**

Most e-commerce sites that sell a wide variety of products are actually electronic catalogs. In a paper catalog, a customer looks up a product in the index, finds the number of the page that contains a description of the product, and then thumbs through the catalog to find the page. On a Web site, a customer clicks a series of links and moves from a broad overview of the company's products to specific product categories, to product descriptions, and finally to even more detailed information, depending on how deep the electronic catalog has been designed to go. Customers can locate a product by exploring the product links or by using a search tool.

► **Catalog Construction**

Electronic catalogs are constructed to access product information from databases. The term **database-driven system** describes a dynamic online catalog that can be updated quickly and easily when the company changes product descriptions or adds new products. With a database-driven system, a change made to the database is instantly reflected in all related Web pages. This system contrasts with the more common static catalogs that are constructed as a series of linked Web pages. In a **static catalog**, if a product name appears on 50 pages in a Web site and the product name is changed, then all 50 pages need to be changed—a process that could require considerable time and can introduce many opportunities for error.

FIGURE E-7: Database functions

Simple database table

ID	Sale Date	Sale Day	Product	Category	Buyer Location	Sale
1	10/1/01	Thursday	Resume Writing	Business	Canada	$19.95
2	10/2/01	Friday	Astrology Kit	Lifestyle	United States	$24.95
3	10/2/01	Friday	Eat Right	Lifestyle	England	$25.95
4	10/3/01	Saturday	Card Games Plus	Entertainment	United States	$30.95
5	10/3/01	Saturday	Astrology Kit	Lifestyle	United States	$24.95
6	10/3/01	Saturday	Word Games	Entertainment	Canada	$19.95
7	10/3/01	Saturday	Typing Tutor	Business	France	$22.95
8	10/4/01	Sunday	Wills & Estates	Business	United States	$24.95
9	10/4/01	Sunday	Cartoon Clips	Entertainment	Australia	$25.95
10	10/4/01	Sunday	Astrology Kit	Lifestyle	Japan	$24.95
11	10/4/01	Sunday	Astrology Kit	Lifestyle	Australia	$24.95
12	10/4/01	Sunday	Eat Right	Lifestyle	Canada	$25.95
13	10/4/01	Sunday	Photo Gallery	Business	United States	$24.95
14	10/4/01	Sunday	Card Games Plus	Entertainment	United States	$30.95
15	10/4/01	Sunday	Wills & Estates	Business	United States	$24.95
16	10/5/01	Monday	Resume Writing	Business	Canada	$19.95
17	10/6/01	Tuesday	Card Games Plus	Entertainment	England	$30.95
18	10/6/01	Tuesday	Eat Right	Lifestyle	England	$25.95
19	10/7/01	Wednesday	Photo Gallery	Business	France	$22.95

Information about a product that a customer puts into a shopping cart is retrieved from a database

Data, such as the date of a sale, is entered into a form and sent to a database

Information about customers, such as their location, is stored in a database

FIGURE E-8: SQL tutorial

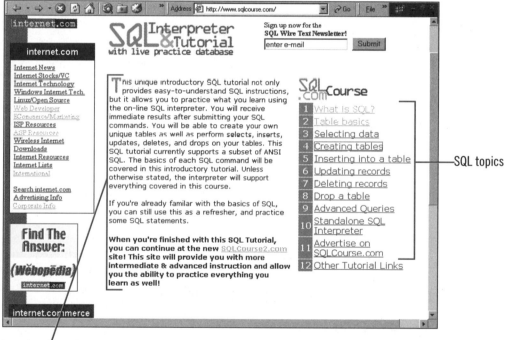

SQL topics

Introduction to SQL

Catalog Considerations

Companies that frequently change product descriptions or add new products might need to create dynamic catalogs that consist of pages generated on the fly from databases. The term on the fly means that an HTML Web page is generated only in response to a customer's request. Large companies with extensive, frequently changing inventories use this method to access and present data. Companies with a relatively stable and limited inventory could effectively use a static catalog that consists of normal HTML Web pages.

E-Commerce

E-Commerce

Understanding Forms

An e-commerce-enabled Web site must include mechanisms for customers to enter information such as their name, address, and credit card number. This information is then stored in a database. Web site developers create **forms** for customers to complete. Most electronic forms combine text boxes and drop-down lists. Text boxes accept content that the customer enters. These text boxes can be programmed to accept only content that conforms to specific criteria, such as a five-digit postal code or a certain date format. Drop-down lists offer a customer several options from which to choose when completing a form. The data entered into an online form is sent directly to a company via e-mail or, more commonly, is transmitted via a CGI script to a company database. Very often, a new page of information is generated from the information a customer enters in the form. This page is then sent directly to the user's computer, where it appears in the browser as a new Web page. Javad asks you to investigate how forms are created. He also wants you to research the technology required to generate Web pages from the information entered in a form.

Details

► Form Design

When you design a form, you first need to determine its purpose. For example, will the form be used to gather information about the customer, or will the form be used to gather information about the product that the customer wants to purchase? As a rule, you need to make forms short and simple to complete. Figure E-9 shows a sample form. As you can see, the various parts of the form are clearly labeled and attractively presented. The form also includes drop-down lists so that users can quickly enter information such as dates and numbers. A poorly designed form frustrates customers and creates a negative shopping experience that could transform a potential customer into a lost customer.

► Form Construction

You can construct a form by entering HTML tags, or you can use a software program, such as Adobe PageMill or Microsoft FrontPage to help you construct a form. The <FORM> tag appears at the top of a form and the </FORM> tag appears at the bottom of the form. Long forms can be broken into multiple pages so that customers feel they are making progress towards a tangible goal. These kinds of progressive forms are often used as part of the checkout process.

► Form Validation

Web developers often use JavaScript to ensure that the data entered into a form conforms to specific criteria. For example, you can check to make sure that the e-mail address a customer enters uses the correct e-mail **syntax**, the rules for arranging an e-mail address correctly. The e-mail address must include an @ sign, and a top-level domain such as .com, .org, or .ca.

► Form Processing

Even the best designed and constructed form on a Web page will not be useful unless a method is devised to handle the data that customers enter into the form. Generally, two methods are used to handle data generated by a form. The simplest method is to enter an HTML tag that instructs the server to e-mail the data back to the company as soon as the customer clicks the Submit button. A more reliable method is to use a CGI script to send the data to the server, where it interfaces with the company database. The server processes the data that a customer enters into a form, and then generates a new Web page. For example, after you enter your contact information into a form and click the Submit button, the server would generate a confirmation page for your order. You can then verify that the information is correct, or you can click the Back button and fix the errors. Figure E-10 shows an example of a Web page generated from data entered into a form. Web developers can use CGI or Active Server Pages (ASP) technology to generate these results pages.

FIGURE E-9: Sample form

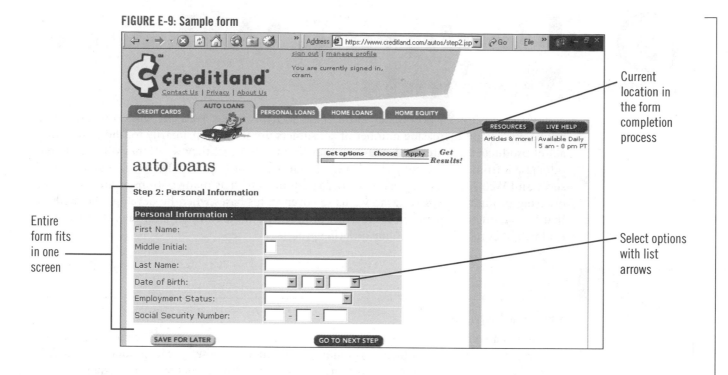

Current location in the form completion process

Entire form fits in one screen

Select options with list arrows

FIGURE E-10: Web page generated from data entered into a form

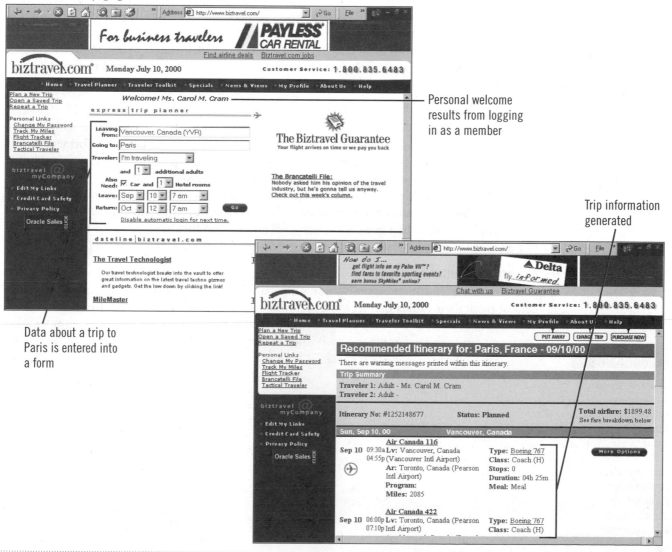

Personal welcome results from logging in as a member

Trip information generated

Data about a trip to Paris is entered into a form

Identifying Ordering Methods

Not every consumer who decides to purchase an item from a Web site will do so exclusively online. In fact, an increasing number of consumers use the Web primarily to find information about products that interest them. Once they find the product they want, they often choose to purchase it from the company's brick and mortar outlet, or to place a fax or telephone order. A successful Web site must, therefore, provide customers with as many options as are feasible for ordering products. ▬▬▬ Javad wants to cover all his bases when he develops the methods that MediaLoft customers will use to order products from the company Web site. He asks you to explore issues related to the online ordering process.

Details

▶ Ordering Instructions

You cannot assume that everyone who visits your Web site is an experienced Web surfer. Therefore, you need to provide your customers with simple instructions on how to order products. Figure E-11 shows the step-by-step ordering instructions provided on a Web site that sells fitness equipment.

▶ Alternate Methods

Many customers prefer to complete their orders by phoning the company directly, by sending a fax, or by visiting the store. You want to make sure customers are aware that they can choose any of these ordering methods as an alternative to placing an order online. Many online businesses also provide customers with a toll-free number, their hours of operation, and a mailing address. Figure E-12 shows a Web page that lists a variety of ordering methods.

▶ Tracking

A customer who finally clicks the Send or Process button to finalize an order is making a great leap of faith. With one quick motion, they've sent their credit card and contact information into the formless void of cyberspace. Will they actually receive the product they've just paid for? Online businesses can ease these justifiable concerns and build customer loyalty by providing customers with a tracking mechanism. Several e-commerce software packages include tracking tools that a business can use to inform customers of their current status in the order process. For example, has the order been acknowledged? Has the product been retrieved from the warehouse? Is the product already on a truck speeding towards the customer's house?

▶ Acknowledgement

At a minimum, customers appreciate an e-mail acknowledgement of their orders, even if they cannot track their orders online. Most online companies immediately send their customers an automatically generated e-mail acknowledgement that usually includes an order number. The company can then send another e-mail when the product has been shipped.

e-byte

"Research by Jupiter Communications reveals that 28 percent of attempted online shopping transactions are not completed because of confusing navigation schemes and ordering processes." *Source: WebBusiness.com[1]*

FIGURE E-11: Ordering instructions

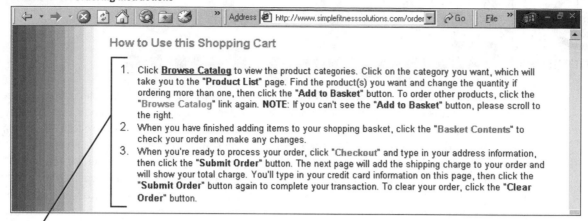

> **How to Use this Shopping Cart**
>
> 1. Click **Browse Catalog** to view the product categories. Click on the category you want, which will take you to the **"Product List"** page. Find the product(s) you want and change the quantity if ordering more than one, then click the **"Add to Basket"** button. To order other products, click the **"Browse Catalog"** link again. **NOTE**: If you can't see the **"Add to Basket"** button, please scroll to the right.
> 2. When you have finished adding items to your shopping basket, click the **"Basket Contents"** to check your order and make any changes.
> 3. When you're ready to process your order, click **"Checkout"** and type in your address information, then click the **"Submit Order"** button. The next page will add the shipping charge to your order and will show your total charge. You'll type in your credit card information on this page, then click the **"Submit Order"** button again to complete your transaction. To clear your order, click the **"Clear Order"** button.

Step-by-step ordering instructions

FIGURE E-12: Ordering methods

Address http://www.crcpress.com/www/order.htm

Ordering Methods

We offer many convenient methods to place your orders. Please select any of the following:

- **Online Ordering**
  Connect to our **Secure Server** to place your order online.

- **Ordering outside the United States/Canada:**
  Order via our international representatives.

- **Phone Orders**
  - US and Canada - **800-272-7737**
  - Europe, Middle East and Africa - **44-1462-488900**
  - India, Asia, South America, and Australasia- **561-994-0555**

- **Fax Orders**
  - US and Canada - **800-374-3401**
  - Europe, Middle East and Africa - **44-1462-483011**
  - India, Asia, South America, and Australasia- **561-989-8732**

- **Mail Orders**
  Write to us at:

In North and South America and Asia	In Europe, Middle East and Africa	In Australia and New Zealand
CRC Press LLC 2000 NW Corporate Blvd Boca Raton, FL 33431	**Turpin Distribution Services Limited** Blackhorse House	**DA Information Services PTY LTD** 648 Witehorse Road

Understanding Shopping Carts

So many online stores have used the image of a shopping cart to characterize the online shopping process that shopping carts are now considered a standard component of all online stores. In cyber terms, a **shopping cart** is the ongoing results of the ordering process; those results are generated from a database. In the browser, these results appear on a Web page that is updated every time a customer adds an item. The shopping cart information usually includes a description of each item, the number of items currently in the cart, the price of each item, and the total cost. Sometimes, shipping costs and taxes, based on the customer location, are also displayed. Shopping carts are set up so that a customer can view their contents at any time, remove items, or add new items. Javad asks you to find out how he can include a shopping cart on MediaLoft's new Web site.

Details

► Purpose

A shopping cart is designed so a customer can buy more than one item in a single shopping session. Just like real-world businesses, online businesses want customers to gather and pay for several items at once. The business saves money by processing only one transaction and the customer can save money on shipping costs.

► Construction

A shopping cart is actually an interface between the customer who visits the Web site, and the database that provides the information the customer requests. A customer selects a product, then clicks a button to add the product to an electronic shopping cart. Figure E-13 shows how a book is selected from the Barnes and Noble Web site. Figure E-14 shows the page of information that is then generated after the book is selected. The customer can click Back To Shopping to add other items to the shopping cart, or they can proceed directly to Checkout to purchase just the one book.

► Database Interaction

The most important element in shopping cart technology is the database. The database stores all the information about products and customers. When a customer selects a product, a message is sent from the Web page to the server on which the database is located. The database is always located on a server, which can be an ISP or an in-house server. Most small-to-medium-sized companies store their databases on the same server that hosts their Web site. As you learned in a previous lesson, various applications, such as ODBC, SQL, CGI, and ASP are used to connect with the database, find information about the product, and then generate a product description.

► Options

Three principal options are available to help you add shopping cart capabilities to your Web site. Table E-1 describes these options.

FIGURE E-13: Adding a product to a shopping cart

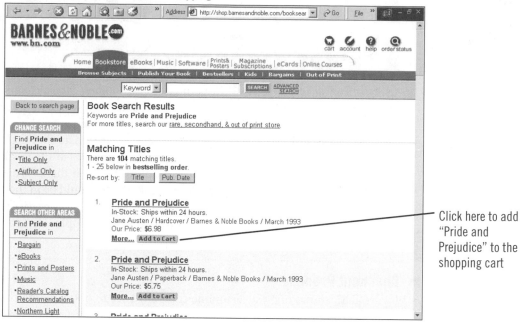

Click here to add "Pride and Prejudice" to the shopping cart

FIGURE E-14: Shopping cart contents

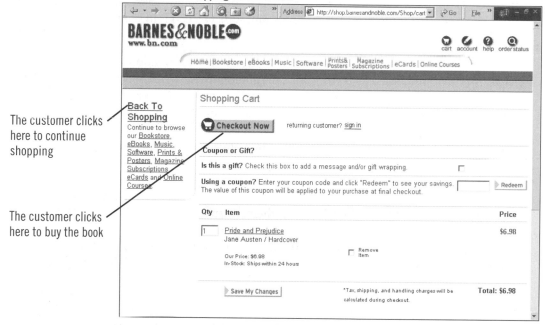

The customer clicks here to continue shopping

The customer clicks here to buy the book

TABLE E-1: Shopping cart options

option	description
Shopping cart software	You can install shopping cart software directly to the Web server. For most programs, you need to provide the domain name of your Web site and the ODBC data source. Hundreds of shopping cart software programs are available, including PerlShop, EasyCart, and NetPay. The expertise required to use these programs varies considerably. Some programs provide CGI scripts that you need to install yourself. Other programs use point and click methods and templates to guide you through the process of installing and activating a shopping cart. A company can install shopping cart software on an existing Web site to make it e-commerce-enabled, rather than design a new Web site from scratch.
E-commerce packages	If you use an e-commerce software package to build your Web site, various levels of shopping cart capabilities are included as part of the package. E-commerce software packages range from small-business do-it-yourself versions to large-scale e-business solutions.
Low-cost/free solutions	The Web is overflowing with free and low-cost shopping cart solutions of varying degrees of quality. Many of these solutions are targeted at individuals or small businesses that want to cash in on the e-commerce revolution.

Exploring Checkout Procedures

Details

After reviewing and approving the contents of a shopping cart, a customer proceeds to the cyber equivalent of the checkout counter. A checkout counter is located on a secure server that protects the customer's payment information during its transmission. The entire checkout procedure needs to be streamlined and convenient, yet assure customers that their payment information is secure. Just as people do not want to wait in checkout lines at the local supermarket, neither do they want to be frustrated by slow checkout procedures on the Internet. In fact, Web surfers are possibly less tolerant of delays on the Internet than they would be in the real world. ⟶ Javad asks you to examine issues related to checkout procedures. He's particularly interested in learning about express checkouts and the reasons why so many shopping carts are abandoned at the point when the customer is asked to confirm payment.

► Checkout Process

Figure E-15 shows one way an online company tries to optimize the checkout process. The form requesting shipping information includes a check box for customers to select if they want the product shipped to the same address they just entered on the previous screen. Note how the current step in the checkout procedure is highlighted so that customers know their status in the checkout procedure. You can use this method to reassure customers that an end is in sight (or on the site!).

► Express Checkout

If your customers have previously entered their contact information into the system (such as when they first purchased an item), your site should provide a method for them to immediately proceed to the final steps in the checkout process. You can supply an Express Checkout option for customers who have already registered or set up an account. Because the customer needs to enter contact information only once, the next time the customer arrives at the Web site and selects products to purchase, the required information is already stored in the company database.

► Logins

Some Web sites even include Smart Login or a similarly named feature that customers can select to log into a site without entering their username and password. A Web site accomplishes this level of customization by storing the login information as a cookie on the user's computer. The next time the user visits the Web site, the information in the cookie is recognized, and the user is immediately admitted. As a result, many Web sites can greet returning customers by name.

► Escape Routes

You always want to include an unambiguous escape hatch so that people can cancel their order at any point in the ordering process, even after they have placed the order. Some Web sites inform customers that they can cancel their order online within a specific time frame (such as 30 minutes), or sites provide a toll-free number that customers can call if they change their minds. Providing these escape routes helps build customer loyalty and reduces unnecessary processing costs.

► Reasons for Abandoning Carts

More often than most online businesses like, customers add items to a shopping cart, proceed to the checkout system, and then suddenly click away without completing the purchase. The abandoned cart rolls off into cyberspace, never to be seen again. An online business needs strategies to minimize the number of abandoned shopping carts. A good starting point is to understand the shopping experience from the customer's point of view, and then try to anticipate why a customer abandons a filled shopping cart. Figure E-16 lists some of these reasons.

FIGURE E-15: Step in the checkout procedure

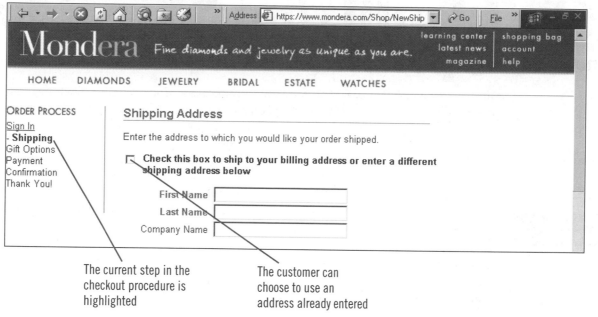

The current step in the checkout procedure is highlighted

The customer can choose to use an address already entered

FIGURE E-16: Reasons for abandoning a shopping cart

Window Shopping

Another common reason for abandoning shopping carts is simply that the customer did not intend to buy in the first place. In effect, they were doing the cyber-equivalent of window-shopping. Because the Internet at least feels relatively anonymous, surfers can indulge themselves by filling a shopping cart with luxury items that they are not able to purchase. The good news is that these same customers might one day return to the Web site with money to spend—if their fantasy shopping experience was enjoyable. To accommodate these customers, many Web sites now include wish lists, which allow customers to preselect the items that they would like to buy. When the customer is ready to buy an item, they can return to the site at any time, open their wish list, select the item, and proceed directly to checkout.

Identifying Shipping Options

Once a customer has made a commitment to purchase a product online, few things turn off a customer more than not receiving the product ordered. As a result, ensuring that shipping procedures are firmly in place should be an online company's top priority. Efficient shipping procedures are particularly important at holiday periods. Most people do not want to receive a URL address in a birthday card in lieu of a gift. In its retail operations, MediaLoft uses the postal service to ship special orders to customers. Now that they are exploring options for taking their business online, MediaLoft needs to recognize that their competitors might offer more convenient shipping options. Javad asks you to investigate some of the issues and options related to shipping goods that customers have purchased online.

▶ **Shipping Methods**

The two most common shipping methods are a private courier service or the postal service. Each of these services offer additional options, most of which relate to speed. The faster the shipping, the higher the price. Some companies even offer free shipping as an incentive, although customers need to ensure that product prices have not been inflated to cover the alleged free shipping costs. Figure E-17 shows the shipping options that customers can select if they order from the etoys Web site. Notice how shipping charges are calculated in relation to the size of the products (little thing, medium thing, big thing) and the speed of the delivery (4-10 business days, 3-6 business days, or 2-3 business days).

▶ **Shipping Dates**

Online companies selling gift products often provide their customers with a series of Order By dates. For example, a customer might need to order Valentine's Day chocolates by February 4 to ensure ground delivery by February 14, but they might wait until February 12 if they are willing to pay for overnight shipping.

▶ **Shipping Costs**

From the customer's point of view, shipping costs are a major concern. Therefore, an online business needs to make sure that customers always know the shipping cost of their order. Many online businesses include shipping costs in the running totals that customers can view as they add items to their shopping carts. Figure E-18 shows a sample running total on the illuminations.com Web site. If the customer is registered with the company, the actual shipping costs, based on the customer's geographical location and shipping preferences, are included. In addition to shipping costs, customers need to be informed of any broker or handling fees. A good way to persuade a customer to click away from making a large purchase is to suddenly inform them that a 10% handling fee is added to the order, or that undisclosed broker fees might be added at the time of delivery.

▶ **Shipping Internationally**

As you already know, customers can come from anywhere to shop at an online store. As a result, online businesses that plan to sell to customers in other countries need to pay special attention to shipping costs. Another good strategy is to inform customers as soon as possible (maybe even on the home page) about international shipping options. A customer from Canada, for example, does not want to fill a shopping basket only to be informed that orders are shipped only within the continental United States.

FIGURE E-17: Sample shipping methods

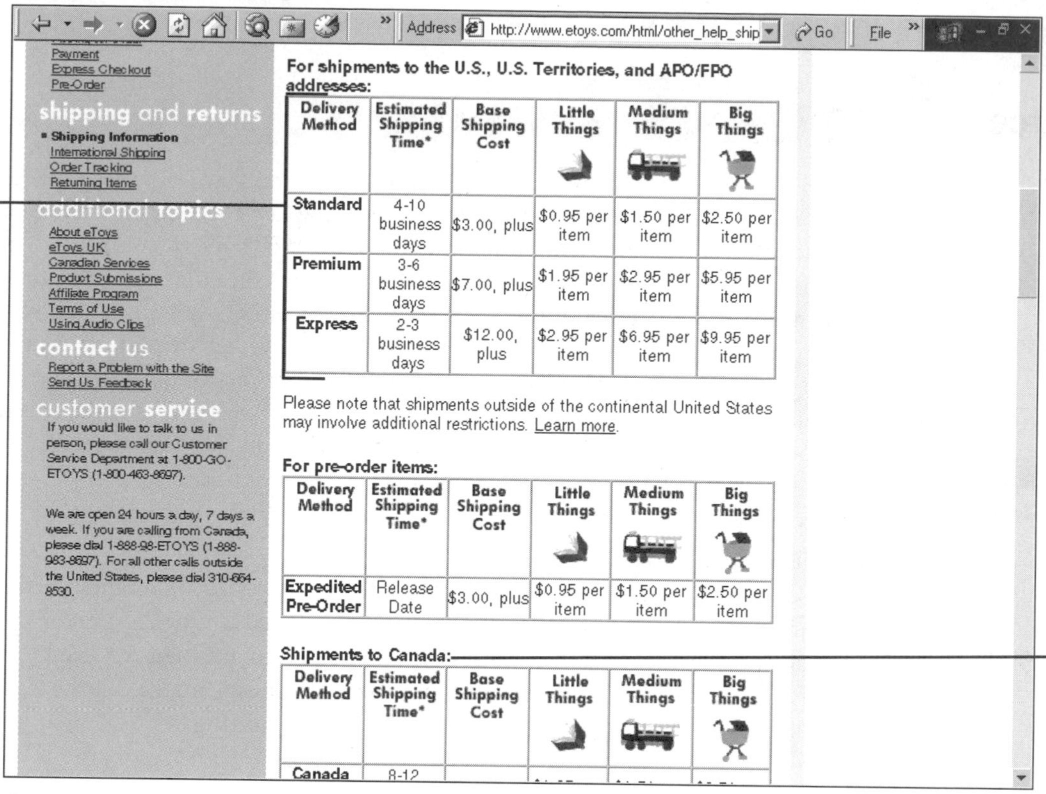

Prices depend on shipping times

Shipping options for Canadian customers

For shipments to the U.S., U.S. Territories, and APO/FPO addresses:

Delivery Method	Estimated Shipping Time*	Base Shipping Cost	Little Things	Medium Things	Big Things
Standard	4-10 business days	$3.00, plus	$0.95 per item	$1.50 per item	$2.50 per item
Premium	3-6 business days	$7.00, plus	$1.95 per item	$2.95 per item	$5.95 per item
Express	2-3 business days	$12.00, plus	$2.95 per item	$6.95 per item	$9.95 per item

Please note that shipments outside of the continental United States may involve additional restrictions. Learn more.

For pre-order items:

Delivery Method	Estimated Shipping Time*	Base Shipping Cost	Little Things	Medium Things	Big Things
Expedited Pre-Order	Release Date	$3.00, plus	$0.95 per item	$1.50 per item	$2.50 per item

Shipments to Canada:

Delivery Method	Estimated Shipping Time*	Base Shipping Cost	Little Things	Medium Things	Big Things
Canada	8-12				

Sidebar navigation:

Payment
Express Checkout
Pre-Order

shipping and returns
• Shipping Information
International Shipping
Order Tracking
Returning Items

additional topics
About eToys
eToys UK
Canadian Services
Product Submissions
Affiliate Program
Terms of Use
Using Audio Clips

contact us
Report a Problem with the Site
Send Us Feedback

customer service
If you would like to talk to us in person, please call our Customer Service Department at 1-800-GO-ETOYS (1-800-463-8697).

We are open 24 hours a day, 7 days a week. If you are calling from Canada, please dial 1-888-98-ETOYS (1-888-983-8697). For all other calls outside the United States, please dial 310-664-8530.

Address: http://www.etoys.com/html/other_help_ship

FIGURE E-18: Running totals that include shipping costs

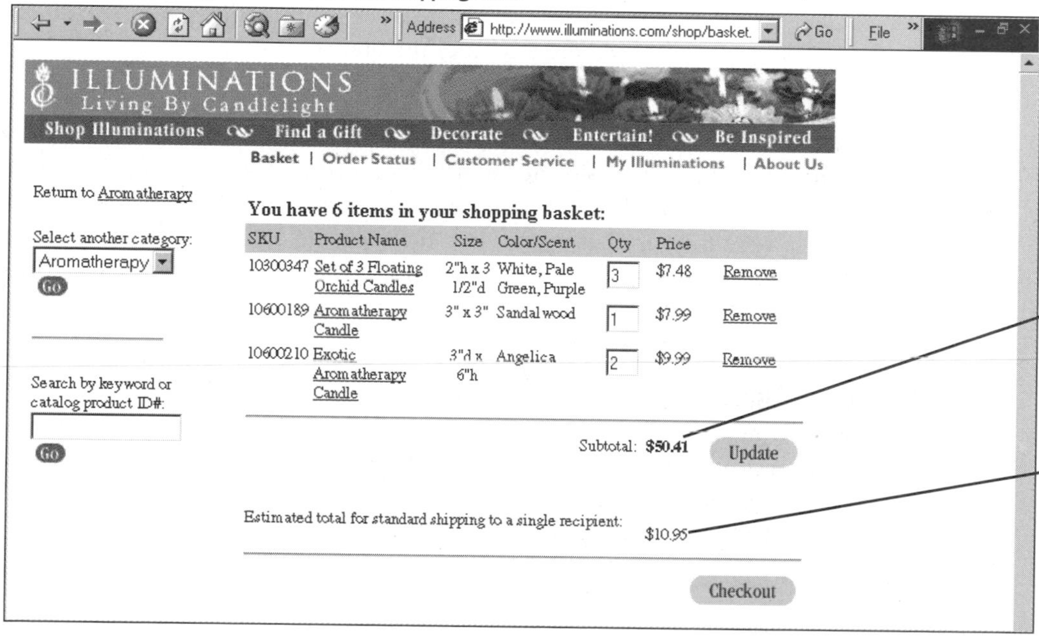

Subtotal for six items

Estimated shipping costs

Address: http://www.illuminations.com/shop/basket.

ILLUMINATIONS
Living By Candlelight

Shop Illuminations | Find a Gift | Decorate | Entertain! | Be Inspired

Basket | Order Status | Customer Service | My Illuminations | About Us

Return to Aromatherapy

Select another category:
Aromatherapy
GO

Search by keyword or catalog product ID#:
GO

You have 6 items in your shopping basket:

SKU	Product Name	Size	Color/Scent	Qty	Price	
10300347	Set of 3 Floating Orchid Candles	2"h x 3 1/2"d	White, Pale Green, Purple	3	$7.48	Remove
10600189	Aromatherapy Candle	3" x 3"	Sandalwood	1	$7.99	Remove
10600210	Exotic Aromatherapy Candle	3"d x 6"h	Angelica	2	$9.99	Remove

Subtotal: **$50.41**   Update

Estimated total for standard shipping to a single recipient: $10.95

Checkout

E-Commerce

Monitoring Speed Issues

A slow-loading site loses customers. Web surfers are generally an impatient lot, particularly if they are experienced users and are accustomed to visiting fast-loading sites. Three factors influence how quickly a site downloads: the bandwidth of the Web surfer's computer connection, the bandwidth of the server, and the size and type of the various files that comprise the Web site. An online business can't do much about the bandwidth of either the surfer's connection or the server's connection. However, an online business can ensure that the data transmitted from its Web site uses as little bandwidth as possible. You can use a variety of tools to make sure that your site loads quickly. Then, once you have created a Web site, you can monitor the speed with which it loads, depending on the connection method. Javad asks you to learn about the various ways in which a Web site can be tuned up to function smoothly.

Details

► Image Compression

You can use various compression programs to reduce the size of images so that they load quickly. Some programs such as GIF Wizard can be accessed online. You enter the URL of an online image and the GIF Wizard compresses the image. You are then required to register with the company and pay a fee if you want to use the compressed image. Figure E-19 shows the results of the compression when applied to an image of a painting.

► Graphics

The trend in recent years has been to minimize the number of images on a page. In the past, many navigation links were buttons that were actually separate picture files. If the picture files were large, the buttons could take quite some time to load, and the surfer could not quickly select items and progress through the Web site. Because customers do not appreciate waiting for graphics to load before they can read text links, developers are increasingly using text-only links. Some experienced surfers even set their browsers so that only text appears. Web sites constructed of all graphic images will not appear on browsers where graphics are disabled. Sites that open with a visually complex introduction consisting of animations or movies often offer a Skip Intro option so that surfers can directly enter the site.

► Web Site Analyzers

Several sites on the Web will scan a Web site and return a description of any errors or anomalies found. Figure E-20 shows a Web site analysis returned by NetMechanic. In this example, two links were incorrect, two HTML errors were discovered, and 15 problems related to browser compatibility were found. That means that the Web site analyzed might not load well on all browsers. In addition, the analysis uncovered 11 possible spelling errors. On the bright side, the analysis gave the Web site five stars for loading time. You can view more details about the analysis of these features by clicking the report links.

► Web Speed Analysis

Some Web site analyzers also monitor the speed with which your site loads, depending on the Internet connection of the surfer. When you design a Web site, you need to know how fast it loads with a 14.4 modem all the way up to a T1 connection. Remember that even Web surfers with low bandwidth connections are potential customers.

FIGURE E-19: GIF Wizard compression results

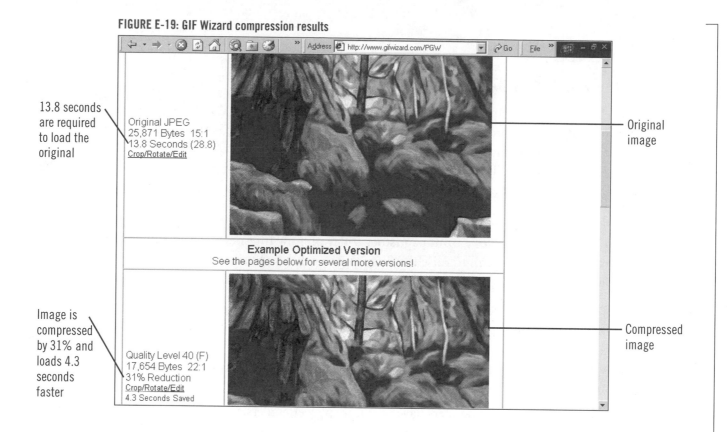

13.8 seconds are required to load the original

Original image

Image is compressed by 31% and loads 4.3 seconds faster

Compressed image

FIGURE E-20: NetMechanic Web site analysis results

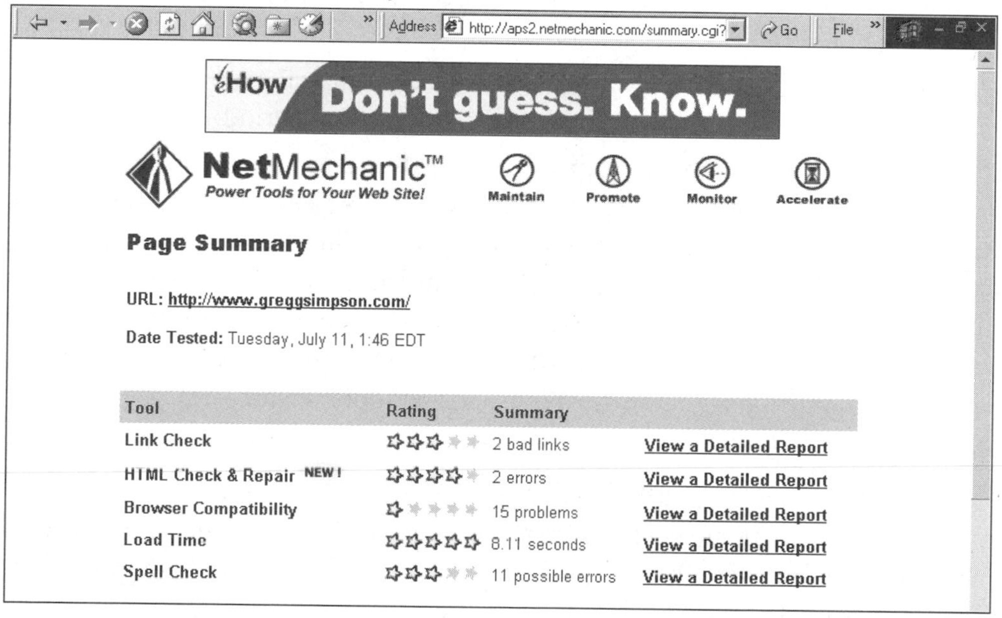

Focus

Is Internet Retailing Doomed?

The eRetailNews site ran the article shown below on April 4, 2000. It discusses issues related to the rapid growth of e-commerce. To visit the eRetailNews Web site, open your Web browser, go to the Student Online Companion at *www.course.com/illustrated/ecommerce*, click the link to Unit E, then click the link to Focus. The eRetailNews site runs a variety of interesting articles each week. Read the article shown below, then open your word-processing program and answer the questions that follow.

The Wall Street Journal includes a front page story today on how Internet Retailer, Pupule Sports Inc., has found it increasingly difficult to raise the financing to get their business off the ground. The market has shifted as investors begin to worry about seeing a return on investment.

As predicted in the 2000-1 eRetailNews Report, pure online eRetailers are beginning to show signs of problems stemming from tough competition from traditional brick and mortar players. The initial surge of optimism for Internet Retail is now being replaced by pragmatism. With so many companies competing for traffic, not everyone can generate the volume needed to build a profitable business model. Not even Amazon.com has achieved that milestone yet, and it has far more traffic than any other online retailer.

Given the advantage traditional retailers have over pure play eRetailers, we predict a big shake out of the market this year.

Watch for many online retailers to be acquired as their stock prices fall, making them attractive to traditional retailers wanting to leverage the online traffic and enhance their own online offerings.

The online retail model is far from doomed. We are entering a phase in the US market that will result in consolidation of the market.

This is not unusual. The online retail market is following a traditional market life cycle. We have passed through the initial boom period and are entering the consolidation period.

Investors increasingly want to see a business model that yields a return on their investment. eRetailers need to adopt strategies that will build long term customer loyalty (see eRetailNews 2000-3 and Commerce Cubed). Expect to see some eRetailers run out of funding this year, as investors require a return on existing investments. Investors will be very willing to sell budding eRetailers to traditional stores or larger competitors, if they see this as the best way to get a return on their investment. This isn't necessarily a bad thing. It can give eRetail more strength, being able to leverage traditional store's merchandising skills and develop economies of scale through a consolidated supply chain.

Consolidation among pure play eRetailers will increase traffic, helping drive economies of scale. The companies to watch will be the ones acquiring their less fortunate brethren.

Is there room for new online retailers? There is still room for new entrants in this market. To succeed, new entrants must have a sustainable competitive advantage, and they need to demonstrate fiscal responsibility from the outset.

Slow and steady may yet win the race. As many new start-up companies have discovered, cash-flow management is crucial to the survival of a new company. Spending $50m on advertising may generate traffic, but what use is it if the company cannot generate the revenue to keep the doors open?

Given the unwillingness of venture capital companies to add more fuel to the fire, new start-ups will need to show a faster or more guaranteed return on investment.

Source: eRetailNews[3]

Explore Further...

1. The article states that "The market has shifted as investors begin to worry about seeing a return on investment." Do you think this statement is valid now? Spend some time collecting articles, either from the Internet or from print sources, that discuss the issues of e-commerce and investment. What is the prevailing opinion about the future of e-commerce? Write a one-page paper that summarizes at least three articles related to investors and e-commerce sites. Your goal is to determine how the situation has changed (or not changed) since the eRetailNews article was written.

2. Consider the statement that "eRetailers need to adopt strategies that will build long term customer loyalty." What strategies do you think eRetailers could adopt to build customer loyalty? Check out at least three Web sites that you think are making efforts to build customer loyalty. What exactly are these sites doing? How successful do you think their efforts are (or will be)? Write a two-page report that summarizes the strategies that you think eRetailers could adopt to build long-term customer loyalty. Use the Web sites you have viewed as examples of what strategies work (or do not work).

3. The article advises readers to "Watch for many online retailers to be acquired as their stock prices fall, making them attractive to traditional retailers wanting to leverage the online traffic and enhance their own online offerings." Find recent articles (either online or in print) that discuss takeovers of online retailers by traditional retailers. What advantages do you think are gained by the takeovers? Do you think the takeovers will be successful? Why or why not? With these questions in mind, write a one-page summary of one of the takeovers you researched.

4. Note the following paragraph: "With so many companies competing for traffic, not everyone can generate the volume needed to build a profitable business model. Not even Amazon.com has achieved that milestone yet, and it has far more traffic than any other online retailer." Check out print and online sources to find the latest information about Amazon.com. Are they profitable, and how is profitable defined? Write a summary of Amazon's current position. Your goal is to analyze how the "big kid" on the block is surviving.

Practice

► Review

Fill in the blank with the best answer.

1. A Web site is a collection of pages connected by _____.

2. Hyperlink text, buttons, or other graphic elements are often used as _____ aids.

3. Some Web page designers maintain that no more than six or seven items should appear on a navigation bar. True/False? _____

4. Instead of frames, Web page designers use _____ to divide a page into several sections.

5. The term inline _____ refers to embedding a customer's information in a Web page.

6. Most Web site search tools use indexing _____ that electronically visit a site, follow the links, and index the contents.

7. A collection of information such as names, addresses, product descriptions, and prices is called a _____.

8. The term Open Database _____ defines the standard interface used to access a database from another source, including a Web page.

9. Structured _____ Language (SQL) is the standardized language used to request information from a database.

10. The term database-driven system describes a static online catalog that can be updated easily when changes are made to product descriptions. True/False? _____

11. Most electronic forms combine text _____ and drop-down lists.

12. Some Web developers use JavaScript to ensure that data entered into a form conforms to specific criteria. True/False? _____

13. Many online companies send the customer an immediate e-mail _____ that usually includes an order number.

14. A _____ cart is the ongoing results of the ordering process that have been generated from a database.

15. You can supply an Express _____ option for customers who have previously registered or set up an account.

16. You use an image _____ program to reduce the size of an image so that it loads quickly.

► Independent Challenges

1. Web sites that make their customers wait too long or provide difficult checkout procedures lose customers. However, customers are likely to return to sites that they can navigate quickly, and then, with a minimum of effort, enter credit card information and purchase products. You can learn a great deal about how to design an efficient e-commerce Web site by checking out how other sites facilitate online purchasing.

To complete this independent challenge:

a. Open your Web browser, go to the Student Online Companion at *www.course.com/illustrated/ecommerce*, click the link for Unit E, then click the link for Independent Challenge 1.

b. Select two of the companies listed, or go to the Web sites of two companies of your choice. Make sure the companies you choose sell products online.

c. Explore the Web sites you have selected to determine how the checkout procedures are handled. Note that you will need to add one or two products to your shopping cart, and then follow the required procedures up to the point where you need to enter payment information. At that point, you will need to abandon the shopping cart.

d. Open the Project File ECE-02.doc in your word-processing program. This document contains the table you will use to enter information about the checkout procedures on the two Web sites you have selected.

e. Save the document as *Checkout Procedures*.

f. Identify the name of the company, and the URL of each Web site in the tables provided.

g. Answer the questions for both of the Web sites you chose. Your goal is to analyze the efficiency of the checkout procedures, and to determine, where possible, how these procedures can be improved.

h. Type **Your Name** at the bottom of the document, save it, print a copy, then close the document.

2. Many Web sites provide search tools that you can download and install on your own site. These tools range from simple search tools that are provided for free, to ongoing search services, to full-scale search tools that allow entry of keywords and misspellings, and link to one or more databases. You will compare three search tools that offer similar functionality.

To complete this independent challenge:

a. Open your Web browser, go to the Student Online Companion at *www.course.com/illustrated/ecommerce*, click the link for Unit E, then click the link for Independent Challenge 2.

b. Select three of the companies listed.

c. Explore the Web sites you have selected to find search tool packages that are similarly priced and offer similar functions. Your goal is to compare three search tools at the same level. Note that several of the Web sites offer more than one search tool package.

d. Open the Project File ECE-03.doc in your word-processing program. This document contains the checklist that you will use to compare the three search tools you selected.

e. Save the document as *Web Site Search Tools*.

f. Identify the name of the company, and the URL of each Web site in the table provided.

g. Complete the checklist for each of the search tools you selected.

h. Answer the questions provided. Your goal is to identify the search tool that you think is the most useful in offering customers increased access to products on a Web site.

i. Type **Your Name** at the bottom of the document, save it, print a copy, then close the document.

3. Reading a page of source code requires some practice, but soon you will be able to identify some of the most common HTML tags. In this independent challenge, you decide to check out the HTML codes used to create various navigation bars.

To complete this independent challenge:

a. Find a Web site that includes a navigation bar. You can select a Web site you worked with in another independent challenge for this book, or you can select a new Web site.

b. View the source code for the page that includes an example of the component. To view source code, click View on the menu bar in your browser, then click Source or Page Source. The Web page's source code opens in a separate window.

c. In the window containing the source code, scroll down the page to view its length. If the source is just a few pages long, print a copy. In Internet Explorer, click File on the menu bar in the Notebook window, then click Print. In Netscape Navigator, press [Ctrl][P], then click OK. Alternatively, you can find the HTML tags you think are related to the component you are interested in, use your mouse to select the tags, press [Ctrl][C] to copy them, open a blank document in your word-processing program, press [Ctrl][V] to paste them, then print the document.

d. Print a copy of the Web page.

e. Compare the printout of the source to the printout of the Web page.

f. Use a highlighter to mark the HTML tags that you think were used to create the navigation bar. Try to identify the various parts of the navigation bar. For example, you should see references to image files and hyperlink text.

g Highlight at least two tags that are unfamiliar to you.

h. Open your Web browser, go to the Student Online Companion at *www.course.com/illustrated/ecommerce*, click the link to Unit E, then click the link to Independent Challenge 3.

i. Follow links to one of the HTML sources listed.

j. Find definitions for the two tags you selected.

k. Open a document in your word-processing program, write a paragraph that describes the tags that were used to create the navigation bar. Include the definitions of the two tags that were unfamiliar to you.

l. Type **Your Name** in the bottom of the document, save the document as Source Code Analysis, print a copy, then close the document.

4. Hundreds of shopping cart software programs are available on the Web, so finding the best program for your online business might not be an easy task. Many programs appear to offer everything a business needs to turn the humblest Web site into an e-commerce giant. You decide to evaluate two of these programs with the hope that you can find one that would be suitable for a small business.

To complete this independent challenge:

a. Fill in the box below with the name or description of a business you'd like to pursue, and a description of the products you'd like to sell. Select a business that sells products related to one of your own interests. For example, if you are interested in photography, you might choose to sell products such as darkroom equipment, photographic paper, or camera cases.

Business name/description ....

Products ....

b. Open your Web browser, go to the Student Online Companion at *www.course.com/illustrated/ecommerce*, click the link to Unit E, then click the link to Independent Challenge 4.

c. Explore the links provided to find two Web sites that appear to offer similar shopping cart packages. Choose packages at the same price level. If you want, you can select and compare free packages.

d. Open the Project File ECE-04.doc in your word-processing program. This document contains the table that you will use to compare the two Web sites you've selected.

e. Save the document as *Shopping Cart Comparison*.

f. Complete each table with information related to the Web sites you chose. Your goal is to evaluate not only the shopping cart packages offered, but how the Web site inspires—or does not inspire—confidence in the reliability and quality of the products offered.

g. Type **Your Name** at the bottom of the document, save it, print a copy, then close the document.

▶ Up to Date

Several online companies will analyze a Web site with relation to a variety of factors such as load speed, use of HTML codes, spelling errors, and broken links. For example, Figure E-21 shows the NetMechanic's analysis of how fast a Web site loads at five different modem speeds. You can learn a great deal about effective Web site design by studying the results provided by Web analysis tools.

To complete the Up to Date Challenge:

a. Go to one of the e-commerce sites that you have visited during the last week or two, keeping in mind the surfing policies of your educational institution or company. If possible, find a site that loaded quite slowly, or that you feel needs to be redesigned.

FIGURE E-21: NetMechanic load time analysis

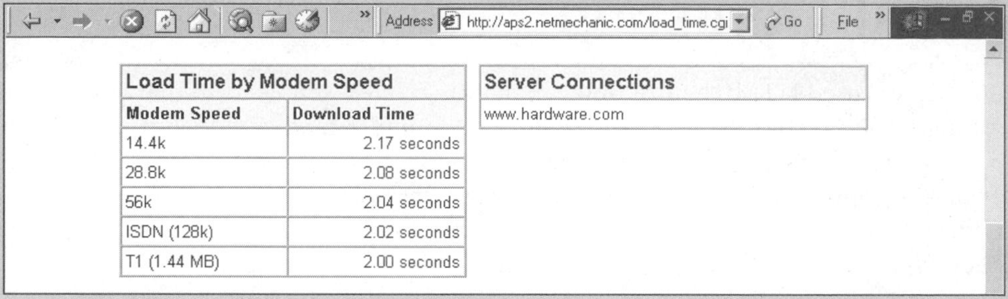

Load Time by Modem Speed		Server Connections
Modem Speed	Download Time	www.hardware.com
14.4k	2.17 seconds	
28.8k	2.08 seconds	
56k	2.04 seconds	
ISDN (128k)	2.02 seconds	
T1 (1.44 MB)	2.00 seconds	

b. Copy the URL of the site by clicking in the Address box to select the URL, then pressing [Ctrl][C] to activate the Copy command.

c. Go to the Student Online Companion at *www.course.com/illustrated/ecommerce*, click the link to Unit E, then click the link to Up to Date.

d. Follow one of the links provided to find a Web site analysis service.

e. Paste the URL you copied into the appropriate location on the Web site analysis site. Figure E-22 shows the location where you would paste a URL in the NetMechanic site.

FIGURE E-22: NetMechanic home page

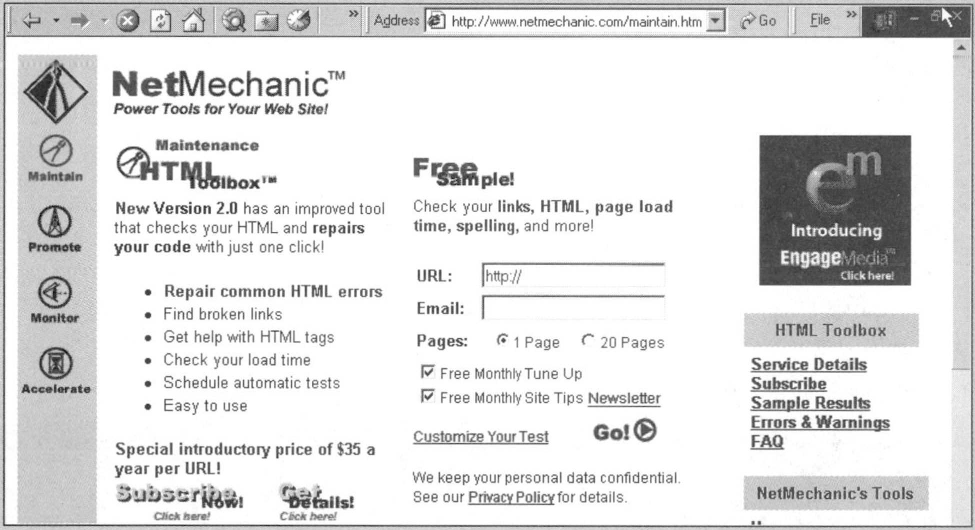

f. If necessary, enter your e-mail address. Note that some sites might provide results in your browser.

g. Launch the Web site analysis. You might need to wait some time for the analysis to be completed, depending on the complexity of the Web page you selected.

h. When the analysis is completed, print a copy from the browser, or check your e-mail for results. Print as much information as provided, so you can determine the areas where the Web site requires work.

i. In your word-processing program, write a paragraph or two summarizing the results of the Web site analysis. If appropriate, briefly describe what steps are required to fix the Web site.

j. Type **Your Name** at the bottom of the document, save the summary as *Online Web Site Analysis*, print a copy, attach it to the printed results of the analysis, then close the document.

► Visual Workshop

Even if you've never used HTML before, you can quickly create a simple form that you can then send to yourself via e-mail. Getting some practice using HTML will help you understand how Web pages are structured, which will, in turn, help you add and modify components on a Web page, or communicate with a Web page designer. You can get more information about building forms by checking out the many HTML tutorials available on the Internet. See your Student Online Companion for a list. To complete the Visual Workshop, click Start, Programs, Accessories, click Notepad then type the text shown in Figure E-23 below.

FIGURE E-23: HTML codes in Notepad

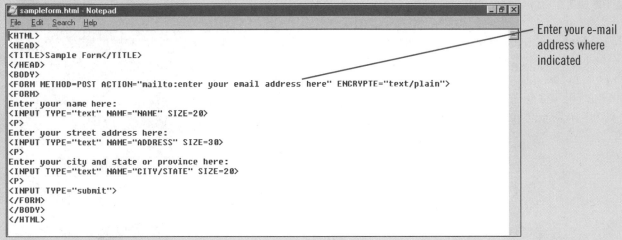

Enter your e-mail address where indicated

Save the file as *sampleform.html*. Make sure you enter your own e-mail address where indicated. Save the completed form, then open the sampleform.html file in your browser. The form should appear as shown in Figure E-24. Enter your name and address in the form boxes, click the Submit Query button, then check your e-mail. Information from your first form will be sent to you! If you need help, or don't receive the form, go to the Student Online Companion at *www.course.com/illustrated/ecommerce*, click the link for Unit E, then click the link for Trouble.

FIGURE E-24: Form viewed in the browser

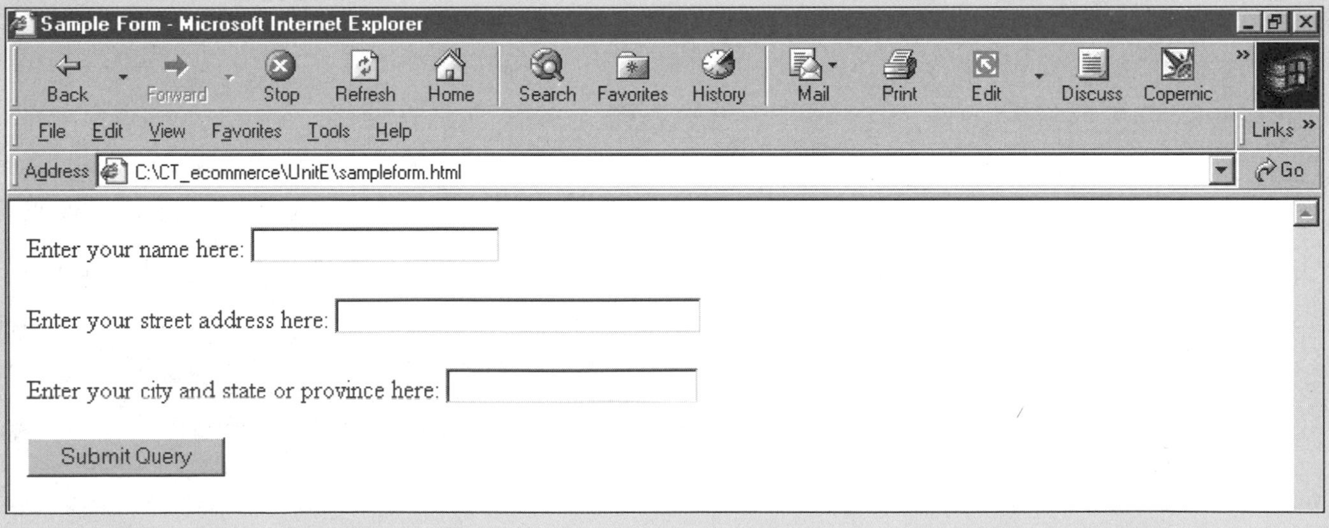

Unit F

Payment
Processing

- ▶ Define electronic payments
- ▶ Explore electronic payment issues
- ▶ Identify e-payment options
- ▶ Explore e-cash
- ▶ Understand credit card issues
- ▶ Define merchant accounts
- ▶ Explore online payment services
- ▶ Understand transaction processing
- ▶ Identify taxation issues
- ▶ Understand taxation requirements
- ▶ Exploring m-commerce

The single most important feature that sets an e-commerce Web site apart from other kinds of Web sites is that an e-commerce site receives payment information online. In this unit, you will review the issues related to electronic payments, explore some of the current e-payment options, and identify the steps involved in processing online transactions. You will also consider the impact that mobile-commerce (m-commerce) might have on how people use the Internet to purchase goods and services and examine the taxation issues related to the online purchases. ✐ Matt Jefferson has worked for several years in the financial department at MediaLoft's head office. While he is familiar with the forms of payment accepted at MediaLoft's many retail outlets, he asks you to investigate how to set up the new Web site to accept payments online.

Defining Electronic Payments

Traditionally, all payment transactions involved some form of paper, whether a check, an invoice, a credit card slip, or cash. Now you can pay all of your monthly bills with a few clicks of the mouse, purchase products without leaving your desk or sofa, and have your paycheck directly deposited into your bank account. ◄▬▬ Since you have just joined Matt's team to research payments options for MediaLoft, you decide to explore the characteristics of an electronic payment and check out its current and projected role in e-commerce.

Details

► Characteristics

An **electronic payment** is a payment that is transmitted electronically either over telephone lines, or between Web sites on the Internet. No tangible currency such as a bank note or check changes hands. Any information required to make the payment, such as a credit card number or Personal Identification Number (PIN), exists only in digital form.

► Projected Growth

The use of electronic methods to pay bills and purchase products online is growing as the Internet grows. Figure F-1 shows the projected growth of revenue from online purchases since 1998, and Figure F-2 shows the average amount of B2C and B2B online transactions. The average B2C transaction is shown to be $244, while the average B2B transaction is shown to be $800. Both these graphs are included on the epaynews.com Web site, an online business that provides ongoing statistics related to e-commerce[1].

► Electronic Payment Categories

You can divide electronic payments for B2C into two categories—payments made for goods and services purchased online, and payments made in response to bills or invoices. In the first instance, the consumer selects a product, completes an online form, and selects a payment method, such as credit card, debit card, e-cash, or e-check. In the second instance, a consumer authorizes a bank to transfer money from a bank account to specified recipients, such as the telephone company or a utility company.

► Electronic Data Interchange

Electronic Data Interchange (EDI) describes the electronic transfer of data between companies engaged in B2B e-commerce. EDI relates to most of the activities required to do business with trading partners, and has existed in various forms for many years. Activities suitable for EDI include placing orders with suppliers, issuing invoices, and processing payments. EDI can also be described as **paperless trading**. Table F-1 describes some of the benefits of EDI for B2B e-commerce.

► Electronic Payment Process

A customer who decides to purchase an item from an online business is transferred to a secure server where he or she enters a credit card number into a form. The information entered into the secure server is encrypted using security technologies. The payment information moves to the online transaction server, where the payment is authorized (or declined), depending on whether the credit card number is valid and the customer has sufficient credit to cover the purchase. If the credit card information is valid and funds are available, the information is transmitted to the institution or organization that receives payments owed to the merchant, and a deposit is made to the merchant's bank account. The consumer is informed that the transaction has been processed, and shipping the goods has been initiated. If the goods are shipped electronically, such as a downloadable computer game, then the entire process could take no more than a minute or two from the time the customer submits the payment to the time that the file appears on the customer's hard drive, depending on the size of the file and the computer's download speed.

FIGURE F-1: Electronic payment statistics

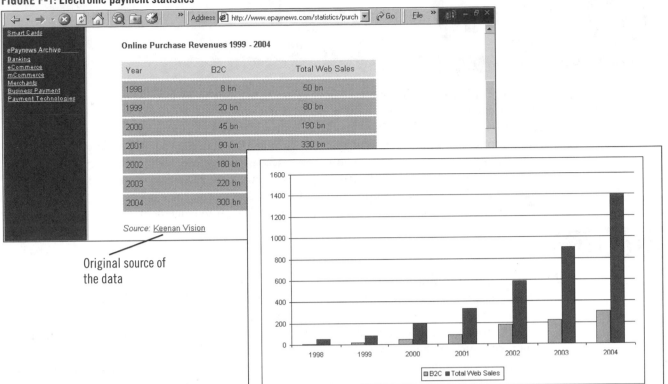

Online Purchase Revenues 1999 - 2004

Year	B2C	Total Web Sales
1998	8 bn	50 bn
1999	20 bn	80 bn
2000	45 bn	190 bn
2001	90 bn	330 bn
2002	180 bn	
2003	220 bn	
2004	300 bn	

Source: Keenan Vision

Original source of the data

FIGURE F-2: Comparison of online transaction amounts

Transaction Size At Commerce-Enabled Web Sites

Size	Sample	B2C	B2B
$1 - 50	20%	22%	5%
$51 - 100	13%	15%	5%
$101 - 500	27%	26%	36%
$501 - 1000	9%	10%	5%
$1000 - 10,000	23%	20%	41%
+ $10,000	8%	8%	8%
Average	$4622	$4450	$5580
Median	$300	$244	$800

Source: ActivMedia Research

Original source of the data

TABLE F-1: Benefits of Electronic Data Interchange

- Increases processing efficiency and data reliability because information is entered only once, which saves time and reduces the risk of error.

- Eliminates payment-processing delays that are related to the postal system.

- Allows inventory to be ordered on an as-needed or just-in-time (JIT) basis, which reduces expensive warehousing costs.

- Reduces the amount of space and number of facilities needed to store paper records.

- Reduces the cost of doing business by decreasing telephone and postage costs.

Exploring Electronic Payment Issues

The increasing dependence on using electronic methods to process payments has its benefits and its challenges. On the one hand, electronic payments can be less expensive to process than paper payments. On the other hand, the perceived risk of fraud might worry some vendors, while concerns about the security of electronic transactions and the buying patterns they divulge might discourage some consumers. ✎ Lately, Matt feels as if every time he picks up a newspaper or surfs the Internet, he sees a news story related to some aspect of electronic payments. He asks you to clarify some of the issues related to the e-payment of goods and services purchased online so that he can report to MediaLoft management.

Details

▶ Costs and Benefits

Electronic payments are intended to lower transaction costs significantly—sometimes by 60 percent or more. Since fewer paper resources are used to process an online payment, the environment may benefit from a decreased demand for paper products. On the other hand, significant technical resources, such as high-speed Internet connections, secure servers, and computers capable of processing high-volume transactions, are required. Once these technological resources are in place, however, businesses can achieve real cost savings, particularly for B2B transactions. Figure F-3 illustrates the potential environmental benefits that could result when a company uses only electronic means to bill customers and receive payments.

▶ Security

For many consumers, the issue of security remains paramount. Stories about credit card number harvesting, teenagers hacking into celebrity bank accounts, and Internet fraud help to fuel skepticism. On the other hand, documented evidence of people losing money because of someone stealing their credit card number from the Internet is still rare. Online businesses must ensure that their customers enter credit card information only on a secure server, and then provide customers with accurate information about the security measures in place. Figure F-4 shows how L.L. Bean informs customers about the process required to pay online using a credit card.

▶ Privacy

Consumers are also concerned about the privacy of Internet transaction information. When they pay for a product online, is the information about their purchase sold or given to other businesses? Are companies creating personal profiles of consumers, based in part on information obtained from tracking their online buying habits? While many consumers understand that their credit card numbers are transmitted securely, they are not nearly as convinced that their personal information is kept confidential. Privacy concerns related to what goods and services are purchased online will continue to be controversial as governments debate the need for legislation to regulate e-commerce activities. Most online stores now post privacy policies on their Web sites.

e-byte

"As E-Transactions radically alter the nature of sales processing, increasing sales potential and lowering costs of transaction, they expose business to new and different fraud and security hazards."
Source: ActivMedia Research[2]

FIGURE F-3: E-payment environmental benefits

FIGURE F-4: Ordering online in a secure environment

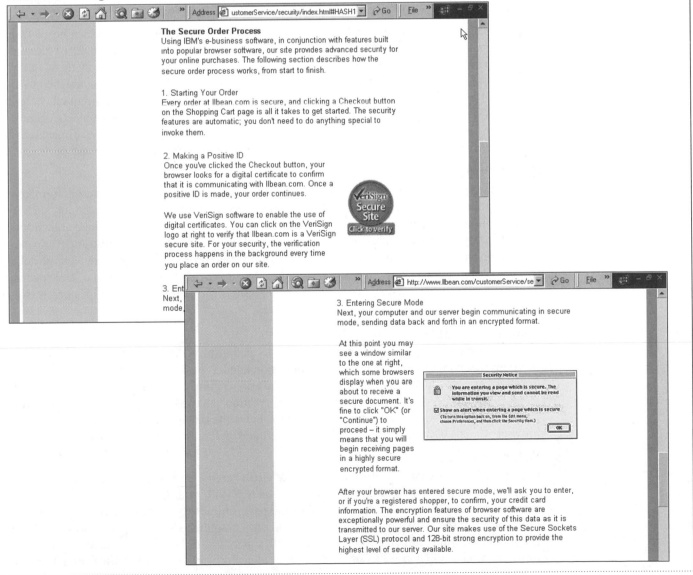

Address ⓔ ustomerService/security/index.html#HASH1 ▾ | Go | File »

The Secure Order Process
Using IBM's e-business software, in conjunction with features built into popular browser software, our site provides advanced security for your online purchases. The following section describes how the secure order process works, from start to finish.

1. Starting Your Order
Every order at llbean.com is secure, and clicking a Checkout button on the Shopping Cart page is all it takes to get started. The security features are automatic; you don't need to do anything special to invoke them.

2. Making a Positive ID
Once you've clicked the Checkout button, your browser looks for a digital certificate to confirm that it is communicating with llbean.com. Once a positive ID is made, your order continues.

We use VeriSign software to enable the use of digital certificates. You can click on the VeriSign logo at right to verify that llbean.com is a VeriSign secure site. For your security, the verification process happens in the background every time you place an order on our site.

VeriSign Secure Site – Click to verify

Address ⓔ http://www.llbean.com/customerService/se ▾ | Go | File »

3. Entering Secure Mode
Next, your computer and our server begin communicating in secure mode, sending data back and forth in an encrypted format.

At this point you may see a window similar to the one at right, which some browsers display when you are about to receive a secure document. It's fine to click "OK" (or "Continue") to proceed – it simply means that you will begin receiving pages in a highly secure encrypted format.

*Security Notice
You are entering a page which is secure. The information you view and send cannot be read while in transit.
☑ Show an alert when entering a page which is secure
(To turn this option back on, from the Edit menu, choose Preferences, and then click the Security item.)
OK*

After your browser has entered secure mode, we'll ask you to enter, or if you're a registered shopper, to confirm, your credit card information. The encryption features of browser software are exceptionally powerful and ensure the security of this data as it is transmitted to our server. Our site makes use of the Secure Sockets Layer (SSL) protocol and 128-bit strong encryption to provide the highest level of security available.

Identifying E-Payment Options

The methods used to pay for products and services online include credit cards, electronic cash (e-cash), software wallets or purses, and smart cards. Matt is interested in learning more about the various forms of electronic payments. While credit cards rule the cyber waves now, other forms of e-payment could soon replace them.

Details

► Credit Cards

A credit card provides a consumer with a preset spending limit, such as $2,000, $5,000, or $10,000. Customers can charge items up to their spending limit each month, and then either pay off the entire credit card balance, or pay a minimum amount and then pay interest on the unpaid balance. Some analysts maintain that up to 90 percent of all consumer transactions are made with a credit card such as Visa or MasterCard.

► E-Checks

An **e-check** is an encrypted representation of a paper check. Consumers fill in the check online, then send it via a secure server to the recipient. The amount specified on the e-check is electronically withdrawn from the sender's account, and then deposited into the recipient's account.

► E-Cash

E-cash is also referred to as **Scrip**, **digital cash**, or **digital coins**. A consumer can buy e-cash and store it in a digital wallet on a hard drive. The digital wallet is electronically linked to the consumer's bank account and can be refilled at any time. Since e-cash is drawn directly from a bank account, it very much resembles real cash. While credit card payments are always attached to an individual or a company, payments made with e-cash are preauthorized and anonymous. E-cash is often used to pay for electronic goods, such as software, games, and reference materials, received over the Internet. Some forms of e-cash can be purchased online and then e-mailed to a recipient, who then can use it to purchase products from Web sites that accept e-cash payments.

► Smart Cards

Smart cards look like credit cards, but are embedded with a low-cost integrated microprocessor chip that provides the consumer with the means to conduct everyday transactions, such as making phone calls, accessing an Automatic Teller Machine (ATM), and paying for public transportation. Smart cards are also used to store personal identity, medical, and insurance information. Many smart cards are used in conjunction with a password or PIN. Already very popular in Europe in the form of phone cards and transportation cards, worldwide use of smart cards could dramatically increase as they become more sophisticated and capable of storing electronic cash for use in handling online transactions.

► Electronic Wallets

Electronic wallets, or e-wallets, are also referred to as **digital wallets**. An **e-wallet** is a software program that contains a user's payment information in encrypted form to ensure its security. For example, an individual's e-wallet could contain credit card numbers, bank account numbers, contact information, and shipping location. This information can then be automatically and securely transferred to an online order form. Figure F-5 shows the dialog box in the Internet Explorer browser where a user sets up an e-wallet that will reside on the user's computer.

► Virtual Credit Cards

Closely allied to e-wallets is the concept of the virtual credit card. A **virtual credit card** is an image of a credit card placed on the computer desktop. With one click of the credit card image, the cardholder accesses account information and pays for online purchases. Customers can even drag and drop the virtual card from the desktop onto an online checkout page. The credit card number and contact information is automatically entered into the checkout form, and the customer just needs to enter a PIN or other form of identification to authorize the transaction.

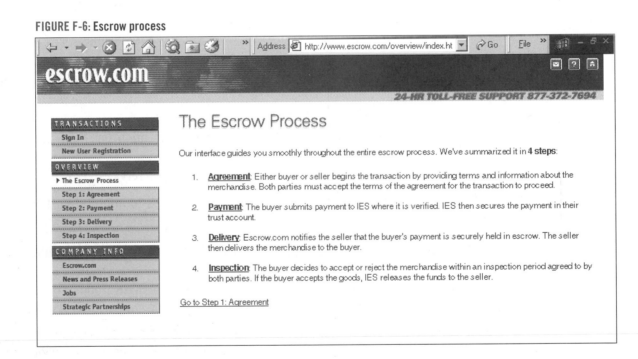

Visa card information
already loaded

Adding MasterCard
information

FIGURE F-6: Escrow process

The Escrow Process

Our interface guides you smoothly throughout the entire escrow process. We've summarized it in **4 steps**:

1. **Agreement**: Either buyer or seller begins the transaction by providing terms and information about the merchandise. Both parties must accept the terms of the agreement for the transaction to proceed.

2. **Payment**: The buyer submits payment to IES where it is verified. IES then secures the payment in their trust account.

3. **Delivery**: Escrow.com notifies the seller that the buyer's payment is securely held in escrow. The seller then delivers the merchandise to the buyer.

4. **Inspection**: The buyer decides to accept or reject the merchandise within an inspection period agreed to by both parties. If the buyer accepts the goods, IES releases the funds to the seller.

Go to Step 1: Agreement

Escrow

Escrow is the term used to refer to the holding of a buyer's payment by a third party. The seller of a product receives payment when the buyer has inspected and accepted the product. If the buyer returns the product, a refund is granted after the seller has inspected and accepted the returned product. Buyers and sellers who participate in online auctions often use escrow companies such as escrow.com to handle payments so that both parties are protected from fraud. Figure F-6 describes the escrow process as explained on the escrow.com Web site.

E-Commerce

Exploring E-Cash

The future of e-cash could be bright, or it could fade into oblivion as other forms of e-payment win the race to be the online payment method of choice. At present, e-cash (also called **digital cash**) is making some inroads into people's wallets, often in the form of gift certificates that are transferred via e-mail. One advantage of e-cash is that it can be spent in very small increments, called **micro payments**. Because most credit cards can't handle payments under $1.00 or even $5.00, people might start using e-cash to make payments in very small amounts, such as 10 or 20 cents, to receive products in digital form. For example, a micro payment of 20 cents could be required to download an article or a chapter of an electronic book (or e-book). Some online search engines already charge $.50-$1.00 for a downloadable copy of a newspaper article.

Other e-cash options take the form of tokens or icons that consumers can collect and trade for products on selected Web sites. Figure F-7 shows an information page from the Beenz Web site, and Figure F-8 shows an information page from the InternetCash Web site. E-cash concepts such as Beenz, Flooz, RocketCash, and InternetCash will be interesting to track to see if they catch on. A good way to learn about e-cash and how consumers can use it to purchase products online is to explore the services offered by some e-cash providers. While Matt anticipates that most of MediaLoft's customers will continue to use credit cards for a few more years, he is interested in how customers can use e-cash to purchase products. He asks you to explore two companies that offer e-cash services.

Steps

1. Open your Web browser, go to the Student Online Companion at *www.course.com/illustrated/ecommerce*, click the link for **Unit F**, then click the link for **Exploring e-cash**

2. Select two sites from the list provided

3. Open the Project File **ECF-01.doc** in your word-processing program, then save it as **E-cash Services**
   The document contains a series of questions about online e-cash services.

4. Go to one of the sites you chose in Step 2, then follow links to information about its e-cash services

5. Enter the name and URL of the company you've chosen, then answer the questions provided
   Your goal is to find information about how e-cash is used to purchase products online, and to evaluate the effectiveness of the e-cash system offered by the company you have chosen.

6. Repeat Steps 4 and 5 to gather information about a second e-cash provider
   If possible, try to select a company that offers a different kind of e-cash service. For example, if the first company offers tokens, make your second selection a company that offers digital coins or another form of e-cash that is debited directly from a consumer's bank account.

7. When you have completed all the questions for each e-cash company, type **Your Name** at the bottom of the document, save it, print a copy, then close the document

FIGURE F-7: Information about using Beenz

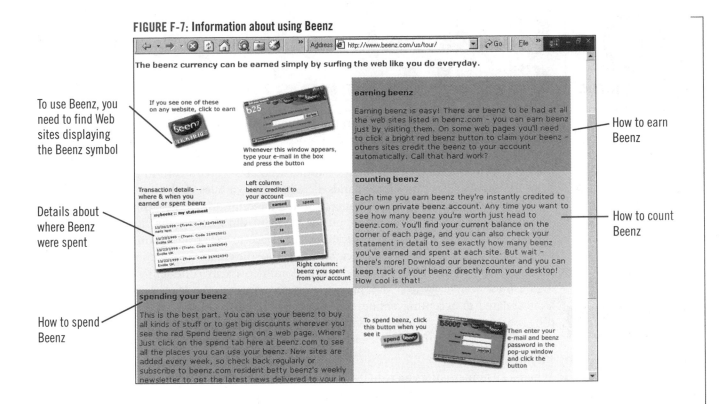

To use Beenz, you need to find Web sites displaying the Beenz symbol

Details about where Beenz were spent

How to spend Beenz

How to earn Beenz

How to count Beenz

FIGURE F-8: Information about using InternetCash

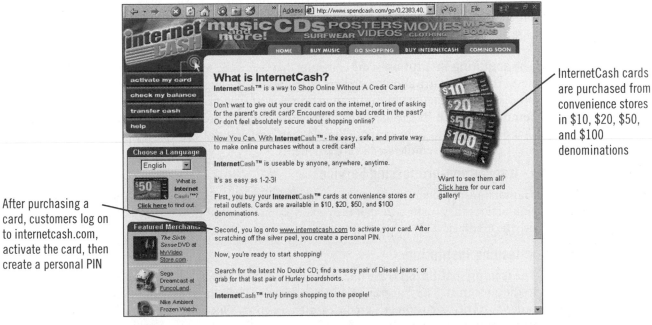

After purchasing a card, customers log on to internetcash.com, activate the card, then create a personal PIN

InternetCash cards are purchased from convenience stores in $10, $20, $50, and $100 denominations

E-Commerce

Understanding Credit Card Issues

For an online business, credit card transactions are essential for fiscal survival. On the negative side, a wide range of costs are involved in processing credit card payments. In addition, companies are increasingly concerned about the risk of fraud that results from the anonymity made possible by buying on the Internet. A customer who uses a credit card to purchase an item in a brick and mortar store physically hands a credit card to a sales clerk who then swipes the card through a credit card reader. The reader produces a receipt, which the customer must then sign. The clerk can check if the signature on the payment slip matches the signature on the credit card, or ask to see additional identification. These face-to-face transactions provide some measure of security. In an online credit card transaction, the customer is anonymous, often several thousands miles away from the merchant, and not necessarily conducting the transaction during business hours. ➤ Matt plans to present a report to the MediaLoft management about issues related to accepting online credit card payments. In particular, he plans to define the processes required to conduct an online credit card transaction.

Details

► Payment Process

When a customer enters a credit card number into an online form and then clicks the Submit button, a series of transactions is set in motion. The process is described in Table F-2, and then graphically displayed in Figure F-9.

► Options

Two principal options are available to a company that wants to accept credit card payments online. The first option is to obtain a merchant account, and either purchase transaction-processing software, or pay a transaction-processing service. The second option is to select a payment-processing service or packaged e-commerce solution that will handle all the transactions and activities related to accepting, verifying, and processing online credit card payments.

► Transaction-processing Participants

As you can see from the activities shown in Table F-2, processing credit cards requires the participation of three companies or organizations: the acquiring institution, the transaction-processing service, and the issuing institution.

• Acquiring Institution

The **acquiring institution** is the company that issues the merchant account to the online business. You will learn about merchant accounts in the next lesson The acquiring institution processes and clears credit card transactions for a fee and can be the same bank with which the company does all its business, or it can be an online merchant account provider. A company that does not want to or cannot obtain a merchant account can choose to pay an Internet payment provider to handle credit card payments.

• Transaction-processing Service

Transaction-processing services such as Authorize.Net and CyberCash authorize the credit card transaction; they make sure that the person using the credit card is the person who is entitled to use the credit card.

• Issuing Institution

The **issuing institution** is the financial organization (usually a bank) that issues the credit card to the consumer. The transaction-processing service will interact with the issuing institution in order to verify a customer's credit card transaction. Once the issuing institution assures the transaction-processing service that the customer's credit is good, the transaction can be processed so that the customer receives the product ordered, and the vendor receives the payment to which they are entitled.

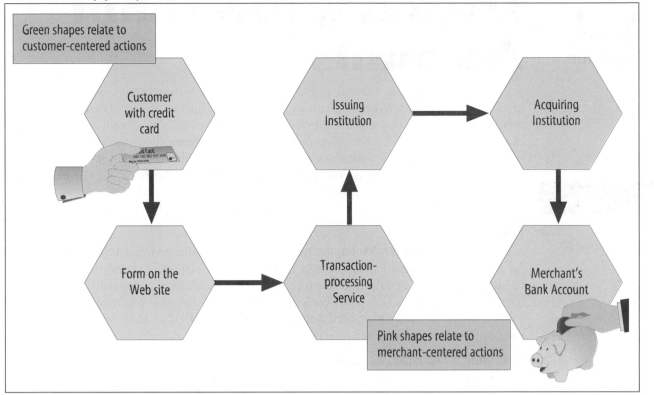

TABLE F-2: Online payment process

participant	activity
Customer	Obtains a credit card such as a Visa or MasterCard from an issuing institution such as a bank or credit union.
Issuing institution	Issues the credit card and sets the credit limit based on the customer's credit history.
Customer	Visits a Web site, selects a product, fills out a form with contact and credit card information, then submits the form via a secure server.
Vendor	Receives an e-mail with details about the transaction, but usually not the credit card number itself, which is sent in encrypted (scrambled) format to the transaction-processing company.
Transaction-processing company	Checks that the credit card is valid and that the issuing bank will release enough money to pay for the product, based on the amount of credit the customer has available.
Issuing institution	Receives the request, approves it (or rejects it), marks the customer's credit card account with the amount of the charge, then sends a message to the vendor's acquiring institution to confirm the order.
Customer	Receives confirmation via e-mail that the order has been processed.
Vendor	Ships the order to the customer.
Acquiring institution or Internet payment-processing service	Deducts transaction charges from the purchase amount, then deposits the balance to the vendor's bank account, or sends the payment directly to the vendor.
Customer	Receives the product.

E-Commerce

Defining Merchant Accounts

A business operating in the real world must obtain a merchant account in order to accept credit card payments. When a business goes on the Internet, it can choose to upgrade its existing merchant account to accept online credit card payments, obtain a new online merchant account, or use a payment-processing service. ◄═══ Because MediaLoft is a large and established business, Matt does not anticipate any problems with obtaining a merchant account that accepts online payments. However, he needs to clarify the fees involved and the criteria required to obtain an online merchant account.

Details

► **Purpose**

A company sets up a **merchant account** with a bank to handle credit card transactions—usually for a fee. When a customer uses a credit card to purchase a product, money from the bank that holds the consumer's credit card account (the issuing institution) is deposited directly into the company's merchant account. The bank or financial institution that sets up a merchant account for a company is called a **Merchant Account Provider (MAP)**. The MAP verifies the credit card, processes the transactions, and then deposits the amount into the merchant's account.

► **Obtaining a Merchant Account**

A merchant account is classified according to how payments will be received. Internet payments are classified as **Card Not Present (CNP)** or **Mail Order/Telephone Order (MOTO)**. Even if a company already has a merchant account set up with an acquiring institution, the company will probably need to modify the account to accept payments online. A business with a merchant account has **merchant account status**.

► **Criteria**

An acquiring institution must determine if the online business will deliver products to its customers, will remain financially stable, and will not be a victim of e-shoplifting or fraudulent charge backs. See the In The Know for information about charge backs. Acquiring institutions generally classify companies by the perceived level of risk involved in their business. Figure F-10 shows the list of businesses that one online MAP specifies as high risk.

► **Fees**

Most MAPs charge a fixed per-transaction fee ranging from approximately $.30 to $1.00 per transaction. In addition, MAPs might charge a percentage of the sale price, a fixed monthly fee, and a one-time setup fee. Some MAPs might also require a minimum monthly order, and require an online business to purchase or lease special hardware and software systems necessary for processing the transactions. The fees charged for merchant accounts vary, depending on the perceived level of risk to the MAP. Because a merchant account is a form of credit, many MAPs also require merchants to provide security deposits. A real-world store usually provides a percentage of its estimated annual sales (for example, 10 percent) as a security deposit.

► **Acquiring Institutions**

A company can obtain a merchant account from a bank that handles the credit card the company wants to accept, or it can obtain a merchant account from an online merchant account provider. The Web sites of most banks provide information about the merchant account packages they have available for online businesses. Careful research is required to sort out the reputable companies from the fly-by-nighters that hope to cash in on the e-commerce gold rush.

► **Credit Card Processing**

Figure F-11 displays how the CyberSource credit card services function. In this process, CyberSource acts as the intermediary that receives the credit card payment, transfers it to the issuing bank, receives confirmation (or rejection), and then deposits the money in the merchant's account (or cancels the transaction).

FIGURE F-10: High-risk merchant list from Absolute-Merchant-Accounts

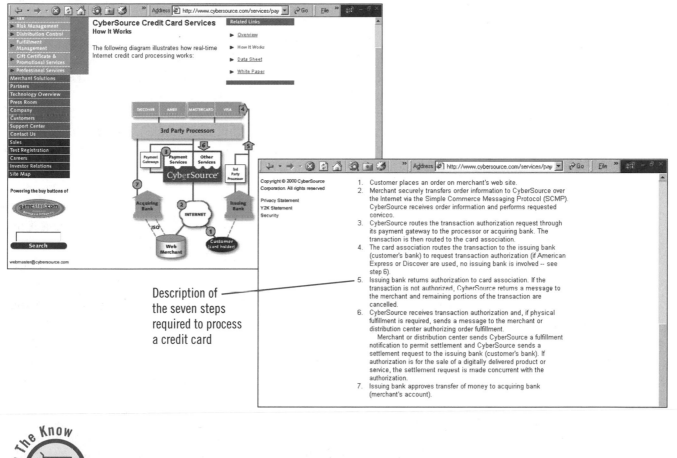

Special "High Risk" Merchant List

- Adult Entertainment and/or Materials
- Airports
- Attorneys/Bankruptcy
- Auto Dealers (used cars)
- Buying/Shopping Club
- Business Opportunity
- Carpeting (custom)
- Check Cashing Services
- Collection Agencies/ Debt Collection
- Credit Restoration And/Or Repair Services
- Cruise Lines
- Direct Outbound Telemarketing
- Dating Services
- Furniture (custom)
- Future Service Liability Greater Than One Year
- Hair Loss Products
- Horoscope & Fortune Teller Services
- Investment Opportunity
- Membership Business (longer than one year)
- Mortgage Services
- MLM Sign Up Fees/Business Opportunity
- Outbound Telemarketing
- Pornographic Materials
- Products/Services With Unreasonable Guarantees
- Racing, Car, Horse, Dog
- Time Share Rentals
- Travel Agencies (selling travel/tour packages)
- Water Purifiers
- Window Treatments (custom)
- Wall Covering (custom)

FIGURE F-11: CyberSource credit card processing

CyberSource Credit Card Services
How It Works

The following diagram illustrates how real-time Internet credit card processing works:

Related Links
▶ Overview
▶ How It Works
▶ Data Sheet
▶ White Paper

Copyright © 2000 CyberSource Corporation. All rights reserved

Privacy Statement
Y2K Statement
Security

Description of the seven steps required to process a credit card

1. Customer places an order on merchant's web site.
2. Merchant securely transfers order information to CyberSource over the Internet via the Simple Commerce Messaging Protocol (SCMP). CyberSource receives order information and performs requested services.
3. CyberSource routes the transaction authorization request through its payment gateway to the processor or acquiring bank. The transaction is then routed to the card association.
4. The card association routes the transaction to the issuing bank (customer's bank) to request transaction authorization (if American Express or Discover are used, no issuing bank is involved -- see step 6).
5. Issuing bank returns authorization to card association. If the transaction is not authorized, CyberSource returns a message to the merchant and remaining portions of the transaction are cancelled.
6. CyberSource receives transaction authorization and, if physical fulfillment is required, sends a message to the merchant or distribution center authorizing order fulfillment.
   Merchant or distribution center sends CyberSource a fulfillment notification to permit settlement and CyberSource sends a settlement request to the issuing bank (customer's bank). If authorization is for the sale of a digitally delivered product or service, the settlement request is made concurrent with the authorization.
7. Issuing bank approves transfer of money to acquiring bank (merchant's account).

In The Know

Charge Backs

A charge back is a reversed purchase—one that a customer either no longer wants or did not receive. Charge backs occur when the customer disputes having made the transaction in the first place, when the customer claims that the product or service was not received, or when the customer wishes to return goods because they are not satisfactory. Problems can occur when merchants cannot prove that the customer did not receive the goods or services ordered. The term **e-shoplifting** is used to describe fraudulent charge backs. These occur when customers refuse to pay for goods that they actually received. One of the major risks facing online businesses is the growing incidence of charge backs, both legitimate and fraudulent.

E-Commerce

Exploring Online Payment Services

An online business can accept credit card orders by setting up an account with an online payment service. These services are also variously referred to as credit card-processing services, Internet payment providers, and online payment-processing services. Some online payment services process credit card payments for an online business without requiring the business to have merchant account status, some provide merchant accounts at reduced rates, and some will process credit card payments for companies that do not have merchant accounts. Figure F-12 shows the services available on the CyberCash Web site.

Some online payment services are also turnkey e-commerce systems. A **turnkey system** is one that supplies all the hardware and software required for a full e-business solution that in turn allows a business to accept credit cards, process transactions securely, fulfill orders, and provide full customer service. Figure F-13 compares the fees charged by some of the companies that provide turnkey e-commerce systems. Sorting out the different online payment services can be a challenge. Making the right choice requires having a fairly accurate count of the number of transactions a business anticipates, because a transaction fee must be paid for each credit card purchase. Matt recently visited a cyber trade show where he heard about the services offered by several online payment providers. He asks you to compare three of these services so that he can gain a clearer idea of what services are offered for an online business, the costs involved, and what other software or hardware is required.

Steps

1. Open your Web browser, go to the Student Online Companion at *www.course.com/illustrated/ecommerce*, click the link for **Unit F**, then click the link for **Exploring online payment services**

2. Select three sites from the list provided

3. Open the Project File **ECF-02.doc** in your word-processing program, then save it as **Payment Services**
   The document contains the table that you will use to compare the products and services offered by three online payment-service providers.

4. Go to one of the sites you chose in Step 2, then follow links to information about the online payment services

5. Enter the fees charged for each of the items listed in the table
   You might not be able to find fee information for all the items. Type NA for Not Applicable, where required.

6. Answer the questions provided
   Your goal is to analyze the Web sites you have visited, and determine if the services they offer will help an online business conduct transactions efficiently, and at a reasonable cost. Study each Web site critically, and ask yourself if you would do business with them. If you would not, identify your reasons. For example, the company Web site may not include real-world contact information, or the pages may contain more advertising hype than useful information.

7. When you have completed all the questions for each payment provider, type **Your Name** at the bottom of the document, save it, print a copy, then close the document

FIGURE F-12: Sample online payment services

Services —

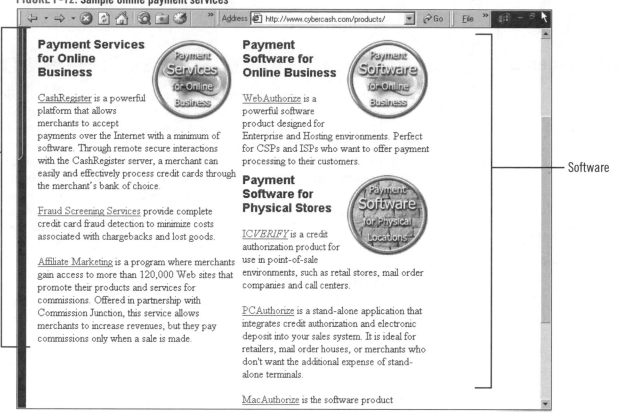

— Software

FIGURE F-13: Comparison of fees for turnkey solutions

Merchant Account Providers Offering Turnkey Solutions

Name	Internet Rate	Trans Fee	Case Rate	Case Fee
1st Merchant Card Services	1.48% to 2.39%	$1.48 to $2.39	2.10%	$0.30
Berryhill Financial Group Inc - Berryhill Financial Services	1.49% to 2.50%	$0.20 to $0.30	2.10%	$0.30
Credit Card Provider	1.50% to 3.50%	$1.50 to $3.50	5.00%	$2.00
CreditCardSolutions.Net	1.59% to 2.95%	$0.20	2.25%	$0.20
0 Down Merchant Services	1.77% to 2.39%	$0.00	1.95%	$0.25
USAbankcards.com	1.95% to 2.49%	$0.25 to $0.30	2.31%	$0.27
Bankcard Solutions	1.95% to 2.50%	$0.30 to $0.35	1.99%	$0.30
Capital Bankcard	1.97% to 2.45%	$0.23 to $0.30	2.12%	$0.28
A-Quick Credit Card Services - Accept Credit Cards!	1.98% to 2.14%	$0.30	1.98%	$0.30
Cardservice Great Lakes - Cardservice International	2.00% to 2.35%	$0.25 to $0.35	2.35%	$0.25
1st National Bankcard Services	2.00% to 2.35%	$0.28 to $0.35	2.15%	$0.28
Merchantbankcard.com - Internet Credit Card Processing	2.00% to 2.35%	$0.28 to $0.35	2.15%	$0.28
Heartland Payment Systems	2.00% to 2.50%	$0.20 to $0.30	2.35%	$0.25
Matrix.com - e-Business Solutions	2.00% to 2.50%	$0.30	2.00%	$0.30
Technocheck Systems	2.00% to 2.55%	$0.25 to $0.35	2.15%	$0.20
Infinity Merchant Services	2.05% to 2.35%	$0.30 to $0.35	2.35%	$0.30

Navigation sidebar: Articles · Turnkey · International · Provider Profiles · Other Providers · Rates Comparison · Merchant Search · Glossary · MerchantWorkz · Get Listed · Contact · MerchantWorkz · workz.com

Understanding Transaction Processing

An online transaction-processing company will authorize and approve credit card orders placed at an online store so that shoppers with valid credit cards can complete their purchases in real time. One of the largest transaction-processing businesses is Authorize.Net. Other companies include CyberCash, ClickPay, and InternetSecure. Some transaction-processing companies provide complete e-business solutions that include the set-up and maintenance of a merchant account. Other transaction-processing services require that business have its own merchant account set up before credit card orders can be processed. ◄━━━ Once MediaLoft upgrades its merchant account to accept online orders, Matt will need to determine how the credit card orders should be processed. He asks you to research real-time authorization, the activities performed by a transaction-processing service, and how to add payment-processing capabilities to a Web site.

Details

► Real-time Authorization

Transaction-processing services verify credit card payments in real time. The term **real time** refers to activities that occur within a few minutes of the time the transaction occurs. A real-time transaction will be processed as soon as the consumer clicks the Submit or Process button to send a credit card number over a secure server to pay for a product or service.

► Options

A business with a merchant account can accept credit card payments online. However, a business cannot process the payments online in real time without the assistance of a transaction-processing service (also called a gateway service). A Web site without a connection to a gateway service would need to go offline to process credit card payments using a credit card reader, just as they would in a retail store. An online business needs to choose whether to use a transaction-processing service to process credit card payments in real time, or to process credit card payments in batches at intervals, such as once an hour or once a day.

► Payment-processing Procedure

Here's one way a company can e-commerce-enable a Web site that they have already built using an e-commerce software program:

1. Obtain a merchant account.

2. Purchase a digital certificate to securely identify the company.

3. Set up a contract with a gateway or transaction-processing service such as InternetSecure or Authorize.Net.

4. Configure the software program to communicate with the transaction-processing company. Figure F-14 shows how to use EC Builder to select payment options, and then set up a connection with a transaction-processing company.

When a customer makes a credit card payment from the Web site, the payment is transferred securely to the transaction-processing service where the payment is authorized. A message is then sent back (usually within seconds) to inform the customer that the payment is verified.

► Verification Activities

A principal role of the transaction-processing service is to ensure the validity of the credit card number a consumer enters. Figure F-15 shows a page on the TechWeb site that describes four areas that a transaction-processing service can check to verify a credit card payment. The fourth area—Velocity—relates to finding credit cards that have a history of charge backs. A customer who frequently uses a credit card, and then cancels the payment might not be approved by a transaction-processing service that verifies only credit cards with a very limited charge back record.

FIGURE F-14: Selecting transaction-processing options in EC Builder

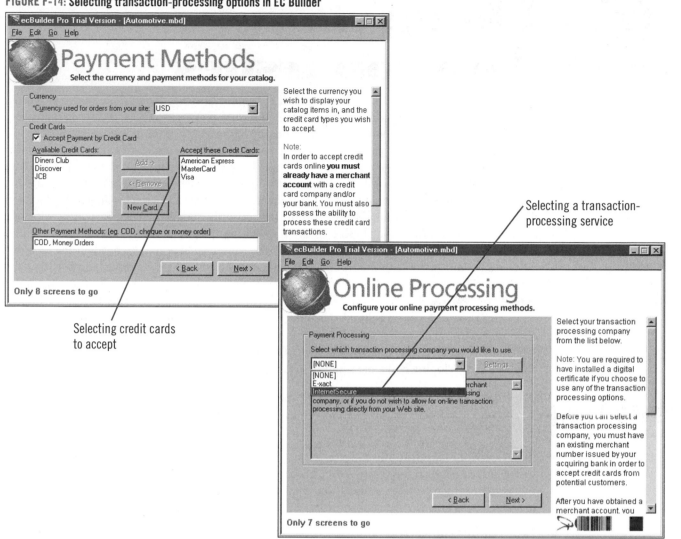

Selecting credit cards
to accept

Selecting a transaction-
processing service

FIGURE F-15: Verification guidelines

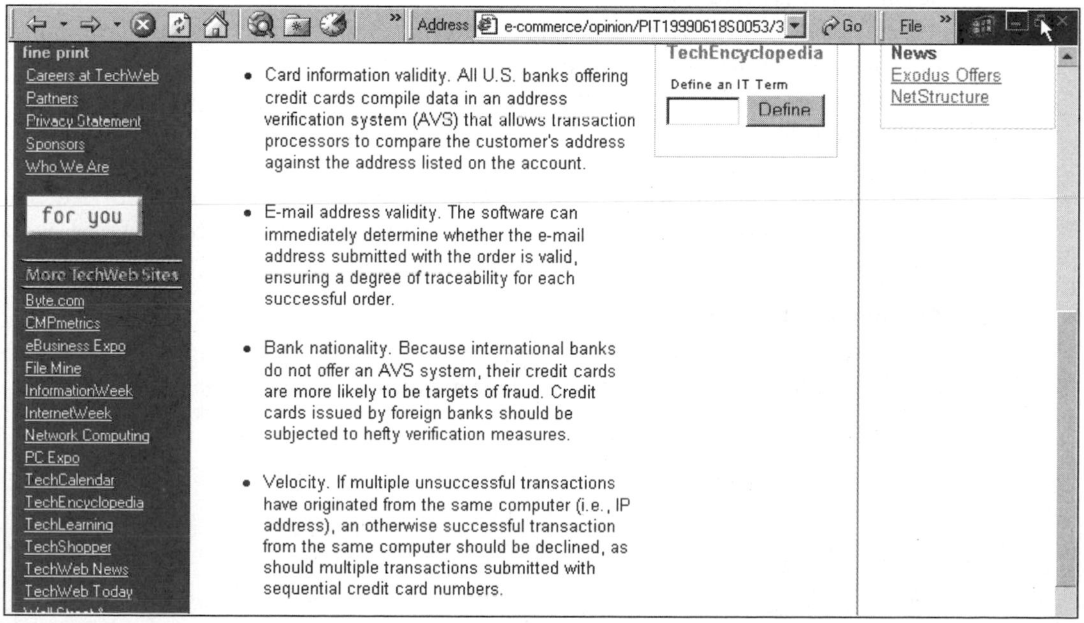

Unit F

E-Commerce

Identifying Taxation Issues

When a customer purchases a product in a brick and mortar store, the total purchase price often includes a sales tax. The amount of this tax depends on a variety of factors, including the nature of the product, and the physical location where the transaction took place. In some states or provinces, a consumer will pay no sales tax, while in others they might pay up to 17 percent for selected products. Now, what happens when the same consumer purchases the same product from an online store that could be located just about anywhere in the world? Is the sales tax applied according to the location of the server that hosts the Web site, or according to the location of the purchaser? To compound the confusion, the server that hosts the Web site could be located thousands of miles from the physical location of the company that maintains the Web site and supplies the products. The situation gets even more complicated when the product that is being purchased is not tangible in the traditional sense; that is, it is a digital product, such as digitally developed film that a consumer downloads directly from a company's server to the consumer's hard drive. ◀━━ Like everyone else, Matt is uncertain about how Internet taxation will proceed once the moratorium is lifted. The only certainty at present appears to be the difficulty of obtaining agreement between all the parties involved in taxation—from the consumer to the merchant, to all levels of government. Matt asks you to define some of the issues and vocabulary involved in developing equitable taxation for Internet financial transactions.

Details

▶ **Internet Tax Freedom Act**

In 1998, the U.S. Congress passed the Internet Tax Freedom Act (ITFA) to impose a three-year moratorium on new Internet taxation. Figure F-16 shows a portion of the act. Note that the moratorium is only on the imposition of *new* taxes, so existing taxes will still be collected.

▶ **Taxation Questions**

Figure F-17 illustrates just some of the questions related to imposing taxes on Internet transactions, and collecting existing taxes. Some of the issues related to Internet taxation have no precedent, particularly issues related to the taxation of digital products.

▶ **Level Playing Field**

In an earlier unit, you learned about the level playing field in relation to the universality of the Internet. All Internet businesses, no matter how small or large, have access to the same markets. In taxation terms, the level playing field concept means that the same tax is applied to the same purchase, regardless of whether it is made online or in a brick and mortar store. Since at present most countries and states within countries have widely different tax regulations, the level playing field concept may not be feasible. Some analysts are particularly worried that inequities could occur if products purchased from a brick and mortar store are taxed, while the same products purchased from an online store are not taxed.

▶ **Anonymous Transactions**

The advent of e-cash as an anonymous payment method also might hinder efforts to collect taxes. Transactions that are delivered electronically and paid for with electronic cash could be difficult to trace.

FIGURE F-16: Excerpt from the Internet Tax Freedom Act

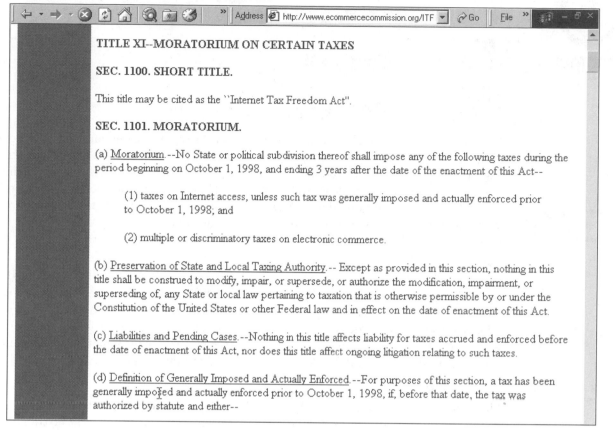

TITLE XI--MORATORIUM ON CERTAIN TAXES

SEC. 1100. SHORT TITLE.

This title may be cited as the ``Internet Tax Freedom Act''.

SEC. 1101. MORATORIUM.

(a) Moratorium.--No State or political subdivision thereof shall impose any of the following taxes during the period beginning on October 1, 1998, and ending 3 years after the date of the enactment of this Act--

    (1) taxes on Internet access, unless such tax was generally imposed and actually enforced prior to October 1, 1998; and

    (2) multiple or discriminatory taxes on electronic commerce.

(b) Preservation of State and Local Taxing Authority.-- Except as provided in this section, nothing in this title shall be construed to modify, impair, or supersede, or authorize the modification, impairment, or superseding of, any State or local law pertaining to taxation that is otherwise permissible by or under the Constitution of the United States or other Federal law and in effect on the date of enactment of this Act.

(c) Liabilities and Pending Cases.--Nothing in this title affects liability for taxes accrued and enforced before the date of enactment of this Act, nor does this title affect ongoing litigation relating to such taxes.

(d) Definition of Generally Imposed and Actually Enforced.--For purposes of this section, a tax has been generally imposed and actually enforced prior to October 1, 1998, if, before that date, the tax was authorized by statute and either--

FIGURE F-17: Taxation questions

How does the virtually unlimited mobility of Web servers affect tax collection?

How can taxes be applied to digital products that can be downloaded anywhere in the world?

How can taxes be applied to products and services sold across international boundaries in cyberspace?

Can a Web site be taxed as a physical entity?

Will consumers pay one tax to buy a product in a brick and mortar store, and pay another tax–or no tax–to buy the same product from an online store?

Who is responsible for sales taxes–the buyer or the seller?

How will Value Added Tax be collected?

Will customs officials collect sales taxes on international purchases?

Does a vendor in Indiana need to calculate taxes on a purchase made by a consumer in Montreal?

E-Commerce

Understanding Taxation Requirements

At present, a customer is charged tax when he or she lives in the same state in which the online company has its location. For example, you will be charged sales tax if you live in California and buy a product online from a company that also is located in California. As you will learn in this lesson, the concept of Permanent Establishment that has influenced taxation laws for many years is now being called into question. Matt asks you to check out taxation requirements related to doing business both in the United States and globally.

► Permanent Establishment

A company is generally taxed according to its **Permanent Establishment (PE)**, defined as the physical location of the business. With e-commerce, the concept of tax rules that are dependent on location raises challenging questions, because an e-commerce business can exist only in cyberspace, and its Web site hosted by a server that can be easily moved. Figure F-18 summarizes some of the PE-related premises put forth by a Working Party subgroup of the Organization for Economic Cooperation and Development (OECD) Committee on Fiscal Affairs[3].

► Digital Downloads

Many analysts predict that existing tax legislation is sufficient to handle the purchase of physical goods from online stores. However, how can the transfer of digital products be taxed? For example, a consumer in Italy could download software from a vendor located in Japan who actually operates from a server located in the Bahamas. Which jurisdiction collects tax and, what's more important, what methods can be used to collect the taxes? Online sales of products such as e-books, movies, and music are expected to rise dramatically as bandwidths increase, and more consumers begin purchasing digital versions of products that they once bought in physical form. Governments will need to develop clear tax policies to avoid a drop in tax revenues.

► International Issues

Because tangible products that are shipped internationally will cross a border, customs duties and other taxes can be imposed as the products enter the country. The sheer volume of Internet-purchased goods being shipped internationally might, however, make tax collection difficult. In addition, shipping digital products over the Internet bypasses international boundaries, just as it does state or provincial boundaries. In the United Kingdom, a recently issued paper on e-commerce tax policies points to tax haven use, anonymous transactions, and digital cash as situations that will make tax collection difficult. Check the In The Know for an excerpt from this paper.

► Value Added Tax

As explained in the vat.com Web site, Value Added Tax (VAT) is an indirect tax on consumer expenses that is charged and collected at each stage of the production process and on the final sale. VAT is normally borne by the consumer in the price paid for goods and services. Because many countries around the world also add VAT to purchases, it might play a significant role in global solutions related to applying tax to Internet transactions.

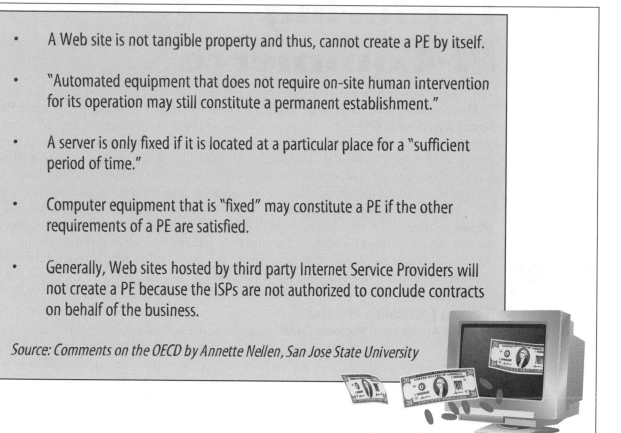

- A Web site is not tangible property and thus, cannot create a PE by itself.

- "Automated equipment that does not require on-site human intervention for its operation may still constitute a permanent establishment."

- A server is only fixed if it is located at a particular place for a "sufficient period of time."

- Computer equipment that is "fixed" may constitute a PE if the other requirements of a PE are satisfied.

- Generally, Web sites hosted by third party Internet Service Providers will not create a PE because the ISPs are not authorized to conclude contracts on behalf of the business.

Source: Comments on the OECD by Annette Nellen, San Jose State University

In The Know

Global Taxation Solutions

"The international nature of e-commerce brings with it the need to find global solutions to the taxation issues that it raises. If international trading is to be encouraged, business needs certainty and clarity over how international tax rules will work. At the same time, the Government needs to ensure that the rules work in a way that does not lead to a loss of tax revenue. Working with other governments and business to achieve these aims is essential. If countries take different approaches or act unilaterally, there could be:

- double taxation or unintentional non-taxation;
- excessive compliance burdens for business; and
- opportunities for the dishonest to evade or avoid taxes."

Source: United Kingdom Inland Revenue[4]

Exploring M-Commerce

Some analysts predict that mobile-commerce will fuel the next great surge in e-commerce activity. **Mobile-commerce** refers to the use of a wireless device such as a cellular phone or **Personal Digital Assistant (PDA)** to access the Internet to purchase products or services. M-commerce is expected to gain popularity first in Europe and Japan, where the use of mobile technology is already widespread. Technology companies are exploring m-commerce payment methods that range from upgrading existing smart cards, to creating e-wallets and virtual credit cards. Already, consumers are using mobile devices to connect to the Internet, send e-mail, and view Internet Web sites that are specially produced for the small screens on cellular telephones and PDAs. You've read a few articles about m-commerce and decide to research it further so that you can prepare a report for Matt. The information you provide will be included in a presentation Matt plans to give to MediaLoft management. The presentation will focus on future methods consumers might use when making online purchases.

Details

► Wireless Application Protocol

Wireless Application Protocol (WAP) is the standard being developed for the delivery of content over mobile communicators, such as cellular phones and PDAs. This content will be presented in the form of Web-like applications such as browsers that are accessed over wireless networks. The development of WAP is being governed by the WAP Forum, which is a democratic consortium of wireless technology developers. The Forum defines WAP as "an open, global specification that empowers mobile users with wireless devices to easily access and interact with information and services instantly."[5] Figure F-19 shows a portion of the WAP Forum FAQ page, and describes some uses for WAP.

► M-Commerce Challenges

Web-based applications that can be accessed by wireless devices must be designed to handle the challenges particular to the transmission of data over wireless networks. At present, the bandwidth available to transmit data is limited to the 9.6 kbps range. As increased bandwidth is made available to mobile devices, increased usage is expected to occur because waiting times will be reduced. Another challenge involves the presentation of Web-based applications. Small screens, a lack of color, and limited graphics capabilities are all factors that WAP applications must be designed to overcome.

► Wireless Markup Language (WML)

WML is a markup language similar to HTML, except that WML is used to create pages for WAP applications that will be viewed on wireless devices. Instead of creating pages, developers use WML to create decks that consist of one or more cards. The **WMLScript** is a scripting language similar to JavaScript, that is used to produce pages for WAP applications.

► M-Commerce Characteristics

Durlacher Corporation, a European research group that focuses on emerging technology and media, has identified seven attributes of mobile communications that will influence the development of m-commerce. Figure F-20 defines each of these attributes. At present, the final three attributes—localization, instant connectivity, and personalization—are still in the planning stages. The success of m-commerce may depend on how well these attributes are made possible technologically, and then to what extent consumers perceive their benefits. For example, will consumers want to use a mobile device to store personal preferences so that they can instantly book a hotel room in the right price range and location?

FIGURE F-19: WAP Forum FAQ

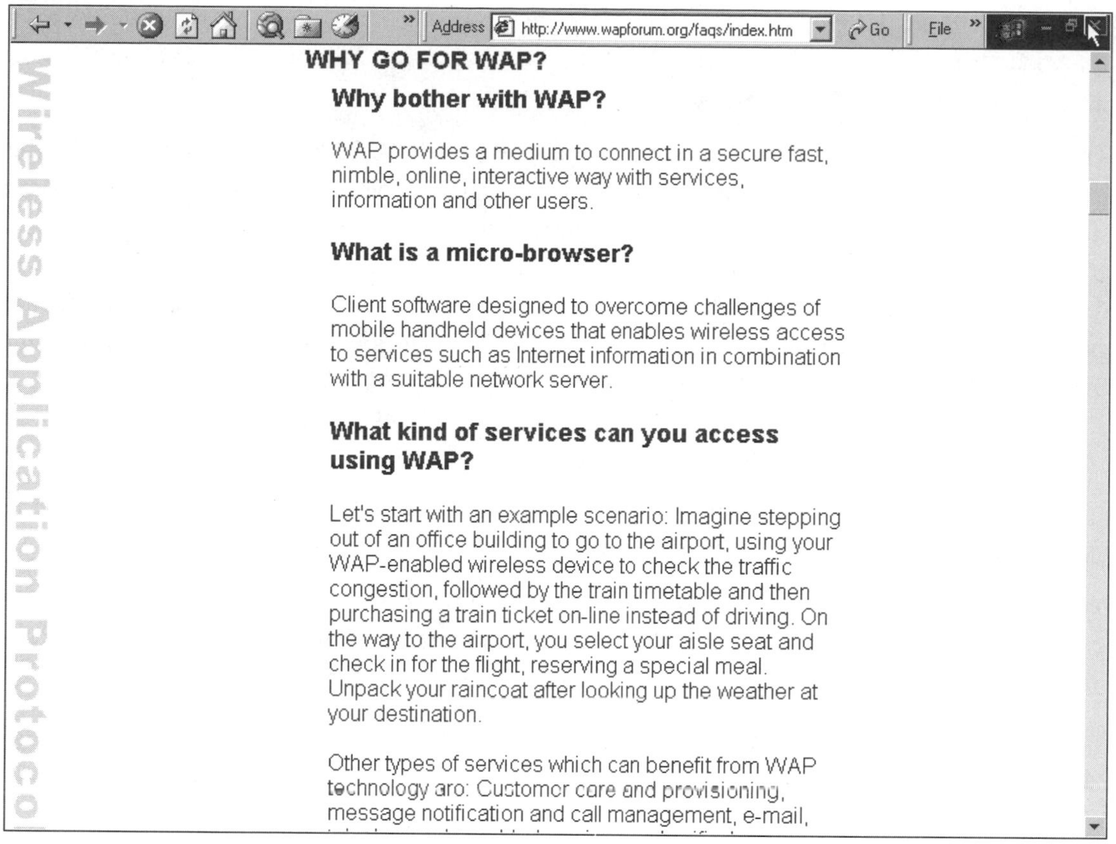

Address: http://www.wapforum.org/faqs/index.htm

Wireless Application Protocol

WHY GO FOR WAP?

Why bother with WAP?

WAP provides a medium to connect in a secure fast, nimble, online, interactive way with services, information and other users.

What is a micro-browser?

Client software designed to overcome challenges of mobile handheld devices that enables wireless access to services such as Internet information in combination with a suitable network server.

What kind of services can you access using WAP?

Let's start with an example scenario: Imagine stepping out of an office building to go to the airport, using your WAP-enabled wireless device to check the traffic congestion, followed by the train timetable and then purchasing a train ticket on-line instead of driving. On the way to the airport, you select your aisle seat and check in for the flight, reserving a special meal. Unpack your raincoat after looking up the weather at your destination.

Other types of services which can benefit from WAP technology are: Customer care and provisioning, message notification and call management, e-mail,

FIGURE F-20: Durlacher's mobile communication attributes

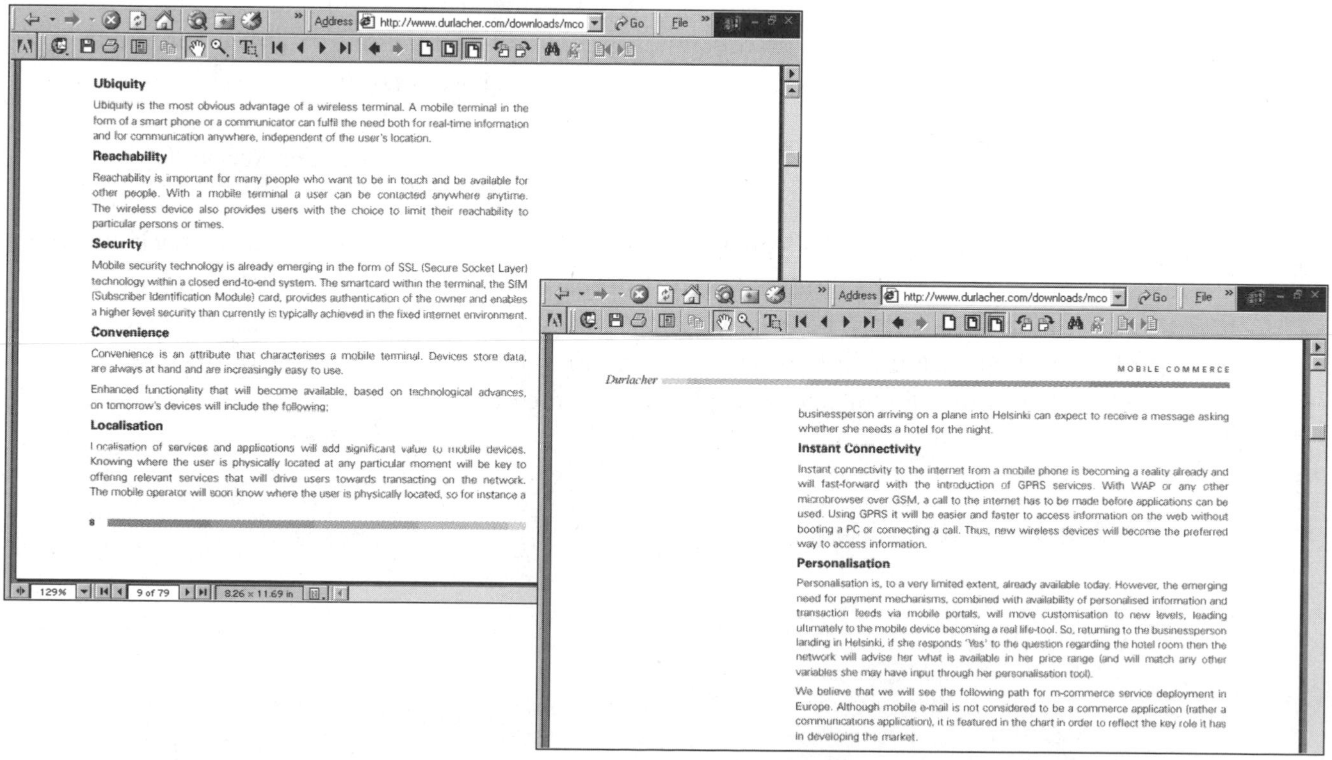

Address: http://www.durlacher.com/downloads/mco

Ubiquity

Ubiquity is the most obvious advantage of a wireless terminal. A mobile terminal in the form of a smart phone or a communicator can fulfil the need both for real-time information and for communication anywhere, independent of the user's location.

Reachability

Reachability is important for many people who want to be in touch and be available for other people. With a mobile terminal a user can be contacted anywhere anytime. The wireless device also provides users with the choice to limit their reachability to particular persons or times.

Security

Mobile security technology is already emerging in the form of SSL (Secure Socket Layer) technology within a closed end-to-end system. The smartcard within the terminal, the SIM (Subscriber Identification Module) card, provides authentication of the owner and enables a higher level security than currently is typically achieved in the fixed internet environment.

Convenience

Convenience is an attribute that characterises a mobile terminal. Devices store data, are always at hand and are increasingly easy to use.

Enhanced functionality that will become available, based on technological advances, on tomorrow's devices will include the following:

Localisation

Localisation of services and applications will add significant value to mobile devices. Knowing where the user is physically located at any particular moment will be key to offering relevant services that will drive users towards transacting on the network. The mobile operator will soon know where the user is physically located, so for instance a

8

129%   9 of 79   8.26 x 11.69 in

Address: http://www.durlacher.com/downloads/mco

Durlacher   MOBILE COMMERCE

businessperson arriving on a plane into Helsinki can expect to receive a message asking whether she needs a hotel for the night.

Instant Connectivity

Instant connectivity to the internet from a mobile phone is becoming a reality already and will fast-forward with the introduction of GPRS services. With WAP or any other microbrowser over GSM, a call to the internet has to be made before applications can be used. Using GPRS it will be easier and faster to access information on the web without booting a PC or connecting a call. Thus, new wireless devices will become the preferred way to access information.

Personalisation

Personalisation is, to a very limited extent, already available today. However, the emerging need for payment mechanisms, combined with availability of personalised information and transaction feeds via mobile portals, will move customisation to new levels, leading ultimately to the mobile device becoming a real life-tool. So, returning to the businessperson landing in Helsinki, if she responds 'Yes' to the question regarding the hotel room then the network will advise her what is available in her price range (and will match any other variables she may have input through her personalisation tool).

We believe that we will see the following path for m-commerce service deployment in Europe. Although mobile e-mail is not considered to be a commerce application (rather a communications application), it is featured in the chart in order to reflect the key role it has in developing the market.

Focus

M-Commerce Issues

The Register Web site ran the article shown below on March 24, 2000. Titled "Don't Believe the M-commerce Hype," the article maintains that consumers might not be as willing to embrace m-commerce as suppliers of wireless technology hope they will. To visit the Register's Web site, open your Web browser, go to the Student Online Companion at *www.course.com/illustrated/ecommerce*, click the link to Unit F, then click the link to Focus. The Register is based in the United Kingdom, and runs articles that critically examine new Information Technology (IT) trends. As its logo says, the Register is "Biting the hand that feeds IT." Read the article shown below.

The current frenzy about gizmo mobile phones providing wireless access to the Net is nothing short of hype, according to a report by analysts Ovum.

In its report Mobile E-commerce - Market Strategies, Ovum claims those involved in this fledgling industry should concentrate on providing "genuinely unique and compelling services" rather than trying to excite the market with over-hyped messages of "cool new technology."

The report claims that there are perfectly good alternatives to buying goods and services without having to resort to m-commerce.

"What's to persuade someone to order a pizza using a mobile application, rather than just picking up the phone?" asked report author Duncan Brown.

"There would have to be a significant value-add to change habits: perhaps discounts, an up to date menu on screen - easy selection of pizza and toppings with a few key presses - and no waiting for engaged tones or overworked staff," he said.

What's more, Brown claims the demand for m-commerce is being driven by suppliers, rather than customers. "It's debatable whether ordinary consumers are actually demanding mobile e-commerce services right now," he said. "It's more a case of suppliers sensing an opportunity to make money, and pushing the idea at them," said Brown.

Source: The Register[6]

To answer the following questions, you will need to read the Focus article, and also check out some of the articles included on the Student Online Companion. To access these articles, open your Web browser, go to the Student Online Companion at *www.course.com/illustrated/ecommerce*, click the link for Unit F, then click the link for Focus Articles. You can then follow some of the links provided to check out other articles related to m-commerce.

Explore Further...

1. The author of the article asks why people would use their mobile device to order a pizza online instead of just making a phone call. The article then goes on to state: "There would have to be a significant value-add to change habits: perhaps discounts, an up to date menu on screen - easy selection of pizza and toppings with a few key presses - and no waiting for engaged tones or overworked staff." Do you agree with the author's skepticism about the future of m-commerce? Research some of the ways in which consumers might use mobile devices to conduct online transactions, and then think of some ways yourself. Since no one can yet predict the exact nature of m-commerce transactions, the ideas you develop could be just as valid as any you'll find in articles on the Internet. Write a short paper describing the types of m-commerce transactions that you think consumers will want to make. Alternatively, give reasons why you think consumers will not be eager to use a mobile device to conduct online transactions. Support your point of view with examples from your research.

2. The article titled "Where's the WAP?", included in the Student Online Companion for the Focus section of this Unit, explores why the development of Wireless Application Protocol in North America lags behind Europe and Asia. Search the Internet for articles that relate to m-commerce developments in North America. Your goal is to determine some current developments, the major companies involved, how you think m-commerce will develop (or not develop) in North America, and if you think demographics or cultural differences might lead to a disparity in WAP usage. Do you think that North Americans will be as eager to adopt m-commerce as the Europeans and Asians are expected to? Write a short paper describing how you think the technology will develop in North America. Include references to the articles you've read.

3. The article titled "Japanese Combine Mobile Phone, Web Craze," included in the Student Online Companion for the Focus section of this Unit, describes the state of wireless technology in Japan as of June 2000. Note the names of the technology companies cited in the article, then search for their Web sites. Find information about the current state of the technology being developed by each company. If you can't find information about the companies cited, search for "wireless technology companies." Your goal is to learn about some of the latest developments being made by companies developing wireless technology and m-commerce solutions. Select one or two companies that you think are on the cutting edge, then write a short paper describing the technology being developed.

Practice

► Review

Fill in the best answer

1. An electronic payment is one that is transmitted _____ over the Internet.

2. The term Electronic Data _____ is used to describe the electronic transfer of data between companies engaged in B2B e-commerce.

3. EDI is also described as paperless _____.

4. An encrypted representation of a paper check is called an _____.

5. A low-cost integrated microprocessor chip is embedded in a _____ card.

6. An e-wallet is actually a _____ program that contains all the information required to process a credit card transaction.

7. The term that refers to a buyer's payment being held by a third party is _____.

8. Payments in very small increments are called _____.

9. The bank that provides a consumer with a credit card is called the _____ institution.

10. The term _____ is used to describe a reversed purchase.

11. Customers who refuse to pay for goods that they actually received may be guilty of _____.

12. A _____ account is one that a company sets up with a bank to handle credit card transactions.

13. A MAP is a _____ _____ _____.

14. The acronym MOTO stands for Mail Order/_____ Order.

15. A _____ system is one that supplies all the hardware and software required for a full e-business solution that in turn allows a business to accept credit cards, process transactions securely, fulfill orders, and provide full customer service.

16. Transactions that occur immediately are referred to as _____-time transactions.

17. A principal role of the transaction-processing service is to ensure the _____ of the credit card number a consumer enters.

18. WAP stands for Wireless _____ Protocol.

19. Pages for WAP applications are created by _____, a markup language similar to HTML.

20. The concept of a _____ playing field means that the same tax is applied to the same purchase, regardless of where it is made.

▶ Independent Challenges

1. An online business needs to apply to a bank in order to obtain a merchant account. The fees charged and policies of banks can vary considerably. Some banks are more inclined than others to deal with businesses that want to conduct transactions online. One of the best ways of learning more about merchant accounts is to investigate the policies of one or two real-world banks that you deal with locally.

To complete this independent challenge:

a. Fill in the box below with the name of the business that you might want to pursue online. Include a description of the products or services your Web site will sell. Make sure you select a business that sells products related to one of your own interests.

Business category ....

Products or services ....

b. Identify two financial institutions in your area that issue merchant accounts for either Visa or MasterCard.

c. Visit each institution's Web site or the brick and mortar bank, and obtain merchant account brochures. Find as much information as you can about obtaining a merchant account.

d. Open the Project File ECF-03.doc in your word-processing program. This document contains the table where you will enter information about the merchant account services at the two institutions you have selected.

e. Save the document as *Merchant Accounts*.

f. Answer the questions for both of the institutions you chose. Your goal is to determine how—and if—you would obtain a merchant account from a real-world financial institution.

g. Type **Your Name** at the bottom of the document, save it, print a copy, then close the document.

2. Smart cards may well become the technology used most often to make online electronic payments. Online businesses need to familiarize themselves with the latest developments regarding smart cards. Fortunately, the Web contains numerous sites that feature information about smart cards and how they can be used to facilitate online purchasing.

To complete this independent challenge:

a. Open your Web browser, go to the Student Online Companion at *www.course.com/illustrated/ecommerce*, click the link for Unit F, then click the link for Independent Challenge 2.

b. Open the Project File ECF-04.doc in your word-processing program. This document contains a list of questions related to smart cards.

c. Save the document as *Smart Card Questions*.

d. Search the sites listed in the Student Online Companion for Independent Challenge 2 to find answers to the questions provided in your Project File document. (*Hint:* Check FAQ pages whenever possible.) Your goal is to learn as much as you can about smart cards—how they are made, and how they might be used in the future to facilitate e-commerce transactions.

e. Type **Your Name** at the bottom of the document, save it, print a copy, then close the document.

3. The concepts and activities associated with processing online payments are not always straightforward. To help you make sense of the sometimes conflicting information available, you can explore several transaction-processing services to find answers to specific questions. Your goal is to find the common ground among all the transaction services available.

To complete this independent challenge:

a. Open the Project File ECF-05.doc in your word-processing program. This document contains a list of Frequently Asked Questions related to processing online payments.

b. Save the document as *Online Payment Processing*.

c. Open your Web browser, go to the Student Online Companion at *www.course.com/illustrated/ecommerce*, click the link for Unit F, then click the link for Independent Challenge 3.

d. Search two or three of the sites listed in the Student Online Companion for Independent Challenge 3 to find answers to the questions provided in your Project File document. (*Hint:* Check FAQ pages whenever possible.) Your goal is to learn as much as you can about transaction processing. You are also checking to see if information about similar topics varies from site to site. Note that you can choose to answer each question from just one site, or you can provide answers from two or three sites.

e. Type **Your Name** at the bottom of the document, save it, print a copy, then close the document.

4. Taxation issues related to Internet payments for goods and services, including digital goods, give rise to considerable controversy. Some critics advocate the dismissal of all taxes on products bought online. Other critics advocate the introduction of a Value Added Tax similar to that used in Europe and other countries. To help you make sense of the many opinions and controversies surrounding taxation, you will explore several Web sites that carry articles related to Internet taxation, and then you will answer a series of questions.

To complete this independent challenge:

a. Open the Project File ECF-06.doc in your word-processing program. This document contains four questions related to Internet taxation.

b. Save the document as *Internet Taxation Issues*.

c. Open your Web browser, go to the Student Online Companion at *www.course.com/illustrated/ecommerce*, click the link for Unit F, then click the link for Independent Challenge 4. Here you will find links to sites that provide information related to each of the four questions in the *Internet Taxation Issues* document.

d. Search the provided sites to find information appropriate for each of the four questions. Note that no right answer exists. Your goal is to analyze what other people have said about the issues, and then to form your own opinion.

e. Type **Your Name** at the bottom of the document, save it, print a copy, then close the document.

► Up to Date

Figure F-21 shows a Web site that carries articles on international taxation issues related to e-commerce. You need to find more recently published articles so that you can learn about the latest developments in Internet taxation.

FIGURE F-21: International e-commerce taxation issues

To complete the Up to Date Challenge:

1. Open your Web browser, go to the Student Online Companion at *www.course.com/illustrated/ ecommerce*, click the link for Unit F, then click the link to Up to Date.
2. Follow the link to a list of current articles related to taxation issues and e-commerce.
3. Follow links to three articles. At least two of the links you follow should relate to Internet taxation issues in a country other than your own, or they should relate to Internet international taxation issues that affect how companies in your country do business with companies in other countries.
4. Open a document in your word-processing program, write two or three paragraphs that summarize each of the three articles you chose. Include the URL of the article and the date it was written. Your goal is to determine some of the issues related to Internet taxation at the international level.
5. Type **Your Name** at the bottom of the document, save it as *International Internet Taxation Articles*, print a copy, then close the document.

► Visual Workshop

A great way to determine how various e-payment methods are developing is to check out the Web sites of leading online companies. Figure F-22 shows the payment methods accepted by Amazon.com. As you can see, four payment methods are acceptable: credit card, check or postal order, purchase order, and gift certificate. At the time this book was published, other forms of electronic payment such as e-cash and e-checks were not listed; however, when you visit the page, additional payment methods may be included. Open your Web browser, go to the Student Online Companion at *www.course.com/illustrated/ecommerce*, click the link for Unit F, then click the link for Visual Workshop. Follow links to three of the companies listed to find out what payments methods they accept. As you gather information, complete the box below.

FIGURE F-22

company	payment methods

E-Commerce

Security

Issues

Objectives

► **Define security issues**

► **Identify security threats**

► **Explore consumer security issues**

► **Explore business security issues**

► **Identify security procedures**

► **Understand encryption**

► **Understand digital certificates**

► **Define SSL and SET technologies**

► **Explore authentication and identification**

► **Explore security providers**

► **Explore privacy policies**

► **Define legal issues**

Security is a major concern of just about everyone—whether it involves personal security, financial security, or national security. We all want and need to feel safe. This basic need also determines how both businesses and consumers use the Internet to communicate, to make purchases, and to transfer data. In this unit, you will examine general security issues and security threats for both consumers and businesses, and then you will examine some of the technologies such as SSL, SET, encryption, and digital certificates that are being developed to prevent unauthorized access to information. You will also explore some of the services offered by security providers, and you will analyze privacy policies. Finally, you will define some of the legal issues related to doing business over the Internet. ◀━━ Merilee Bonnard has joined the Online Development Group to implement security strategies for MediaLoft's new e-commerce Web site. She asks you to help her identify the principal security issues, and help her learn about the various tools and technologies available to ensure the security of an online store.

E-Commerce

Defining Security Issues

You can define security in the real world as the freedom from danger and from risk. You feel secure when you know you are safe from physical, mental, and emotional harm. With relation to e-commerce and the Internet, **security** refers primarily to the techniques used to store and transmit data, to form policies that govern how data is used, and to protect networks and equipment from potential harm or failure. The potential growth of e-commerce depends on people believing that surfing the Internet and buying and selling online are safe activities that will not result in financial loss or an invasion of privacy. Figure G-1 shows the home page of one of the many Web sites dedicated to informing the public about Internet security issues. New articles appear regularly. ► To help Merilee introduce her report on Internet-related security issues, you decide to learn about the nature of online security and the requirements of an effective security system.

Details

► **Internet Security**

The TCP/IP protocol used to transmit data over the Internet was not designed to be secure, which means that data transmitted from computer to computer can be intercepted, read, and even altered. For example, a **sniffer** program can record information that passes through a computer (or router) on its way to a destination computer, unless that information is scrambled. Security breaches can occur when many e-mails and files are transmitted in their original form.

► **Security Requirements**

The security of an individual's computer, a corporate Intranet, and an online store depends on four requirements: Identification, Access, Protection, and Validity. Figure G-2 summarizes each of these requirements as they relate to the security of an online store.

► **Identification**

In the real world, most people carry some form of paper identification to prove their identity. In the cyberworld, identification methods include the use of passwords, Personal Identification Numbers (PINs), digital signatures, and digital certificates.

► **Access Control**

A company's Web site is designed to communicate to the world. However, the company certainly does not want the world to have access to confidential information, such as the names and addresses of employees, the credit card numbers of customers, and internal memos that refer to proprietary business information. A security system is required to identify individuals according to their access rights. For example, the casual Web surfer can only view public pages on the Web site, while the company's Web developer can post updated Web pages to the site. Within most organizations, various levels of access to information are clearly defined, often with the aid of an Access Control List (ACL).

► **Protection**

The Internet is a wide-open land populated by the same ratio of responsible and irresponsible individuals found in any real-world land. While the majority of Web surfers—just like the majority of citizens—are law-abiding individuals, certain measures are required to guard against the activities perpetrated by "bad apples." A consumer surfing the Web needs to feel that strangers can't learn personal information about them, that thieves can't steal their credit card numbers, that viruses will not attack the data on their computers, and that cyberstalkers can't harm their children. Methods used to protect both individuals and data from damage, loss, or unauthorized use include technical solutions such as the encryption of data, and social solutions such as the enforcement of privacy policies.

► **Validity**

When you send an e-mail message to a friend or a colleague, you don't expect its contents to be modified in transit. Similarly, no online business expects its Web site to be tampered with. Security measures should ensure the validity of information by protecting it from unauthorized modification.

FIGURE G-1: Security-related news articles

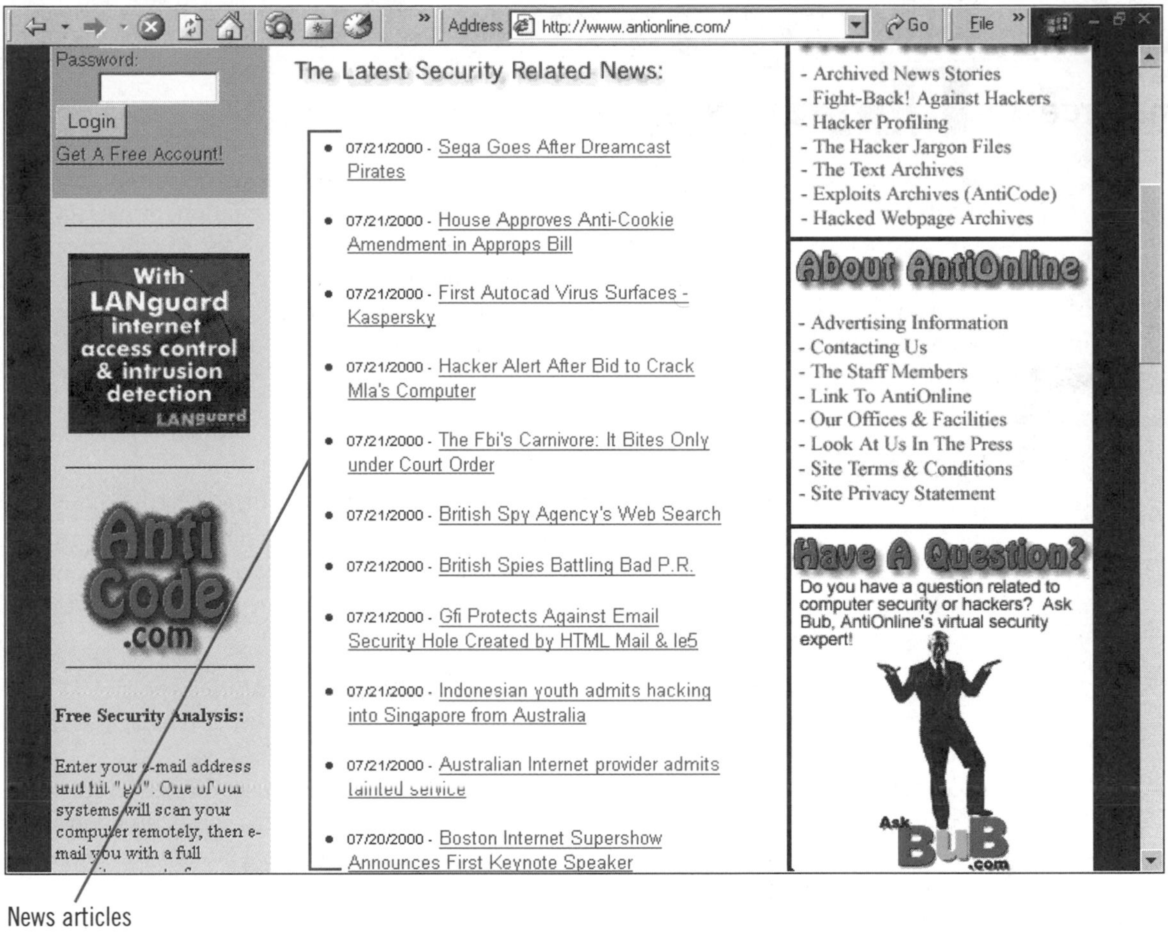

Address: http://www.antionline.com/

Password:

Login
Get A Free Account!

With LANguard internet access control & intrusion detection
LANguard

AntiCode .com

Free Security Analysis:

Enter your e-mail address and hit "go". One of our systems will scan your computer remotely, then e-mail you with a full

The Latest Security Related News:

- 07/21/2000 - Sega Goes After Dreamcast Pirates
- 07/21/2000 - House Approves Anti-Cookie Amendment in Approps Bill
- 07/21/2000 - First Autocad Virus Surfaces - Kaspersky
- 07/21/2000 - Hacker Alert After Bid to Crack Mla's Computer
- 07/21/2000 - The Fbi's Carnivore: It Bites Only under Court Order
- 07/21/2000 - British Spy Agency's Web Search
- 07/21/2000 - British Spies Battling Bad P.R.
- 07/21/2000 - Gfi Protects Against Email Security Hole Created by HTML Mail & Ie5
- 07/21/2000 - Indonesian youth admits hacking into Singapore from Australia
- 07/21/2000 - Australian Internet provider admits tainted service
- 07/20/2000 - Boston Internet Supershow Announces First Keynote Speaker

- Archived News Stories
- Fight-Back! Against Hackers
- Hacker Profiling
- The Hacker Jargon Files
- The Text Archives
- Exploits Archives (AntiCode)
- Hacked Webpage Archives

About AntiOnline

- Advertising Information
- Contacting Us
- The Staff Members
- Link To AntiOnline
- Our Offices & Facilities
- Look At Us In The Press
- Site Terms & Conditions
- Site Privacy Statement

Have A Question?

Do you have a question related to computer security or hackers? Ask Bub, AntiOnline's virtual security expert!

Ask BuB .com

News articles

FIGURE G-2: Security requirements

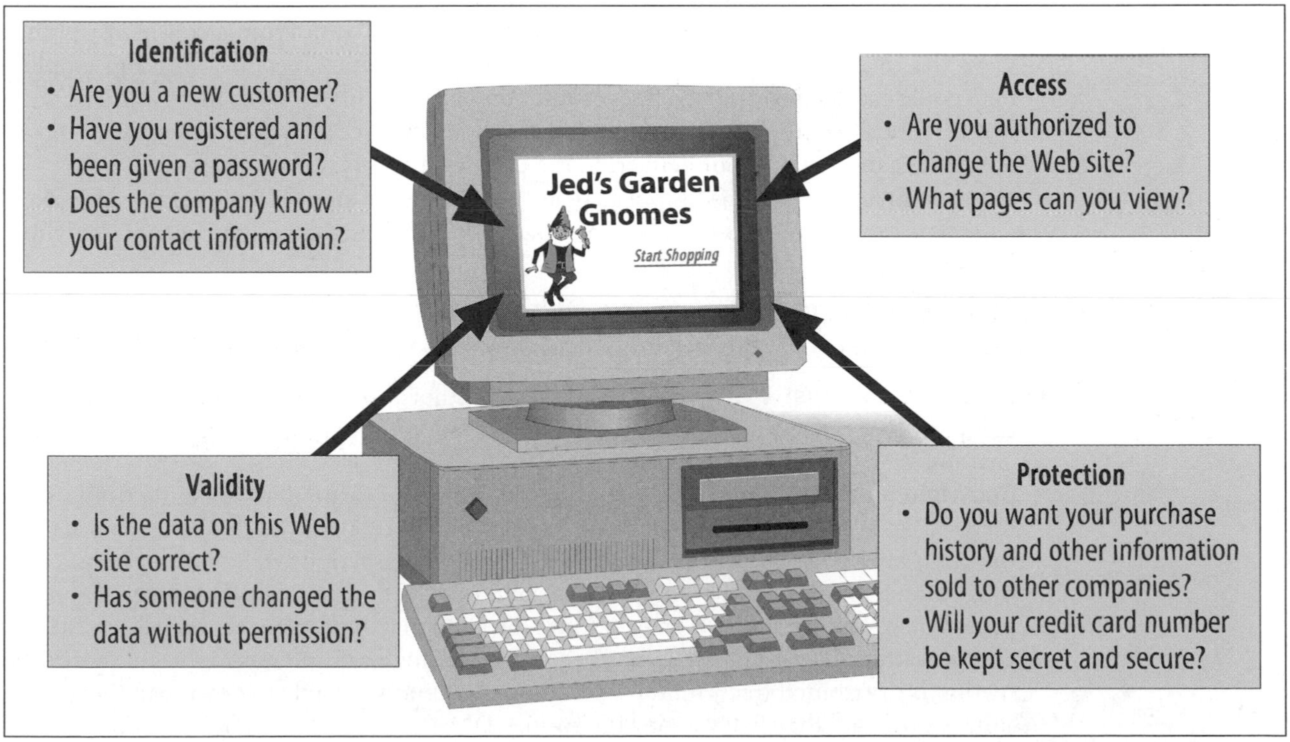

Identification
- Are you a new customer?
- Have you registered and been given a password?
- Does the company know your contact information?

Access
- Are you authorized to change the Web site?
- What pages can you view?

Jed's Garden Gnomes
Start Shopping

Validity
- Is the data on this Web site correct?
- Has someone changed the data without permission?

Protection
- Do you want your purchase history and other information sold to other companies?
- Will your credit card number be kept secret and secure?

Identifying Security Threats

E-Commerce

Security on the Internet relates primarily to data. When unauthorized persons access or sell data, damage can occur resulting in a loss of money, time, personal information, or privacy. Figure G-3 shows how security breaches can affect the integrity of a company's list of employees. Table G-1 relates each of the security threats discussed in this lesson to the e-commerce activities of Gandolf Foods, a fictional company that sells gourmet party foods online. Merilee asks you to explore the security risks associated with the damage, loss, and unauthorized use of data.

Details

► Damage to Data

Companies and individuals depend on the integrity—or truth—of the data that they access from the Internet. For example, a customer will make a purchasing decision based on the price shown on a Web page. If this price has been altered because of a security breach, the online company could risk losing money, the customer, or both. Damage to data can occur from viruses, vandalism, and technical breakdown.

- **Viruses:** Some viruses can wipe out or seriously damage computer systems. When viruses are transmitted over the Internet—often as attachments to e-mail messages—one infected computer can quickly infect thousands more computers.
- **Vandalism:** Vandalism on the Internet usually takes the form of modifying or erasing data. For example, a company could access its Web site one morning to find a competitor's address in place of its own. Another form of vandalism occurs when an individual attempts to crash computers and servers by sending huge files or thousands of messages to the same e-mail address at once.
- **Technical Breakdown:** All computers are at risk from power surges, physical threats such as floods, tornadoes, and hurricanes, and damage caused by faulty software.

► Loss of Data

Loss or unauthorized use of data can be attributed to three causes: theft, fraud, and human error.

- **Theft:** Consumers worry that their credit card number could be stolen on its way across the Internet, particularly if they send it in unscrambled form. From a company's point of view, the theft of confidential information such as product specifications and employee data could have a devastating effect on the company's ability to serve its customers.
- **Fraud:** Fraud occurs when a customer uses a stolen credit card, or a company takes a customer's money without delivering the promised goods or services.
- **Human Error:** Data can disappear from a computer system if an operator mistakenly deletes it or fails to make backup copies to replace files that might become corrupted because of software errors.

► Unauthorized Use of Data

Two issues related to unauthorized use of data are privacy violations and copyright infringement.

- **Privacy Violations:** Privacy relates to the unauthorized use of personal information. A company that sells a customer's personal information to marketers without informing the customer may be guilty of privacy violations.
- **Copyright Infringements:** The Web is a gold mine of information—ranging from printed materials to artwork to sound files to video files. However, all of the people who create these materials are not necessarily compensated. Frequently, copyright violations occur as a result of ignorance. The teen who downloads a sound file of the latest hip-hop hit that someone posted on a Web page may not realize that the band playing the music receives no financial compensation. Copyright issues may become increasingly complex as more and more information is distributed freely on the Internet. If consumers are able to download the latest hit song for free, are they likely to buy the entire CD?

FIGURE G-3: Data security issues

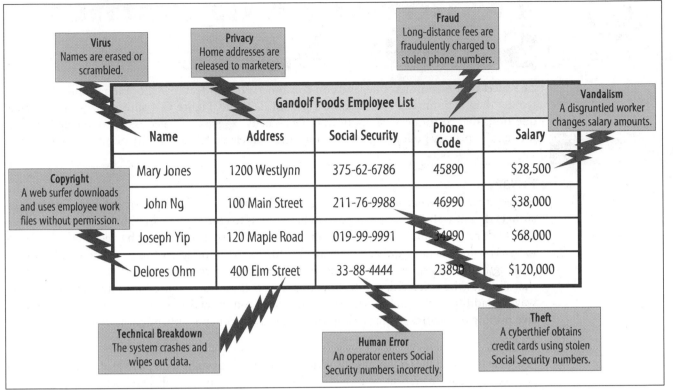

TABLE G-1: Implications of Security Risks

risk	e-commerce example
Damage to Data	
Viruses	Over one weekend, every e-mail acknowledgement that Gandolf sends carries a disk-eating virus.
Vandalism	Customers cannot access the Web site because thousands of messages from a disgruntled former employee jam Gandolf's server.
Technical breakdown	The Web server carrying Gandolf's Web site crashes with a denial of service to its customers, who can't access the site for several days during a holiday season—Gandolf's busiest period.
Loss of Data	
Theft	A competitor breaks into Gandolf's computer, steals proprietary information, creates similar products with almost identical names, then sells them at a lower price.
Fraud	A customer falsely claims not to have received an order for $500 worth of lobster tacos charged to a credit card. If Gandolf Foods can't prove the order was received, they must absorb the charge back.
Human error	An employee incorrectly inputs an order with the result that the customer who ordered the Cozy Romantic Dinner Deal receives the Football Party Pack.
Unauthorized Use of Data	
Privacy violations	A customer discovers that Gandolf Foods sold confidential information about her food and wine preferences to several companies that sell gourmet food and lifestyle products. As a result, the customer receives numerous catalogs and telemarketing phone calls.
Copyright infringement	A surfer downloads recipes published on Gandolf's Web site and publishes them in a cookbook without permission.

Exploring Consumer Security Issues

Details

The success of e-commerce depends on consumers. If they feel that shopping online is safe and secure, then e-commerce will become a part of daily life. Figure G-4 summarizes the principal questions that consumers ask about Internet security. Merilee asks you to help her write Medialoft's privacy policy by gathering information related to the security of online transactions.

► Privacy

Privacy relates to *what* information is gathered about an individual. For example, many consumers do not want just any company to have access to contact information such as their name, street address, e-mail address, and phone number. The issue of privacy has been around for as long as businesses have gathered consumer information to build customer profiles and compile mailing lists. The explosion in interest in Internet privacy relates to the *volume* of information that can now be collected, and to how this information may be used in potentially damaging ways. In addition, consumers are very concerned about how they may be affected by the extensive mining of personal information from databases made possible by computer technology.

► Cookies

A cookie is a small file containing information, such as your name and password, that is stored on your computer by a Web site you've visited. The next time you visit this Web site, the information is sent back to the site so the site recognizes you. Cookies can simplify your surfing activities by saving you the trouble of reentering identity information at a particular Web site. However, cookies might also be used to track your buying habits and how you navigate a Web site.

► E-mail

If you have an e-mail account, you've probably received unsolicited e-mail messages. Most of these messages will tell you that you can unsubscribe from the mailing list just by sending a reply. Unfortunately, by replying to these unsolicited e-mail messages, you inform the sender that your e-mail address is real—which could lead to the receipt of even more unsolicited e-mail messages. Most e-mail programs include features to block unsolicited e-mails.

► Surfing History

When you land on a Web site, the information about you that is transmitted to that site includes the URL of the Web site you just visited, the type of browser you use, the location of your ISP, and the language you speak. You can pay a service such as Anonymizer.com to act as a **proxy** that will intercept and encrypt or scramble all the data that a Web server sends to your computer, so that no one but you knows which sites you've visited.

► Confidentiality

Confidentiality relates to *how* the information about an individual is used. Consumers want to make sure that any information they provide is kept confidential, and for the use of only companies they've authorized. Another concern is that companies or organizations may use confidential information to make value judgments and decisions that affect people's lives. Figure G-5 describes medical information brokering, which many people are anxious to prevent by legislation.

► Children

Parents can install products such as NetNanny and Child Block to prevent access to Web sites containing inappropriate content, while security companies might soon develop technology to monitor incoming e-mails or other forms of contact.

► Cyber Revenge

Individuals can easily modify photographs and data to create damaging personal images and misinformation. Legislation is pending to address this new crime.

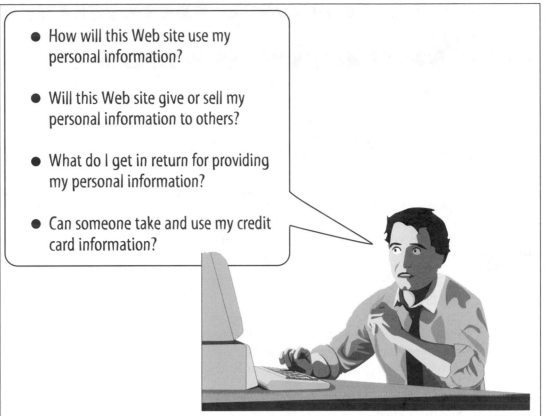

- How will this Web site use my personal information?

- Will this Web site give or sell my personal information to others?

- What do I get in return for providing my personal information?

- Can someone take and use my credit card information?

FIGURE G-5: Medical information brokering

A potential employer buys your surfing history. They find out that you've checked out Web sites on Repetitive Strain Injury (RSI), purchased therapeutic wrist braces, and joined an online support group for sufferers of Carpal Tunnel Syndrome, a condition that can affect your ability to use a keyboard efficiently for long periods of time.

Can an employer refuse to hire you because your preexisting condition could:
1. Make you unsuitable or unable to work long hours at a keyboard?
2. Make the employer vulnerable to a lawsuit if your condition worsens on the job?

E-Commerce

Exploring Business Security Issues

Very few real-world businesses would leave their premises unlocked or ask a stranger off the street to come on into the back office and shred company records. The same attention to security that a company pays to its real-world premises must be paid to its online premises. The difference between an online thief and a real-world crook is that access to goods and data is gained via electronic means, rather than with a crowbar or picklock. In addition to safeguarding its data, a company must ensure its customers feel completely confident that adequate security measures are in place to protect personal and financial information from unauthorized use.

Before MediaLoft commits significant funds to protect its e-commerce site, management wants a risk analysis. Merilee asks you to help her prepare the analysis by listing key questions related to security, and then by identifying specific security flaws that she will need to address when developing a security plan.

► Security Questions

Before a business can implement effective security precautions and procedures, it must identify its needs. Figure G-6 lists several key questions that an online business should ask when analyzing current and expected levels of risk. The process of answering these questions leads to the development of systems and procedures designed to prevent security breaches, and to fix them when they occur.

► Security Flaws

Security flaws result from vulnerabilities that the system administrator needs to identify and eliminate. Table G-2 describes some of the most common security flaws.

TABLE G-2: Common security flaws

security flaw	description
Accidental damage	Suppose an employee working on the company Web site copies data from a floppy disk or from an e-mail infected with a virus. The resulting damage, because the employee did not first scan the disk for viruses, is compounded if the employee does not report the error. The virus could then be spread through active content embedded in the company's Web site.
User identification	Company employees—particularly those who work on the company Web site—might use predictable passwords that anyone can guess. The intuitive vandal can then access the company's Web site, and modify its content in unexpected ways.
Global file sharing	One of the great things about the Internet is that it allows an employee working from a ski chalet in the Swiss Alps to upload files directly to his company's network in Dublin. However, if the file sharing system is not set up correctly, critical files could be accidentally exposed to unauthorized users.
Software	Software used to run Web servers is highly complex, which means that bugs are almost unavoidable. These bugs can lead to security holes that system administrators need to recognize and then fix. Sometimes these holes do not get fixed simply because of time constraints.
Active content	As you learned in a previous unit, some Web sites contain active content—small programs that run within a Web page. When you open a Web page containing active content that downloads automatically, harmful viruses embedded in the active content might invade your computer. Most browsers are set to disable active content that is not authenticated with a digital certificate.
CGI programs	CGI programs are often used to collect data such as customer contact information, and then to transfer the data to the Web server for processing. Some CGI programs are not adequately secured, and creative vandals can often infiltrate a program to change Web page content, or even to steal credit card numbers that have not been encrypted.

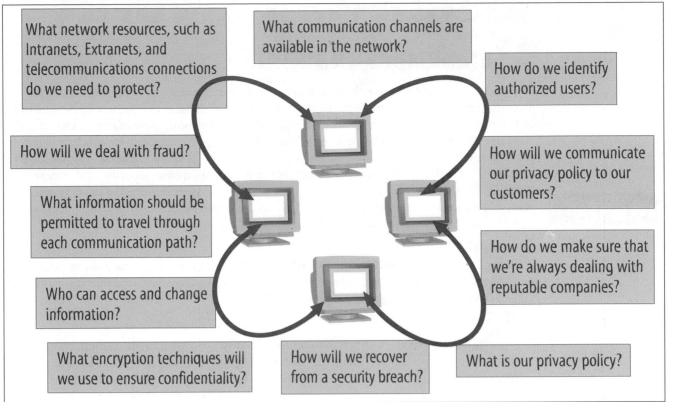

What network resources, such as Intranets, Extranets, and telecommunications connections do we need to protect?

What communication channels are available in the network?

How do we identify authorized users?

How will we deal with fraud?

How will we communicate our privacy policy to our customers?

What information should be permitted to travel through each communication path?

How do we make sure that we're always dealing with reputable companies?

Who can access and change information?

What encryption techniques will we use to ensure confidentiality?

How will we recover from a security breach?

What is our privacy policy?

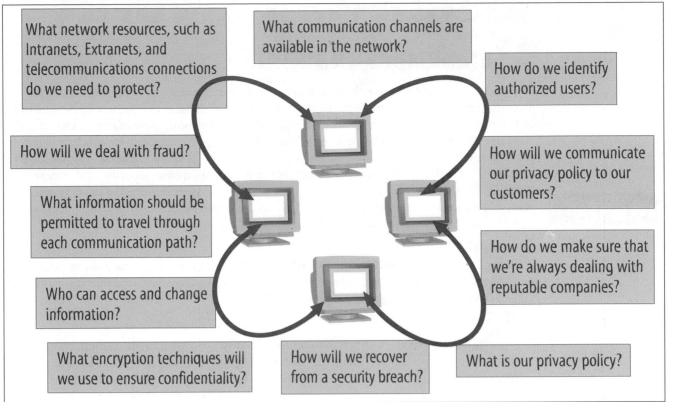

In The Know

Hacking and Cracking

The words hacker and cracker are often used interchangeably to refer to people who gain unauthorized entry to computer systems. The distinction is that a **hacker** enjoys the challenge of breaching seemingly watertight security systems, while a **cracker** seeks to damage, steal, or modify data. From a company's point of view, *any* unauthorized access to information must be prevented. Many security companies deliberately recruit "ethical hackers" to help identify security risks. If a hacker can breach the security system, then the company can take steps to prevent similar breaches.

E-Commerce

Identifying Security Procedures

Companies that use their computers to access the Internet and process orders must develop security procedures to prevent unauthorized access to their systems, to protect data transmitted over the Internet from loss or damage, and to safeguard customer information from unauthorized use. A company also must use the available technology to keep its system safe before competitors and others use that same technology to gain unlawful access. ✐ Merilee needs to develop a comprehensive security plan that will maintain the security and integrity of MediaLoft's Web site. She asks you to help her identify the steps required to develop a security plan, and to determine what measures she can take to protect against specific threats.

Details

▶ Security Plan

A security plan—also called a security policy—grows and changes as new risks are identified, and old risks are removed by the development of new technology. Six steps that companies can take to develop a security plan are described below.

1. Erect Firewalls

Many organizations erect a **firewall** to protect a network or even a single computer from unauthorized intrusions. The firewall itself can be a computer, a router, or another kind of communications device. A company that erects a firewall between its network and the Internet usually allows authorized persons such as employees to send and receive e-mail and to visit Web pages, but does not allow access to outside users. A firewall is often used to safeguard a company's Intranet from unauthorized users. Figure G-7 shows a diagram of a network system connected to the Internet. Note the presence of firewalls to protect company networks.

2. Employ Encryption Methods

Encryption is the process of scrambling information into an unreadable form. Companies can safeguard information outsiders should not see by encrypting that data before transmitting it over the Internet.

3. Issue and Monitor Passwords

Companies can establish procedures for developing a password system that cannot be easily violated by outsiders.

4. Develop Access Control Lists

The **Access Control List (ACL)** specifies which users are allowed to access which data to perform which functions.

5. Obtain Digital Certificates

A digital certificate verifies the identity of the company or individual that created the Web site and is responsible for its content.

6. Monitor Active Content

Companies can ensure that any active content downloaded from Web sites comes from trusted sources.

▶ Prevention

Table G-3 describes some ways to guard against common security risks.

▶ Disaster Recovery Plan

A disaster recovery plan must be a part of an online company's security strategy. Questions that will help a company develop a workable plan include: How long can we afford to be without our Web site before we start sustaining serious financial losses? How will we respond if unauthorized modifications to our Web site result in angry or confused customers? What will we do if confidential company information is leaked to our competitors?

FIGURE G-7: Virtual Private Network (VPN) diagram showing Internet security systems

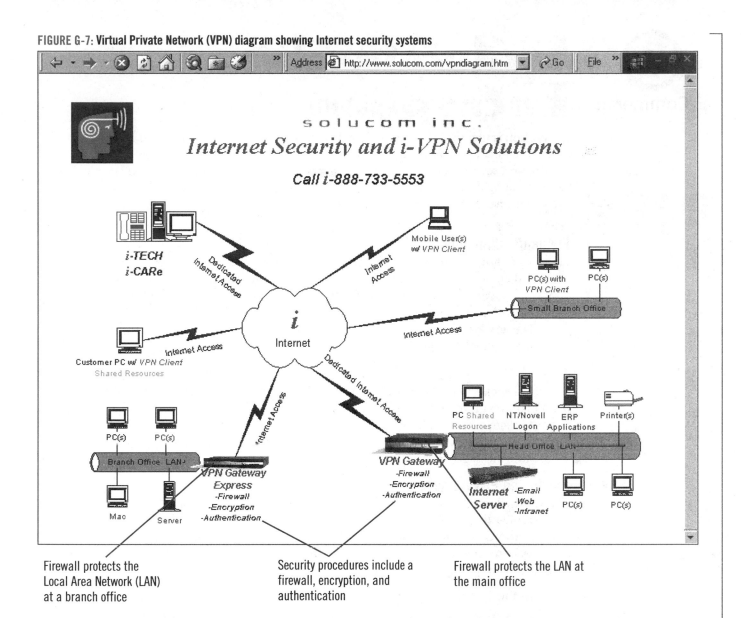

Firewall protects the Local Area Network (LAN) at a branch office

Security procedures include a firewall, encryption, and authentication

Firewall protects the LAN at the main office

TABLE G-3: Prevention Methods

threat	sample preventative measures
Active content	Allow active content to run only if it is verified by digital certificates that identify its creator. Note that a browser can be set to download only active content that meets certain security specifications, such as the presence of a digital certificate from a trusted source.
Attempts to crash systems	Use security software to turn off connections to suspicious sources.
Copyright	Use software to embed digital watermarks into images so that they cannot be copied, and use document security services to lock files that contain information that's offered for sale over the Internet.
Credit card theft	Use encryption technologies to scramble credit card numbers in transit.
Technical breakdowns	Implement a system to regularly back up data, store back up tapes offsite, and use multiple servers in different locales.
Unauthorized modification of data	Use firewalls to prevent unauthorized access.
Viruses	Install antivirus software to monitor the contents of e-mails, attachments, and downloaded files. Conscientiously keep virus-checking activities and software up-to-date to catch new viruses as they appear.

Understanding Encryption

Encryption is the process of scrambling data into a secret code that can be broken only by complicated mathematical algorithms. To date, encryption is still the safest method used to transmit information securely over the Internet. Merilee needs to learn how encryption works because the MediaLoft e-commerce site will be set up to handle credit card payments. She asks you to summarize the elements of an encryption system.

► Elements of an Encryption System

Figure G-8 shows the four elements that make up an encryption system: the plain text, a cipher, a key, and cipher text. This simple example of encryption is known as a substitution cipher, or Caesar cipher, because its earliest known use was by Julius Caesar. The **plain text** message "Meet me at 2 p.m." is encrypted using a **cipher** that will add a specific number of characters to each letter. The **key** is the exact number of letters that will be added. Because the key is 3, the resulting **cipher text** is *phhw ph dw 5 sp.*

► Keys

An effective encryption method requires two keys—one key is used to encrypt the message from plain text into cipher text, and another key is used to decrypt the message from cipher text into plain text. An additional layer of security is added when the key used to encrypt the message produces different cipher text every time it is applied—even when applied to the exact same message.

► Public and Private Keys

The key used to encrypt a message is called the **public** key. The key used to decrypt the message is called the **private** key. Because two different keys are used, the encryption system is referred to as **asymmetric encryption**. You also will see the term public-key encryption used. When both keys are the same, the system is referred to as **symmetrical encryption, private key encryption**, or **single-key encryption**.

► Keys on the Internet

Public-key encryption is usually used to secure small amounts of data, such as credit card numbers, because the procedure requires a relatively long processing time. Figure G-9 illustrates how public-key encryption works to ensure the privacy of a transaction. Private-key encryption—where the same key encrypts and then decrypts the message—is used to transfer long messages and files between two trusted sources.

► Using Keys

Only the holder of the private key can decode the message. The computer system keeps private keys secret, while public keys are widely available. Incoming messages are secure when the computer system controls the distribution of private keys. The complicated mathematical algorithms used to encrypt data mean that someone who just has access to the public key would not be able to figure out the private key required to decrypt the message—or at least not without considerable computing effort.

e-byte

"According to RSA Data Security, it would take a hacker a trillion × a trillion years to break a 128-bit encryption using current technology."
Source: VeriSign.com[1]

► Pretty Good Privacy

One of the most popular public-key systems is Pretty Good Privacy (PGP), a software program developed by Philip Zimmerman for encrypting messages. With PGP, you distribute a public key to all the people from whom you want to receive messages. These people then use this public key to encrypt their messages. When you receive an encrypted message back, you use a private key, known only to you, to decrypt the message. A **unique private key** is generated from a public key only once, used by the recipient only for a specific transaction, and then discarded.

FIGURE G-8: Simple encryption example

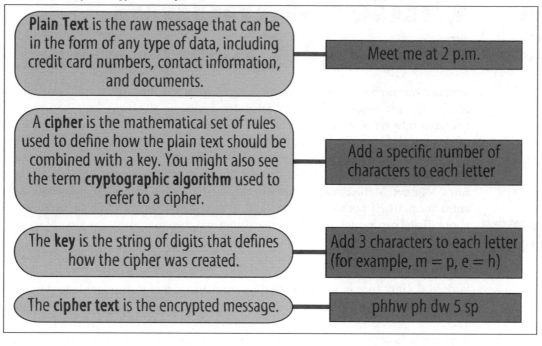

Plain Text is the raw message that can be in the form of any type of data, including credit card numbers, contact information, and documents.

> Meet me at 2 p.m.

A **cipher** is the mathematical set of rules used to define how the plain text should be combined with a key. You might also see the term **cryptographic algorithm** used to refer to a cipher.

> Add a specific number of characters to each letter

The **key** is the string of digits that defines how the cipher was created.

> Add 3 characters to each letter (for example, m = p, e = h)

The **cipher text** is the encrypted message.

> phhw ph dw 5 sp

FIGURE G-9: Public key encryption used to ensure privacy

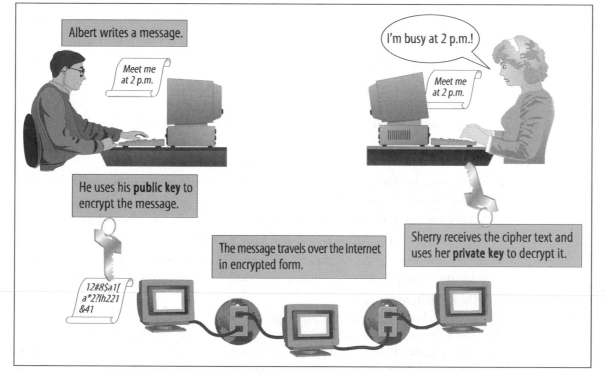

In The Know

Encryption Levels

Both 40-bit and 128-bit encryption is used. The number of bits relates to the number of possible keys available to unlock the cipher used to encrypt the message. For example, several billion possible keys are available to decrypt a 40-bit encryption, while 300 billion trillion times as many keys are available to decrypt a 128-bit encryption.

Understanding Digital Certificates

Suppose you need to know that the person receiving your message is really the person who should receive the message—and not an imposter. Figure G-10 shows how you can use public key encryption to verify someone's identity. This process is called **authentication**. For small amounts of data, such as credit card numbers, public key encryption works fine. However, using this method to scramble long messages puts a considerable strain on computer resources. Two tools have been developed to facilitate the identification process: digital certificates and digital signatures. Merilee realizes that MediaLoft will need to obtain a digital certificate so that it can authenticate itself both to suppliers and to customers. She asks you to summarize information about digital certificates and digital signatures, and then to find out how to obtain and use them.

Details

▶ **Digital Signatures**

A **digital signature** is an authentication mechanism that is impossible to duplicate or forge. In fact, a digital signature is actually a digest of text that is encrypted and then sent along with a text message. A **digest** is a single string of numbers that is created with a formula called a **one-way hash function**. When you use a private key to encrypt a digest, you create a digital signature. You create a digital signature when you want to ensure that a message or document originated with the person who signed it, and that the message was not changed during transit.

▶ **Using a Digital Signature**

Figure G-11 shows how digital signatures authenticate both the sender and the recipient of a message. Following are the steps that match the figure:

1. Frank creates a text message that tells Sherry where they will meet.

2. Frank uses a hash function to create a digest of the message—a string of numbers.

3. Frank uses his private key to encrypt just the digest. This process produces a digital signature.

4. Frank uses the public key both he and Sherry can access to encrypt *both* the original message and the digital signature.

5. Frank sends the message over the Internet.

6. Sherry receives the message, and then uses her private key to decrypt the text message and extract the encrypted digital signature.

7. Sherry uses her public key to decrypt the digital signature and extract its digest.

8. Sherry also extracts the message digest from the text.

9. Sherry compares the digest extracted from the digital signature to the digest of the text message. If the digests match, then Sherry knows for certain that the message came from Frank.

▶ **Digital Certificates**

Digital signatures verify that a message originated with a specific individual and was not changed in transit. However, digital signatures do not ensure that the person with whom the message originated is the *right* person. A **digital certificate** is needed to verify that the sender of a message is who he or she claims to be. Digital certificates also provide the person who receives the message with the public key required to encrypt a reply. Note terms such as Web certificate and Digital ID also are used to refer to digital certificates. Digital certificates are available for a variety of purposes. For example, a Web server would obtain a server certificate to verify its identity to the computers that it hosts. Wireless server certificates are also available.

▶ **Certificate Authority**

A **Certificate Authority (CA)** is the trusted third party that issues digital certificates to companies and individuals. One of the largest CAs is Entrust. Check the In The Know to learn about the information included in a digital certificate issued by a CA.

FIGURE G-10: Public key encryption used to authenticate a user's identity

FIGURE G-11: Using a digital signature

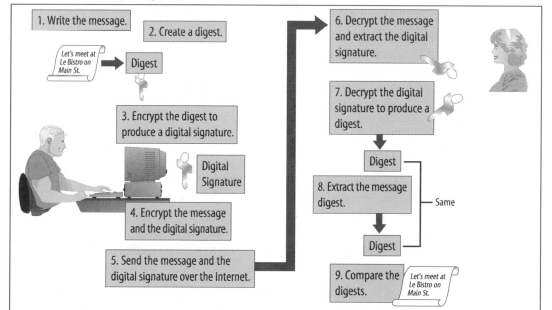

In The Know

Information Required for a Digital Certificate

A certificate typically includes a variety of information pertaining to its owner and to the **Certificate Authority** (CA) that issued it, including:

- the name of the holder and other identification information required to uniquely identify the holder, such as the URL of the Web server using the certificate, or an individual's email address;
- the holder's public key which can be used to encrypt sensitive information for the certificate holder;
- the name of the CA that issued the certificate;
- a serial number; and
- the validity period (or lifetime) of the certificate (a start and an end date).

In creating the certificate, this information is digitally signed by the issuing CA. The CA's signature on the certificate is like a tamper-detection seal on a bottle of pills—any tampering with the contents is easily detected.

Source: Copyright Entrust Technologies, Inc. Reprinted with permission.[2]

Defining SSL and SET Technologies

SSL, which stands for **Secure Socket Layer**, is the principal technology used to transmit encrypted data from computer to computer over the Internet. Another technology being developed is SET, which stands for **Secure Electronic Transaction**. E-commerce Web sites frequently include statements such as "Your order is encrypted using SSL technology" or "Your order is handled on our secure server" to reassure customers that their transactions are being securely transferred. Merilee is confident that MediaLoft will process orders through a secure server. She asks you to further define SSL, learn about the new SET technology, and summarize the ordering process from a security point of view.

Details

▶ **Secure Sockets Layer**

SSL was developed by Netscape in order to send documents securely over the Internet. SSL uses a private key to encrypt data that is then transmitted over the SSL connection. You can use SSL to send documents securely from Web sites viewed in either Netscape or Internet Explorer.

▶ **Consumer Needs**

When customers land on a Web site and start shopping, they want to be sure that the data they send is strongly encrypted, and that they are dealing with the company they think they are dealing with—and not an imposter. The SSL protocol ensures that the data is encrypted and, as you learned in a previous lesson, digital certificates are used to verify the identity of the Web site owner.

▶ **SSL Evidence**

You can easily check whether the Web site you've landed on will securely transmit any data you enter. First, you will see that the "http" in the URL has changed to "https" to signify that the SSL protocol is being used to encrypt any information that is entered and then sent from the secure page. Second, a security symbol will appear on the status bar. In Internet Explorer and later versions of Netscape Navigator, this symbol appears as a closed lock. You can double-click this symbol to view the digital certificate that has been attached to the Web site, and verify its identity. Figure G-12 shows a secure Web page and its digital certificate.

▶ **SSL Process**

Figure G-13 shows the procedures required to secure a transaction using the SSL protocol. You can summarize the SSL process by stating that it allows the consumer to verify the identity of a vendor, and then to transmit confidential information such as credit card information in a secure, encrypted format.

▶ **SET**

The SET protocol goes one step further than SSL and verifies the identity of the consumer. As a result, use of the SET protocol helps to protect the merchant from fraud, which some analysts maintain is a greater risk than any faced by the consumer regarding credit card information stolen while in transit over the Internet. SET was developed by Visa and MasterCard specifically to ensure the security of Internet credit card transactions. SET uses digital certificates to identify both the buyer and the seller, and then encrypts the information before sending it over the Internet. The credit card number is transferred directly to the credit card issuer where the purchase amount is verified, and the customer's credit card account is billed. The merchant never sees the credit card number.

FIGURE G-12: Viewing a secure Web page

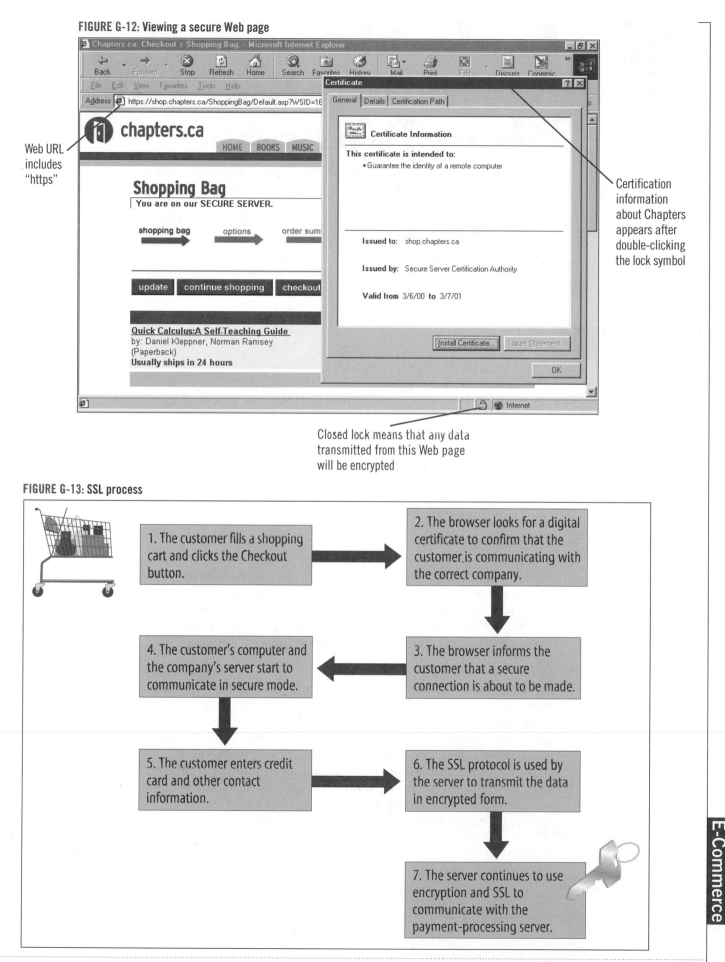

Web URL includes "https"

Certification information about Chapters appears after double-clicking the lock symbol

Closed lock means that any data transmitted from this Web page will be encrypted

FIGURE G-13: SSL process

1. The customer fills a shopping cart and clicks the Checkout button.

2. The browser looks for a digital certificate to confirm that the customer is communicating with the correct company.

3. The browser informs the customer that a secure connection is about to be made.

4. The customer's computer and the company's server start to communicate in secure mode.

5. The customer enters credit card and other contact information.

6. The SSL protocol is used by the server to transmit the data in encrypted form.

7. The server continues to use encryption and SSL to communicate with the payment-processing server.

Exploring Authentication and Identification

A crucial part of any security system is knowing who is doing what, and whether they are supposed to do what they are doing. When individuals can buy just about any product from just about anywhere in the world from companies they may never deal with again, any integrity that may have arisen as a result of personal interaction no longer exists. In this lesson, you will look at how users of a system (or customers to an online store) can be identified and authenticated.

As a network manager, Merilee is familiar with the use of passwords to authenticate users. She is now interested in investigating other authentication methods, including new trends toward the use of biometrics. She asks you to help her compile a descriptive list of the most popular methods used to identify and authenticate users.

Details

► Passwords

One of the most common ways in which individuals are identified is through the use of passwords. The use of passwords as an identification method can be problematical, primarily because many people use the same password for all their online accounts. To make matters worse, the password used is very often a word that just about any mildly creative thief could guess. Popular choices for passwords include a first or middle name, a spouse's name, a child's name, a pet's name, or a birthdate. One of the first—and easiest—precautions that consumers can take to protect themselves is to choose a hard-to-guess password, as described in Figure G-14 on the National Institute of Health's Web site.

► Access Control List

An **Access Control List (ACL)** contains the names of individuals who are permitted to access and or/modify specific information. Some people on the list may be authorized to view just content, while other individuals may have the passwords and authorization required to actually modify content in specific areas. A company needs to create a comprehensive ACL that clearly specifies which individuals are permitted to access and modify what kinds of data on the company's Web site, Intranet site, and Extranet site.

► Biometrics

The use of an individual's physical characteristics to identify him or her is called **biometrics**. Biometric methods include fingerprints, speech recognition, and eye scanning. Some analysts predict that the future of e-commerce security lies in the development of effective biometric techniques. Perhaps the day will come when computers and Personal Digital Assistants are equipped with eye scanners that unequivocally identify you, along with information about your current residence, your financial information, and how many calories you consumed at lunch. Figure G-15 defines biometrics, and describes how it might be used to verify identity. A company needs to calculate whether an investment in biometrics will yield significant benefits in terms of the money saved by eliminating or reducing fraud.

FIGURE G-14: Choosing a password

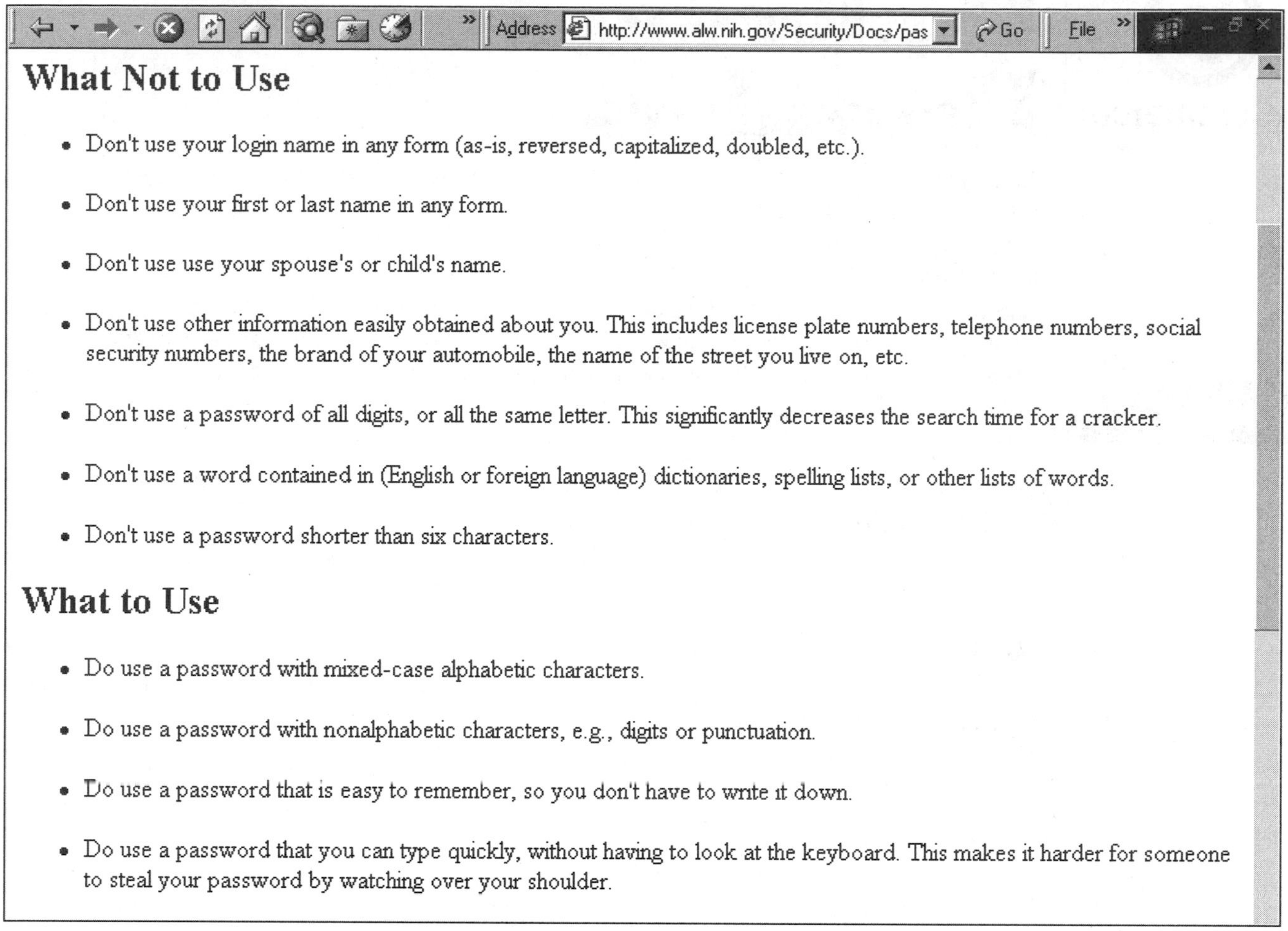

```
←  ·  →  ·  ⊗  ⟳  ⌂  ⊕  ▣  ✦  ⊛      »   Address  🔲 http://www.alw.nih.gov/Security/Docs/pas ▼  ⟳Go    File »   ▨ − ⬚ ✕
```

What Not to Use

- Don't use your login name in any form (as-is, reversed, capitalized, doubled, etc.).

- Don't use your first or last name in any form.

- Don't use use your spouse's or child's name.

- Don't use other information easily obtained about you. This includes license plate numbers, telephone numbers, social security numbers, the brand of your automobile, the name of the street you live on, etc.

- Don't use a password of all digits, or all the same letter. This significantly decreases the search time for a cracker.

- Don't use a word contained in (English or foreign language) dictionaries, spelling lists, or other lists of words.

- Don't use a password shorter than six characters.

What to Use

- Do use a password with mixed-case alphabetic characters.

- Do use a password with nonalphabetic characters, e.g., digits or punctuation.

- Do use a password that is easy to remember, so you don't have to write it down.

- Do use a password that you can type quickly, without having to look at the keyboard. This makes it harder for someone to steal your password by watching over your shoulder.

FIGURE G-15: Biometrics description

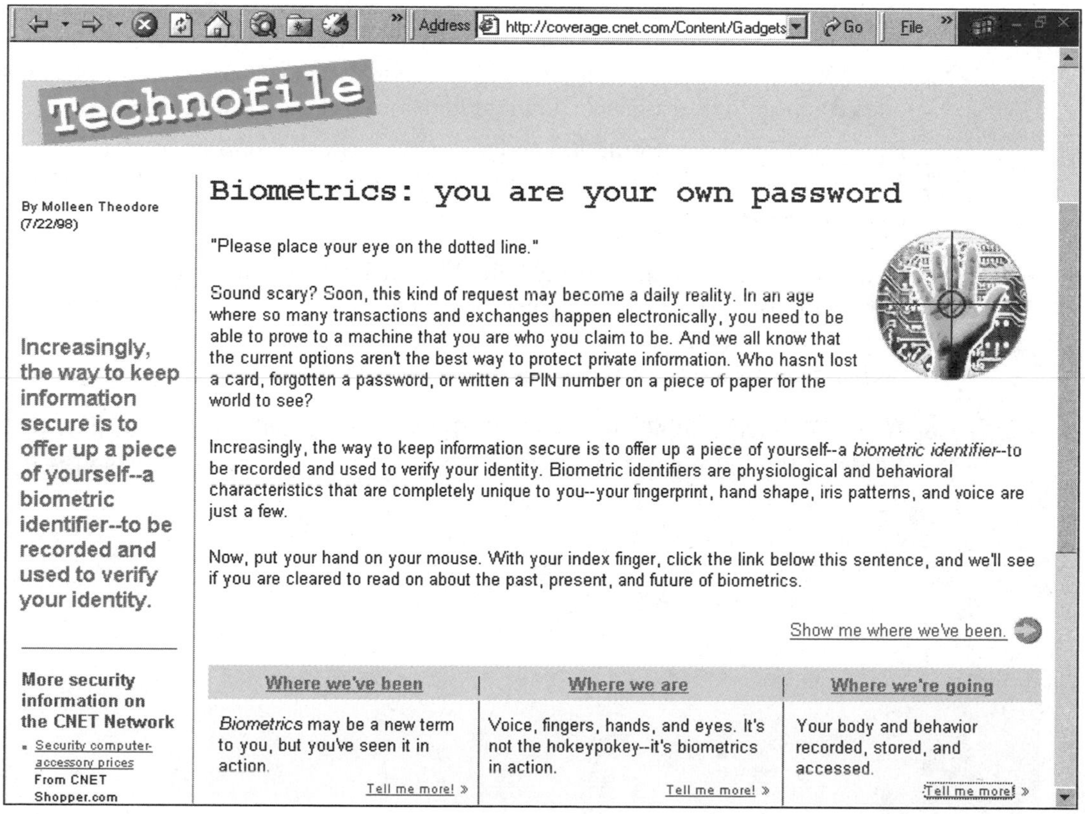

```
←  ·  →  ·  ⊗  ⟳  ⌂  ⊕  ▣  ✦  ⊛      »   Address  🔲 http://coverage.cnet.com/Content/Gadgets ▼  ⟳Go    File »   ▨ − ⬚ ✕
```

Technofile

Biometrics: you are your own password

By Molleen Theodore
(7/22/98)

"Please place your eye on the dotted line."

Sound scary? Soon, this kind of request may become a daily reality. In an age where so many transactions and exchanges happen electronically, you need to be able to prove to a machine that you are who you claim to be. And we all know that the current options aren't the best way to protect private information. Who hasn't lost a card, forgotten a password, or written a PIN number on a piece of paper for the world to see?

Increasingly, the way to keep information secure is to offer up a piece of yourself--a biometric identifier--to be recorded and used to verify your identity.

Increasingly, the way to keep information secure is to offer up a piece of yourself--a *biometric identifier*--to be recorded and used to verify your identity. Biometric identifiers are physiological and behavioral characteristics that are completely unique to you--your fingerprint, hand shape, iris patterns, and voice are just a few.

Now, put your hand on your mouse. With your index finger, click the link below this sentence, and we'll see if you are cleared to read on about the past, present, and future of biometrics.

Show me where we've been. ➤

More security information on the CNET Network

- Security computer accessory prices
  From CNET Shopper.com

Where we've been	Where we are	Where we're going
Biometrics may be a new term to you, but you've seen it in action.	Voice, fingers, hands, and eyes. It's not the hokeypokey--it's biometrics in action.	Your body and behavior recorded, stored, and accessed.
Tell me more! »	Tell me more! »	Tell me more! »

E-Commerce

Exploring Security Providers

A company that wants to ensure the security of its transactions will most likely need to hire an Internet security provider. Companies such as RSA Security and VeriSign provide the software applications, development kits, and services required to encrypt data, authenticate transactions, issue Web site and server digital certificates, and verify users. Figure G-16 shows two security packages available from VeriSign. ➤ Thanks to all the research you've done about e-commerce security technologies, Merilee realizes that she will need some assistance to develop effective security systems for MediaLoft. She asks you to investigate some of the products and services offered by security providers.

Steps

1. Open the Project File **ECG-01.doc** in your word-processing program, then save it as **Security Providers**

   The document contains the table that you will use to compare the products and services offered by two security service providers.

2. Open your Web browser, go to the Student Online Companion at *www.course.com/illustrated/ecommerce*, click the link for **Unit G**, then click the link for **Exploring Security Providers**

3. Select two sites from the list provided

4. Follow links to information about security services related to e-commerce, then answer the questions provided

   Your goal is to determine if the Web sites you've chosen provide you with enough information to make a relatively informed decision about the security package you'd need for a medium-sized online business. Study the Web sites critically. Ask yourself if the description of products and services would encourage you to do business with the sites. Base your analysis on factors such as the design and tone of the Web site, the amount of information provided, the "reader-friendliness" of the information, whether the information seems useful and up-to-date, and whether the services offered appear to be reasonable solutions for a medium-sized online business.

   Figure G-17 shows information about general security requirements on @stake's Web site. As you can see, the information is easy to understand and includes references to many of the technologies explained in this unit.

5. In the space provided, indicate which service you would choose

   Make sure you give reasons for your choice. For example, the Web site may include plenty of easy-to-understand information about its services, rather than pages of advertising hype, or perhaps the products offered appear to incorporate the latest technology.

6. When you have completed all the questions for each security service provider, type **Your Name** at the bottom of the document, save it, print a copy, then close the document

FIGURE G-16: Security packages from VeriSign

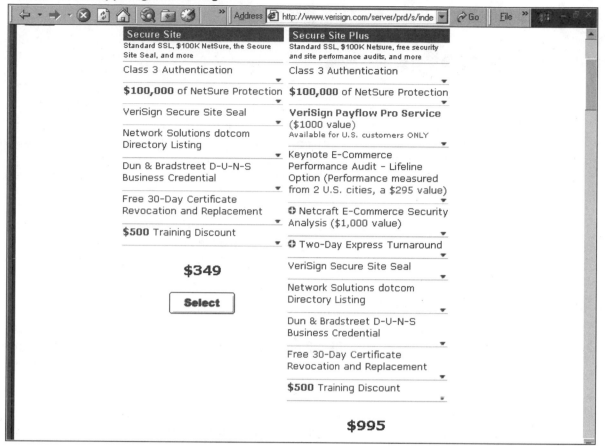

Secure Site	Secure Site Plus
Standard SSL, $100K NetSure, the Secure Site Seal, and more	Standard SSL, $100K Netsure, free security and site performance audits, and more
Class 3 Authentication	Class 3 Authentication
$100,000 of NetSure Protection	**$100,000** of NetSure Protection
VeriSign Secure Site Seal	**VeriSign Payflow Pro Service** ($1000 value) Available for U.S. customers ONLY
Network Solutions dotcom Directory Listing	Keynote E-Commerce Performance Audit – Lifeline Option (Performance measured from 2 U.S. cities, a $295 value)
Dun & Bradstreet D-U-N-S Business Credential	✪ Netcraft E-Commerce Security Analysis ($1,000 value)
Free 30-Day Certificate Revocation and Replacement	✪ Two-Day Express Turnaround
$500 Training Discount	VeriSign Secure Site Seal
	Network Solutions dotcom Directory Listing
$349	Dun & Bradstreet D-U-N-S Business Credential
Select	Free 30-Day Certificate Revocation and Replacement
	$500 Training Discount
	$995

FIGURE G-17: General security information provided by @stake

Address http://www.atstake.com/acrobat/architectu

Network Security

How secure is your network? Placing firewalls at the boundaries of your network helps protect against external attacks, but it won't protect you from internal threats - the most common form of attack. Security must be distributed to protect all elements of the network, and should extend from operating systems configurations to access control lists. Inadequate network security leads to unexpected downtime and lost time and money.

Application Security

Do you really know who is logging on to your system? Simple username and password combinations can be compromised, allowing attackers to access the system under the guise of someone you trust. Strong authentication mechanisms can be implemented to verify the identities of your users.

Once a user is logged in, how are they authorized to access content? Do you have a scalable, reliable way of controlling access to applications and data on your networks? As your business grows, access control lists can become cumbersome to manage and slow to process. The use of additional technologies and products can help ease this burden.

@stake can assist you in designing security mechanisms such as strong authentication and access controls for your systems and applications. Since the right approach depends on your environment, applications, and user-base, @stake will work with you to select and design a custom solution, aligned with your business goals.

Data Security

Is your data secured? Organizations are distributing information beyond traditional corporate walls to establish connections with suppliers, partners, and customers. These connections increase the risk associated with unauthorized data access. Strong encryption and digital signatures strengthen data security, both inside and outside the enterprise. We have the knowledge and experience to secure your data.

@stake   Securing the Internet Economy℠

125%   1 of 4   8.5 x 11 in

Exploring Privacy Policies

Customers want and need to be sure that the Web site from which they purchase products does not lose their credit card information, sell their personal information, or take their money fraudulently. To address these concerns, most online companies provide links to both a security policy and a privacy policy. The security policy describes the security systems in place. These systems could include use of the SSL protocol, 128-bit encryption, and digital certificates. As online transactions become more commonplace, some consumers might begin taking security precautions for granted. However, many consumers still have concerns about their personal information and how it will be used. A company's privacy policy tells consumers how the company will use any information collected about them. Figure G-18 shows the privacy policy page on the Barnes & Noble Web site. Here, the privacy policy is presented in the form of FAQs. These questions provide a good overview of the issues that privacy policies usually address. Figure G-19 provides information about how Nordstrom's Web site uses cookies. ⚓ Merilee has begun writing a privacy policy for MediaLoft. She asks you to check out the privacy policies included on the Web sites of three prominent online businesses so that she can explore the issues involved.

Steps

1. Open the Project File **ECG-02.doc** in your word-processing program, then save it as **Privacy Policies**
   The document contains a series of questions about privacy policies.

2. Open your Web browser, go to the Student Online Companion at *www.course.com/ illustrated/ecommerce*, click the link for **Unit G**, then click the link for **Exploring Privacy Policies**

3. Select three sites from the list provided

4. Go to one of the sites listed in the Student Online Companion for this lesson, then follow the links to its privacy policy

5. Enter the name and URL of the company you've chosen, then answer the questions provided
   Your goal is to determine what kind of information is included in the privacy policy. Then you will evaluate how the policy would help a consumer make an informed decision about the safety of providing personal information to the online business.

6. Repeat Steps 4 and 5 to gather information about the privacy policies at two more Web sites

7. When you have completed all the questions for each privacy policy, type **Your Name** at the bottom of the document, save it, print a copy, then close the document

FIGURE G-18: Privacy policy introduced as a series of questions

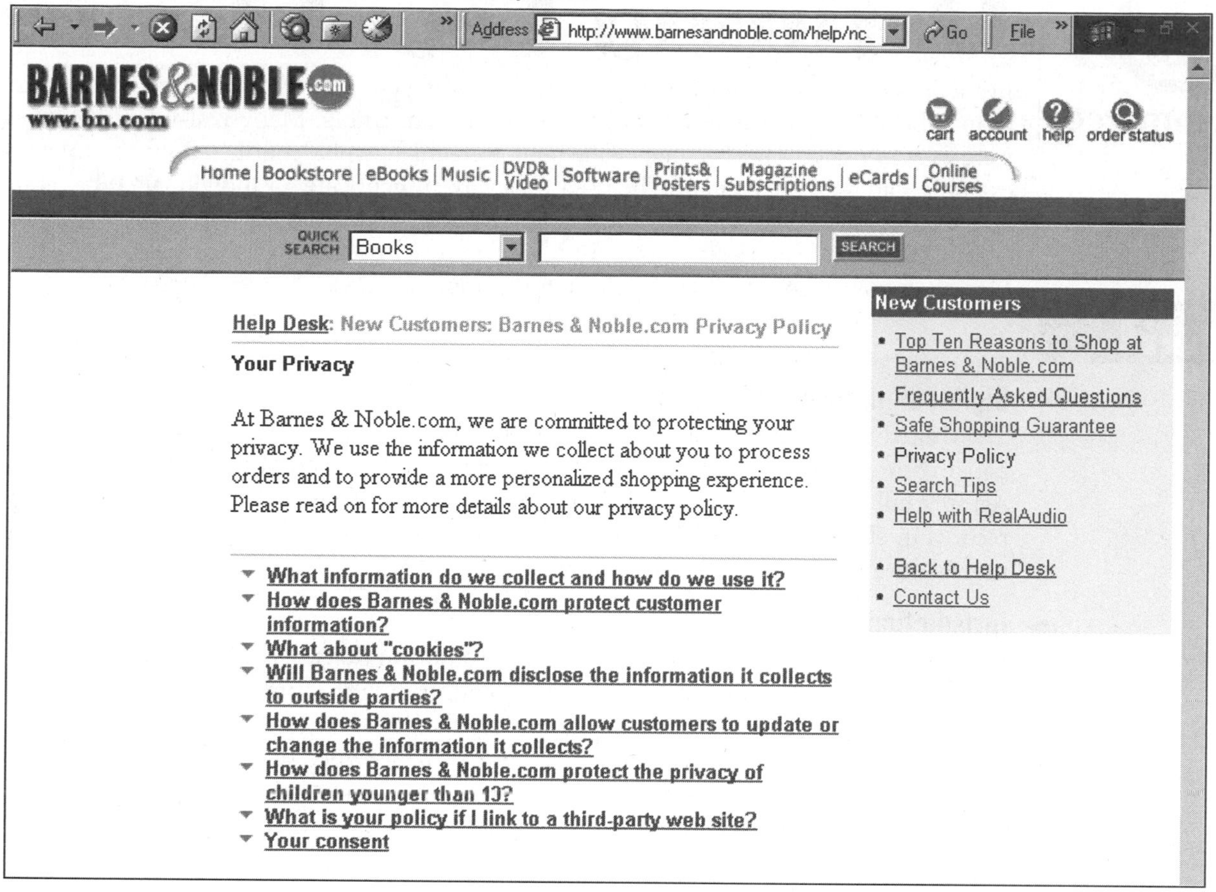

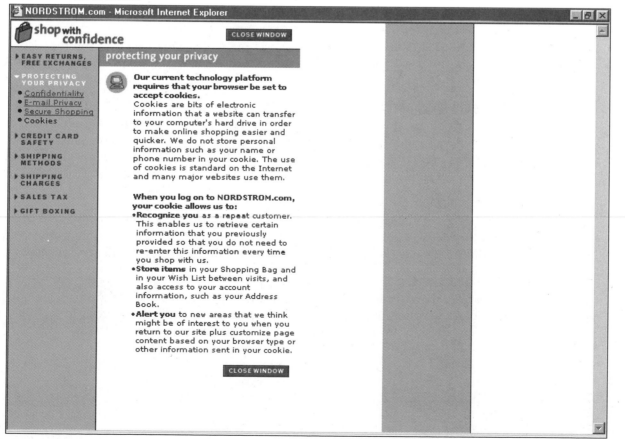

FIGURE G-19: Use of cookies

Unit G

E-Commerce

Defining Legal Issues

Just a decade ago, most of the legal issues surrounding e-commerce activities did not exist. The term cybersquatting was unknown, and cookies were edible. Many real-world activities that were easy to police have become challenging to regulate when conducted on the Internet. For example, can a digital signature be used to legally authenticate an individual? What copyright laws relate to online content? Who owns the rights to words that are also brand names or concepts? ◄▬▬▬ Merilee asks you to put together a brief overview of the major legal issues that MediaLoft may encounter as it develops its e-commerce services.

Details

► **Digital Signature Legislation**

The United States has passed legislation that grants electronic contracts the same legal status as paper contracts that include handwritten signatures. Called the Millennial Digital Commerce Act, the bill establishes a national standard for the legal validity of contracts, signatures, and records in electronic form. This law could help facilitate e-commerce by providing a cheaper, more secure alternative to paper documents.

► **Jurisdiction**

In the real world, a governing body can impose laws and exact penalties from people within its jurisdiction—usually a city, state, province, or country. On the Internet, the concept of jurisdiction can be problematical. For example, how can the government of Country A prosecute a citizen of Country B who creates a virus that destroys data owned by citizens in Country A, when Country B has no laws against cybercrime? From an e-commerce perspective, businesses, and consumers need guidelines relating to the feasibility of litigation and prosecution.

► **Privacy**

Privacy legislation relates to what kind of information transmitted over the Internet can—or should—be accessible to governing bodies, businesses, and other individuals. At least three Internet privacy issues relate to the future of e-commerce: how personal information is collected and used for marketing purposes, how businesses use e-mail to generate new business, and how the Web surfing habits of consumers are tracked and evaluated. Over the next several years, companies will need to pay close attention to how all of these activities are regulated, both in their home country and globally.

► **Intellectual Property**

Consumers can use the Internet to quickly and cheaply obtain copyrighted materials that can be easily digitized and then distributed online. These materials include books, music, and videos. Companies need to develop new business models that generate profit by providing consumers with convenient, inexpensive, and legal access to intellectual property.

► **Self-Regulation**

Some groups of e-tailers are attempting to head off government regulation of e-commerce and other Internet activities by setting up self-regulation policies. Figure G-20 shows the ten commandments included on the Web site sponsored by the Electronic Retailing Association.

► **Legal Questions**

Figure G-21 shows a page on the Law for Internet Web site that asks and answers common legal questions related to doing business over the Internet. Companies can refer to this and other Web sites to keep as up-to-date as possible on current and pending legislation.

FIGURE G-20: Self-regulation policies

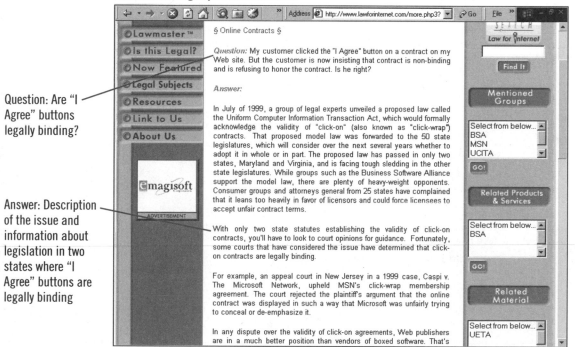

> retailing.org
>
> home   about ERA   savvy shopper   help   join now   privacy policy
>
> ## REGULATORY & CONSUMER INFORMATION>Commandments
>
> **Ten Commandments of Electronic Retailing**
>
> As a condition of membership, ERA members subscribe to the "Ten Commandments of Electronic Retailing":
>
> 1. Tell the truth, the whole truth, and nothing but the truth.
> 2. If you share factual information, make sure you can prove it.
> 3. If it's a commercial, call it a commercial.
> 4. You can compare your product to others, but don't disparage others.
> 5. Don't market to children.
> 6. Don't use indecency.
> 7. Use only bonafide experts and testimonials, and if you pay for them, say so.
> 8. Disclose all the costs associated with a purchase.
> 9. Let the consumer know everything they need to know about the product.
> 10. If you make a guarantee, make it clear and honor it.

FIGURE G-21: Legal questions answered

Question: Are "I Agree" buttons legally binding?

Answer: Description of the issue and information about legislation in two states where "I Agree" buttons are legally binding

> Lawmaster ™
> Is this Legal?
> Now Featured
> Legal Subjects
> Resources
> Link to Us
> About Us
>
> emagisoft
> ADVERTISEMENT
>
> § Online Contracts §
>
> *Question:* My customer clicked the "I Agree" button on a contract on my Web site. But the customer is now insisting that contract is non-binding and is refusing to honor the contract. Is he right?
>
> *Answer:*
>
> In July of 1999, a group of legal experts unveiled a proposed law called the Uniform Computer Information Transaction Act, which would formally acknowledge the validity of "click-on" (also known as "click-wrap") contracts. That proposed model law was forwarded to the 50 state legislatures, which will consider over the next several years whether to adopt it in whole or in part. The proposed law has passed in only two states, Maryland and Virginia, and is facing tough sledding in the other state legislatures. While groups such as the Business Software Alliance support the model law, there are plenty of heavy-weight opponents. Consumer groups and attorneys general from 25 states have complained that it leans too heavily in favor of licensors and could force licensees to accept unfair contract terms.
>
> With only two state statutes establishing the validity of click-on contracts, you'll have to look to court opinions for guidance. Fortunately, some courts that have considered the issue have determined that click-on contracts are legally binding.
>
> For example, an appeal court in New Jersey in a 1999 case, Caspi v. The Microsoft Network, upheld MSN's click-wrap membership agreement. The court rejected the plaintiff's argument that the online contract was displayed in such a way that Microsoft was unfairly trying to conceal or de-emphasize it.
>
> In any dispute over the validity of click-on agreements, Web publishers are in a much better position than vendors of boxed software. That's
>
> SEARCH
> Law for Internet
> Find It
> Mentioned Groups
> Select from below...
> BSA
> MSN
> UCITA
> GO!
> Related Products & Services
> Select from below...
> BSA
> GO!
> Related Material
> Select from below...
> UETA

Focus

Biometrics

As you learned in the lesson on identification and authentication, biometrics might be the technology used to positively identify users in the 21st Century. However, some controversy surrounds the use of biometric technology. For example, some people consider eye scanning intrusive, while others may not be willing to be fingerprinted. Figure G-22 shows a description of the various ways in which biometrics could be used to identify individuals in the electronic age. Read the descriptions, then answer the questions below.

FIGURE G-22: Biometric security methods

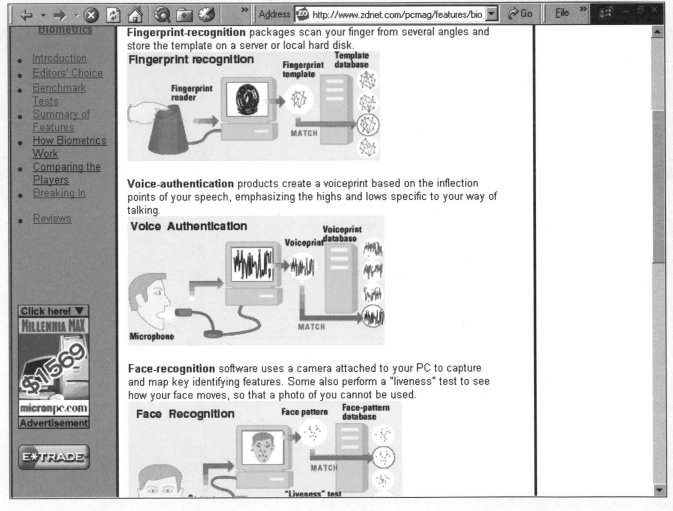

Explore Further...

To complete the following questions, you'll need to conduct some research about biometrics. First, start your Web browser, go to the Student Online Companion at *www.course.com/illustrated/ ecommerce*, then click the link to Focus. You will find links to articles related to biometrics. Spend some time following the links and scanning some of the articles. Your goal is to learn about the topics and familiarize yourself with some of the current controversies. Complete the following questions.

1. What objections do you think a person might have to biometric identification methods? For example, some people might feel that face-scanning equipment is not hygienic. Write a one-page paper that summarizes some of the objections that consumers could have. Include your opinion—either for or against—regarding the validity of these objections.

2. What are some security issues related to biometrics? Can electronic fingerprints or voice scans be stolen? Can someone use your electronic identity to hack into a secure area with the result that you are liable for any damages that occur? Write a one-page paper that describes some of the issues related to the security of biometric identification. You may need to conduct searches for recent articles that link biometrics to fraud or other cybercrimes.

3. Suppose you were a business interested in using biometric technology to identify and authenticate your employees. Follow links to find information about some of the biometrics products available, then write a one-page paper that presents some options. Include information about price and technology requirements. Do you think that using biometrics technology is currently viable?

4. Select one of the biometrics technologies such as face or voice recognition, then write a one-page paper describing the technology. Give reasons why you do—or don't—think the technology you chose will replace traditional identification methods.

► Review

1. Security on the Internet refers primarily to techniques used to store and transmit _____.

2. The _____ protocol used to transmit data over the Internet was not designed to be secure.

3. A _____ program can record information that passes through a computer (or router) on its way to a destination computer.

4. A security system must include procedures to identify individuals according to their _____ rights.

5. You ensure the _____ of information transmitted over the Internet by protecting it from unauthorized modification.

6. Attempts by individuals to crash computers and servers by sending hundreds of huge files to the same e-mail address at once is a form of _____.

7. Privacy relates to the unauthorized use of _____ information.

8. A _____ is a small file containing information, such as your name and a password, that is stored on your computer by a Web site you've visited.

9. _____ relates to *how* the information about an individual is used.

10. A _____ enjoys the challenge of breaching seemingly watertight systems, while a cracker seeks to damage, steal, or modify data.

11. A company that erects a _____ between its network and the Internet usually allows authorized persons such as employees to send and receive e-mail and to visit Web pages, but does not allow access to outside users.

12. _____ is the process of scrambling information into an unreadable form.

13. A _____ certificate verifies the identity of the company or individual who created the Web site and is responsible for its contents.

14. A _____ is the mathematical set of rules used to define how plain text should be combined with a key.

15. The key used to encrypt a message is called a _____ key.

16. When both keys are the same, the system is referred to as _____ encryption, or private key encryption.

17. One of the most popular public-key systems is Pretty _____ Privacy (PGP), a software developed by Philip Zimmerman for encrypting messages.

18. A digest is a single string of numbers that is created with a formula called a one-way _____ function.

19. Digital certificates also provide the person who receives the message with the _____ key required to encrypt a reply.

20. A Certificate _____ (CA) is the trusted third party that issues digital certificates to companies and individuals.

21. SET stands for Secure _____ Transaction.

22. SSL was developed by _____ in order to send documents securely over the Internet.

23. The 'http' in a URL changes to _____ to signify that the SSL protocol is being used to encrypt information that is entered and then sent from the secure page.

24. SET uses digital _____ to identify both the buyer and the seller, and then encrypts the information before sending it over the Internet.

25. An Access _____ List (ACL) contains the names of those individuals who are permitted to access and or/modify specific information.

26. A company's _____ policy tells consumers how any information collected about them will be used.

27. Companies need to develop new business _____ that generate profit by providing consumers with convenient, inexpensive, and legal access to intellectual property.

28. Some groups of e-tailers are setting up self-_____ policies to prevent undue government control over e-commerce.

► Independent Challenges

1. In this unit, you were introduced to a great deal of technical information, particularly in the lessons related to security technologies such as encryption, SSL, SET, and digital certificates. Much of the information was presented as simply as possible to give you an overview of the various technologies. The actual procedures involved are considerably more complicated. To help you develop a more comprehensive understanding of some of these technologies, you decide to explore some of the Web sites that provide in-depth information.

To complete this independent challenge:

a. Select one of the following technologies to focus on: Public Key Encryption, SSL, or Web Server Certificates.

b. Open a new document in your word-processing program, enter the name of the technology you've chosen, then save the document as *More Information on [Technology]*. Make sure you substitute the technology you've chosen (for example, Public Key Encryption) for "Technology."

c. Open your Web browser, go to the Student Online Companion at *www.course.com/illustrated/ecommerce*, click the link for Unit G, then click the link for Independent Challenge 1.

d. Search two or three of the sites listed in the Student Online Companion for Independent Challenge 1 to find more information about the technology you've selected. Note that much of the information will be very technical. Your goal is to confirm what you've already learned, and then to find additional information that broadens your understanding of the technology.

e. Write a one- or two-page summary of what you've learned about some of the definitions and procedures that were not covered in the related lesson.

f. Enter **Your Name** at the bottom of the document, save it, print a copy, then close the document.

2. Viruses are one of the major security threats, and affect every user with a computer. With frightening speed, a virus can leapfrog from computer to computer over the Internet, until millions of computers are infected, and system after system crashes. Companies and individuals both need to employ strict procedures to guard against virus invasions. You decide to check out the tools available for protecting your own computer against viruses.

To complete this independent challenge:

a. Open your Web browser, go to the Student Online Companion at *www.course.com/illustrated/ecommerce*, click the link for Unit G, then click the link for Independent Challenge 2.

b. Open the Project File ECG-03.doc in your word-processing program. This document contains a list of questions related to viruses and virus protection.

c. Save the document as *Virus Protection*.

d. Search the sites listed in the Student Online Companion for Independent Challenge 2 to find answers to the questions provided. Your goal is to learn as much as you can about viruses and how to protect your own computer from virus invasions.

e. Type **Your Name** at the bottom of the document, save it, print a copy, then close the document.

E-Commerce

3. Privacy on the Internet is likely to be a hot topic for several years to come as new technologies both for protecting privacy and for invading privacy are developed. Figure G-23 shows a Web site dedicated to bringing surfers up-to-date news about privacy issues related to the Internet.

FIGURE G-23: Internet privacy issues

Address http://www.cptech.org/privacy/

Privacy

Some Current Privacy Disputes

- Children's Privacy
  - The Child Online Protection Act (COPA)
    - EPIC's COPA Litigation Page.
    - June 22, 2000. Decision of the US Court of Appeals, Third Circuit striking down COPA.
    - June 22, 2000. ACLU statement on COPA.
  - The Childrens' Online Privacy Protection Act of 1998 (COPPA).
  - KidsPrivacy.org: A Parent's Guide to Online Privacy.
- US/ EU Settlement on Safe Harbor
  - June 9, 2000. U.S. Department of Commerce Draft Safe Harbor Privacy Principles.
  - The TransAtlantic Consumer Dialogue's Statements on Safe Harbor
    - March 30, 2000. TACD Statement on U.S. Department of Commerce Draft International Safe Harbor Privacy Principles and FAQs.
    - TACD Resolution On Safe Harbor Negotiations.
    - TACD Comments on the US Department of Commerce "Safe Harbor" Proposal.
    - TACD Safe Harbor Proposal and International Convention on Privacy Protection.
- The Clinton Administration's "Critical Infrastructure Protection" project.
  - January 22, 1999, President Clinton's annoucement of new program to combat cyber terrorism.
  - 1998, EPIC's Critical Infrastructure Protection and the Endangerment of Civil Liberties An Assessment of the President's Commission on Critical Infrastructure Protection (PCCIP).
- Intel's new CPU id
  - Junkbusters, Intel and the Processor Serial Number Rationale · Boycott FAQ Our assessment of the risks and benefits of the PSN
  - January 25, 1999, Ted Bridis, Associated Press, Intel Agrees To Change Its Chips.

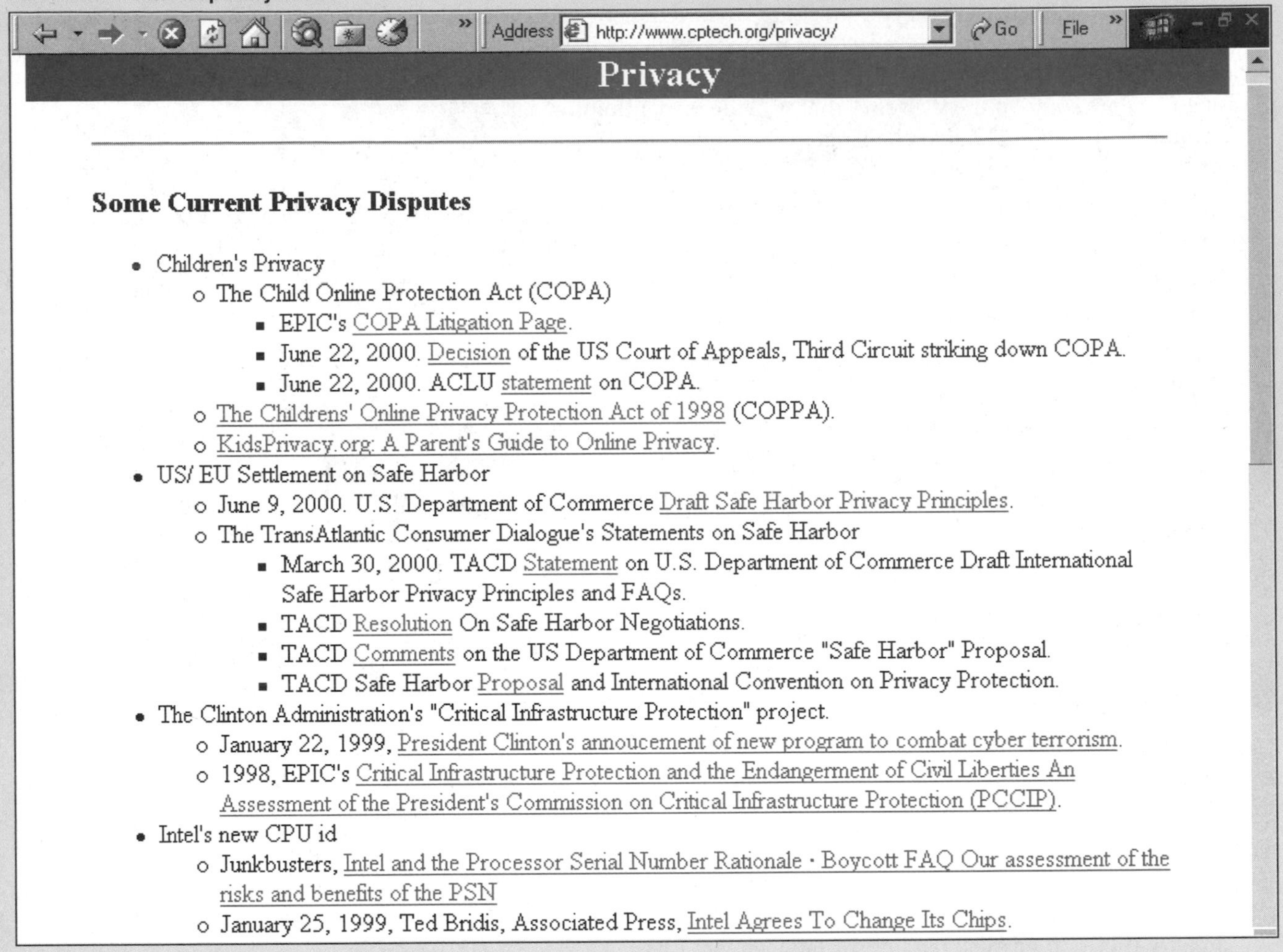

You decide to explore some Web sites that deal with privacy issues so you can develop an understanding of upcoming trends. To complete this independent challenge:

a. Open your Web browser, go to the Student Online Companion at *www.course.com/illustrated/ecommerce*, click the link for Unit G, then click the link to Independent Challenge 3.

b. Follow the link to a current list of articles related to Internet privacy issues, particularly articles that relate privacy issues to e-commerce activities.

c. Follow links to three articles.

d. Open a document in a word-processing program, and write two or three paragraphs that summarize each of the three articles you chose. Make sure you include the URL of the article, the name of the author, and the date it was written. Your goal is to determine some of the issues related to Internet privacy.

e. Write a paragraph or two that summarizes your own opinions about privacy on the Internet, based on information you learned from the articles. Your goal is to identify the principal issues as you see them, and then to determine what actions you think should be taken to protect the privacy of Web surfers.

f. Type **Your Name** at the bottom of the document, save it as *Current Privacy Issues*, print a copy, then close the document.

4. While some forms of security breaches are difficult to prevent, consumers can prevent the unauthorized collection of data by modifying settings on their browsers. Figure G-24 shows some of the Internet security options Internet Explorer 5 provides in its Internet Options dialog box. In this dialog box, which is accessible from the Tools menu, users can choose to disable cookies, specify how ActiveX content should be handled, set security levels, and block sites that conform to specific criteria.

FIGURE G-24: Security settings in Internet Explorer

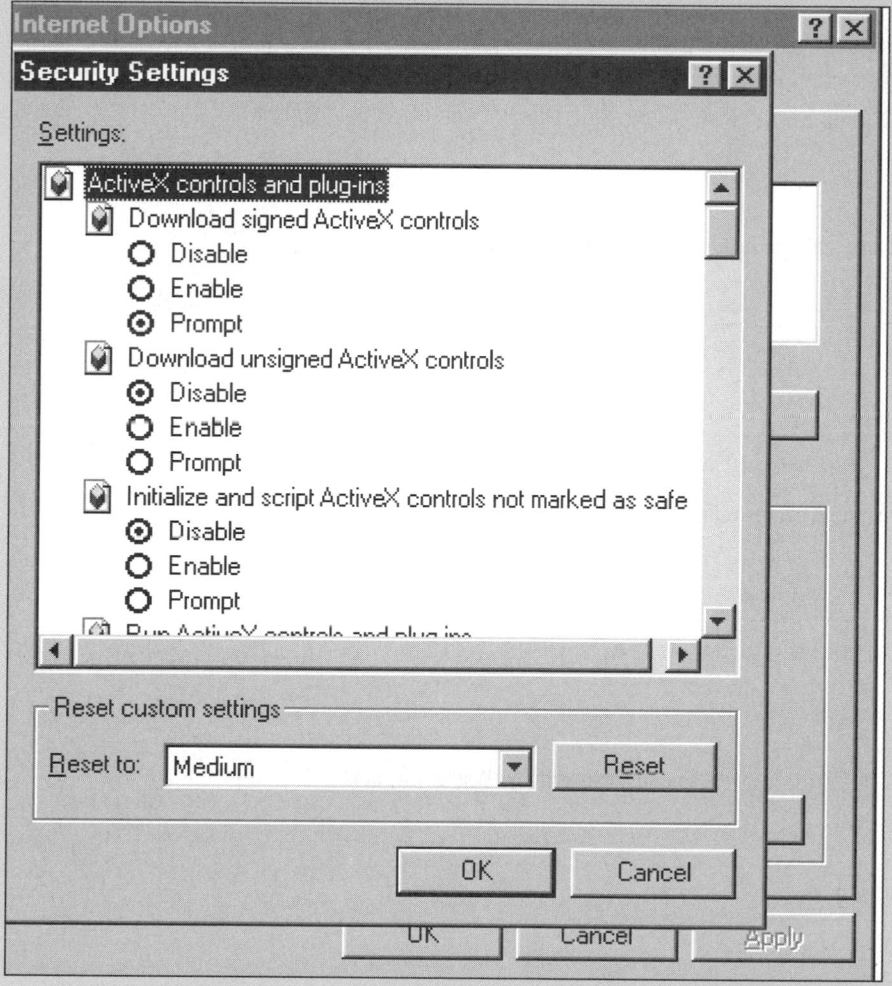

You decide to explore the security-related options that are available on the browser you use.
To complete this independent challenge:

a. Open the Project File ECG-04.doc in your word-processing program. This document contains a list of questions related to the security tools available on your browser.

b. Save the document as *Browser Security Settings*.

c. Explore the security settings on your browser to answer the questions provided. In Internet Explorer, select Internet Options from the Tools menu. In Netscape Navigator, select Security Info from the Tools option in the Communicator menu. (*Note:* Do not change any of the settings unless you are authorized to do so.)

d. Type **Your Name** at the bottom of the document, save it, print a copy, then close the document.

▶ Up to Date

As more and more Web surfers learn about cookies and how to disable them, their effectiveness may be diminished. However, the demise of cookies does not necessarily mean that tracking activities will stop. A technology often referred to as a Web bug is actually a 1-pixel gif (picture file) that is embedded in Web sites to help track a consumer's progress from Web site to Web site. For marketers, information about the Web surfing habits of a target market can be invaluable. You decide to investigate the latest information about Web bugs.

To complete this Up to Date challenge:

a. Open your Web browser, go to the Student Online Companion at *www.course.com/illustrated/ecommerce*, click the link for Unit G, then click the link to Up to Date.

b. Follow links to articles about Web bugs, then answer the questions below.

Current Date: ....

What exactly is a Web bug and how is it used to track Web surfers?

....

....

....

....

Summarize one or two recent events related to how Web bugs are being used.

....

....

....

Do you think that Web bugs pose a threat to consumer privacy? Why or why not?

....

....

....

....

▶ Visual Workshop

Every week, new articles related to Internet security appear. One week, cybersquatting might hit the news when some-one registers a celebrity's name as a domain name and then demands payment. Another week, a cracker might successfully vandalize a government Web site with predictably embarrassing results. In still another week, a brand new killer virus may crash computer systems around the world. Figure G-25 shows a selection of stories included on the zdnet.com Web site. As you can see, at least three stories directly relate to Internet security issues. Open your Web browser, go to the Student Online Companion at *www.course.com/illustrated/ecommerce*, click the link for Unit G, then click the link to Visual Workshop. You'll see a list of news-related Web sites. Visit some of the sites to find current news articles related to Internet security, then complete the table below.

FIGURE G-25: Visual workshop

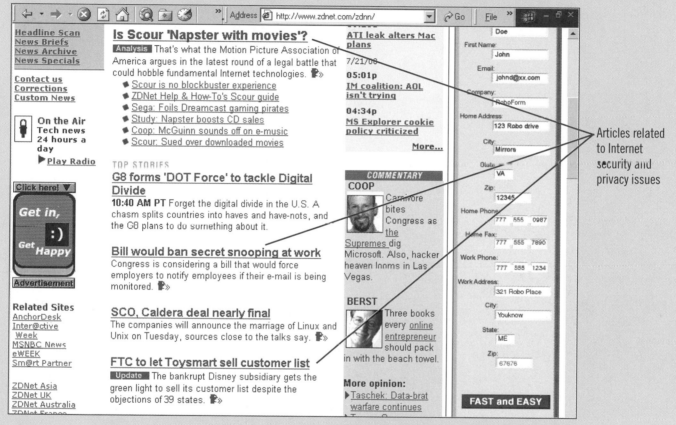

Current Date: ....

Titles and summaries of three articles related to Internet security:

Customer
Service

Objectives

- ► Define customer service issues
- ► Identify customer service options
- ► Develop FAQs
- ► Understand e-mail support
- ► Understand telephone support
- ► Explore live help services
- ► Understand customer discussion forums
- ► Explore value-added options

An online business has the best chance of staying in business when it offers people a product they want, at a price they are willing to pay, from an easy-to-use Web site—and when the company backs up the shopping experience with superior customer service. In this unit, you will explore issues related to customer service, and then look at some of the customer service options available to online businesses. These options include FAQ pages, e-mail support, telephone support, customer discussion forums, and live, online support. Teresa Ramirez has been working with MediaLoft's customer service team since she joined the company five years ago. Now she's been tasked with helping the Online Development Group establish viable options for providing customer service to its online customers.

E-Commerce

Defining Customer Service Issues

Most people have at least two or three favorite stores in the real world that they like to visit because the sales staff recognize them and sometimes are even familiar with their buying preferences. Many Web analysts predict that the most successful Web stores will be those that can duplicate this personal shopping experience—only online, and for many more customers than can possibly be served from a brick and mortar store. The key component will be customer service, or E-service. **E-service** is defined as the methods that a company uses to provide customer service directly from its Web site. ~~Teresa~~ Teresa suspects that many Web surfers are becoming less inclined to spend lots of time surfing the Web looking for the best deal. Instead, they are interested in finding and sticking with just a handful of companies that offer good products backed up by great service. She is convinced that MediaLoft's success as an online business will depend on building a loyal base of repeat customers who are greeted and served every time they arrive at the Web site. She asks you to explore ways that MediaLoft's online shopping experience could integrate traditional and new forms of customer service.

Details

► Personal Interaction

Web surfing is an intensely personal activity. You are alone in front of your monitor with only your mouse to keep you company. You arrive at a Web site, see a product that interests you, and then follow links to learn more. Suddenly, you have a question about the product. In a real-world store, you could find a sales clerk and, hopefully, have your question answered within minutes. As a Web surfer, you have become accustomed to finding out information for yourself, but when you can't find it immediately, what do you do? Chances are good that you click away. The implication for online businesses is that they must provide as many ways as possible to satisfy customer queries *immediately*.

► Customer Service Activities

Figure H-1 lists a selection of activities that contribute to excellent customer service. An online business needs to find ways of engaging in these activities from its Web site. For example, how can the Web site make personal recommendations, reward loyal customers, and provide help? In the real world, procedures are already in place for these activities. In the cyberworld, new procedures need to be developed. For example, a Web site might incorporate live online help, or login procedures to identify returning customers. A customer should be required to provide identifying information only once—whether on the Web site, during an in-store visit, or from contact with a sales representative.

► Relationship Building

The goal of all customer service activities is to build a one-on-one relationship with each individual customer. When they are ready, online customers want instant access to customer help that makes them feel as if personal attention is being paid to them. All customers want their lives made easier, and online shoppers appreciate Web sites that achieve that goal.

► Personalization

Many companies are developing personalization strategies to make customers feel at home on a Web site. Cookies, Web bugs, and logins are used to collect information about surfers so that they can be greeted upon arrival at a Web site, and so that the ads they see and the products that are highlighted relate to their particular interests. Figure H-2 shows the list of articles about personalization that are included on the personalization.com Web site, along with a page showing one of the link-to articles. The featured article describes how companies engaging in B2B e-commerce can use "three-dimensional point and click product descriptions" that let customers drill down to progressively greater detail. The goal is to provide customers with easy access to as much—or as little—product information as they need.

FIGURE H-1: Customer service activities

FIGURE H-2: Articles on the personalization.com Web site

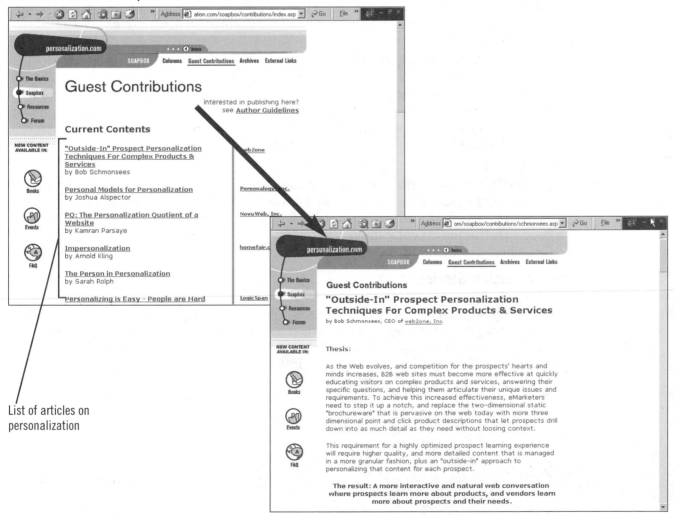

List of articles on personalization

Identifying Customer Service Options

When a new brand of Personal Digital Assistant hits the streets, the Web-savvy shopper can go to one of several online stores to find the best deal. Which store they eventually choose to do business with will depend on several factors—not all of them related to price. In fact, one of the principal determining factors probably will be access to superior customer service. As with all areas of the Web, consumers demand the power of choice, which means they want to select from several different customer service options. ➤ Teresa asks you to review the customer service options available, and then to explore ways that MediaLoft can use preemptive measures to make its customer service activities efficient and effective.

Details

► **Summary of Options**

Figure H-3 presents several customer support options available to online businesses. You can divide these options into two categories—online customer support and offline customer support.

• **Online Customer Support** Online customer support is provided directly from the company's Web site. For customers who connect to the Internet via a phone line, online customer support is preferable because it does not require customers to have two phone lines or to disconnect from the Internet. The least expensive online customer support option usually directs customers to information on the Web site. This information is presented as a FAQ page. Other online customer support options shown in Figure H-3 include e-mail, customer discussion forums, chat rooms, and live help. Many analysts predict that the live help option will become extremely popular as more online customers start expecting customer service from real people 24 hours a day.

• **Offline Customer Support** The telephone is the most popular medium for providing offline customer support, since e-mail has all but replaced traditional letter writing (snail mail). Although expensive, telephone support will likely continue to be an attractive option—at least to consumers who appreciate the connection with a real person. The challenge for online companies is to make telephone support profitable. Many companies outsource telephone support to call centers that can provide 24-hour support at a reasonable cost.

► **Costs**

Figure H-4 shows a price comparison of customer service responses. Compiled by Forrester Research, the chart indicates that answering a customer's query by telephone costs $33, while answering the same query with information on a Web page costs $1.17. On the other hand, some analysts maintain that the increased cost of telephone support is offset by the higher sales possibilities gained from a customer service representative interacting with a customer.

► **Preemptive Service**

Forrester Research defines preemptive service as "service that exceeds customer expectations by resolving issues before they become problems."[2] Providing preemptive service means anticipating and solving customer support issues before customers are even aware of them by providing unexpected levels of customer service. The goal is for customers to be impressed first and foremost by how well the Web site has helped to fulfill their needs—whether for a reasonably priced product, timely delivery, or information.

FIGURE H-3: Customer service options

Online customer support

FAQ pages

Live help

E-mail

Chat rooms and discussion forums

Offline customer support

Snail mail

Telephone support

FIGURE H-4: Comparison of customer service costs

Figure 2 - "Cost And Growth Per Channel" - Microsoft Internet Explorer

Fig 2   Cost And Growth Per Channel   > GET DATA

Channel	Cost	Annual growth rate	Percentage of incidents handled through these channels	
			Today	2002**
Telephone	$33	90%	54%	13%
Email	$9.99	111%	9%	4%
Chat*	$7.80	N/A	<1%	4%
Message boards*	$4.57	178%	<1%	2%
Knowledge base/Web	$1.17	407%	37%	87%

* Low penetration among firms reporting
** Projected

Reported by 46 responding companies providing business-to-business customer service

Source: Forrester Research, Inc.

E-Commerce

Developing FAQs

Frequently Asked Questions pages have become a standard element on Web sites, supporting everything from pet food to luxury yachts. The goal of a FAQ page is to provide customers with a quick, easy, and inexpensive way to find answers to common questions. Figure H-5 shows the FAQ page included on the Charles Schwab investment Web site. Note the links to additional help options. FAQ pages are designed to capitalize on the self-serve nature of the Web, and work successfully when they are well written and logically organized. FAQ pages are also the most inexpensive customer service option because personally responding to a customer query is always going to be much more expensive than developing a simple FAQ page. ➤ Teresa is familiar with the kinds of questions that MediaLoft customers ask in the brick and mortar stores. However, she realizes that many of the questions that online customers ask will relate to situations unique to online shopping. Because these situations are often similar across Web sites, she asks you to explore the FAQ pages of three bookstores to determine the kinds of questions MediaLoft should address.

Steps

1. Open your Web browser, go to the Student Online Companion at *www.course.com/illustrated/ecommerce*, click the link for **Unit H**, then click the link for **Developing FAQs**

2. Select three sites from the list provided

3. Open the Project File **ECH-01.doc** in your word-processing program, then save it as **FAQ Comparison**
   The document contains a series of questions related to FAQ pages from three online bookstores.

4. Go to one of the sites listed in the Student Online Companion for this lesson, then follow the links to its FAQ page
   Note that you may need to search around to find the FAQ page. Some Web sites include only a link to Help on the main page; from there you need to follow additional links to find the FAQ page.

5. Enter the name and URL of the company you've chosen, then answer the questions provided
   Your goal is to determine what kinds of questions are asked and how these questions are organized, so that you can evaluate their usefulness in assisting consumers. As you evaluate the site's FAQ pages, refer to the FAQ tips shown in Figure H-6.

6. Repeat Steps 4 and 5 to gather information about the FAQ pages at two additional Web sites

7. When you have completed all the questions, list which FAQ page you think is most successful in the space provided at the bottom of the document
   Make sure you give reasons for your choice. If you don't think that any of the FAQ pages work well, describe how they could be improved.

8. Type **Your Name** at the bottom of the document, save it, print a copy, then close the document

FIGURE H-5: Sample FAQ page

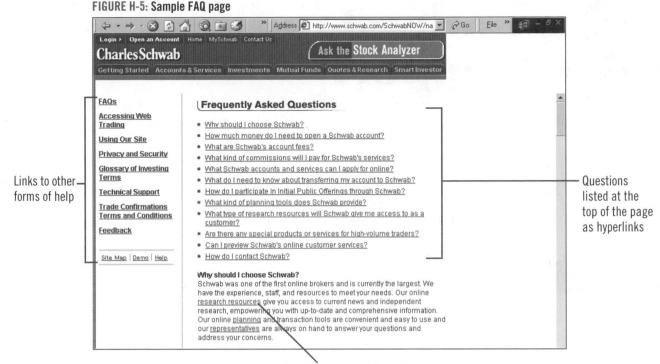

Links to other forms of help

Questions listed at the top of the page as hyperlinks

Hyperlinks to more information included in answers

FIGURE H-6: FAQ tips

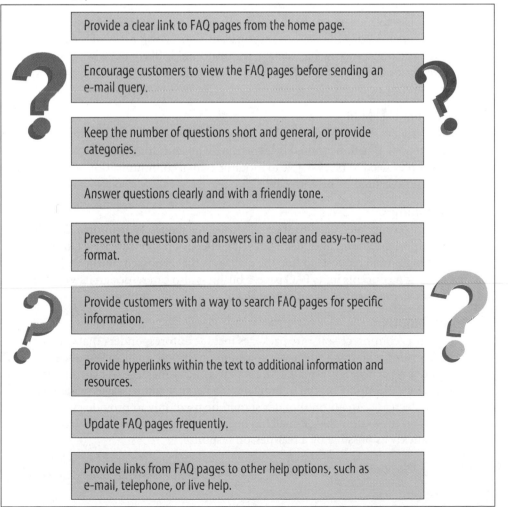

Provide a clear link to FAQ pages from the home page.

Encourage customers to view the FAQ pages before sending an e-mail query.

Keep the number of questions short and general, or provide categories.

Answer questions clearly and with a friendly tone.

Present the questions and answers in a clear and easy-to-read format.

Provide customers with a way to search FAQ pages for specific information.

Provide hyperlinks within the text to additional information and resources.

Update FAQ pages frequently.

Provide links from FAQ pages to other help options, such as e-mail, telephone, or live help.

Understanding E-Mail Support

E-mail is an attractive support option because it costs less than telephone support and does not necessarily require 24-hour attention. E-mail support attracts customers because it allows them to stay online while they shop, yet enables them to ask questions at any time of the day or night. In the early days of e-commerce, e-mail support was considered the answer to all customer support issues. The theory was that all a company needed to do was include a link to an e-mail address on its Web site, and then wait for the questions to roll in. The reality is proving to be more complex. Companies are finding that e-mail support is most successful when they treat it nearly the same as a chat function. That is, they reply promptly to every inquiry, and they carefully monitor and manage their e-mail communication policies. Teresa certainly plans to include a link to e-mail support on the MediaLoft Web site. However, she wants to understand the issues related to e-mail support so that she can make sure customers are effectively served.

Details

► E-Mail Scenarios

E-mail support is effective when it answers customer questions promptly and helps forge a positive relationship. Figure H-7 illustrates how a customer *should* receive e-mail support. The flip side is shown in Figure H-8. Here a customer describes all the ways in which he didn't receive e-mail support.

► Response Time

In the hurry-up-and-serve-me climate of the Web, expecting a customer to wait days for a response to an e-mail query will result in a lost customer. A customer might wait until the next business day to receive a response, but rarely will a customer want to wait any longer. By the time the company has replied, the customer is likely to be long gone to a competitor's Web site. A good policy is to inform your customers exactly when they can expect a response to an e-mail inquiry.

► Handling E-Mail

An efficient e-mail support system requires personnel. Some online companies might need to create new positions staffed by personnel who communicate effectively in writing. In addition, resources need to be available to monitor e-mail communications to ensure that the company is well represented 24 hours a day.

► Tracking

Online companies need to track all customer requests for information. The goal is to identify common questions, and then to develop effective responses. In fact, most FAQ pages are built by mining e-mail requests to find the questions that are asked most often. In addition to addressing common concepts in its FAQ page, a business also can re-design its Web site or streamline procedures so the events that prompted the questions do not recur.

► Automation

Many e-commerce software packages include autoresponders that can be used to automatically acknowledge orders and answer common questions. An **autoresponder** is a mail server that will send a reply to each e-mail address that sends a message. As consumers become more accustomed to shopping on the Internet, their tolerance for messages generated from autoresponders may decrease. An autoresponder should be used only to provide customers with an immediate reply so they know their e-mail has been received. Autoresponder replies must then be followed as quickly as possible by a real-person response.

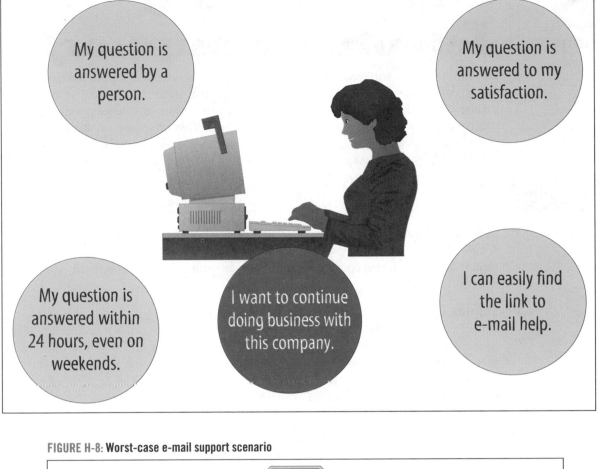

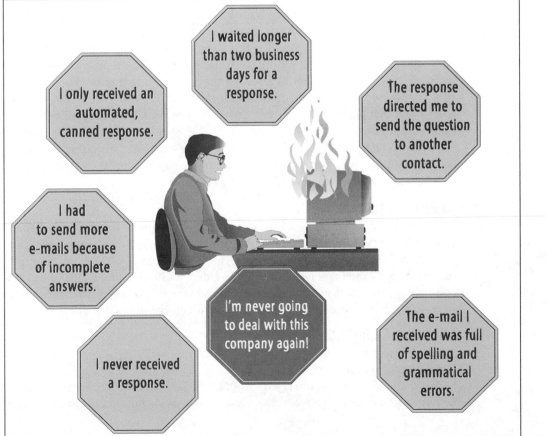

E-Commerce

Understanding Telephone Support

For most customers, the telephone is still the lifeline to service and support. When the going gets tough, customers want access to a toll-free number that leads to a pleasant voice with a helpful manner. The challenge from a company's perspective is how to provide telephone support that will contribute to the profit margin, rather than become a drain on resources. Teresa predicts that MediaLoft will need to expand its existing call center to handle queries and orders from online customers. She asks you to investigate some of the issues related to telephone support.

Details

► Call Center Construction

A **call center** handles incoming calls from both online and offline customers. For many customers, the only human contact with the company will be made through the call center, particularly if the company does not maintain a real-world presence.

► Staffing Options

An online company can set up and staff its own call center, or it can use a call center service. Call center services can be too impersonal because they are often in a different physical location, they service several companies simultaneously, and their knowledge of the product often comes only from catalog descriptions. A company needs to ensure that call center staff can adopt the company persona, and be extremely courteous and professional. Figure H-9 shows the form one service company includes on its Web site to help businesses determine the level of telephone support they need to offer.

► Sales Opportunities

When a customer talks directly with a sales representative, the sales representative has an opportunity to create an additional sale. When a skilled customer service representative takes the order and engages in up-selling and cross-selling, the customer may be persuaded to buy additional products. **Cross-selling** informs customers about an accessory or additional product that they can add on to the product they are already buying. For example, the customer service representative at an online clothing store could ask if the customer would like to add a shirt and belt to go with the jeans they just ordered. **Up-selling** means to promote a model that includes more features and is generally higher priced. For example, the representative at the online clothing store could suggest that the customer purchase the designer sweater or buy two pairs of jeans for just $10 more than one pair. For most companies, telephone support is only cost-effective when it helps to increase sales.

► Support Requirements

A wide range of communications and sales skills are required to handle customer calls effectively. Customer support representatives first need to identify the customer, and then they need to determine the customer's needs. Suppose, for example, that you operate an online gift store. Your call center personnel will need to serve the elderly customer who wants to buy a gift for a grandchild but is not accustomed to shopping online very differently from the experienced Web surfer who wants to pre-purchase birthday presents for an entire family.

► Telephone Support Software

As companies recognize the potential benefits of providing customers with access to telephone support, the market for software designed to set up and maintain telephone support systems will continue to grow. Figure H-10 shows a list of call center software packages that specialize in helping companies provide effective Customer Relationship Management (CRM).

e-byte

"People still need people. Sites with no possibility of human contact for the customer are at a disadvantage. Shoppers want to be able to talk to a real person in real time. Toll-free numbers are big winners." *Source: E-Commerce Times*[3]

FIGURE H-9: Call center requirements

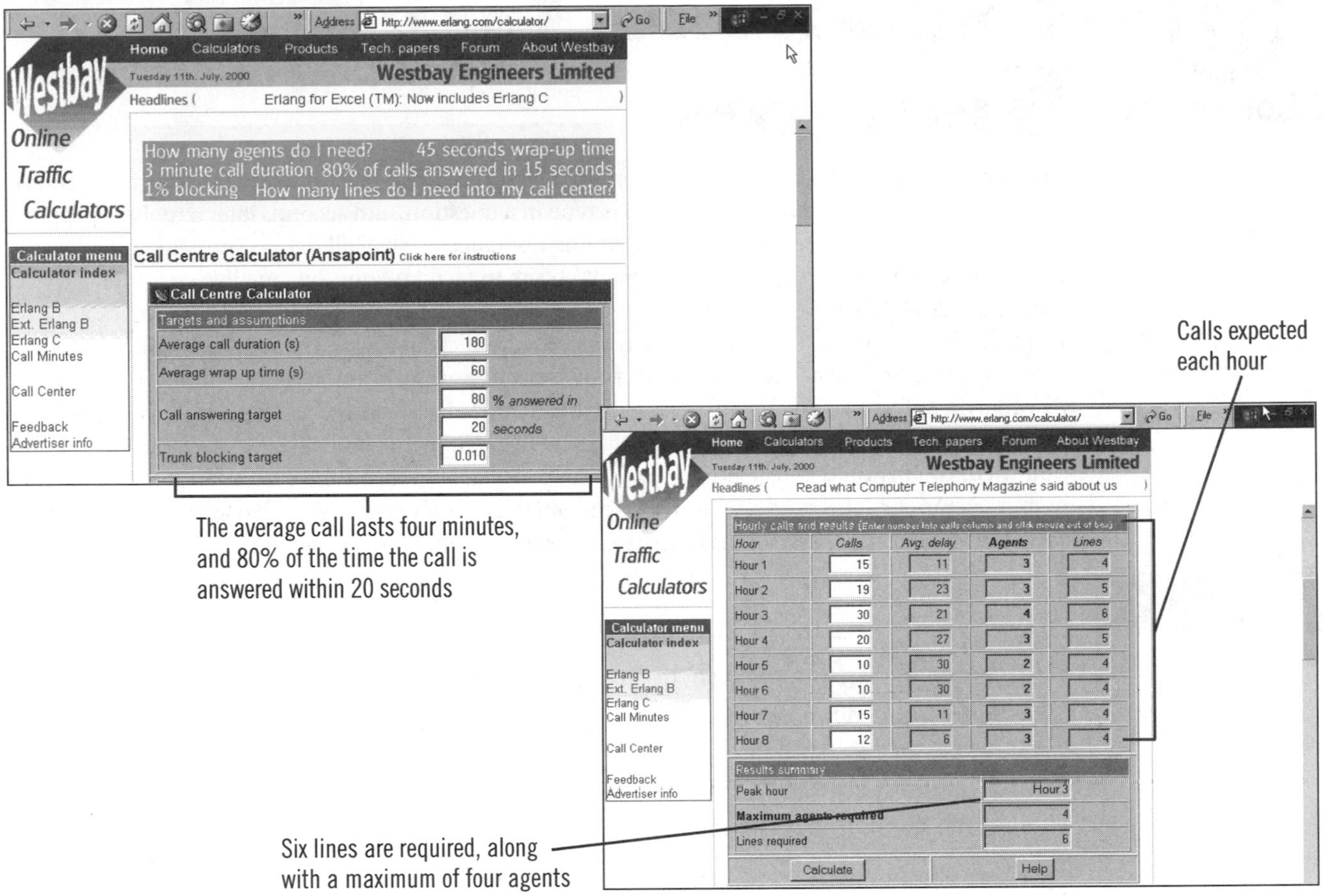

The average call lasts four minutes, and 80% of the time the call is answered within 20 seconds

Calls expected each hour

Six lines are required, along with a maximum of four agents

FIGURE H-10: Call center software

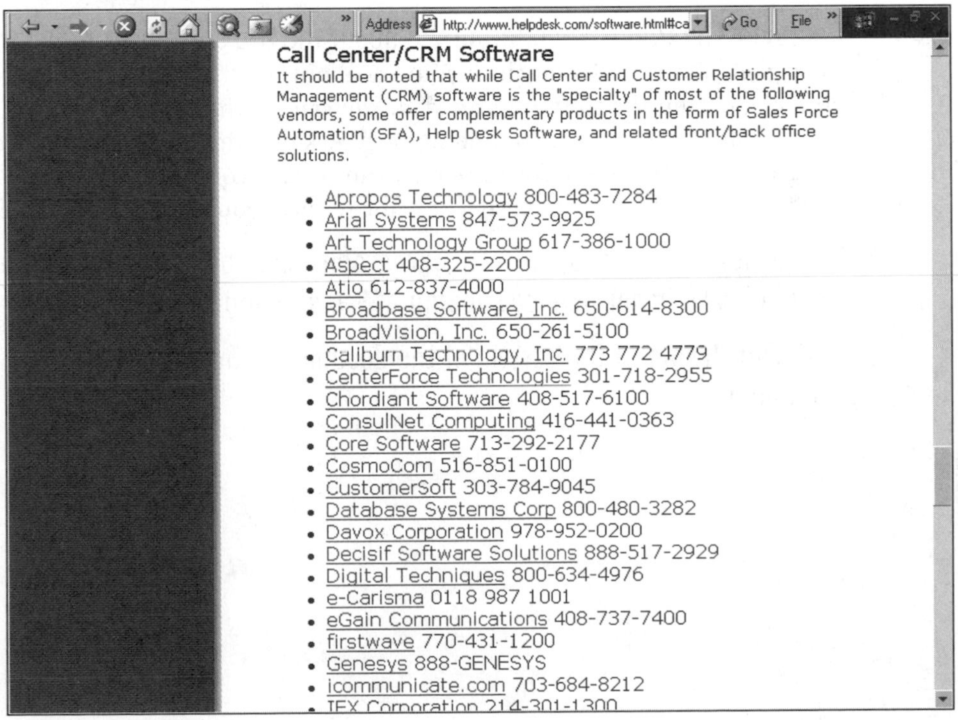

Call Center/CRM Software

It should be noted that while Call Center and Customer Relationship Management (CRM) software is the "specialty" of most of the following vendors, some offer complementary products in the form of Sales Force Automation (SFA), Help Desk Software, and related front/back office solutions.

- Apropos Technology 800-483-7284
- Arial Systems 847-573-9925
- Art Technology Group 617-386-1000
- Aspect 408-325-2200
- Atio 612-837-4000
- Broadbase Software, Inc. 650-614-8300
- BroadVision, Inc. 650-261-5100
- Caliburn Technology, Inc. 773 772 4779
- CenterForce Technologies 301-718-2955
- Chordiant Software 408-517-6100
- ConsulNet Computing 416-441-0363
- Core Software 713-292-2177
- CosmoCom 516-851-0100
- CustomerSoft 303-784-9045
- Database Systems Corp 800-480-3282
- Davox Corporation 978-952-0200
- Decisif Software Solutions 888-517-2929
- Digital Techniques 800-634-4976
- e-Carisma 0118 987 1001
- eGain Communications 408-737-7400
- firstwave 770-431-1200
- Genesys 888-GENESYS
- icommunicate.com 703-684-8212
- IEX Corporation 214-301-1300

E-Commerce

Exploring Live Help Services

Many companies offer their customers online help from a real person who responds to questions in real time. All the customer needs to do is type in a question, and seconds later a reply appears on the screen. Figure H-11 shows a sample online exchange at SkiMall.net, a company in Colorado. HumanClick software was installed on the Web site to facilitate one-on-one live customer service. Figure H-12 shows how an online exchange using NetAgent from eShare Technologies appears from the live agent's point of view. Many analysts predict that live help software will become the most efficient and cost-effective way to provide superior customer support online in real time. Another benefit of live help software is that it standardizes the type of support each customer receives. Teresa is intrigued by the new live help software packages available, and thinks that MediaLoft should consider making live help available to its online customers. She asks you to help her compare the products and services offered by two companies that provide online help software, so that she then can make a presentation to MediaLoft management.

Steps

1. Open your Web browser, go to the Student Online Companion at *www.course.com/illustrated/ecommerce*, click the link to **Unit H**, then click the link to **Exploring Live Help Services**

   You will see a list of links to Web sites that provide tools that Web developers can use to provide live online customer support.

2. Open the Project File **ECH-02.doc** in your word-processing program, then save it as **Live Help Services**

   This document contains a table that compares the products and services offered by two live help services.

3. Select two companies from the list, then follow the links to explore how they can help companies add online help to their Web sites

4. Complete the table with information about the two services you have chosen

   Your goal is to learn as much as you can about the live help services you've selected. If possible, try out the software provided. You can say that you are researching the options available for providing live online support. Ask questions about the products so that you can learn how the live agent responds, and so that you can evaluate the response speed and usefulness. You need to learn how the services you've selected assist customers.

5. In the space provided, write a paragraph describing which live help service you would choose if you were developing a Web site and wanted to include live help

6. Type **Your Name** at the bottom of the document, save it, print a copy, then close the document

FIGURE H-11: Sample live help exchange with HumanClick

Click the link to open a chat window

Type a question here, then click Send

Consumer questions are in red, and company responses are in blue

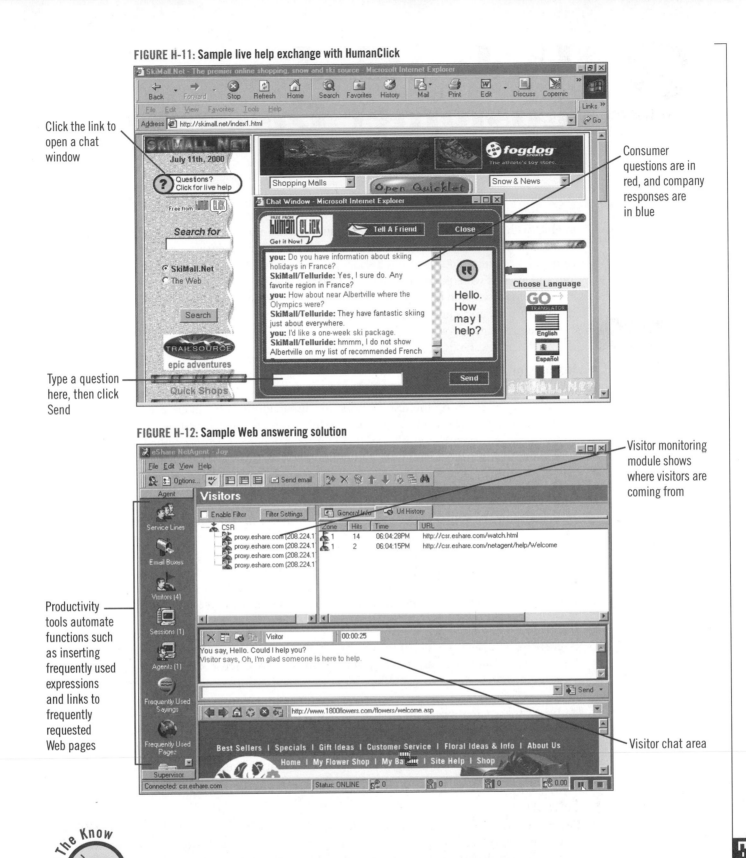

FIGURE H-12: Sample Web answering solution

Visitor monitoring module shows where visitors are coming from

Productivity tools automate functions such as inserting frequently used expressions and links to frequently requested Web pages

Visitor chat area

Reducing Customer Anxiety

"Customer service is important in any business but increasingly customer service has a direct impact on browse-to-buy ratios. Personal online live service reduces the browser's most common shopping anxieties because, typically, online shoppers want to know *who* they are buying from."

Source: 121 Internet Marketing[5]

Understanding Customer Discussion Forums

A common buzzword associated with the growth of e-commerce activities is *community*. Many online businesses are concentrating their efforts on developing communities of customers who will interact with each other to obtain and share information and tips. The goal of these interactions is to increase customer loyalty, while decreasing the need for expensive customer support. Online companies can install customer discussion forums and chat rooms on their Web sites for surfers to join and interact with like-minded people. ◢━━━ Teresa is excited about the possibility of including an online discussion forum or maybe even a chat room on the MediaLoft Web site. She envisions several forums and chat rooms that will appeal to the varying reading tastes of MediaLoft customers. She asks you to investigate further.

Details

▶ Discussion Forums

A discussion forum provides Web surfers with the tools they need to communicate with others about topics of common interest. Visitors to a discussion forum can choose to post questions, or they can simply browse through the questions and answers posted by other visitors. Some companies even provide multiple discussion forums. Figure H-13 shows the range of customer discussion forums included on the PhotoShopper Web site, and Figure H-14 shows one of the postings from the Darkroom Forum.

▶ Chat Rooms

In a chat room, customers can conduct live conversations in real time. An online business needs to ensure the integrity of the chat room, while also ensuring each customer's privacy is protected. Customers who perceive chat rooms only in frivolous terms might not be inclined to use them to find product information. As a result, the online business needs to reassure customers that the chat room is monitored, that they can use it to quickly learn about the company products, and that they can interact with other customers in a safe and informative environment.

▶ Benefits

A great benefit of discussion forums and chat rooms is they can make customers feel they know from whom they are buying, which can lead to a sense of security and, ultimately, customer loyalty. From a company's point of view, the postings to a discussion forum and interactions in a chat room can provide valuable information about customer needs and wants. In addition, these venues provide customers with a way to help themselves. Instead of e-mailing the company to ask a question, a customer can browse through past discussion forums or post a question for other participants. From the customer's point of view, the postings in a customer discussion forum might have more credibility because the people who wrote them are not expected to espouse the company line.

▶ Software

Several software programs are available to add discussion forums and chat rooms to a Web site. The Web developer installs the software on the Web server. Figure H-15 describes the features of one of the free discussion software tools available for download.

FIGURE H-13: List of discussion forums on PhotoShopper.com

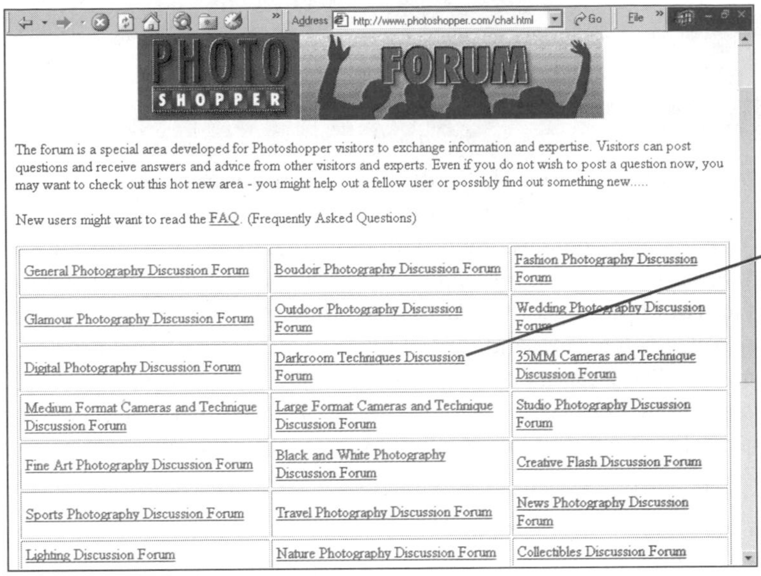

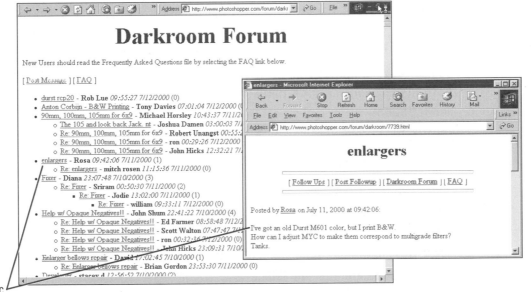

Click a topic to view the discussion forum

FIGURE H-14: Discussion forum in action

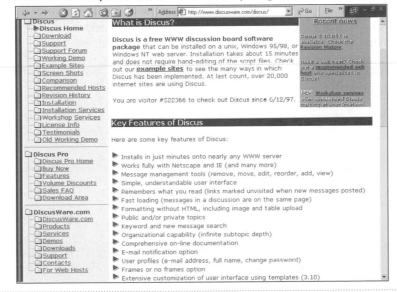

Click a topic to see the question

FIGURE H-15: Sample discussion board software package

Exploring Value-Added Options

A **value-added option** is one that enhances the customer's shopping experience by providing extra service, complimentary items, or customized products. You can summarize a value-added option as one that provides customers with more than they bargained for—but in a positive way! For example, a financial advisor could inform you of a new stock or a high-yield investment, or a travel service could put together a customized itinerary of your next trip, and include directions to recommended restaurants and virtual tours of local attractions. Figure H-16 shows the links that accompanied an itinerary developed by Travelocity for a trip to Nice, France. From this page, customers can view information about Nice, book additional services such as accommodations and transportation, and even follow a link to create their own mini-guide of Nice.

Figure H-17 shows the same-day shipping option provided by Outpost.com as part of its True-Price service. In this lesson, you will explore the value-added options on some Web sites, and determine what they are doing to make the customer feel special, to raise customer loyalty, and to provide excellent customer service. Teresa recognizes that most online bookstores are striving to provide value-added options such as wish lists, personalized notifications, and gift-wrapping services. She wants you to check out the value-added options other kinds of online stores offer, and identify which options MediaLoft could modify to suit the consumers MediaLoft aims to attract.

Steps

1. Open your Web browser, go to the Student Online Companion at *www.course.com/ illustrated/ecommerce*, click the link to **Unit H**, then click the link to **Exploring Value-Added Options**

   You will see a list of links to Web sites that provide various kinds of value-added options designed to build customer loyalty and a sense of community.

2. Open the Project File **ECH-03.doc** in your word-processing program, then save it as **Value-Added Options**

   This document contains questions related to the value-added options available on two Web sites.

3. Select two companies from the list, then follow the links to explore the value-added options that customers can select

4. Complete each table in the document with the required responses

   Your goal is to evaluate the value-added options offered by both of the Web sites you selected. Think carefully about the options—do you think they add to a customer's shopping experience, or do you think that customers would not be interested?

5. Type **Your Name** at the bottom of the document, save it, print a copy, then close the document

e-byte

"Since it is roughly six times less expensive to sell to an existing customer than to acquire a new one, the value of customor loyalty and repeat sales is just too compelling to ignore."
Source: E-Commerce Times[6]

FIGURE H-16: Links to travel information

Personalized message relating to trip destination

Current weather in Nice

Link to tool for creating a personal custom travel guide

Links to more travel services and products

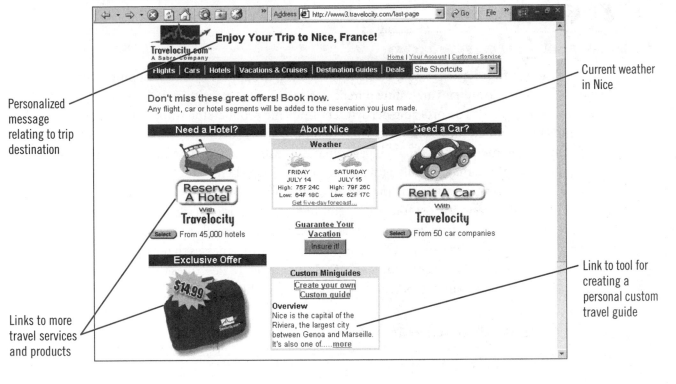

FIGURE H-17: Free shipping option at Outpost.com

Same-day shipping cost

Links to various value-added features

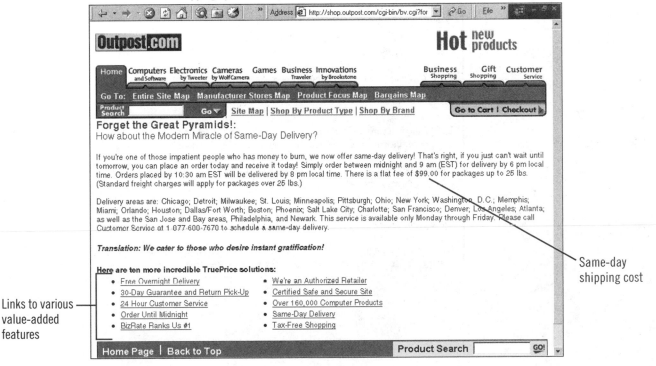

Focus
Backend Integration

Backend integration relates to all the activities required to support online shopping. For example, when a customer completes an online purchase, a series of events within various departments in the company is triggered. The ordering department finds the product, the shipping department packages and ships the product, the accounting department processes payment for the product, the post-sales marketing department tracks the Web pages that the customer visited before finalizing the purchase, and so on. One of the major challenges that businesses face when trying to sell products and services over the Internet is integrating existing systems with online systems to ensure smooth, seamless, and efficient order processing. Most full-scale e-commerce solutions include backend integration systems. However, these solutions usually are beyond the reach of most small- to medium-sized businesses. These smaller businesses need to outsource to other online businesses that can handle some of the procedures required to serve customers effectively. Figure H-18 describes the ways in which UPS works with online companies to streamline shipping operations.

FIGURE H-18: UPS services for online companies

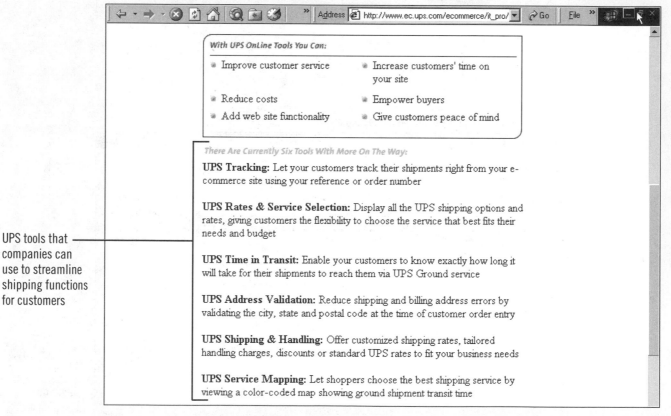

UPS tools that companies can use to streamline shipping functions for customers

Explore Further...

The Focus questions provided below ask you to explore some of the B2B services available to help online companies better serve their customers.

To complete the following questions, you'll need to conduct some research. First, open your Web browser, go to the Student Online Companion at *www.course.com/ illustrated/ ecommerce*, then click the link to Focus. You will find a series of links to various categories of businesses that provide services to support online businesses. Spend some time following the links and scanning some of the services provided. Your goal is to learn how online businesses can partner with various service providers to integrate the many procedures related to doing business online. Complete the following questions.

1. What services offered by online financing companies do you think would help an online business better service its customers? Explore the links in the Financial Services category in the Student Online Companion to learn about some of the services offered to businesses. Write a one-page description of these services, and state whether you think they would be cost effective.

2. What business services could an online business take advantage of to better serve its customers? Explore the links in the Business Services category in the Student Online Companion to learn about some of the ways companies can partner with online businesses. Try following links to pages that provide information for companies rather than consumers. Write a one-page description of some of the services that you think might help an online company.

3. How could an online company benefit from hiring a service to manage employee benefits and other activities related to human resources? Explore the links in the Human Resources category in the Student Online Companion to learn about the services provided by online human resources companies. Write a one-page description of the services that you think might help an online company better serve its employees.

Practice

► Review

1. You can define _____ as the methods that a company uses to provide customer service directly from its Web site.

2. A goal of all customer service activities is to build a one-on-one customer _____.

3. A company that develops _____ strategies is attempting to make customers feel at home on its Web site.

4. Because most consumers have a separate phone line for their Internet connection, most customer support issues should be handled over the telephone. True/False? _____

5. One of the least expensive customer service options is to provide customers with a Web page containing a list of Frequently _____ Questions.

6. The most costly way to answer a customer's query is via the telephone. True/False? _____

7. Service that exceeds customer expectations by resolving issues before they become problems is referred to as _____ service.

8. E-mail customer support is usually fast, effective, and very reliable. True/False? _____

9. A(n) _____ is a mail server that sends a reply to each e-mail address that sends a message.

10. Incoming calls from both online and offline customers can be handled by a _____ _____.

11. The term _____ refers to promoting a model that includes more features and is generally higher priced than the model currently being purchased by the customer.

12. The term CRM refers to Customer _____ Management.

13. Many online businesses use customer discussion forums to develop _____ of customers interacting with each other.

14. A _____-added option is one that enhances the customer's shopping experience by providing extra service, complimentary items, or customized products.

▶ Independent Challenges

1. As you've learned in this unit, most sites provide surfers with several help options—ranging from simple FAQ pages to online customer service. You decide to check out how three companies selling similar products offer help to their customers.

To complete this independent challenge:

a. Fill in the box below with a short description of the type of product that interests you. For example, you could compare the Help options on Web sites that sell real estate, gemstones, craft supplies, or herbal skin rejuvenators.

> **Product Description** ....
>
> ....
>
> ....

b. Open the Project File ECH-04.doc in your word-processing program, then save it as *Help Options*. This document contains the table that you will complete to compare the Help options offered on each of the three online businesses you select.

c. Conduct searches for three companies that sell the product you identified.

d. For each company you choose, explore links to as many Help options as you can, then complete the table.

e. In the space provided, describe which of the three companies offered the best range of help services. Alternatively, describe what services you think should have been offered, but were not.

f. Type **Your Name** at the bottom of the document, save it, print a copy, then close the document.

2. Many online companies are installing customer discussion forums and live chat rooms on their Web sites in order to encourage a sense of community among customers and participants. You decide to explore the available options for including this interactive tool on a Web site. Your goal is to find a solution that is cost effective and easy to use.

To complete this independent challenge:

a. Open your Web browser, go to the Student Online Companion at *www.course.com/illustrated/ecommerce*, click the link for Unit H, then click the link for Independent Challenge 2.

b. Select two sites from the list provided.

c. Open the Project File ECH-05.doc in your word-processing program, then save it as *Discussion Options*. The document contains a table that you can complete to compare the products offered by two companies that sell the software for installing customer discussion forums on a Web site.

d. Follow links on the two Web sites you selected to find the information required for the table.

e. In the space provided, describe the option you would choose if you wanted to add a customer discussion forum to your Web site.

f. Type **Your Name** at the bottom of the document, save it, print a copy, then close the document.

3. Exchanges and returns are a fact of retail life. In the real world, you can easily take a product back to a store to obtain a refund or to make an exchange. Obtaining a refund or exchanging a product in cyberspace might not be so easy. From the customer's point of view, a company needs to provide a clear exchange and return policy that it honors. From the company's point of view, procedures need to be in place to guard against fraud, while still providing excellent customer service. You decide to check out how two companies selling a product of your choice handle exchanges and refunds.

To complete this independent challenge:

a. Fill in the box below with a short description of the type of product that interests you. For example, you could compare help options on Web sites that sell foreign language courses, luggage, model airplanes, or bed linens.

> **Product Description** ....
>
> ....
>
> ....

b. Open the Project File ECH-06.doc in your word-processing program, then save it as *Exchange and Return Options*. This document contains the table that you will complete and use to compare the exchange and return options offered on each of the three online businesses you selected.

c. Conduct searches for companies that sell the product you identified.

d. For each company you choose, explore links to a page that provides information about the company's exchange and return policy.

e. Answer the questions provided about the exchange and return options offered by each of the three companies you chose.

f. In the space provided, describe which of the two companies presented the fairest exchange and return policy. Alternatively, describe what you would consider to be a fair exchange and return policy for an online business.

g. Type **Your Name** at the bottom of the document, save it, print a copy, then close the document.

4. How do you get people to return to your Web site? That question, of course, is on the mind of every business hoping to run its Web site at a profit. No definitive answer exists, which means you are free to think creatively about the many ways you can build your Web site so that each customer will be a repeat customer. You decide to brainstorm at least five ways you could attract customers to return to a Web site that sells a product or service of your choice.

To complete this independent challenge:

a. Fill in the box below with the name of a Web business you'd like to pursue, and a description of its products and/or services. For example, you could call your company Atlantis Lobsters, and describe it as an online cooking utensil company specializing in lobster dishes and lobster-themed kitchen products.

> **Company Name** ....
>
> **Description** ....
>
> ....
>
> ....

b. Open a document in your word-processing program, and list five ways you could encourage customers to return repeatedly to your Web site. Describe each way as fully as possible.

c. Format the list attractively, type **Your Name** at the bottom of the document, save the document as *Sticky Site Strategies*, print a copy, then close the document.

► Up to Date

Many analysts predict that online customer service will become increasingly popular as more and more companies recognize the need to provide excellent customer service in real time, any time. Figure H-19 shows an article on online customer service included on the E-Commerce Guide site. You decide to find more recent articles about online customer service, so that you can determine if it continues to be as important and as neglected an issue as described in the sample article.

To complete this Up to Date challenge:

FIGURE H-19: Article on online customer service

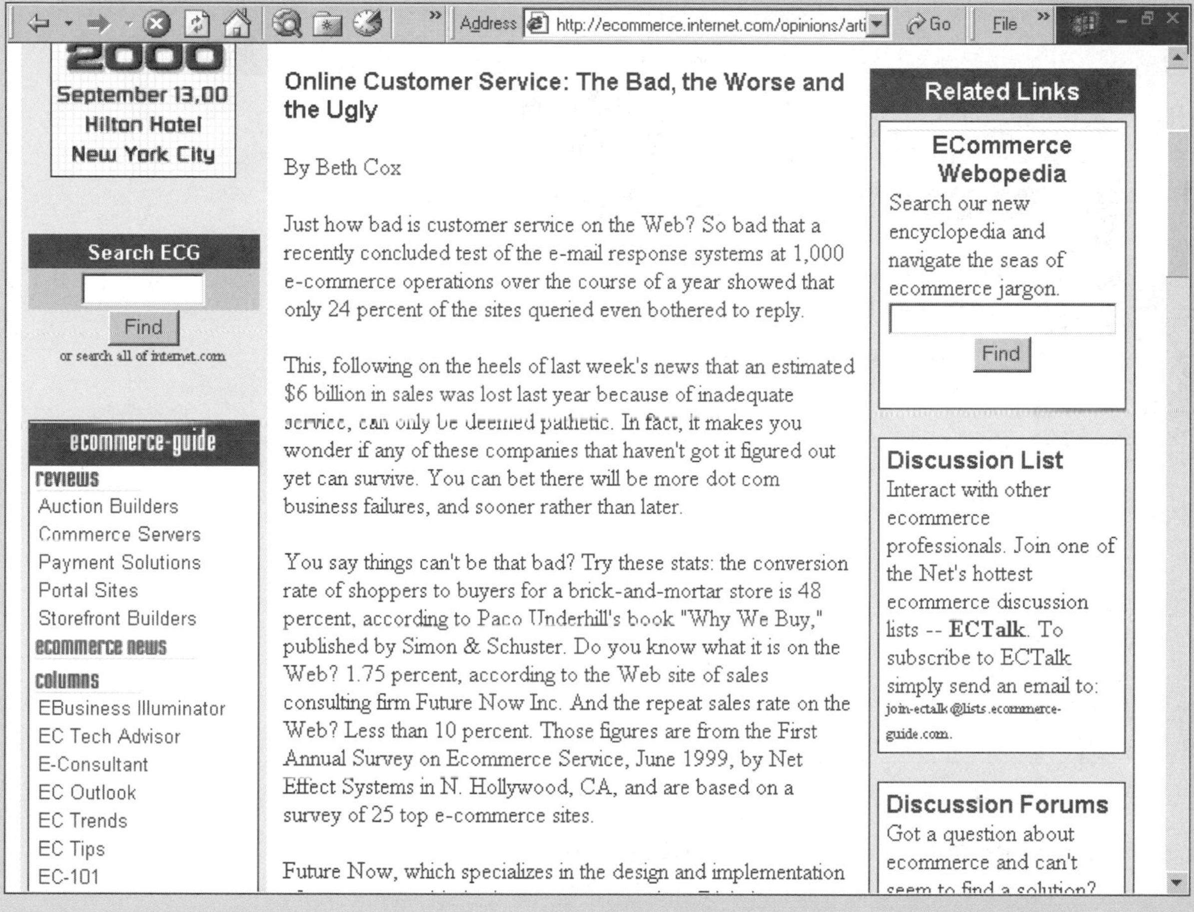

a. Open your Web browser, go to the Student Online Companion at *www.course.com/illustrated/ecommerce*, click the link for Unit H, then click the link for Up to Date. You can read the full text of the article shown in Figure H-19 by following the link provided.

b. Explore the links to find two articles related to the latest developments in online customer service. To quickly find appropriate articles, search for customer service on the various Web sites, then sort the results in date order.

c. Open the Project File ECH-07.doc into your word-processing program, then save it as *Customer Service Articles*. This document contains the table you will use to enter information about the articles you have found.

d. Complete the table with information about each of the articles you have chosen. If you cannot find information such as the author's name or the date the article was written, indicate Not Available in the appropriate table cell. Note that the Date Accessed is the date that you found and read the article.

e. Summarize each article in approximately 100-200 words.

f. Type **Your Name** at the bottom of the document, save it, print a copy, then close the document.

► Visual Workshop

Figure H-20 shows a page of topics included in an online discussion forum on the Baby Express Web site. You can often learn a great deal about a company's products and services by checking out the discussion forums. Open your Web browser, go to the Student Online Companion at *www.course.com/illustrated/ecommerce*, click the link for Unit H, then click the link for Visual Workshop. Here you will view a list of companies that include online discussion forums. Select one of the companies, then follow links to a discussion forum on a topic that interests you. Read some of the postings, then complete the table below.

FIGURE H-20: Visual workshop

Current messages

Are the topics organized so that you can easily find a topic that interests you?

How do you think the discussion forum helps to build customer loyalty for the company? What was the best point? What was the weakest point?

Describe at least one benefit the company receives from hosting the discussion forum.

Describe at least one benefit the customer receives from participating in the discussion forum.

References

Books:

Carroll, Jim, and Rick Broadhead, *Selling Online,* Macmillan, Toronto, 1999.

Flanders, Vincent, and Michael Willis, *Web Pages That Suck,* Sybex, San Francisco, 1996.

Rosen, Anita, *The e-commerce: Question and Answer Book: A Survival Guide for Business Managers,* Amacom, New York, 2000.

Schneider, Gary P., and James T. Perry, *Electronic Commerce,* Course Technology, Cambridge, MA, 2000.

Seybold, Patricia B., *Customers.com: How to Create a Profitable Business Strategy for the Internet and Beyond,* Times Business: Random House, New York, 1998.

Tiernan, Bernadette, *E-Tailing,* Dearborn, Chicago, 2000.

Helpful Web Sites:

About E-Commerce: *http://ecommerce.about.com/smallbusiness/ecommerce/?once=true&*

ClickZ Network: *http://www.zdnet.com/*

Commerce.net: *http://www.commerce.net/resources/*

ComputerWorld: *http://www.computerworld.com/*

Datamonitor: *http://www.datamonitor.com*

Durlacher Research: *http://www.durlacher.com/*

EC Now: *http://ecnow.com/*

E-Commerce Times: *http://www.ecommercetimes.com*

Forrester Research: *http://www.forresterresearch.com*

Internet News: *http://www.internetnews.com/*

Internet World: *http://www.iw.com/*

Internet.com: *http://www.internet.com*

Jupiter Communications: *http://www.jupitercommunications.com*

Neilson Net Ratings: *http://www.nielsen-netratings.com/*

The Register: *http://www.theregister.co.uk/*

U.S. Government e-commerce site: *http://www.ecommerce.gov*

Web Developer: *http://www.webdeveloper.com/*

Web Monkey: *http://hotwired.lycos.com/webmonkey/*

Web Reference: *http://www.webreference.com/*

Web Tools: *http://www.webtools.com/*

Webopedia.com: *http://www.webopedia.com*

World Wide Web Consortium (W3C): *http://www.w3.org/*

ZD Net News: *http://www.zdnet.com/*

E-Commerce

Endnotes

Unit A:

1 William M. Daley, "White Paper on E-Commerce," March 2000, <*http://www.esa.doc.gov/de2k.htm*> (June 2000).

2 Mick Brady, "Reality Check: The State of E-Commerce, Part II," *E-Commerce Times*, (July 12, 2000). <*http://www.ecommercetimes.com/news/articles2000/000705-4.shtml*> (July 18, 2000).

3 "A Framework for Global Electronic Commerce," *The White House*, July 1, 1997, <*http://www.ecommerce.gov/framewrk.htm*> (July 12, 2000).

4 Paul A. Greenberg, "B2B E-Commerce: The Quiet Giant," *E-Commerce Times*, January 4, 2000, <*http://www.ecommercetimes.com/news/articles/000104-1.shtml*> (August 11, 2000).

5 Margaret Kane, "'Cybermediaries': The Net's New Kings," *ZDNet News*, June 7, 1999, <*http://www.zdnet.com/zdnn/stories/news/0,4586,2265299,00.html*> (March 10, 2000).

6 Linda Frum, "From Little Acorns Grow," *The National Post*, March 25, 2000.

7 Nathaniel Borenstein, Harry Hochheiser, and Andy Oram, "One Planet, One Net: Principles for the Internet Era," *Computer Professionals for Social Responsibility*, December 8, 1999, <*http://www.cpsr.org/program/nii/onenet.html*> (March 30, 2000).

Unit B:

1 "Organizing for E-Commerce," *Boston Consulting Group*, April 1, 2000, <*http://57.68.7.209/publications/files/Organizing%20ECommerce%20Apr%2000.pdf*> (August 11, 2000).

2 Eric Schmitt, "Commerce Software Takes Off," *Forrester Research*, March 2000, <*http://www.forrester.com/ER/Research/Report/0,1338,8994,FF.html*> (July 15, 2000).

3 Barbara Gass, Multiactive Software, telephone interview with author, June 19, 2000.

4 Schneider, Gary P., and James T. Perry, *Electronic Commerce.* Course Technology, Cambridge, 2000.

Unit C:

1 "Income and Age, Not Ethnicity, to Remain Largest Gap for US Digital Divide," *Jupiter Communications*, June 15, 2000, <*http://www.jupitercommunications.com/company/pressrelease.jsp?doc=pr000615&query=ethnic*> (July 7, 2000).

2 Susan McKenna, Marketing Manager at DigitalThink, telephone interview with author, July 7, 2000, <*http://www.digitalthink.com*>.

3 Keith Regan, "Report: E-Mail Marketing To Reach $7.3B by 2005," *Ecommerce Times*, May 9, 2000, <*http://www.ecommercetimes.com/news/articles2000/000509-4.shtml*> (July 7, 2000).

4 Jackie Monticup, MagicTricks, telephone interview with author, June 29, 2000, <*http://www.magictricks.com*>.

Unit D:

1 Vincent Flanders, "Solve My Problems Now," *Web Sites That Suck,* 1996–2000, <*http://www.webpagesthatsuck.com/lawyersgunsandmoney.html*> (July 4, 2000).

2 Olin Lagon, "Web Globalization Trends," *Design Shops*, May 27, 2000, <*http://www.designshops.com/pace/ds/pub/2000/05/global052200.html*> (July 3, 2000).

3 "Small and Mid-Sized Business Owners Optimistic About the Year Ahead," Arthur Andersen, June 21, 2000 *<http://www.arthurandersen.com/website.nsf/content/MediaCenterNewsDesk119?OpenDocument>* (July 4, 2000).

4 *ASP Industry Consortium,* 1999, *<http://www.aspindustry.org/faqs.html>* (July 4, 2000).

Unit E:

1 Emelie Rutherford, "Online Customer Service Gets Real," *Web Business,* February 2000, *<http://webbusiness.cio.com/archive/021700_customer_service.html>* (July 10, 2000).

2 Mark Hawkins, "Get a Grip and Learn to Ship," *E-Commerce Times,* March 10, 2000, *<http://www.ecommercetimes.com/small_business/strategy/grip.shtml>* (July 11, 2000).

3 "Is Internet Retailing Doomed?" *E-Retail News,* April 4, 2000, *<http://www.eretailnews.com>* (July 11, 2000).

Unit F:

1 "Statistics for Online Purchases," *ePaynews,* 2000, *<http://www.epaynews.com/statistics/purchases.html#1>* (July 16, 2000).

2 "Real Numbers Behind E-Transactions, Fraud & Security 2000," *ActivMedia Research* *<http://www.activmediaresearch.com/e-transaction__fraud___securit.html>* (July 16, 2000).

3 Annette Nellen, "Comments on the OECD's Proposed Clarification of the Commentary on Article 5 of the OECD Model Tax Convention—Permanent Establishment & E-Commerce," *San Jose State University,* February 2000, *<http://www.cob.sjsu.edu/facstaff/NELLEN_A/OECD-PE.html>* (June 9, 2000).

4 "Electronic Commerce: The UK's Taxation Agenda: Chapter 3: The International Scene," *UK Inland Revenue,* November 1999, *<http://www.inlandrevenue.gov.uk/taxagenda/ecom3.htm>* (June 10, 2000).

5 Wireless Application Forum (WAP), 2000, *<http://www.wapforum.org/what/index.htm>* (June 19, 2000).

6 Tim Richardson, "Don't believe the m-commerce hype," *The Register,* March 24, 2000, *<http://www.theregister.co.uk/content/archive/9958.html>* (June 18, 2000).

Unit G:

1 Form for the "Guide to 128-bit SSL Encryption," *VeriSign,* 2000, *<https://www.verisign.com/cgi-bin/clearsales_cgi/leadgen.htm?form_id=0008&toc=w016712980008000&email>* (June 30, 2000).

2 "What is PKI?" *Entrust Technologies,* 2000, *<http://www.entrust.com/resourcecenter/dcs/pki.htm#whatis>* (June 23, 2000).

Unit H:

1 "Personalization Strategies to Attract and Retain Customers," *Office.com,* 2000, *<http://www.office.com/global/tools/frameset?parameter=ob_tools/sales/custom.html>* (June 30, 2000).

2 Paul R. Hagen, "Tier Zero Customer Support," *Forrester Research,* December 1999, *<http://www.forrester.com/ER/Research/Report/0,1338,8641,FF.html>* (June 30, 2000).

3 Paul A. Greenberg, "Savvy Shoppers Spark New Online Trends," *E-Commerce Times,* November 29, 1999, *<http://www.ecommercetimes.com/news/articles/991129-6.shtml>* (July 9, 2000).

4 Press Release, Datamonitor, July 7, 2000, *<http://www.datamonitor.com/press/prtemplate.asp?id=tc000707+US+mkt+Inet+cust+serv>* (September 7, 2000).

5 John Rennie, 121 Marketing, telephone interview with author, July 12, 2000, *<http://www.121internetmarketing.com>*.

6 Gail F. Goodman, "Driving Repeat Sales With Loyalty E-Mail," *E-Commerce Times,* December 14, 1999, *<http://www.ecommercetimes.com/news/special_reports/repeatsales.shtml>* (July 11, 2000).

E-Commerce

ECommerce

Project Files List

File Listing for Unit A

Location	Provided File Name	Saved File Name
Lessons	ECA-01.doc	Online Shopping.doc
Independent Challenge 1	ECA-02.doc	E-Commerce Articles.doc
Independent Challenge 2	Student-generated	E-Commerce Solutions.doc
Independent Challenge 3	ECA-03.doc	E-Commerce Intermediaries.doc
Independent Challenge 4	ECA-04.doc	Neighborhood E-Commerce Solutions.doc

File Listing for Unit B

Location	Provided File Name	Saved File Name
Independent Challenge 1	Student-generated	Web Needs Analysis.doc
Independent Challenge 2	ECB-01.doc	E-Commerce Developer Comparison.doc
Independent Challenge 3	ECB-02.doc	Template Services Comparison.doc
Independent Challenge 4	Student-generated	My Glossary.doc

File Listing for Unit C

Location	Provided File Name	Saved File Name
Lesson: Understanding Domain Names	ECC-01.doc	Domain Names.doc
Lesson: Monitoring Customer Visits	ECC-02.doc	Site Trackers.doc
Lesson: Exploring Incentives	ECC-03.doc	Incentives.doc
Independent Challenge 1	ECC-04.doc	Competitor Analysis.doc
Independent Challenge 2	Student-generated	Mailing List Critique.doc
Independent Challenge 3	Student-generated	Sample Survey.doc
Independent Challenge 4	ECC-05.doc	Search Engine Analysis.doc

File Listing for Unit D

Location	Provided File Name	Saved File Name
Lesson: Exploring Site Maps	ECD-01.doc	Exploring Site Maps.doc
Lesson: Developing Content	ECD-02.doc	Content Evaluations.doc
Lesson: Exploring Web Site Design Principles	ECD-03.doc	Design Comparisons.doc
Independent Challenge 1	ECD-04.doc	Web Site Goals.doc
Independent Challenge 2	ECD-05.doc	International Business.doc
Independent Challenge 3	Student-generated	Job Descriptions.doc
Independent Challenge 4	Student-generated	Web Developer Information.doc

File Listing for Unit E

Location	Provided File Name	Saved File Name
Lesson: Exploring Navigation Aids	ECE-01.doc	Navigation Aids.doc
Independent Challenge 1	ECE-02.doc	Checkout Procedures.doc
Independent Challenge 2	ECE-03.doc	Web Site Search Tools.doc
Independent Challenge 3	Student-generated	Source Code Analysis.doc
Independent Challenge 4	ECE-04.doc	Shopping Cart Comparison.doc
Up to Date	Student-generated	Online Web Site Analysis.doc

File Listing for Unit F

Location	Provided File Name	Saved File Name
Lesson: Exploring E-Cash	ECF-01.doc	E-cash Services.doc
Lesson: Exploring Online Payment Services	ECF-02.doc	Payment Services.doc
Independent Challenge 1	ECF-03.doc	Merchant Accounts.doc
Independent Challenge 2	ECF-04.doc	Smart Card Questions.doc
Independent Challenge 3	ECF-05.doc	Online Payment Processing.doc
Independent Challenge 4	ECF-06.doc	Internet Taxation Issues.doc
Up to Date	Student-generated	International Internet Taxation Articles.doc

File Listing for Unit G

Location	Provided File Name	Saved File Name
Lesson: Exploring Security Providers	ECG-01.doc	Security Providers.doc
Lesson: Exploring Privacy Policies	ECG-02.doc	Privacy Policies.doc
Independent Challenge 1	Student-generated	More Information on Web Server Certificates.doc *Note:* file names could also be More Information on SSL or More Information on Public Key Encryption.
Independent Challenge 2	ECG-03.doc	Virus Protection.doc
Independent Challenge 3	Student-generated	Current Privacy Issues.doc
Independent Challenge 4	ECG-04.doc	Browser Security Settings.doc

File Listing for Unit H

Location	Provided File Name	Saved File Name
Lesson: Developing FAQs	ECH-01.doc	FAQ Comparison.doc
Lesson: Exploring Live Help Services	ECH-02.doc	Live Help Services.doc
Lesson: Exploring Value-Added Options	ECH-03.doc	Value-Added Options.doc
Independent Challenge 1	ECH-04.doc	Help Options.doc
Independent Challenge 2	ECH-05.doc	Discussion Options.doc
Independent Challenge 3	ECH-06.doc	Exchange and Return Options.doc
Independent Challenge 4	Student-generated	Sticky Site Strategies.doc
Up to Date	ECH-07.doc	Customer Service Articles.doc

E-Commerce

Glossary

Access Control List (ACL) Specifies which users are allowed to access which data to perform which functions.

Acquiring institution The company that issues the merchant account to the online business.

Active Server Pages (ASP) Provides Web developers with a server-side scripting environment for creating Web pages that are produced in direct reaction to events caused by the Web visitor.

ActiveX controls Objects on Web pages that perform specific tasks such as displaying a drop-down menu in a form, or showing an up-to-date- calendar.

Architecture Configuration of computers in a large system; used to refer to either hardware or software of a combination.

Asymmetric encryption An encryption system that involves the use of two different keys.

Authentication The process used to ensure that the person receiving a message is really the person who should receive the message, and not an imposter.

Autoresponder A mail server that will automatically send a reply to each e-mail address that sends a message; autoresponders are generally used assure customers that their e-mail has been received.

Bandwith The number of simultaneous visits a site can handle in a given time period.

Benchmark A reference or standard used for measurement or comparison purposes.

Bits per second (bps) How quickly data moves across the Internet.

Branding The association of a company with a particular logo, image, or characteristic, such as high quality or reliability.

Brick and mortar Retail location in the real world.

Brochureware A small site (an 'electronic brochure') that includes limited information about the company and its products.

Business-to-Business e-commerce (B2B) Sales made by one business to another.

Business-to-Consumer e-commerce (B2C) Sales made to consumers using the Internet to buy a product or service.

Call center Handles incoming telephone calls from both online and offline customers.

Card Not Present (CNP) A credit card transaction is made without the credit card itself being physically handled by the vendor.

Certificate Authority (CA) The third party that issues digital certificates to companies and individuals.

Cipher An encryption method that adds a specific number of characters onto each letter.

Cipher text The text that results after a cipher is applied to plain text.

Click and mortar Companies that sell products or services both in the real world and online.

Client Any computer that requests information from the server.

Client-side applications Includes tasks and applications that are run on the user's computer rather than on the server.

Cookie A small text file that contains information for a specific Web site such as a password and username; these text files are stored on the user's computer.

Commerce All the activities in which a company or individual engages to complete a transaction.

Common Gateway Interface (CGI) script Script used to transfers information from a computer on the Internet to the host computer.

Component outsourcing When a company hires an outside company to handle specific portions of an e-commerce initiative.

Content Interesting articles, games, questionnaires, and other materials of interest to a market included on a Web site to encourage surfers to stay on the site as long as possible.

Corpographics The gathering of data about corporate structure, purchasing history, and personnel.

Cracker A person who breaks into computer systems to damage, steal, or modify data.

Cross-selling Informs customers about an accessory or additional product that they can add on to the product they are already buying.

Customization Serving the individual needs of each customer that visits a Web site and purchases products or services.

Cyberintermediaries Individuals who develop Internet-based intermediation solutions.

Cybermalls A Web site that contains links to a broad selection of online stores organized by categories, similar to a real world mall.

Cybersquatting Registering a company name and then trying to resell it to its lawful owner at a profit.

Data mining A class of database applications that searches for patterns within selected groups of data.

Database A collection of data, such as names and addresses, that is organized so that a computer can quickly retrieve specific information.

Database-driven system A term used to describe a dynamic online catalog that can be updated quickly and easily.

Decks Used to refer to one or more cards containing content for pages created with Wireless Markup Language (WML).

Digest A single string of numbers that is created with a formula called a one-way hash function.

Digital certificate Verifies that the sender of a message is who he or she claims to be, and provides the person who receives the message with the public key required to encrypt a reply.

Digital signature An authentication mechanism that is impossible to duplicate or forge.

Digital wallet/e-wallet Software program that contains a user's payment information in encrypted form to ensure its security.

Disintermediation The process of edging out traditional middlemen as a result of the self-serve activities made possible by the Internet.

Domain name The address of a Web page that can contain two or more groups of words separated by periods; an example of a domain name is "course" in the Web address "www.course.com".

Dot.com Companies that conduct most or all or their business online.

Dynamic HTML (DHTML) Used to create Web sites with which a Web surfer can interact without needing to download additional plug-in programs.

Early outsourcing When a company hires an outside consultant to design its Web site.

E-cash Digital cash that is drawn directly from the consumer's bank account and stored in a digital wallet on a hard drive; e-cash is also known as Scrip, digital cash, or digital coins.

E-check An encrypted representation of a paper check.

E-commerce Using the Internet to assist in the trading of goods and services.

Electronic Data Interchange (EDI) The electronic transfer of data between companies engaged in B2B e-commerce.

Electronic data transmission Use of an electronic method to conduct business; methods include phones, faxes, e-mail, Personal Digital Assistants (PDAs), and Web sites.

Electronic payment A payment that is transmitted electronically either over the telephone line, or between Web sites on the Internet.

E-mail Sending of messages from one computer to another computer over the Internet.

E-marketing Using the Internet to market products and services.

Encryption The process of scrambling data into a secret code that can only be broken by complicated mathematical algorithms.

Escrow The holding of a buyer's payment by a third party.

E-service The methods that a company uses to provide customer service directly from its Web site.

E-shoplifting When customers refuse to pay for goods that they actually received.

Executable file A file created in a format that a computer can run independently of the programming language environment in which the program was written.

eXtensible Markup Language (XML) A programming language used in conjunction with HTML to create new sets of custom tags to describe content.

Extranet An extension of a company's Intranet that is made accessible to selected people or groups outside the company.

File Transfer Protocol (FTP) Allows the transfer of documents and files from one computer to another computer over the Internet.

Firewall Surrounds an Intranet to prevent unauthorized access by examining each message that enters and exits the Intranet, then blocks messages that do not conform to specific criteria.

Forms Collection of text boxes and drop-down lists that users complete to submit information from a Web site.

Graphical User Interface (GUI) Use of pictures, icons, and other graphical elements to help users easily view content and navigate from page to page on a Web site.

Hacker A person who breaks into computer systems for the challenge of breaching a seemingly watertight security system.

Hyperlink Highlighted text on a Web page that allows a Web surfer to go to another page on the same Web site, or to another Web site anywhere on the Web.

Hyperlinks Also known as links, they connect the pages in a Web site.

HyperText Markup Language (HTML) The formatting language used to identify the structure and layout of a Web document.

Indexing robots A software program that search engines use to find pages that contain keywords related to specific topics.

Inline personalization Embedding information that has been generated as a result of a customer's request.

Interactive Web site A Web site that displays pages based on user input.

Interface A program or actual device that connects two entities.

Intermediary Similar to a middleman, a businessperson such as an agent, broker, or sales representative, who negotiates transactions between a business and the consumer.

Internet Short for interconnected, a network of computers all over the world that are linked together to exchange data.

Internet Service Provider (ISP) Connects a computer to the Internet; a basic account with an ISP provides customers with an e-mail address and limited or full access to the Internet.

Intranet A group of connected networks owned by a company or organization and used for internal business purposes.

Issuing institution The financial organization that issues a credit card to a consumer.

Java applets Programs written in the Java programming language that users can download safely from the Internet and run on any system.

JavaScript A scripting language used to provide feedback to the Web surfer, to generate new Web pages, and to execute tasks defined by the user.

Just-In-Time (JIT) Products are ordered and then manufactured on an as-needed basis to reduce warehousing costs.

Key The exact number of letters that will be added when a cipher is used.

Late outsourcing When a company designs its Web site on their own and then hires outside consultants to maintain it.

Level playing field All online businesses, regardless of size, have access to the same markets all over the world; also used to refer to the same regulations applied to all participants.

Local hyperlink A hyperlink to another page on the same Web site; also called an internal hyperlink.

Mail Order/Telephone Order (MOTO) Similar to a Card Not Present (CNP) credit card transaction where the credit card transaction is made without the credit card itself being physically handled by the vendor.

Merchant account Account that a vendor sets up with a bank or other financial institution in order to accept credit card payments from customers.

Merchant Account Provider (MAP) The financial institution that sets up a merchant account for a company.

Merchant account status A vendor that is authorized to accept credit card payments from customers.

Meta tag The HTML code used to enclose a description of a site's content.

Methods The actions performed with an object or performed on an object.

Micro payments Very small payments (e.g., less than $1.00) usually made with e-cash to purchase goods and services online.

Middlemen People such as agents, brokers, and sales representatives, who negotiate transactions between a business and the consumer.

Mobile-commerce The use of a wireless device such as a cellular phone or Personal Digital Assistant (PDA) to access the Internet to purchase products or services.

Navigation aid Visual aids, such as button, hyperlink text, or other graphic elements, that help surfers find their way around a Web site.

Navigation bar A series of tabs or links on a Web site along the top of the screen that leads to the site's main sections.

On the fly An HTML Web page is only generated in response to a customer's request.

One-way hash function Formula used to created a digest for a digital signature.

Opt-in E-mail campaigns in which customers have agreed to participate.

Opt-out E-mail options that customers must deselect if they do not want to receive e-mail.

Outsourcing When a company hires another company to handle some of the tasks related to the creation and maintenance of a Web site.

Paperless trading Another term for Electronic Data Interchange (EDI).

PERL A programming language used to write scripts required to run a CGI program.

Permanent Establishment (PE) Physical location of an organization or business for taxation purposes.

Personal Digital Assistant (PDA) Hand held device that includes computing, telephone/fax, and networking capabilities.

Private key The key used to decrypt a message.

Private key encryption See Symmetrical encryption.

Properties The characteristics of an object, such as height and color.

Proxy Intercepts and encrypts or scrambles all the data that a Web server sends to a computer.

Psychographics The study of how people think and feel with relation to what they buy.

Public key The key used to encrypt a message.

Public-key encryption A method of encryption used to secure small amounts of data.

Qualified traffic Visitors to a Web site who already match the profile of previous buyers.

Real time Activities that occur within a few minutes of the time the transactions are made.

Re-intermediation The new type of intermediation being pursued by Web entrepreneurs who are exploiting markets that could not have existed before the Internet.

Remote hyperlink A hyperlink to a different Web site; also called an external hyperlink.

Scalability The ability to move easily from a low-cost, low-maintenance e-commerce solution to a higher-level solution without disrupting service to customers.

Secure Electronic Transaction (SET) A new technology being developed as a way to transmit encrypted data between computers.

Secure server The computer that handles the e-commerce transaction so that customer information cannot be accessed or stolen.

Secure Socket Layer (SSL) The principal technology used to transmit encrypted data from computer to computer over the Internet.

Security With regard to the Internet, the techniques used to store and transmit data, to form policies that govern how data is used, and to protect networks and equipment from harm or failure.

Self-serve economy The willingness of consumers to help themselves and to make new technologies part of their daily lives.

Server The Web host's computer.

Server-side The scripts that a Web developer writes to run on the server rather than on the Web surfer's own computer.

E-Commerce

Shopping cart A page listing the ongoing results of the ordering process; for example, the products that a consumer has selected to purchase.

Single-key encryption See Symmetrical encryption.

Site map Illustrates how the Web site is organized into categories and sub-categories.

Snail mail The conventional postal system.

Sniffer A program that can record information passing through a computer on its way to a destination computer, unless that information is scrambled.

Spamming Indiscriminately e-mailing hundreds or thousands of people at once, in the hopes that some of them will respond.

Sticky Web site A Web site that attracts and keeps surfers.

Structured Query Language (SQL) The standardized language used to request information from a database.

Symmetrical encryption The encryption system that involves the use of two identical keys.

Syntax Rules for arranging text; for example, an e-mail address must include an @ sign and a top-level domain such as .com, .org., or .ca.

Tables Used to divides a Web page into several sections, many of which are side-by-side; often used instead of frames.

Tags Used in HTML codes to designate how text and other objects appear on the Web page.

Templates A pre-designed structure for a Web site that includes coordinated styles for elements such as navigation aids, fonts, and images.

Top-level domain In a Web address, the suffix attached to the domain name; current top-level domains include com, org, and gov; country-specific top-level domains such as de for Germany and au for Australia are also used.

Turnkey system Supplies all the hardware and software required for a full e-business solution that allows a business to accept credit cards, process transactions securely, fulfill orders, and provide full customer service.

Unique private key A key that is generated from a public key only once, used by the recipient for a specific transaction, and then discarded.

Upload Sending a copy of a file from a user's computer to a remote computer.

Up-selling Promotion of a model that includes more features then the one the customer is buying, and is generally higher priced.

Variable data A description of products ordered, a customer's contact information, or other information generated as a result of customer input.

Vendor A company that supplies the products sold on the Web site.

Viral marketing Describes a message or giveaway that people receive and then send along to friends and colleagues.

Virtual credit card A picture of a credit card that is placed on a computer desktop, and, when clicked on, allows the cardholder to access account information and pay for online purchases.

Virtual Reality Modeling Language (VRML) Used to create three-dimensional virtual worlds on a Web site.

Web hosting provider The company that hosts a Web site.

Web robot A software program that search engines use to find pages that contain keywords related to specific topics. A Web robot is also known as a spider or bot.

Wireless Application Protocol (WAP) The delivery of content over mobile communicators such as cellular phones and Personal Digital Assistants.

WML Script A scripting language similar to JavaScript that is also used to produce pages for WAP applications.

World Wide Web (Web) Provides easy navigation between Web sites through the use of hyperlinks.

World Wide Web Consortium (W3C) Sets the standards to which browsers and other Web technologies should conform.

WYSIWYG What You See It What You Get refers to the ability to format text in a Web design program just as you would in a word-processing program without having to enter codes.

XHTML A future Web-specific vocabulary that might become the new language of the Web.

XML (Extensible Markup Language) A markup language that can be used in conjunction with HTML to create custom tags that describe, deliver, and exchange structured data.

Index

Index

Index

Index